# BEYOND CHARITY

The Twentieth Century Fund is a research foundation undertaking timely analyses of economic, political, and social issues. Not-for-profit and nonpartisan, the Fund was founded in 1919 and endowed by Edward A. Filene.

# BEYOND CHARITY

## International Cooperation and the Global Refugee Crisis

Gil Loescher

A Twentieth Century Fund Book

*New York   Oxford*
OXFORD UNIVERSITY PRESS
1993

## Oxford University Press

Oxford   New York   Toronto
Delhi   Bombay   Calcutta   Madras   Karachi
Kuala Lumpur   Singapore   Hong Kong   Tokyo
Nairobi   Dar es Salaam   Cape Town
Melbourne   Auckland   Madrid

and associated companies in
Berlin   Ibadan

## Copyright © 1993 by The Twentieth Century Fund

Published by Oxford University Press, Inc.,
200 Madison Avenue, New York, New York 10016

Oxford is a registered trademark of Oxford University Press

Library of Congress Cataloging-in-Publication Data
Loescher, Gil.
Beyond charity : international cooperation and the
global refugee crisis / Gil Loescher.
p. cm.
"A Twentieth Century Fund book."
Includes bibliographical references and index.
ISBN 0-19-508183-8
1. Refugees.   2. Refugees—Services for.
I. Title.
HV640.L62   1993
362.87′8—dc20
92-39365

3 5 7 9 8 6 4 2

Printed in the United States of America
on acid-free paper

# Foreword

While nearly all the traditional wellsprings of refugees—wars, famine, persecution, and strife—still are forcing movements of peoples across national borders, two particular forces seem to be shaping the current contours of this global problem. The end of the cold war and the breakup of the Soviet empire have released ancient communal and regional conflicts long suppressed by communist rule, and the consequences of overpopulation and scarce resources are growing at a rate that may mark the beginning of a great world crisis for the next century.

In these circumstances, it is not surprising that many governments are hardening their positions on support for and admittance of large numbers of new refugees. Even "conventional" problems, such as the dilemma of the Kurds and Haitians, test the political capacity and public goodwill of the major powers. The issue is further complicated by increased blurring of the political and economic bases for refugee movements.

As in the past, leaders are constrained from housing large numbers of refugees by domestic economic pressures and, in some cases, the fear of political instability. Over the years, the world has turned away or remained ambivalent in the face of Jewish, Palestinian, and, most recently, Yugoslavian attempts to escape daunting or life-threatening circumstances. Yet, each of these refugee crises, in its own way, has shown how abiding and even dehumanizing the results of global inaction can be.

The principal international protector of refugees today remains the office of the United Nations High Commissioner for Refugees (UN-HCR), established in 1951 to assist those fleeing totalitarian persecution at the height of the cold war. In 1951, there were 2 million refugees; today, there are close to 20 million. The scope of the crisis has outgrown the UNHCR's effectiveness, which has always been hindered by both its dependence on voluntary contributions to carry out its programs and its need to obtain the acquiescence of host governments.

Gil Loescher, professor of international relations at the University of Notre Dame, sees a significant erosion of the traditional protection for refugees. He argues that we have entered a new era when, fearing the specter of uncontrolled immigration, nations are toughening their stands against even such basic forms of sanctuary as asylum. Loescher calls for reform and strengthening of such existing institutions as the UNHCR and for a concerted strategy by the major nations, including new institutional arrangements.

His practical case rests, in part, on the belief that it is a mistake to think of these problems as "merely" humanitarian or charity issues. The movement of large numbers of people can trigger political events and even set the geopolitical agenda. The outpouring of East Germans after the Soviet Union relaxed its grip on their country, for example, may have been what forced the actions that brought down the Berlin Wall, bringing about a united Germany.

The issues Loescher is addressing in this book are only a part of the complex dynamics involved in the movement of peoples. The Fund has and is continuing to examine the problem, exploring the refusal of nations to allow emigration in Alan Dowty's *Closed Borders* and the economic effects of immigration in Thomas Muller's *Immigrants and the American City,* and through work being done on international organizations, particularly the specialized agencies of the United Nations.

Gil Loescher makes clear that whether the UNHCR can serve as a catalyst for multinational cooperation depends upon the commitment of political leadership from the United States and other nations. The prescriptions he offers merit serious attention from those who must find the will to lead on these issues. On behalf of the Trustees of the Twentieth Century Fund, I thank him for his contribution to the debate about how to respond to this intensifying world problem.

Richard C. Leone, *President*
*The Twentieth Century Fund*
*February 1993*

# Acknowledgments

This book was researched and written during tumultuous years in which fundamental changes have occurred in international politics. Refugee movements helped shape these changes, when tens of thousands of East Germans fled West, bringing down the Berlin Wall, the paramount symbol of the Cold War and the old world order. In recent years, the control of populations and refugee movements has been the very subject of conflicts in the Balkans, the ex–Soviet Union, and parts of the Third World. International relations in the 1990s seem to be characterized by an increasingly chaotic and potentially explosive mixture of unreconciled tendencies toward self-determination, democratization, religious revival, and ethnic aspirations. As yet, great uncertainty surrounds the question of what will actually replace the bipolar world, and whether satisfactory international mechanisms exist to manage the complex problems of the new era. Clearly, refugee and international migration has emerged as a central theme in international politics for the post–Cold War world. In every region of the globe, refugee flight, economic migration, massive internal displacement of populations, and problems associated with the care and maintenance, integration, or safe return of displaced persons to their home countries are issues that dominate national and international agendas.

I am grateful to the Twentieth Century Fund for having had the foresight to support this study before the dizzying geopolitical events of the past few years began to unfold, and to the University of Notre Dame for permitting me to take two years' leave from teaching. The Refugee Studies Programme at Oxford University provided me with an institutional base as a Senior Research Fellow during 1987–1989. During 1990–1991, I continued work on the security aspects of refugee movements while I was a Research Associate at the International Institute for Strategic Studies in London.

Numerous institutions and individuals have assisted me and offered me their hospitality during the research and writing of this book. Early on in the project, I benefited from a five-week stay as a Scholar in Residence at the Rockefeller Study Center at the Villa Serbollini in Bellagio. In the limited space available, I can only mention a few of the many individuals who provided essential assistance to this project either in the form of information and insights or in the form of logistics, such as transport to remote refugee camps and settlements. They include Dennis McNamara from the UN Transitional Authority in Cambodia; Sadako Ogata, Hans Thoolen, Rick Stainsbury, Irene Kahn, Johan Cels, Salvatore Lombardi, Jeff Crisp, Louise Drüke, Karola Paula, Fiorella Badiani, Alfredo Del Riyo, Maureen Connelly, Patricia Weiss Fagen, Kofi Asomani, Samshul Bari, Iain Guest, Jamie Lynch, and Gervase Coles from the UNHCR; Jim Purcell and Reinhold Lohrmann from the International Organization for Migration; Gilbert Jaeger, Bernard Alexander, Joachim Henkel, and Anders Johnson formerly of the UNHCR; Philip Rudge from the European Consultation on Refugees; Bernd Mesovic from Arbeiter Wohlfahrt; Roger Winter, Ginny Hamilton, Bill Frelick, Jacqueline Stromberg, Court Robinson, and Hiram Ruiz from the U.S. Committee for Refugees; Beth Ferris, formerly of the World Council of Churches; Jacques Cuenod, Dennis Gallagher, and Susan Forbes Martin from the Refugee Policy Group; Jonas Widgren and Cengiz Aktar from the Secretariat for Intergovernmental Consultation; Guy Goodwin-Gill from Carleton University; Julia Taft formerly of the U.S. Refugee Coordinator's Office; Joe Stern formerly of the Canadian Refugee Status Advisory Committee; John Chipman and Francois Heisbourg from the International Institute for Strategic Studies; Dennis Clagget formerly of the International Catholic Migration Commission; Arthur Helton from the Lawyers' Committee for Human Rights; Barbara Harrell-Bond, Nick Van Hear, and Andrew Shaknove from the Refugee Studies Programme in Oxford; Mary McClymont, Bill Klausner, and Emma Playfair from the Ford Foundation; Saeed Ahmad Akhtar, formerly Deputy Commissioner for Afghan Refugees; Dennis Grace from the International Rescue Committee; Clandena Skran from Appleton University; Norman and Naomi Zucker from the University of Rhode Island; Demetrious Papademetriou from the U.S. Department of Labor; Jeremy Azrael from the Rand Corporation; Doris Meissner from the Carnegie Endowment for International Peace; and finally to my colleagues and students at Notre Dame and Oxford. I am grateful to many others who helped me along the way—whether at Notre Dame, Oxford, Geneva, Tegucigalpa, Peshawar, or along the Thai–Cambodia border—and to those who provided information, documents, and comments while requesting anonymity.

For this book I have interviewed the present UN High Commissioner for Refugees, Sadako Ogata, and most of her predecessors, as well as many of the heads of leading voluntary agencies. During the past several years, I have also interviewed government policymakers in the United States, in Canada, in most West European countries, and in several capitals in developing countries. I have also visited refugee camps in Southeast Asia and Hong Kong, Central America and Mexico, South Asia, and North Africa, as well as refugee holding and detention centers in Europe and North America. In preparing this study, I have interviewed or spoken with hundreds of officials, refugee workers, researchers, refugees, and asylum seekers on practically every continent.

In addition to the generous support of the Twentieth Century Fund, field and library research have been funded by various sponsors, including the Kellogg Institute for International Studies, the Joan Kroc Institute for International Peace Studies, the Institute for the Study of Liberal Arts, and the Jesse Jones Faculty Travel Fund at the University of Notre Dame; the National Endowment for the Humanities; and the Institute for the Study of World Politics. During the final stages of writing, I was engaged in a consultancy for the Ford Foundation which enabled me to interview many of the senior executives and management of the most important international humanitarian, development, and political agencies in New York, Washington, D.C., Geneva, and London regarding the dominant refugee themes of the 1990s.

Over the past several years, I have presented portions of this study to seminars and audiences at a number of different places. These include the University of Lund in Sweden, Oxford University, the University of Notre Dame, Webster University in St. Louis, Grinnell College in Iowa, the UNHCR in Geneva, the Royal Institute for International Affairs in London, the Ford Foundation in Cairo; at the U.S. Army, Europe, in Heidelberg; and at conferences and meetings at Ditchley Park and Wilton Park in England, The Hague in the Netherlands, the International Studies Association meeting in London, and the American Political Science Association meeting in San Francisco. These occasions have provided opportunities for discussion and helpful criticism of my work.

Some passages in the present work originally appeared in an Adelphi Paper I wrote for the International Institute for Strategic Studies entitled *Refugee Movements and International Security* (Summer 1992) and in my previously co-authored book *Calculated Kindness: Refugees and America's Half-Open Door* (New York: Free Press, 1986). I am grateful to the IISS and to the Free Press for allowing me to use them here.

I have tried to write a book that reaches general readers and policymakers who may have little specific knowledge of the subject, as well as my academic colleagues, some of whom specialize in refugee affairs. I am grateful to the specialists for their patience when reading parts of the book dealing with history or developments that are already familiar to them, but I hope that they will appreciate the overall comprehensiveness of the book and the attempt to indicate directions for more effective approaches to refugee problems at present and in the future. Special debts of gratitude are due to Laila Monahan for her comments and initial editing of the manuscript, to Carol Kahn Strauss of the Twentieth Century Fund for copy-editing the entire manuscript, and to Steven Gray of Oxford University Press for the final copy-editing and for many of his helpful comments, some of which I have incorporated in the text. These editors have helped make the book much more readable and more accessible to a wider audience than might otherwise have been the case. Finally, Beverly Goldberg, Director of Publications at the Twentieth Century Fund, and David Roll and Melinda Wirkus of Oxford University Press, piloted the book to publication. I am grateful for their support and assistance.

G.L.
*Oxford, U.K.*
*December 1992*

# Contents

# BEYOND CHARITY

# Introduction:
# The Global
# Refugee Crisis

Desperate men, women, and children pushed out of their own countries by forces entirely beyond their control are paraded with grim regularity across our television screens. Images of exhausted, destitute mothers cradling emaciated children in some makeshift camp in a remote corner of the world not only evoke the pathos of refugees but graphically illustrate the daily reality of millions of people caught up in the crosscurrents of revolution, war, and famine who have been forced into exile.

That a global refugee problem exists cannot be denied. Refugees are everywhere—a by-product of wars, military coups, and massive human rights violations. Every year, new accumulations of people are displaced as old problems remain unresolved and new ones emerge. Disintegrating nations such as Ethiopia, Liberia, Somalia, the ex–Soviet Union, Sudan, and the former Yugoslavia provide examples of the chaotic conditions and widespread displacement that can easily arise from ethnic, tribal, and religious conflicts.

The largest and most dramatic refugee movements in the post–Cold War era involved the nearly 2 to 3 million Iraqi Kurds and Shi'ites who streamed toward the borders of Iran and Turkey following Saddam Hussein's genocidal attacks; the 2.5 million ex-Yugoslavs expelled from their homes as a result of "ethnic cleansing"; and the millions of starving Somalis forcibly displaced as a result of brutal interclan warfare and food shortages. These new displacements come on top of earlier movements, some going back decades, that have created permanent refugee residents in other countries. The Palestinians, for example, make up at least half of

3

Jordan's 3 million population, and an estimated 1 million Mozambicans have spent over a decade in neighboring Malawi. The majority of today's refugees are the result of intense and long-standing conflicts in Afghanistan, the Horn of Africa, Southern Africa, Indochina, and Central America that began during the last decade and remain largely unresolved as ethnic hatreds have quickly filled the ideological void left after the ending of East–West rivalry in these regions.

Although the demise of the Cold War and the development of regional peace accords raised hopes of finding solutions to long-standing refugee problems in Angola, Cambodia, and Mozambique, little evidence suggests that new refugee movements will not occur in these and other countries in the near future. Population growth, poverty and underdevelopment, famine, political instability, the proliferation of arms in association with increased militarism, and ethnic conflicts all signal continuing mass movements of populations. During recent years, the perpetuation and growth of the refugee problem in the Third World have resulted in an increased number of asylum seekers in the industrialized countries. This increase in South–North movements coincides with the end of the Cold War and the removal of the physical barriers between Eastern and Western Europe. The collapse of communism and the acceleration of political and economic reforms in Eastern Europe have given rise to grave economic dislocation, as well as to the resurgence of long pent-up ethnic hatreds and conflicts. Eruptions in Albania, the former republics of Yugoslavia, and the ex–Soviet Union remind us that upheavals and dislocations on the European continent are not yet finished. In the future, refugees will continue to appear in huge numbers all over the world.

Not only does there appear to be no end in sight to the growing numbers of refugees, but there exists no overall permanent solution—and no "quick fix"—to the problem. Unlike earlier forced movements, which were ultimately resolved by repatriation or overseas resettlement, refugees today come predominantly from Third World countries and find only temporary asylum in neighboring states. The majority of these populations languish in camps or survive illegally without any hope of a permanent place of settlement or eventual return home. Those who do repatriate frequently return to unstable situations where their physical safety is in doubt and where their economic prospects are poor.

## Refugees and the UNHCR in a Changing World

The office of the United Nations High Commissioner for Refugees (UNHCR) is the international community's principal mechanism to assist and to protect refugees. Formally established in 1950 at the height of East–West confrontation, the UNHCR was initially charged with protecting and assisting people displaced in the aftermath of World War II and those fleeing communist persecution in Europe. From the 1960s until recently, however, the focus has shifted away from Europe to the Third World.

During the last 30 years, the majority of the office's budget has been allocated for operations in Africa, Asia, and Latin America. While the assistance contributed by the international community has at times been substantial, the local pressures created by the presence of large refugee populations and sudden mass exoduses in recent years have been enormous.

Over the past decade and a half, the number of refugees in the world has increased alarmingly. The total rose from 2.8 million in 1976 to 8.2 million in 1980 to nearly 18 million at the end of 1992.[1] It is likely that the number will exceed 20 million during this decade. In addition, at least another 20 million people are displaced inside their own country. Authorities fear that many more people could become displaced as ethnic and religious tensions previously suppressed by totalitarian regimes or East–West competition are now unleashed, potentially leading to violence. Thus, in the 1990s, the UNHCR is confronted with profound social and political changes in the Third World, the Balkans, and the ex–Soviet Union that create a number of new dilemmas for managing the refugee problem.

The growth in numbers and the complexity of refugee flows in recent years have presented enormous challenges to UNHCR in planning, managing, and funding its worldwide network of protection and relief programs. It is increasingly asked to bear more responsibility and leadership, but with diminishing resources. The UNHCR is chronically underfunded and understaffed. Although it serves twice the number of refugees it did a decade ago, the financial support levels for basic care and maintenance for refugees worldwide have remained at virtually the same level. Thus, in many cases the UNHCR has been unable to fulfill its mandate in recent years because the office lacks the requisite financial resources and personnel.

## The Refugee Definition and Changing Characteristics of Refugee Flows

According to the 1951 Geneva Convention, a refugee is someone with "a well-founded fear of being persecuted in his country of origin for reasons of race, religion, nationality, membership of a particular social group or political opinion."[2] In practice, the question of who exactly is a refugee is a major point of contention. Even small definitional distinctions and classifications are important, because they may mean the difference between having access to political asylum, receiving aid, and being granted international protection, or being left without any officially recognized status or help at all.

In today's interdependent world, more people are migrating for a wide variety of reasons. Some people leave home, either legally or illegally, primarily for economic reasons and are typically labeled "economic migrants."[3] Others seek to join family members living abroad.[4] And a growing number of people move principally to escape the violence associated with political instability, the denial of human rights, and lack of government protection in their countries.

Because of the close relationship between political conflict and economic and social problems, it is sometimes difficult to distinguish between refugees and migrants. Technically, refugees flee to save their lives, and migrants to improve their economic prospects; but distinguishing between them becomes extremely difficult when people flee from countries where poverty and violence are direct consequences of the political system. For decades, Haitian boat people fled a country impoverished by the corrupt and violent Duvalier family; and they are now fleeing again from the military regime that overthrew Jean-Bertrand Aristide, the elected President of Haiti. The influx of Albanians into Italy continued even after the election of a democratic government in Albania, demonstrating anew the complexity of the problem.

Although anyone uprooted because of exposure to violence and the denial of human rights is commonly referred to as a refugee, the 1951 UN Refugee Convention is much more precise. The key criterion determining refugee status is *persecution,* which usually means a deliberate act of the government against individuals, and thus excludes victims of general insecurity and oppression or systemic economic deprivation, and people who have not crossed national frontiers to seek refuge.[5] From the perspective of international law, the main characteristics of a refugee are that he is outside his home country and that he does not have the protection of his country of origin.[6] Primarily, a refugee is defined as "a person in whose case the normal bond of trust, loyalty, protection and assistance between a person and the government of his country has been broken (or does not exist)."[7]

While the definition contained in the 1951 Refugee Convention remains important as a statement of legal responsibility and international commitment to protect refugees, increasingly large numbers of politically coerced and displaced people do not fall within the Convention's strict definition. As a result, migrants who flee threatening circumstances that do not involve individual persecution have not been widely accepted as refugees, although until recently many have been given humanitarian assistance and treated on an ad hoc basis as de facto or non-Convention refugees. There is a growing perception in the industrialized world, however, that these movements of people can no longer be handled adequately by uncoordinated responses on the part of individual receiving countries.

The stark fact that must be faced is that the world is witnessing a huge growth in forcibly displaced people—those driven from their countries by civil war, by famine, or by grave social injustice, as well as by political oppression and individual persecution. In terms of sheer numbers, non-Convention "refugees" fleeing civil wars, ethnic conflicts, and generalized violence in the Third World or in Eastern Europe are a bigger problem for the international community than Convention refugees. And they are not adequately protected by current international norms.

In recent years, governments all over the world have become less tolerant toward refugees and feel that there is no more room for immigrants of any kind. The refugee problem has reached such a critical point that the very institution of asylum is being threatened. As a consequence, the international community is not meeting its legal and ethical obligations to protect and aid refugees. UNHCR is now facing one of its most serious challenges ever.

## Increased Restrictionism

Although the numbers of refugees coming to the West is still small compared to the numbers given temporary asylum in the Third World, the industrialized countries—European governments in particular—have thrown up barriers to prevent non-European asylum seekers from entering their countries. Even East Europeans are finding entry closed to them, as the ideological and political motives for granting asylum in Western states have largely disappeared with the fall of the Iron Curtain. Industrialized countries are also averse to opening their doors to asylum seekers from the Third World, who are basically perceived as economic migrants in search of a better life. Actual migratory movements from the South and fear of a large exodus from the former Eastern bloc have only served to reinforce this restrictive attitude toward asylum.

Traditionally the principal diplomatic supporters of the international refugee regime, Western governments are now imposing visa requirements, detaining some asylum seekers in centers at airports or nearby, applying sanctions against airlines and carriers that transport asylum seekers, and interpreting the refugee conventions in very restrictive ways. Several European countries have tightened their immigration and asylum laws to restrict further the opportunities for asylum seekers to apply for protection and assistance within Europe. Even in countries with well-established traditions of immigration, such as the United States, concern is expressed in some quarters about the country's ability to absorb more immigrants and refugees and still remain "American."

Throughout the world, the climate of opinion is turning against refugees. The stricter standards for accepting refugees in Europe and in other Western countries have serious repercussions on the willingness of Third World countries to grant refugees asylum. For example, the American policy of intercepting Haitian boat people and returning them home without any possibility of applying for asylum makes it hypocritical for the United States to criticize Malaysia or other Asian states for forcibly turning away boatloads of Vietnamese refugees and refusing to grant them "first asylum" while long-term solutions are sought. Likewise, the forcible return of Albanians, ex-Yugoslavs, Romanians, Tamils, Palestinians, Zaireans, and other asylum seekers to their home countries by European governments in recent years means that Western states can no longer serve as an example in this regard to others.

Western governments' retreat on humanitarian standards and their unwillingness to bear a greater share of the world's refugee burden lend added respectability to restrictionism and naked self-interest. Many nations have introduced measures specifically designed to deter refugees from claiming asylum, and they unabashedly describe such policies as "humane deterrence." Physical harassment of refugees and military attacks on their settlements and camps are growing in scale and frequency. As political and economic pressures build worldwide, refugee protection is weakening everywhere.

## Problems of Host Nations

Most refugees and displaced people move from one Third World country to another and are found in the poorest parts of the world: Sudanese, Somalis, and Ethiopians in the Horn of Africa, Uganda, Kenya, and Yemen; Mozambicans in Malawi; Liberians in West Africa; and Rohingya Burmese in Bangladesh, to give only a few examples. A tradition of hospitality remains remarkably strong in many of these African and Asian states and communities, but the burdens of hosting so many people are great at both national and local levels. Even a modest influx places a severe strain on a poor host country's social services and physical infrastructure and may radically distort local economic conditions. In Malawi, for example, where the GNP per capita is only $170, one in every ten persons is a refugee from Mozambique. This is the equivalent of the United States, a far richer country, suddenly admitting over 25 million Central Americans—the entire population of that region.

Tensions may also arise from the consequences of admitting outsiders into traditional social structures. Frequently, refugees are cultural and economic minorities who seek safety among closely related groups across national frontiers. Many governments are unwilling to admit refugees who will significantly increase a minority group, for fear that they might disrupt the precarious existing order of racial, religious, and ethnic balance.

Some governments also perceive refugees as potential threats to national security. These governments are extremely reluctant to offer asylum to refugees from neighboring countries, for fear of endangering political relations, fear of encouraging a mass influx, or fear of admitting ideologically incompatible groups of persons. Mass migrations are frequently employed as foreign policy tools, and refugees have become instruments of warfare and military strategy. These actions have put refugees at risk of physical attack both by the armed forces of the countries of origin and by the agents of the host countries.

For these wide-ranging economic, social, and political reasons, the majority of the world's refugees are not offered permanent asylum or the opportunity to integrate into local communities by most Third World governments. Rather, they are kept separate and dependent on external assistance provided by the international community. Aid programs remain geared to so-called emergency assistance, in order to provide care until that unknown day when the refugees will return home. But camps do not and cannot constitute socially and economically viable long-term settlements. The international community's apparent inability to provide alternatives is one of the greatest failures of the international humanitarian and political systems.

## Consequences of Current Policies

The consequences of such attitudes and policies have yet to be fully realized. The world has not completely turned its back on refugees, although a steady erosion has occurred in even the minimal protections afforded them by international law. Contemporary refugee crises demonstrate the fragility of the international refugee regime. Multilateral arrangements for addressing these problems are under tremendous strain, and it appears that refugee problems have assumed a magnitude beyond the capacity of national or international humanitarian institutions to respond effectively.

The one certain lesson we can draw from the past is that building walls is no answer against those who feel compelled to move. The refugee crises of the interwar years and the Holocaust demonstrated that refugee problems, when exacerbated by prejudice, isolationism, and restrictionism, can be incalculably worse than had ever been imagined. In the aftermath of World War I, the global commitment to refugees was sporadic and shallow, but not ungenerous. As the Great Depression took hold and the outflow of dispossessed people from Hitler's Germany increased, the generosity dried up. Borders were fenced off with barbed wire; refugees were arrested, detained, and deported; and ships filled with thousands of Jewish asylum seekers were turned away from ports everywhere in the world and ultimately forced back to German-occupied Europe and to their extinction. The Palestinian refugee situation illustrates the incredibly harmful consequences of a protracted and long-term refugee problem whose root causes have never been addressed satisfactorily.

Fifty years after the Holocaust, we are at risk of seeing history repeat itself. In former Yugoslavia, grandmothers, mothers, and children are again packed into cattle trucks and deported while husbands, fathers, and sons are herded into detention camps where they are starved and tortured. In response to Europe's greatest postwar refugee crisis, neighboring states have closed their borders, imposed visa restrictions, and warned refugees to stay at home rather than seek refuge abroad. The refugee crisis in Bosnia-Herzegovina represents a tragic failure. Similar events, if not quite on quite so large a scale, are unfolding in Azerbaijan, in the Caucasus, in Moldova, in Central Asia, and in other parts of the former Soviet Union. Across the Atlantic, the United States has set up a naval blockade off the coast of Haiti to prevent Haitians from fleeing their island. The danger exists that the international community may be in the process of creating situations reminiscent of those of dispossessed Jews in the 1930s and of the Palestinians in the 1950s, where large numbers of unwanted people are barred from entry to any place where they might be able to reestablish themselves.

At no moment has it seemed more appropriate—indeed, more urgent—to reexamine both national and international policies and practices toward refugees. War, persecution, and mass expulsions are not just the refugees' problems; they are also perceived to be a major problem by practically every community and nation in the world, because governments fear the instability that uncontrolled migration might bring. The refugee problem is a challenge to the effectiveness of the United Nations, to the political will of the advanced industrialized democracies to respond to the international crises of the post–Cold War era, and to our common humanity. The challenge for governments is to find formulas and mechanisms that will ensure an effective and humane approach to those forced to move in the Balkans, the ex–Soviet Union, Africa, Haiti, and elsewhere, without at the same time inviting instability, more movement, and resulting chaos.

The objective of this book is to provide policymakers, scholars, students, and the general public with a concise examination of the historical context and present implications of the refugee and asylum problem that faces us today. This book examines the scope and nature of the global refugee problem in the twentieth century and the history of international and national responses to that problem since the first intergovernmental attempts were initiated in the aftermath of World War I. The primary issue addressed by the study, however, is whether the contemporary refugee regime is capable of dealing effectively with the new international refugee crisis that is emerging, the increasingly restrictive asylum and resettlement policies in the industrialized world, and the persistent poverty and instability in Third World countries called upon to provide asylum. The book will argue that in the post–Cold War era it is no longer sufficient to respond to the refugee crisis as a strictly humanitarian problem requiring humanitarian solutions, but that a pressing need exists for a more comprehensive political response to the pressures of refugee generations that lie ahead.

This book presents an opportunity to engage in a profound discussion of a crucial question that will shape the course of history in our time. The first step in engaging in such a discussion must be to understand the causes that drive people to move and the serious political and strategic consequences of refugee movements for governments all over the world. A better understanding of the origins and consequences of the refugee problem will not only help combat the growing hostility toward those who seek asylum; it will ultimately help us find appropriate and long-standing solutions to problems that create refugees.

# 1

# Refugee Movements: Causes and Consequences

Refugee movements constitute one of the most important and difficult problems facing the international community in the post–Cold War era. During the last decade, the forced mass movement of people across international boundaries has appeared with increasing frequency on the agendas of international affairs. It is now clear that we are living in an era in which fundamental political and economic changes in the international system result in large-scale movements of people. It is also a time when mass migrations themselves affect political, economic, and strategic developments worldwide. Indeed, it was the outpouring of refugees from East to West Germany in late 1989 that brought down the Berlin Wall, led to the unification of the two Germanies, and generated the most significant transformation in international relations since World War II. Two years later, in the first major post–Cold War refugee crisis, the huge buildup of Iraqi Kurds at the Turkish and Iranian borders constituted such a serious threat to international security that the UN Security Council authorized an international intervention in the domestic affairs of a member state. In 1992, the Security Council approved a United States–led intervention in Somalia to provide humanitarian relief to starving civilians caught in interclan warfare. In the Horn of Africa, in Southern Africa, in Liberia, in Burma, and most recently in parts of the former Yugoslavia and the ex–Soviet Union, ill-treatment of minorities, forced displacement, famine, and environmental damage are challenging the sanctity of borders and the concept of sovereignty and contributing to the disintegration of nations.

Until recently, it would have been unusual for policymakers to classify

11

refugee flows as significant factors affecting local, regional, and international stability and as national security problems. The common perception was that these issues raised humanitarian concerns and demanded a humanitarian response. In reality, refugee movements have important political and security repercussions for both the sending and the receiving countries. Today, peace is no longer threatened primarily by aggressors marching across the borders of sovereign states. The sources of post–Cold War instability are more diffuse and complex, and they include refugee and mass migration movements. Refugee protection and assistance around the world still depend on generosity, but the refugee problem is essentially political. Its prevention and solution, therefore, are not just matters of international charity or humanitarian action by UNHCR and other agencies; ultimately they depend on wider political and diplomatic actions taken by regional and extra-regional states and international organizations to manage regional and ethnic conflicts and to initiate the reintegration of refugees and other displaced people and the economic reconstruction of war-ravaged areas of the world.

## Causes of Refugee Movements: War and Persecution

The majority of contemporary refugee movements in the Third World are caused by war, ethnic strife, and sharp socioeconomic inequalities. The difficulty of building durable state structures in the context of deep ethnic division, economic underdevelopment, indebtedness, and unresolved boundary and natural resource disputes has resulted in much of the domestic conflict and political instability that developing states have experienced.[1]

## The Colonial Legacy

A majority of Third World states have only gained full political independence in recent decades. One legacy of colonialism in the developing world was the arbitrary creation of borders and the preferential treatment of certain population groups. After achieving political independence, many new nations found that communal conflict, competition for resources, and disputes over territory that had once been suppressed by colonial rule now resurfaced and resulted in unstable political institutions and violent conflict. Even when internal conflicts did not materialize, expansion of the armed forces and their role in society has, for many emerging states, been destabilizing. Frequently, political leaders in developing countries used state power structures to ensure their own self-preservation; and corruption, dictatorial government policies, and weak administration contributed to instability. The clash between demands for self-determination on the part of ethnic minorities and efforts by central governments to maintain territorial integrity and existing state boundaries has been at the root of many internal conflicts. Compounding the internal difficulties were the bipolarity, superpower rivalry, and proliferation of arms that characterized international politics during much of the Cold War. These provided a stimulus to militarization and conflict in the Third World.[2]

## Civil Wars

Since attaining independence, hardly any developing country has avoided violent conflict.[3] The protracted civil wars suffered by some less developed countries—Afghanistan, Burma, Cambodia, Lebanon, Sri Lanka, Uganda, and the countries of Central America, the Horn of Africa, and Southern Africa—dramatically express the failure of developing nations to achieve social and political cohesion. More recently, ethnic conflicts, accompanied by economic deprivation and the absence of a strong civil society, have torn apart the former Yugoslavia and threaten several states in the ex–Soviet Union. Domestic weaknesses and internal divisions in Liberia, Somalia, Sri Lanka, Cambodia, and the former states of Yugoslavia and the Soviet Union, among others, make external mediation by the UN or regional organizations extremely difficult and hazardous for the peacekeepers. In recent years, civil wars have become more frequent and more destructive. With modern weaponry accessible even to the very poorest countries, civil war can quickly devastate their fragile infrastructures. Today's internal conflicts are also taking an increasing proportion of civilian lives. According to the Independent Commission on International Humanitarian Issues: "During World War I, 95 percent of casualties were combatants and only 5 percent civilian. World War II saw a complete reversal of the picture with 75 percent civilian and 25 percent combatant casualties. In some contemporary wars, over 90 percent of casualties are civilians."[4]

With such heavy civilian death tolls, it is not surprising that the countries involved in the most destructive wars of the last decade—Afghanistan, Cambodia, Iran, Iraq, Liberia, Mozambique, Somalia, Sudan, Vietnam, and ex-Yugoslavia—have also been the main sources of refugees. It is also true that the principal sources of the current world refugee problem—Angola, Burma, Ethiopia, Iran, Iraq, Somalia, and Vietnam—are among the world's most repressive societies.[5]

## The Emergence of "Refugee Warriors"

Most conflicts in the Third World have generated not only refugees but also refugee fighters. A significant feature of these conflicts is the political and military role played by the refugees themselves.

Because most Third World states are ethnically plural societies, many individual communal groups have their own separate identities, often rooted in common history, culture, religion, and language.[6] Most of these communal groups are dominated by the ruling majority, lack real power, and thus exist without any means to protect or to promote their special interests. They are typically a marginalized sector of society and are not the beneficiaries of state programs. Ethnic conflicts typically begin when central governments threaten to alter the communal group's precarious status or force its members to change their identity or loyalty by seeking cultural and political homogeneity in the form of a new national identity.[7] Armed separatist movements that have as their objective either to seize power by overthrowing their government or to set apart their own province and establish their own state unit frequently include politically and militarily active refugee groups, termed "refugee warriors."[8]

## Separatist Movements

Struggles over the distribution of power and resources, coupled with ethnic, religious, and ideological differences, have been the principal source of some of the most devastating civil wars and episodes of mass repression during the last decade and more.[9] These conflicts have fragmented into many opposition movements that regularly spawn new groups and factions. As several analysts have noted, separatist and irredentist movements drive the most enduring internal conflicts of the modern world, and ethnic conflicts historically have produced some of the largest flows of refugees.[10] In the Horn of Africa, for example, the root cause of the enduring conflicts has been competition for power among multiethnic groups and clans in Ethiopia, Somalia, and Sudan.[11] In Angola, civil war continues to rage between the Ovimbundu of southern Angola, who largely make up UNITA, and the recently elected government in Luanda. In some internal wars, such as those in ex-Yugoslavia, the former Soviet Union, and northern Iraq, the principal objective has been to create refugee movements by driving people from their homes and villages and razing these to make it impossible for the people ever to return.

## Superpower Intervention and Support
## for Freedom Fighters

The ideological and ethnic conflicts of the 1980s provided an arena for foreign intervention. Warring factions within these countries served as surrogates of the superpowers from whom they received considerable support in the form of weaponry, economic assistance, and military training. During the 1980s, due to the globalization of the East–West struggle, the United States and the Soviet Union perceived virtually every region of the world to be vital to their national security interests. Consequently, the superpowers equipped and trained their respective military clients—the refugee warriors or "freedom fighters" of the Third World.[12]

The nearly 3 million Afghan refugees who fled to Pakistan—a close ally of the United States—formed the base for Afghan mujaheddin resistance to the Soviet-backed Afghan government's control in Kabul. Along the Thai–Cambodian border, China, the United States, and the ASEAN nations supported the Khmer resistance front as a way of maintaining political pressure on Vietnam and on Vietnam's client administration in Phnom Penh. In Central America, Nicaraguan "contras" were supplied by the United States to wage a war of resistance in Nicaragua. The Soviet Union, likewise, considered Muslim refugee groups an important factor in the pursuit of its regional and global strategic objectives. Moscow either generously assisted or abandoned groups it had long sponsored, depending on its current perception of Soviet national interests.

Even smaller countries adopted a major-power role by actively supporting, training, and arming refugee warrior groups or government forces, some of whom were thousands of miles away. Pakistani, Iranian, and Saudi support of Afghan mujaheddin; Sandinista Nicaraguan arms supplies to Salvadoran insurgents; and Indian intervention in Sri Lanka are examples of smaller countries' promoting their own political interests through guerrillas and armed refugee groups. In Southern Africa, the South African military used proxies to destabilize frontline states, especially Angola and Mozambique, resulting in large-scale refugee movements. In the Horn of Africa, regional states intervened repeatedly in the affairs of their neighbors by supporting different groups of rebels. Sudan assisted guerrilla units in northern Ethiopia; and Ethiopia and Libya, in turn, backed the Sudan People's Liberation Army's (SPLA) insurgency in southern Sudan. Libya, Egypt, and Sudan became involved on different sides in Chad, and Somalia supported the guerrilla activities of Ethiopian liberation movements and allowed them considerable freedom of movement within its borders.

External intervention frequently complicated and escalated conflict, thus contributing to the generation of refugee movements. As the structure of conflict in the Third World became increasingly international, internal wars became protracted and devastating affairs that were constantly resupplied with materiel from outside. In the process, they produced endless outpourings of refugees.[13]

The ending of the Cold War and of East–West conflict in the Third World have not diminished the risk of displacement. The number of refugees and displaced people is on the rise all over the world. There is no evidence that communally based conflicts in the developing world are abating. Indeed, we should expect ethnic warfare to flare up repeatedly in the 1990s, particularly in regions where such tensions and hatreds have remained largely dormant or suppressed by totalitarian rule for the past generation. We are likely to witness an increasingly chaotic and potentially explosive combination of unreconciled self-determination, democratization, and ethnic and religious revival. This is most evident in the Balkans, Eastern Europe, and the ex–Soviet Union, where long-standing ethnic rivalries are being pursued more conspicuously than at any time since World War II. Disintegration, civil war, and the redrawing of boundaries are creating massive internal hemorrhaging in ex-Yugoslavia and large numbers of refugees in Germany, Hungary, Austria, and other neighboring states. In the former Soviet Union, the number of internal refugees is rapidly growing. Anti-Russian fervor in parts of former Soviet Central Asia, the Baltic states, and other regions is spurring a flight of Russians from these new states. Armenians and Azeris flee attacks from each other in Nagorno-Karabakh, while conflicts in Georgia and Tajikistan have driven tens of thousands of refugees into neighboring states. Ethnic discrimination within Romania and Bulgaria has already resulted in migratory movements of Romanian Magyars and Bulgarian Turks, and of Romanian gypsies and Bulgarians, across international borders. The breakup of Czechoslovakia could increase tensions between Slovaks and Hungarians. But conflicts are also likely to occur among indigenous populations in Latin America, Southeast Asia, Africa, and elsewhere.

## Push and Pull Factors

Although systemic factors such as warfare, repression, and external intervention are without question the principal causes of contemporary refugee movements, other factors also cause people to flee their homelands. Certain conditions must exist in the states of destination as well. Policymakers and refugee experts now speak of *push* and *pull* factors prompting migration.[14] In the context of contemporary Third World conflicts, it is said that individuals are "pushed out" of their home countries by various disruptive conditions. Push factors are generally negative—conflict, political instability, social inequalities, poor economic opportunities. Policymakers and analysts also speak of "pull" factors, such as higher standards of living, jobs, or freer communities in the country of destination, that "pull" or attract people to them. In addition, ethnic and migrant networks play an important role, informing potential emigrants and refugees of employment and living conditions and offering assistance to co-nationals when they first arrive in host countries. Pull factors are generally positive. Roughly speaking, if you are pushed you are a refugee, and if you are pulled you are an ordinary migrant.

The push–pull approach lends itself to making the differentiations that characterize policy debates over distinctions between economic and political refugees. In practice, however, it may be extremely difficult to assess the relative importance of push and pull factors in any individual decision to leave the home country. Inevitably, there is a mixture of both, particularly when people flee from countries where poverty is a direct consequence of the political system. In Haiti, for example, the state serves as a vehicle for the enrichment of a small elite at the expense of the majority of the population. The Haitians who have fled in the tens of thousands for the past several decades have escaped extreme poverty caused by political exploitation. Thus, distinctions between politically and economically motivated flight that are made by social scientists in a theoretical typology do not necessarily transfer to the policymaking arena.

As another example, throughout the 1980s the British and Hong Kong governments based their policy toward Vietnamese boat people on the assumption that nearly all Vietnamese were attracted to Hong Kong as economic migrants, seeking family reunion and material opportunity. Because it was widely perceived that opportunities for work and resettlement were the factors that motivated the Vietnamese to leave home, deterrence policies (such as denial of resettlement and employment, and crowded, prisonlike living conditions) were introduced as far back as the early 1980s in the expectation that people would not continue to come if they had no access to these attractions and if conditions were miserable. Deterrence policies failed to discourage people from leaving Vietnam, however, thus demonstrating that—at least in the case of the Vietnamese boat people—push factors in the homeland, such as political repression, economic stagnation, and poverty, have been as strong as pull factors in the country of first asylum. Throughout the 1980s, people continued to risk their lives to leave Vietnam.[15]

In a period when it is difficult to maintain clear divisions between immigrants and refugees, the inclination of most governments is to label all unwanted migrants, no matter what their motivations, as economic refugees. Ironically, the term *economic refugees* was first used to describe Jews leaving Germany in the 1930s; they were referred to as the *Wirtschaftsemigranten*.

## European Host Nations

In addition to responding to push–pull factors, population flows are determined by refugee admission and immigration control policies, by welfare systems and standards of living, and even by flight patterns of the major airlines. Because until recently Italy and Spain had less rigid border controls than existed in traditional receiving countries, both countries experienced an upsurge in illegal immigration, particularly from North Africa.

Patterns of migration can also be viewed as being the result of differences in opportunities between various countries or regions.[16] In France until the late 1980s, asylum seekers were able to register at the National Employment Agency and qualify for a maximum of one year's entitlement to an integration allowance, in the same way as refugees. As a result some people who were not refugees made asylum claims in order to receive social assistance. Germany, which until 1993 had incorporated the right to political asylum in its constitution and remains the most prosperous West European state, has consistently attracted more than half of the total asylum applicants on the continent. Cultural affinity and geographical proximity, as well as the relaxation of exit controls in most postcommunist states and huge economic differentials between Germany and the East, have made Germany the destination point for increasing numbers of East Europeans. Moreover, Frankfurt airport is at the crossroads of major international flight patterns and is therefore a gateway for many Third World travelers. Yet, it is not former colonial powers, but Sweden, Australia, and Canada—countries with very high standards of living, liberal social climates, and economies requiring a continuous input of foreign labor—that rank highest among all countries in ratio of refugees to population.[12]

## Resettlement and Asylum in the United States

The United States, likewise, is a draw for millions of immigrants from all over the world. For specific refugee groups, the United States has not only extended asylum, it has positively welcomed them, particularly if they are victims of one of the United States' ideological adversaries. Since the mid-1970s, the United States has admitted well over 1 million refugees, far more than any other nation, and it remains one of the few Western countries that have not significantly cut back on acceptances in recent years.

The United States has sought to cultivate the image of being a country where the politically oppressed might find relief. The importance given to the Statue of Liberty and to the words of Emma Lazarus welcoming the "huddled masses yearning to breathe free" testifies to this desire. Refugees come to the United States because of its cultural diversity and political openness, and because of the prospect of greater economic security. America's appeal is that it offers the largest, most dynamic, and most prosperous economy in the world. For refugees whose migration is frequently motivated by extremely bleak economic conditions, as well as by fear of political persecution or physical violence, the United States promises physical safety and an opportunity for economic betterment.

Many Western countries have special relations with individual developing nations, many of these dating back to the colonial era. These links affect the flow of individual asylum seekers and migrants, and they impose constraints on the way asylum policy is implemented. For example, Cuban and other Latin American exiles often seek asylum in Spain; the United Kingdom has asylum applicants from the Commonwealth; Francophone Africans and Maghrebis seek refuge in France; Zairois flee to Belgium; and Portuguese-speaking Africans go to Portugal. These special historical links impose constraints that are not easy to reconcile with attempts to harmonize asylum and migration policies.

## The Political Uses of Refugees

Large-scale refugee flows are not just the result of wars, internal upheavals, or economic conditions; frequently they stem from officially instigated or organized state actions. Refugee movements are often made to happen by governments in order to reduce or eliminate selected social classes and ethnic groups within their own borders.[18] Conversely, they may be used to affect the policies and politics of their neighbors.

Increasingly in the last decade and a half, states have actively used refugee movements or "push-outs" as tools in their foreign policies.[19] Forced emigration is a policy through which a state can project its economic and political influence, seek to affect the policies and politics of other states, or compel a neighboring state to provide recognition, aid, or credit in return for halting or regularizing the flow.[20]

Some sending countries have even come to see refugee exoduses as an economic resource. The benefits of out-migration may include the export of an unemployed or underemployed population, the hope of maximizing foreign currency earnings through remittances by their expatriate citizens, and the provision of an outlet or "safety valve" for the relief of domestic dissidence and economic pressures. For example, for years refugees constituted one of Vietnam's most valuable exports, and remittances from overseas made up over half of the country's hard currency earnings. In the past some countries of origin have even bartered people in exchange for much-needed foreign currency. For decades, West Germany provided huge sums for East German emigrants and for ethnic Germans from Romania and the Soviet Union. Israel is reported to have paid $2,000 for each of the 16,000 Falashas it evacuated from Addis Ababa after the departure of President Mengistu in 1991.[21]

In addition, governments have employed refugee exoduses to rid themselves of political dissidents, potential challengers to authority, unwanted minorities, and other "undesirables," as well as to destabilize or embarrass their adversaries and to capture the assets of their departing citizens. For example, ASEAN officials claimed during the late 1970s that the expulsion by Vietnam of hundreds of thousands of Vietnamese nationals of Chinese origin was a veiled attempt to create racial and economic problems in Southeast Asia and to infiltrate enemy agents into the region. Similarly, Fidel Castro's deliberate expulsion of a number of criminals and psychotics during the 1980 Mariel boatlift to Key West, Florida, was an attempt to embarrass the United States. Idi Amin ousted Uganda's Asian minority in the early 1970s to rid the country of an unwanted group and to acquire their valuable assets in the process. Entire regions in Ethiopia were deliberately depopulated in an effort to deprive Eritrean and Tigrean opposition movements of their popular bases. In more recent years, the Burmese military drove out hundreds of thousands of its Arakan Muslim minority to rid itself of some of its unwanted citizens, and Serbian militias ruthlessly implemented a policy of "ethnic cleansing" to clear territory it claimed of opposing ethnic groups.

The export of refugees can also be used as a bargaining chip in interstate negotiations over trade and bilateral political recognition. Typically in such situations, the sending state possesses considerable leverage in the bargaining process. By pleading an inability to control the population outflow, or by demonstrating a willingness to manipulate it, the sending state can extract strategic and foreign policy concessions from the receiving state. The Vietnamese government, for example, conditioned its willingness to cooperate on the repatriation of boat people on the West's agreement to secure for Hanoi greater integration into the world economy—especially access to credit—and diplomatic recognition, particularly by the United States. During the mid-1980s, the East German government facilitated the entry into West Berlin of tens of thousands of Third World asylum applicants. The Honecker regime anticipated that West Berlin and West German reception facilities and judicial systems would be unable to cope with such massive numbers of arrivals and would be forced to recognize (at least tacitly) the East German state or to provide it with additional financial credits in returning for halting the flow.

In April 1991, in the aftermath of a mass influx of boat people into Italy, President Ramiz Alia of Albania reportedly agreed to enforce stricter departure controls against his own people in return for Italian food aid and credits to shore up the Albanian economy. When Italy was deemed too slow in releasing this aid, Albanian authorities acquiesced in yet another mass departure of their citizens to Italy in August 1991. In response to this crisis, the Italian government and the European Community promised more emergency aid to alleviate the economic breakdown in Albania. Shortly after the first of these incidents, President Lech Walesa, while on a visit to the United States, warned of an Albanian-like exodus from Poland, should his country not receive sufficient American economic assistance and debt relief.[22] And policymakers in Soviet successor states, trying to broker Western-assisted reform packages for their country, have repeatedly warned the West of the dire strategic and geopolitical consequences of chaos and displacement in the former Soviet Union, should outside aid not be forthcoming.

## Foreign Policy and Admissions Policies

Admissions policies for refugees have also been based on political, ethnic, and ideological sympathies.[23] Thus, for the first two decades after World War II, nearly all refugees who sought asylum in the West fled the political repression and economic hardship of the Soviet-backed regimes of Eastern Europe. Cultural similarity made for relatively easy integration into the host countries, and refugees provided much-needed labor for the expanding economies of the West. Population groups that managed to secure refugee status in the United States generally had powerful domestic lobbies. Soviet Jews and Pentacostals received strong backing from the American Jewish and Evangelical communities, and special provisions assisted their settlement in the United States; Cuban emigrants have found immediate support from a large and vociferous Cuban-American community in Florida; Polish immigrants have benefited from advocates among Polish-Americans; and the large-scale admission of Indochinese refugees was spearheaded by a combination of American religious, ethnic, and refugee resettlement organizations.[24] In the Federal Republic of Germany and in Hungary, ethnic Germans from Eastern Europe and the Soviet Union and Magyars from Romania are automatically considered citizens. Even in the developing world, responses to refugee influxes frequently have been determined by historical connections and ethnic and cultural links. In 1991–1992, Bangladesh, one of the world's poorest countries, received several hundred thousand fellow Muslims from neighboring Burma, despite devastating effects of this policy on the country's local economy and environment.

## The Symbolic Use of Refugees

During the Cold War, for obvious political and ideological reasons, refugees from communism were welcomed in the West. In fact, they were encouraged to "vote with their feet." Until very recently, the West has seen refugees as symbols of foreign policy, to be exploited as part of a continuing propaganda campaign. The terms *refugee* and *defector* became synonymous, particularly at the height of the Cold War. Each defection, each crossing into Austria or West Berlin, was construed as a "ballot for freedom." Large numbers of communist bloc refugees were accepted into Europe without question and without close investigation into their motives.

U.S. refugee admission policy toward communist states has been guided by the belief that refugee outflows serve to embarrass enemy nations and discredit their political systems.[25] The decision to bestow formal refugee status on citizens of a particular state usually implies condemnation of the sending government for persecuting its citizens. A generous admissions policy toward a certain group may in fact encourage them to flee; this flight can then be used for propaganda purposes. It can also be used to encourage "brain drains" and the departure of much-needed skilled and professional workers and to arm opposition groups. Conversely, a decision not to accord refugee status to certain national groups often implies support for the sending government. Such foreign policy considerations explain, for example, the different treatment in recent years accorded by the United States to Salvadorans, Guatemalans, and Haitians, whose domestic patrons lacked political clout, as opposed to Cubans, Indochinese, and Nicaraguans, who had powerful political supporters.

## Anticommunist Bias and Open Admissions

American refugee policy has consistently demonstrated an anticommunist bias, and this has translated into virtually open-ended blanket admissions for individuals fleeing communist regimes.[26] Of the 711,303 refugees admitted to the United States during the Reagan administration, 96 percent were from communist countries.[27] Since the early 1970s, specific legislative measures, such as the Jackson–Vanik amendment, have linked the extension of trade benefits to communist nations with freer emigration from those countries. The beneficiaries of special U.S. anticommunist immigration programs included, from late 1965 to 1973, hundreds of thousands of Cubans who arrived as refugees via an airlift of "freedom flights." The objective was to embarrass and discredit the Castro government.[28]

Similarly, when hundreds of thousands of people fled from Vietnam beginning in the late 1970s, the American obligation to a failed ally, the politicization of the refugee problem as an East–West issue, and the unwillingness of neighboring countries to accept responsibility for the local settlement of any of the boat people forced the Western resettlement states to treat all arriving Vietnamese as refugees.[29]

A policy that indiscriminately offers refugee status to large national groups irrespective of the merits of individual claims frequently attracts large illegal migrant flows and invites abuse of refugee and asylum procedures.[30] Open-ended refugee admissions programs for those leaving communist countries, in combination with policies that fail to address the causes that lead to refugee outflows, create "pull and push" factors that inevitably damage public support for a generous refugee admissions policy. Thus, for example, the 1980 Mariel boatlift and the obvious diversity in the origins of the Cubans arriving on U.S. shores during those hectic months caused the United States to begin questioning whether everyone who left Cuba was a refugee. Similarly, after a decade and a half of giving presumptive refugee status to Vietnamese boat people, many Westerners began to question whether all such people had valid claims to refugee status, whether conditions were improving in Vietnam, and whether many people were leaving Vietnam for allegedly less deserving reasons.

With the collapse of communism and the end of the Cold War, a person's decision to leave an Eastern European state is no longer sufficient grounds, in itself, for a claim to asylum; and Western states are quickly raising new barriers in fear of mass migration from East to West. Italy, for example, recently showed some of Europe's new toughness by forcibly repatriating thousands of Albanians seeking to escape Eastern Europe's poorest country, and several Western European states have refused entry to ex-Yugoslavs fleeing a brutal civil war.

In the United States, too, the value of refugee policy as an instrument of American containment strategies has diminished as changes in the communist bloc have rendered this historical basis of American foreign policy obsolete. New political conditions in the late Soviet Union, in combination with freer emigration policies in the ex-USSR and tighter U.S. budget restrictions, ended *carte-blanche* admission for all Soviet Jews, Armenians, and Evangelical Christians.[31] For years, the difficulty Jews faced in obtaining exit permits and the deprivations they suffered in the process gave U.S. government officials sufficient reason to label all who managed to leave as refugees. Recently, however, emigrés have had to prove, individually, that they would face persecution, if returned. And whereas, in the past, Jews leaving the Soviet Union with Israeli visas could reapply for a U.S. visa once they reached Italy or Austria, by the late 1980s they had to apply directly to the U.S. Embassy in Moscow.

Similar political changes in Eastern Europe have resulted in a similarly dramatic lowering of acceptance rates by U.S. authorities of asylum applicants from that region. Nevertheless, unusually sympathetic responses by the United States continue to mark the treatment of individuals fleeing certain countries. The U.S. Congress, for example, continues to extend legislation giving Jews and Evangelical Christians from the ex–Soviet Union, Ukrainian religious activists, and certain Indochinese groups "presumptive refugee status eligibility," requiring a lower standard of proof for such people leaving those countries.[32] Moreover, the vast majority of refugees who will be admitted in the early 1990s will continue to be from communist or formerly communist countries. Of the estimated 132,000 refugees to be admitted to the United States through the overseas resettlement program in fiscal year 1993,[33] over three-quarters of the places were allocated for Soviets and Indochinese, neither of whom were any longer generally considered to be groups fleeing persecution.[34]

While foreign policy factors appear to play a less important role in other countries than they do in the United States, nearly all governments make it easier for some refugees to enter than for others. *Carte-blanche* admission of refugees occurs in the Third World when those refugees serve the political and military interests of the host country. In Pakistan, for example, Afghans were the beneficiaries of a massive relief effort and were given almost complete freedom of movement, while Iranians were given tenuous temporary asylum and received virtually no government assistance. This also helps explain the past acceptance of Nicaraguans in Honduras, of Cambodians in Thailand, of Mozambicans in Malawi, and of Ethiopians and Eritreans in Sudan.

## Refugee Movements as Security Risks

The specter of refugee influxes is often invoked as a threat to the national security of host governments. But what constitutes "security" or a threat to that security? How do government policies stimulate refugee flows, and what effect do mass displacements have on international stability?

Traditionally, *security* has been defined solely in terms of power relations between states, specifically in terms of preserving the territorial integrity of the state or the physical safety and continuity of a particular government in the face of external or internal military threats. In the post–Cold War era, *security* has acquired a new and more complex significance. To traditional political-military issues at the interstate level must be added many other concerns, including ethnic conflict, refugee and migration flows, and population growth. In addition, national security now includes economic and social factors, such as establishing conditions for economic welfare and preserving intercommunal harmony, as well as consideration of political participation and protection of minority rights.

Undoubtedly, mass influxes of refugees can endanger social and economic security—particularly in countries already suffering from economic underdevelopment, unstable political systems, and ethnic or other social cleavages. The world's refugee burden, for example, is carried overwhelmingly by the poorest states; the twenty countries with the highest ratio of refugees have an annual average per capita income of $700 (see Table 1-1).[35] Refugees compete with already desperate nationals for scarce jobs and service.[36] The strain on social services and physical infrastructure, the distortion of local economic conditions, and the racial and religious tensions that can surface in countries with acute cultural heterogeneity

*Table 1-1*  Refugees in Relation to Local Population and Per Capita GNP of the Asylum Country, 1991

| Country | Ratio of Refugee to Non-Refugee Population | Number of Refugees | Population (in millions) | GNP Per Capita |
|---|---|---|---|---|
| Gaza Strip[a] | 1/1 | 528,700 | 0.6 | N/A |
| West Bank[a] | 1/3 | 430,100 | 1.1 | N/A |
| Djibouti | 1/3 | 120,000 | 0.4 | N/A |
| Jordan | 1/4 | 960,200 | 3.4 | $1,730 |
| French Guiana[a] | 1/10 | 9,600 | 0.1 | N/A |
| Malawi | 1/10 | 950,000 | 9.4 | 180 |
| Lebanon | 1/11 | 314,200 | 3.4 | N/A |
| Guinea | 1/13 | 566,000 | 7.5 | 430 |
| Belize | 1/17 | 12,000 | 0.2 | 1,600 |
| Swaziland | 1/17 | 47,200 | 0.8 | 900 |
| Iran | 1/24 | 3,150,000 | 58.6 | N/A |
| Pakistan | 1/33 | 3,594,000 | 117.5 | 370 |
| Sudan | 1/36 | 717,200 | 25.9 | 420 |
| Syria | 1/44 | 293,900 | 12.8 | 1,020 |
| Namibia | 1/50 | 30,200 | 1.5 | N/A |
| Zimbabwe | 1/50 | 198,500 | 10.0 | 640 |
| Côte d'Ivoire | 1/52 | 240,400 | 12.5 | 790 |
| Mauritania | 1/53 | 40,000 | 2.1 | 490 |
| Burundi | 1/54 | 107,000 | 5.8 | 220 |
| Zambia | 1/60 | 140,500 | 8.4 | 390 |
| Zaire | 1/78 | 482,300 | 37.8 | 260 |
| Hong Kong[a] | 1/98 | 60,000 | 5.9 | 10,320 |
| Ethiopia | 1/100 | 534,000 | 53.2 | 120 |
| Thailand | 1/115 | 512,700 | 58.8 | 1,170 |

[a]Territories, not sovereign countries.

SOURCE: *World Refugee Survey 1992* (Washington, D.C.: U.S. Committee for Refugees, 1992).

constitute legitimate security concerns for many developing countries. In parts of Asia and the Middle East, an influx of refugees has been accompanied by a vast increase in the flows of arms and drugs, which contributed to domestic instability and to the rise in crime and violence in the host countries.

As a general rule, the more racial, linguistic, religious, or cultural characteristics incoming refugees have in common with the native population, the easier integration will be. In the Third World, the remarkable receptivity provided to millions of Afghans in Pakistan and Iran, to ethnic kin from Bulgaria in Turkey, to Burmese Muslims in Bangladesh, to Ethiopians in the Sudan, to Ogadeni Ethiopians in Somalia, to Southern Sudanese in Uganda, and to Mozambicans in Malawi have been facilitated by the ethnic and linguistic characteristics the refugees share with their hosts. The generally celebrated receptivity of African countries to refugees from neighboring countries has been commonly credited to hospitality within related groups of people who straddle borders.

How ready a country has been to respond to the needs of refugees— to offer them temporary asylum or permanent settlement—has always depended on its sense of security as well as on its absorptive capacity. In the past, many of the larger African refugee movements spilled over into border areas of neighboring states occupied by ethnic kin of the refugees. Throughout the 1960s and 1970s, and until Africa's refugee dilemma reached its current alarming scale, most international assistance for African refugees from donor states and relief agencies was directed toward supporting the development of organized rural settlements and to maintaining urban refugees. But the majority of Africa's uprooted people managed to settle themselves in various locations. As a result, the impact of refugee influxes was less noticeable. Where land was relatively abundant, refugees were often welcomed because labor was needed; in places where they put strains on food supplies and other local resources, they were not so well received. Nevertheless, until recent years refugees were often given the opportunity to support themselves and to lead relatively normal lives among people with whom they shared a common history and culture.[37]

Refugees are welcome when they are seen as contributing to the host state's power base, national self-confidence, or dominant ethnic community. The large-scale influx of Soviet Jewish immigrants to Israel, for example, is viewed by Tel Aviv as a welcome demographic boost to the state, stabilizing what was a steady decline of the Jewish people as a percentage of the population of "Greater Israel," and forming a potentially significant part of a future settler community for the West Bank. To Arabs, on the other hand, the Jewish influx creates instability at a time of great upheaval in the region and places renewed pressure on Palestinians to leave the occupied territories and to take refuge in nearby countries such as Jordan, whose economy has already been shattered by the Gulf War.

Even in situations where refugees share similar ethnic and linguistic characteristics with their hosts, hospitality can soon wear thin, especially when strategic and security issues are at stake. Since the late 1980s, the influx of Issaq refugees from Somalia has aggravated Djibouti's ethnic, economic, and security problems, despite the fact that the cultural links of the majority of Issa Djiboutis are with Somalia.[38] Farther south, the refugee population in Kenya increased twentyfold in the 18 months from early 1991 to mid-1992. The Kenyan government, wary of Somalia's territorial claims and anxious to limit the number of starving refugees crossing its borders, took an increasingly tough line with ethnically affiliated Somali refugees who were fleeing vicious interclan warfare and widespread starvation.[39] In other situations, financial and other interests tilt the balance against hospitality to refugees. From the late 1980s on, tens of thousands of Burmese refugees, mainly ethnic minorities and students, sought asylum across the Thai frontier. The Thai government, which had close personal ties with the Burmese military authorities and had considerable interest in exploiting Burma's natural resources, had no political interest in providing refuge and periodically attempted to seal off the nation's borders to refugees from Burma in order to avoid conflict with its neighbor.[40]

## Refugees as Sources of Interstate Tension

In pursuit of national security objectives or regional hegemony, neighboring states employ or even instigate military activity within refugee communities across their common borders. The three major countries in the Horn of Africa (Somalia, Ethiopia, and Djibouti) have all used asylum and assistance as a surrogate form of support for rebel movements in other states.[41] The Eritrean and Tigrean Liberation Fronts for many years maintained a political base in Sudan, while the Sudanese People's Liberation Army was allowed to operate from the refugee-hosting areas of southwest Ethiopia. Depending on the state of relations between Addis Ababa and Mogadishu, Somali opposition groups have at various times been given assistance and shelter by the Ethiopian government.

Similarly, Thailand allowed international humanitarian agencies to provide assistance to some 400,000 Cambodians on its border, as a means of sustaining the Khmer resistance groups and of providing a buffer between it and the Vietnamese army.[42] In Honduras, Salvadorans and Guatemalans were perceived as security threats and were kept in enclosed camps, whereas Nicaraguan exiles were viewed as allies in an anticommunist struggle and consequently enjoyed much greater freedom of movement and were allowed to work outside their camps.[43]

The presence of refugees, therefore, raises what may already be a high level of tension between neighboring countries. Migrant and refugee communities frequently maintain close links with their countries of origin. These diasporas actively lobby their host governments to adopt specific foreign policies toward their former home countries. For the United States, the presence of nearly 1 million Cuban refugees, most of whom are implacably opposed to the Castro regime, has clearly made the normalization of U.S.–Cuban relations more difficult. Similarly, the 600,000-strong Croatian community in Germany lobbied Bonn to take the lead among Western governments in opposing Serbian policies and in recognizing the newly independent republics of Croatia and Slovenia, thereby discrediting Germany as an impartial actor in the civil war raging in ex-Yugoslavia. In other parts of the world, the existence of large numbers of Tamils in Tamil Nadu in southern India has greatly complicated New Delhi's dealings with the Sinhalese government of Sri Lanka.

In many Third World regions of conflict, fighters often mingle among refugee populations, using the camps for rest, medical treatment, and sometimes recruitment. Such actions clearly attract military retaliation. During the 1980s, South Africa, for example, regularly attacked camps in Angola, Botswana, Zambia, and Lesotho; and Vietnamese forces repeatedly shelled Cambodian refugees encamped along the Thai border. Claiming that refugee camps harbored guerrillas and subversives, the Guatemalan army crossed the border into Mexico and ruthlessly attacked refugee settlements in Chiapas. Ethiopia regularly carried out raids against refugees inside the Sudan. Southern Sudanese rebels attacked Ugandan refugee settlements, and Uganda attacked Rwandan refugee settlements. In 1985, Angolan government troops attacked some of the estimated hundreds of thousands of Angolan refugees who had taken asylum in Zambia and Zaire. On several occasions in the past, the Honduran army entered camps for Salvadorans within its own territory and killed or injured refugees living there.

Thus, while refugees are often pawns or victims in relations between states, they are by no means always passive political actors. Frequently, they are part of highly conscious communities with armed leaders engaged in warfare for political objectives, such as to recapture their homeland, to destabilize the ruling regime, or to secure a separate state. Contemporary Third World conflicts have also clearly demonstrated that refugee warriors often pursue independent foreign policies that prove difficult to contain and control. American support for the unsuccessful Bay of Pigs attack against Cuba in 1961, for example, led to a subsequent commitment by the United States to provide political asylum for the participants. For the past several decades, some of these groups have been involved in clandestine armed activities against the Cuban regime; others have been engaged in the enormous narcotics trade in Miami. During the 1980s, Miami also became a center for the recruitment of Nicaraguan contra forces who, like the Cuban "freedom fighters," were difficult to contain and control once they began their armed and political struggle against the Sandinista regime in Managua from their exile bases in Florida.

The actions of refugee warriors during the past decade have also influenced the structure of regional and international peace agreements. In the past, the presence of Afghan refugees and mujaheddin in Pakistan or of Nicaraguan contras in Honduras, for example, have created obstacles to ceasefires and peace agreements in Afghanistan and Central America. As long as these refugee warriors had not achieved their goals, they tended to oppose the repatriation of other refugees, who provided legitimacy and manpower for their political and armed struggles. To give only five examples, the forces of the Khmer Rouge, the Afghan mujaheddin, the Salvadoran FMLN, the Angolan UNITA forces, and the Kurdish peshmergas have in the past either prevented refugees from returning "prematurely" or have encouraged them to go home specifically to provide internal sources of support for their continuing guerrilla struggles.

## The Politicization of Humanitarian Aid

Humanitarianism has been adopted by states as a political tool, for example, to justify arming refugee camps in Thailand, Pakistan, and Honduras, aiding insurgency in Nicaragua, Ethiopia, Iraq, Afghanistan, and Angola, and suppressing insurgency in El Salvador, Guatemala, and elsewhere. The practice of using refugees to serve strategic or military objectives has been used widely by small and big powers and even by refugee warrior groups.[44] Increasingly, the UNHCR and aid agencies must operate in the midst of ongoing conflicts where even the most humanitarian activities are perceived by one or even all parties as a factor affecting the outcome of the confrontation.

Internal wars in the Third World and most recently in parts of ex-Yugoslavia and the ex–Soviet Union have been fought not only by military means but also by preventing international aid from reaching people living in conflict areas.[45] Aid workers have experienced increasingly serious difficulties in gaining access to refugees and displaced people in areas contested by governments and guerrilla groups, such as in Somalia, Liberia, southern Sudan, northern Ethiopia, El Salvador, Sri Lanka, and Bosnia-Herzegovina. In the 1980s, even UN authorities were denied access to some Cambodian refugee camps along the Thai border. The International Committee for the Red Cross (ICRC) was expelled from South Africa in the mid-1980s, leaving only local voluntary agencies and officials of the homelands—both of which were highly vulnerable to South African pressure—responsible for the protection of Mozambican refugees. In Somalia and in ex-Yugoslavia, ICRC, UN, and voluntary agency workers have been attacked and killed. In numerous situations all over the world, voluntary agencies have been requested by governments and military leaders to leave militarily contested areas or even whole countries involved in civil wars and separatist struggles.

In such situations, it is not surprising that food supplies have assumed great strategic significance. This is particularly true in the Horn of Africa, where governments and some guerrilla groups used food aid to advance their political goals. In periods of conflict, no country in the Horn has held back from attacking the civilian food supply in areas controlled by armed opposition groups; and international aid agencies have come under strong pressure to support one side or the other. In 1990, fighting in northern Somalia was accompanied by major restrictions on aid agency activities and blockages of food supplies, while government forces carried out a scorched earth campaign in areas inhabited by actual or potential supporters of the rebels. After the overthrow of Siad Barre in 1991, armed bandits and feuding clans prevented food from reaching millions of starving Somalis, and the country descended into a desperate spiral of anarchy, looting, famine, and self-destruction. Voluntary agencies even hired armed Somalis, and the United States and other states dispatched armed troops, to guard food supplies and to ensure their safe delivery to those needing food and medicines. In neighboring Sudan, voluntary agencies active in areas controlled by the Sudanese People's Liberation Army were ordered to leave the country altogether; and in its bitter struggle with the Sudanese government over control of famine relief, the SPLA at times declared airspace in southern regions off limits to overflight. The government, its officially supported tribal militias, and the Sudanese armed forces all delayed or disrupted attempts to bring food supplies from the north into the south by road, barge, train, or air.[46] In Ethiopia, neither the Haile Selassie regime nor the Mengistu regime allowed shipments of food and other aid from government-held towns into rebel-occupied territory. In 1989, the Ethiopian Army requested that all international agencies vacate Eritrea, to clear the way for their military offensive against the EPLF; and they allowed only limited food aid to be trucked into areas of pressing need. The Ethiopian government also attacked food convoys on their way into the country from Sudan and the food distribution centers established by rebel movements. These policies amounted to de facto depopulation, through enforced famine or through expulsion, as starving local populations left their homes in search of food elsewhere. The Ethiopian government also used international food aid as "bait" to lure peasants into resettlement camps; those who refused to move hundreds of miles from their homes were denied food and were separated from their children.[47]

In civil war conditions, it has at times been virtually impossible for humanitarian aid to get through.[41] Humanitarian agencies face harassment, defamation, or expulsion; and members of their staff—local and expatriate—have been beaten, arrested, kidnapped, tortured, and murdered. The agencies are perceived as working for governments or rebel groups and are thought to have hidden political or religious agendas. In fact, governments have been tightening their controls on aid agencies, attempting to incorporate them into officially managed programs that benefit only their own supporters. Throughout the Third World and most recently in parts of ex-Yugoslavia, agencies have been excluded from war zones—in part to deny supposed civilian supporters of rebel groups or ethnic minorities food or medical aid, and in great measure to prevent independent observers from becoming witnesses to the brutal human rights violations perpetrated on noncombatants. But rebel movements and refugee warrior communities also insist on tight rules over international agency activities, including permits to travel and restrictions on access to certain areas.[49]

Throughout the world the gap between international legal and humanitarian standards and actual state practice appears to be growing. As persons outside their country of origin, refugees are entitled under international law to protection by the UN High Comissioner for Refugees and should be safe from being returned home against their will. In international and regional refugee law, the granting of asylum is described as a non-political, humanitarian act. In practice, governments rarely if ever regard it this way—particularly in Third World regions of conflict, and increasingly in Europe as well.

Refugees are legally entitled to a range of human rights and social and material assistance. Although humanitarianism is a factor in the formulation of government policy toward refugees, it is generally outweighed by political and strategic concerns.[50] One major difficulty inherent in the international refugee regime is the near impossibility of implementing protection through an international agency when decisions on asylum and treatment remain the prerogative of individual states. Thus, the scope and activities allowed to the UNHCR depend on the policies of the host government and on the pressure other countries can be persuaded to bring to bear on it. Even the funds made available to the UNHCR by donor states depend on how useful those states perceive a particular refugee population to be to their ongoing foreign policy. The extent of UNHCR activities and influence is delineated by political constraints. As the promoter and guardian of refugee rules, it can call attention to the legal obligations assumed by governments that are signatories to the UN Refugee Convention and Protocol, but it is limited in available means to change the course of action of a government that is determined to violate international standards.

The UNHCR's humanitarian mission is rendered powerless in situations where certain groups of people are the very subject of civil and ethnic conflict. In the former Yugoslavia, for example, the UNHCR was confronted with the choice of either accepting Muslim and Croatian prisoners whom the Serbian militia handed over to them—which in effect would have made them accomplices in the Serbian policy of ethnic cleansing—or refusing to free them from internment in camps or from risk to their lives in conflict zones. The UNHCR cannot fulfill its mandate in a war of such intensity and cruelty. In many post–Cold War conflicts, humanitarian work is no substitute for concerted political solutions.

Although organized international cooperation on refugees has a long history, the claimed rights of national sovereignty have nearly always been used as a cloak to prevent the international community from intervening in the domestic affairs of other states. Perhaps the most tragic refugee crisis of the twentieth century was precipitated by a national government's massive violations of the human rights of particular minority groups and by the inability of other governments to address the "root causes" of the ensuing refugee movements from Nazi Germany. Then, as now, governments placed numerous restrictions on the High Commissioner for Refugees; but it was the first time a refugee problem was to be the subject of international concern and cooperation. The way the problem was dealt with by the international community offers a number of constructive lessons both for the present and for the future.

# 2

# The Origins of
# the International Refugee
# Regime

Many people today are inclined to perceive refugees as a relatively new phenomenon that primarily occurs in countries in Africa, Asia, and Latin America, and in rapidly disintegrating countries in the Balkans and the ex–Soviet Union. Certainly during the past few decades most refugees have fled violent conflicts or persecution in the developing countries; but mass refugee movements are neither new nor unique to the Third World.[1] They have been a political as well as a humanitarian issue for as long as mankind has lived in organized groups where intolerance and oppression have existed. The difference is that, before this century, refugees were regarded as assets rather than liabilities; countries granted refuge to people of geopolitical, religious, or ideological views similar to their own; and rulers viewed control over large populations, along with natural resources and territory itself, as an index of power and national greatness.[2]

While most refugees of earlier eras found it possible to gain safe haven outside their country of origin, this has not been the case for many refugees in the twentieth century. After both world wars, Europe experienced refugee flows similar to those taking place in the Third World today. Like most contemporary refugee movements, people left their homes for varied and complex reasons, including the severe economic disruption and starvation that accompanied the violence and disruption of war and the upheaval of political and social revolution that followed the breakup of multiethnic empires and the creation of new nation-states. The majority of these people were members of unwanted minority groups, political fugitives, or the victims of warfare, communalism, and indiscriminate violence. Essentially, the refugee problems of the period from 1921 to 1951 were political ones, as they are today.

The international responses to mass expulsions, compulsory transfers of population, mass exits, and arbitrary denial of return were often weak and inconsistent. In circumstances similar to those that exist in parts of the Third World and Eastern Europe today, mass influxes threatened the security of European states, particularly when many refugee crises became protracted affairs that surpassed the capabilities of humanitarian agencies and individual states to resolve.

Organized international efforts for refugees began in 1921, when the League of Nations appointed the first High Commissioner for Refugees. Over the next twenty years, the scope and functions of assistance programs gradually expanded, as efforts were made to regularize the status and control of stateless and denationalized people. During and after World War II, two expensive and politically controversial refugee organizations—the United Nations Relief and Rehabilitation Agency and the International Refugee Organization, each with a radically different mandate—further developed the international organizational framework. Since 1951, an international refugee regime composed of the UN High Commissioner for Refugees and a network of other international agencies, national governments, and voluntary or nongovernmental organizations has developed a response strategy that permits some refugees to remain in their countries of first asylum, enables others to be resettled in third countries, and arranges for still others to be repatriated to their countries of origin. Although unevenly applied, international laws that designate refugees as a unique category of human rights victims who should be accorded special protection and benefits have been signed, ratified, and in force for several decades. Annually, billions of dollars are raised and expended on refugees.

## Refugees as a Modern Problem

Historians have argued that refugees are a distinctly modern problem and that international concern for refugees is a twentieth-century phenomenon.[3] Although refugees have been a feature of international society for a long time, before this century there was no international protection for refugees as we know it today; for the most part, they were left to fend for themselves without any official assistance. Citizens enjoyed the protection of their sovereigns or national governments, but once they broke with their home countries and became refugees, they were totally bereft of protection except as other states or private institutions or individuals might elect to provide it. Asylum was a gift of the crown, the church, and municipalities; and fugitive individuals and groups could expect no response to claims of asylum or protection premised on human or political right.

Refugees have been present in all eras. Refugees from religious persecution proliferated throughout Europe in the sixteenth and seventeenth

centuries.[4] Protestants, Catholics, and Jews were expelled by some regimes and admitted by others according to their beliefs, ideologies, and
economic necessity. By the late seventeenth century, with the achievement
of a high degree of religious homogeneity in most parts of Europe, the age
of religious persecution gave way to an age of political upheaval and
revolution, during which individuals were persecuted for their political
opinions and their opposition to new revolutionary regimes. New waves
of refugees were triggered by these revolutionary conflicts. The nineteenth
century produced many relatively small refugee flows, mostly from other
revolutionary and nationalist movements in Poland, Germany, France, and
Russia. Europeans who feared persecution could move to one of the many
immigrant countries in the New World still eager for an increased labor
force and for settlers to fill empty territories. There they could merge with
other migrant groups and neither regard themselves nor be labeled as
refugees. Consequently, before the twentieth century, there were no
hordes of homeless Europeans cast adrift in a world that rejected them.

## Causes of the 1920s' Refugee Movements

During the late nineteenth and the early twentieth centuries, both the
causes and the dimensions of the refugee problem began to change radically. The changed nature of international warfare, the dissolution of the
old empires in Eastern Europe and the Balkan region, and the expansion
of nation-states, accompanied by the deliberate persecution of minority
and stateless groups and the elimination of former ruling classes and political opposition groups, were the immediate causes of most refugee movements during the first several decades of this century.

Although war has always generated some refugees, only in the twentieth century has international conflict affected entire populations.[5] With
the advent of wider technological, economic, and social changes, the scale
and destructiveness of military conflict grew enormously; enemy civilians
as well as opposing armed forces became military targets. The elimination
of the distinction between combatants and noncombatants produced vast
numbers of refugees who were desperate to escape the ravages of indiscriminate violence.[6]

A second cause of refugee movements during the early part of this
century was the formation, consolidation, and expansion of the state system.[7] In Europe, the multinational Habsburg, Romanov, Ottoman, and
Hohenzollern empires all succumbed to the pressures and conflicts that
accompanied the transition from imperial social and political orders to
successor nation-states. As World War I accelerated the dismantling of
these multiethnic empires into nation-states, masses of people were excluded from citizenship in the new national states on grounds of language,
location, ethnicity, or religious affiliation. One insightful account notes
that newly formed governments in Austria, Czechoslovakia, Estonia,
Hungary, Latvia, Lithuania, Poland, and Yugoslavia tried to eliminate the

old order and consolidate their power by creating culturally and politically homogeneous populations.[8] Approximately 2 million Poles migrated to Poland, and 1 million ethnic Germans moved to Germany from their previous homes in the Russian and Austrian-Hungarian empires.[9] Hungary received several hundred thousand Magyar refugees driven out by the successor states of Romania, Czechoslovakia, and Yugoslavia.

In a continuation of a policy of "ethnic cleansing" begun in the late nineteenth century, the Turks intensified their massacres and genocide of the Armenians. During 1914–1919, between 500,000 and 1 million Armenians died, and survivors fled to Soviet Armenia, Syria, and other parts of Europe and the Middle East.[10]

At the end of World War I, Western powers attempted, in a series of Minority Treaties, to provide for the elementary rights of the ethnic minorities who were threatened as a result of the redrawing of national boundaries.[11] However, as the global economic situation deteriorated following the initial postwar recovery, minorities quickly became scapegoats. Governments defined broad categories of people as belonging to the nation-state and relegated others to the ranks of outsiders and aliens who threatened national and cultural cohesion. Many national minority groups were immediately naturalized by their new country, but some groups were not so fortunate.

As nations redefined their borders and identities and the "unmixing of peoples" was imposed on sometimes reluctant populations, millions of people were rendered stateless. The Balkan Wars and the transformation of the ethnically heterogenous Ottoman Empire into a number of more homogeneous nation-states generated mass refugee movements in the Balkans. Hostilities between Turkey and Greece resulted in the Greco-Turkish War of 1922, which displaced 1 million more Anatolian Greek and Armenian refugees.

To the chaos in southeastern Europe and Asia Minor were added huge refugee movements generated by the collapse of czarist Russia, the Russian Civil War, the Russo-Polish war, and the Soviet famine of 1921.[12] These cataclysmic events dispersed between 1 and 2 million people from the Russian Empire—mainly Russians—mostly to Germany and France, but also to the far reaches of the world, including China in the east and North America in the west. The Russian refugees included many people whom the Communist Party perceived to be obstacles to achieving revolutionary change in the new Soviet Union. The migrants also included soldiers of the defeated White Russian armies who had participated in the Russian Civil War, civilians fleeing the chaos and famine brought about by the revolution and civil war, ethnic Russians fleeing newly independent Poland and the Baltic states, and Russian Jews facing persecution.[13]

The cumulative result of these events was the largest displacement of peoples in Europe in modern times. By the early 1920s, the Soviet Union issued decrees that revoked the citizenship of many of its inhabitants. Vast numbers of Russians wandered all over the European continent, where they became a source of interstate friction because of their lack of national identity papers. The sheer numbers of these refugees, their virtual expulsion from their homeland, and the long years of their displaced wanderings made their collective fate in the twentieth century qualitatively different from that of other groups forced into exile by earlier political or religious upheavals. Refugee movements became a source of interstate tension and far exceeded the limited capacity of individual governments to ameliorate them. Within this context, the first rudimentary international organizations were formed to promote the protection and resettlement of refugees.

## Establishing an International Refugee Regime

Immigration controls were introduced in many Western states in the late nineteenth and early twentieth centuries. After the post–World War I upheavals in Europe, therefore, refugees found themselves subject to increasing government controls over international travel. Refugees could not legally stay, move on, or return to their homes without travel documents or passports.

Particularly affected were Russian refugees who had been rendered stateless when the Soviet Union denationalized them and invalidated their travel documents. Unlike other refugee groups joining new nation-states, the Russians were not quickly naturalized by their host governments. They were said to threaten the national homogeneity of states where an explosive ethnic balance already existed.[14] Moreover, the emigrés, particularly the ex-soldiers among them, were perceived to pose a destabilizing political threat to the newly formed regimes.[15]

Governments thus rushed to erect protective barriers and close borders. Most responded to the plight of refugees by simply expelling as many displaced persons as they could round up. Hundreds of thousands of people were consequently plunged into an endless cycle of illegal entry, clandestine existence, expulsion, and yet further illegal entry.

Not only did this situation bring untold misery to the refugees, it also contributed to friction between European states, which freely resorted to violating the territorial sovereignty of neighboring states by pushing refugees across frontiers. Refugee movements significantly affected the domestic politics and local economies of host countries, and they aggravated bilateral relations between sending and receiving states. By 1921, the resources of voluntary agencies that assisted the stateless Russians were exhausted. The principal humanitarian organizations of the period, headed by the International Committee of the Red Cross, prevailed on the League of Nations to create international machinery for dealing with at least some of the refugees.

## The High Commissioner for Refugees

In 1920, Fridtjof Nansen, the world-famous Norwegian explorer, was given the task of negotiating the repatriation of Russian war prisoners, and a year later he was appointed the first High Commissioner for Refugees, with specific responsibilities for Russian refugees only.

The League established strict guidelines within which refugee work had to take place. Governments mandated that aid be limited to Russian refugees, that League funds be spent only on administration and not on direct relief, and that refugee assistance be considered temporary.[16] For most of the interwar period, the international refugee regime ran on extremely limited ad hoc budgets put together without benefit of long-range planning. Financially the League provided only for administrative costs, and aid to refugees and host governments depended on direct financial assistance from individual states or voluntary agencies. The refugee regime lacked the political and financial support of most League members and later proved to be totally ineffective in responding to the Holocaust. There simply was no widespread agreement that refugee aid should be institutionalized, much less that it should be administered through a permanent international agency.

Despite the much-publicized shortcomings of the interwar refugee regime, the appointment of Nansen as High Commissioner constituted the first formal acknowledgment of international responsibility toward refugees, and Nansen proved to be a highly innovative and successful advocate for them, particularly in facilitating assistance to certain groups of refugees.[17] The interwar period also saw the development of legal norms about the protection of refugees and the establishment of refugees as a special category of migrant within municipal and international law.

Initially, Nansen was concerned with the practical problems of Russian refugees, and in particular with the problems of refugee travel. However, the problem of Russian refugees was extremely complex and could not be resolved quickly. The majority could not simply return home; nor could they settle spontaneously in Europe or easily travel to North America or some other overseas destination for immigration. At first, the High Commissioner's staff attempted to protect them by providing consular services and diplomatic interventions with host governments that threatened their expulsion and deportation. Finally, through skillful diplomacy, Nansen tackled the problem head-on by persuading fifty-one governments to recognize travel documents termed "Nansen passports" for stateless Russians. With these documents, not only Russian refugees but also others[18] could legally move from areas where their stays were temporary and often illegal to more hospitable areas in Europe and elsewhere.

Governments moved quickly to adopt the Nansen passport system and cooperated in the exchange and repatriation of massive numbers of refugees following the Greco-Turkish War of 1922. Nansen negotiated agreements involving the exchange of 1.1 million Turkish nationals of the

Greek Orthodox religion and 380,000 Greek Muslim nationals. Similar population exchanges involving well over 100,000 refugees took place between Greece and Bulgaria.

The number of activities that Nansen undertook on behalf of refugees mushroomed, and the functions of the High Commissioner expanded.[19] Following the exchanges among Bulgaria, Greece, and Turkey, governments and voluntary agencies (under the auspices of the League) financially assisted in resettling, finding employment for, and making economically self-sufficient hundreds of thousands of Greek, Bulgarian, and Armenian refugees. One scholar notes that the international refugee regime grew to encompass refugee settlement, employment opportunities, emigration, and linkage of refugee assistance with economic development.[20] Viewing refugees as part of the problem of general unemployment in Europe, Nansen believed that, by focusing assistance on the creation of employment opportunities for refugees, the international refugee regime would also contribute to solving Europe's economic problems. With direct encouragement from Nansen, the International Labor Organization established a Refugee Section that acted as a clearinghouse for information on employment opportunities for refugees, matching prospective employers in one country with prospective employees in another.[21]

In addition to developing a more comprehensive set of provisions covering employment and social services, governments reached agreements to create a more stable and secure legal status for refugees, including assigning regular consular services to be carried out by the High Commissioner and certifying refugee identity and civil status. In 1928, governments agreed to accept a series of legal provisions relating to the economic, social, and legal status of Russian and Armenian refugees. These initiatives were eventually codified into international law in the 1930s.

In 1933, a convention was drafted that attempted to limit the practice of repatriation and to grant Russian and Armenian refugees rights in their countries of asylum.[22] A number of rights to which refugees were entitled were specified, including education, employment in the receiving country, and travel documents. A similar convention was promulgated in 1938 for the benefit of refugees coming from Germany,[23] which was extended in 1939 to those fleeing Austria.[24]

While neither of these conventions received the signatures of more than eight nations,[25] they were significant as first international efforts to elaborate a body of treaty law designed to afford protection to refugees. Although the language of these conventions was purposely limited to benefit narrowly defined national groups and provided only minimal protection for the members of these groups, they were a step toward the formulation of more permanent international laws and institutions.

At best, however, the measures were only partly successful. Providing identity documents allowed refugees to cross international borders legally, but it did not ensure that a foreign government would actually grant them entry visas. The right to grant or deny admission remained the prerogative of sovereign states, and even those that granted asylum did not necessarily acknowledge any legal obligation to do so. Moreover, many refugees were not covered under international arrangements and continued to lack any travel and identity system.

## The Politicization of Refugee Policy

The emerging international refugee regime operated within a highly politicized context in which governments supported refugee assistance programs for security and foreign policy reasons as much as out of humanitarian concern.

Although the High Commissioner for Refugees was formally independent, Nansen always depended on governments for donations. Without official funding to undertake any relief programs, Nansen's ability to intervene actively was largely determined by his ability to raise funds and to convince governments that they should increase refugee aid, ease immigration barriers, and provide more legal protection for refugees within their borders. And these attempts were made at a time when assistance and protection of refugees was intensely political and thus directly influenced by the foreign policy interests of governments.

The refugee assistance programs of the 1920s especially depended on the financing of the two great powers, Britain and France, and on the support of the smaller European countries. However, the decisions as to which refugees qualified for aid were political ones made by the Council and the Assembly of the League of Nations. Governments were more likely to aid refugees fleeing from their enemies than from their friends. Governments in Eastern Europe, for example, aided refugees from the Soviet Union but not those from Germany. Great Britain aided its strategically important allies, Greece and Bulgaria. Refugees fleeing important political states, on the other hand, were a source of embarrassment; and League members sought to avoid arousing the hostility of other members by refraining from criticizing their human rights records. As a consequence, some major refugee groups—such as refugees from fascist Italy and Spain—were excluded from League assistance altogether. All governments were more willing to act in a nonpolitical, nondiscriminatory fashion toward refugees when they needed immigrant labor.

Aid for Russian exiles was perhaps the most politicized refugee problem dealt with by the League in the 1920s.[26] The concern for Russian refugees resulted at least partly from the fact that the Soviet Union was not a member of the League at that time and was regarded with extreme hostility and suspicion by most of its members. Morever, Great Britain and France felt themselves to be financially and morally responsible for the thousands of defeated White Russian army soldiers whom they had supported during the Russian Civil War. The Soviet Union, in contrast, sharply objected to any international efforts aimed at helping refugees, especially White Russians. Interstate cooperation over the issue was impossible. Furthermore, the League of Nations had been at the forefront of economic and diplomatic efforts to isolate the Soviet Union. For the Russians, the Nansen office was a creature of the League of Nations and of the Western powers that they so profoundly distrusted.

These political difficulties underscored the limitations of humanitarian work. Close coordination between political bodies and humanitarian agencies was needed to ensure that the capabilities as well as the limitations of humanitarian work were taken into account. However, not only did governments keep the mandate of the High Commissioner deliberately narrow throughout this period, but they also refrained from adopting any universal definition of the term *refugee* for fear of opening the door to international recognition of political dissidents in any state, including the Great Powers.

## Antifascist Refugees

In the 1930s, Europe was flooded with new groups of refugees, this time fleeing fascism in Germany, Italy, Portugal, and Spain. The rise of totalitarian governments that demanded total allegiance of the people to the state produced millions of refugees. Perceiving ethnic and minority groups as threats to internal control, the fascist regimes that rose to power in Europe in the 1920s and 1930s adopted state policies that forced out those whom they considered unassimilable. In a radical attempt to create a homogeneous and "racially pure" society, the Nazis purged the country of unwanted elements. The main targets were not only political opponents, such as Communists, Social Democrats, antifascist intellectuals, and pacifists, but also members of "racially inferior" population groups—mainly Jews, Slavs, and Gypsies.

As anti-Semitic legislation and brutal agitation and discrimination were stepped up under the Nazis, the group most severely affected were the Jews. Major waves of emigration took place after the initial Nazi takeover in 1933, again after the passage of the Nuremberg Laws in 1935, and a third time after the devastation of *Kristallnacht* in 1938. Increased pressure was placed on Jews to leave: the German government expelled Jews of Polish origin back across the Polish border; and after the conquest of Poland, Jews in areas annexed by the Nazis were forced to move to other parts of Poland. In 1940, the Nazis began deporting German Jews to Poland; and in October 1941, the "Final Solution"—to exterminate the Jewish people—was adopted as state policy.

The rise of fascism elsewhere in Europe also created refugee movements. In Italy, the reign of Benito Mussolini generated a steady but relatively small flow of refugees, mainly antifascists and political opponents, whose departure the government encouraged. In general, however, Italy made it extremely difficult for its citizens to emigrate, and severe penalties were set for illegal emigration.[27] In Portugal, some 2,000 political opponents of Antonio Salazar fled the country. Much larger refugee movements were generated by the Spanish Civil War and by the creation of a fascist government there. At the conclusion of the war, about 400,000 defeated Spanish Republicans fled to neighboring France.

Refugee movements during this period would have been far greater had it not been for the exit controls and emigration restrictions imposed by a number of governments. Only a trickle of people were fortunate enough to be able to leave the Soviet Union, for example, compared with the estimated 20 to 40 million people who died there under the purges, famines, and forcible relocations during Stalin's murderous "Red Terror."[28] Outside Europe, huge displacements of people occurred in Asia and the Pacific, but most of these population movements involved internal flights and migrations.

## The Closing of Borders

Refugees fleeing Italy, Spain, and Portugal generally found temporary asylum in neighboring countries. Some 10,000 Italians who fled the Mussolini regime found refuge in France among the community of Italian migrants already living there and did not place a relief burden on the French government. Similarly, 400,000 Spanish Republicans were given temporary asylum by the French government, which had supported their cause against Franco.

In contrast to refugees from other fascist regimes, Jews from Germany scattered throughout the world. In the early 1930s, most either went to countries bordering Germany or resettled permanently in Palestine or the United States. Jews who fled later in the decade found it almost impossible to locate a country willing to give them temporary asylum. In writing about this period, Hannah Arendt graphically described the refugee's plight: "Once they had left their homeland, they remained homeless; once they had left their state, they became stateless; once they had been deprived of their human rights, they were rightless, *the scum of the earth*."[29] This absence of a place of refuge and the difficulty of finding a new home distinguished the plight of Jewish refugees from refugees of earlier eras.

The lack of international cooperation regarding refugees during the 1930s is traceable not only to the weakness of the League of Nations and the refugee organizations under its auspices, but also to the absence of any consistent or coherent international commitment to resolving refugee problems. Instead, there was a broad consensus in almost every industrialized nation, particularly during the years of the Great Depression, that national interests were best served by imposing and maintaining rigid limits on immigration; that humanitarian initiatives on behalf of refugees had to be limited by tight fiscal constraints and the need to employ the nation's own citizens; and that no particular foreign policy benefits would accrue from putting political and moral pressure on refugee-generating countries or from accepting their unwanted dissidents and minority groups.

These views were fully operative in the United States and in such Commonwealth countries as Canada and Australia, which prior to World War I had accepted a substantial majority of the world's emigrants and had acted as a safety valve for Europe's forced migrants. Between the two world wars, more and more governments enacted highly restrictive immigration laws to keep out all but selected national groups. In the United States, the Immigration Acts of 1921 and 1924 established a quota system designed to limit total immigration and to ensure a certain ethnic composition among each year's newcomers. The British Dominions enacted restrictions aimed at keeping their population British.[30] Australia restricted immigration by non-British migrants, excluded Asians altogether, and promoted schemes to bring in British settlers. In Canada and Latin America, restrictive policies became general policy.

Restrictionism was exacerbated by deepening worldwide economic depression and massive unemployment. Wherever they went, Jewish refugees encountered a world that was closing its frontiers and reducing its immigrant quotas. Even the United States refused to adjust its quota system to accommodate more of these refugees. About half of the very limited 150,000 places were reserved for the English and Irish immigrants, and most of these openings went unfilled. Nonetheless, to make matters worse, Presidents Hoover and Roosevelt instructed U.S. consuls to withhold visas from any person likely to become "a public charge"—a restrictive clause that had been introduced in the Immigration Act of 1917. The effect of these measures was to limit severely the number of refugees who could enter as immigrants.[31]

Other states resorted to tortuous legal interpretations to prevent the entry of these doomed people. Pleas by representatives of public and private international refugee organizations went unheeded. Isolationism was still a factor in the Western hemisphere and encouraged a growing antipathy to aliens of all kinds. In particular, however, the pervasiveness of anti-Semitism worldwide made immigration almost impossible for Jews fleeing the Third Reich. Potential host governments feared that welcoming Jewish fugitives from Nazism might open the floodgates and provoke the flight of hundreds of thousands more Jews from Eastern Europe.

## The High Commissioner of Refugees from Germany

Fridtjof Nansen died in 1930. During the next ten years, the international refugee regime he had almost single-handedly established proved totally incapable of dealing with the problem of Jewish refugees. In 1930, duties involving protection of refugees were placed under the aegis of the League Secretariat, while responsibility for administering the remaining limited-assistance programs was transferred to an agency that became known as the International Nansen Office.

Responding to the initial outflow of Jewish refugees following Hitler's accession to power in Germany in 1933, the League established yet another fragile refugee organization, the High Commissioner for Refugees from Germany. Out of concern for German sensibilities, the High Commissioner was instructed to avoid discussing causes or stressing the political dimension of the refugee problem. Rather, his tasks were restricted to negotiating with host governments concerning settlement and emigration plans and the questions of work permits and travel documents. To avoid antagonizing Germany at a time when it was still a member of the League, this organization was set up outside the formal structure of the League of Nations;[32] and in contrast to its predecessors, the organization did not even receive funding for the administrative expenses of the High Commissioner from the League.

Similarly, in 1938, the Soviet Union objected to any kind of League protection for the few Russian citizens who were able to flee Stalin's purges and collectivization campaigns. These events occasioned relatively little attention from the outside world, and the League members were hardly inclined to take action.

As the scale of the Jewish refugee problem grew, any will to resolve it faded. Despite the limited international recognition of the rights of refugees that existed at the time, states were unwilling to extend new legal protections to refugees, particularly when these would limit the right of sovereign nations to exclude or deport aliens. In addition, virtually no state was willing to accept refugees as migrants, even when all other means of affording protection had failed.

In the face of such international reluctance to accept Jews or to confront the German government on the refugee issue, the High Commissioner for German Refugees, James G. McDonald, could do little. In frustration, he quit his post in 1936; but in his letter of resignation, he underscored the political roots of the problem and the limitations of the international response:

> The efforts of the private organizations and of any League organization for refugees can only mitigate a problem of growing gravity and complexity. In the present economic conditions of the world, the European States, and even those overseas, have only a limited power of absorption of refugees. The problem must be tackled at its source if disaster is to be avoided.[33]

McDonald believed that it was not enough simply to assist those who fled from the Third Reich. Efforts had to be made to confront the causes that created the refugees and to negotiate with the country that was responsible for the exodus. This was not a function of the High Commissioner's office; it was a political function that belonged to the League of Nations itself, and particularly to the Great Powers. At the time, however, all major governments considered such action to be politically inexpedient.

The High Commissioner's attempt to draw attention to the human rights abuses of Germany as the immediate cause of the Jewish refugee problem did not spur international action against the Nazis. Simply put, Western governments viewed the refugee problem as an internal matter of the German government, particularly since Germany was still a member state of the League. Even after Germany withdrew from the League in 1938, France and Britain sought to appease Germany and, therefore, were reluctant to criticize its persecution of the Jews. Western statesmen could not master the challenge of political events in Europe.

In his letter of resignation, James McDonald referred to the need to set aside state sovereignty in favor of humanitarian imperatives and to resolve the Jewish refugee problem at the level of international politics: "[W]hen domestic politics threaten the demoralization and exile of hundreds of thousands of human beings, considerations of diplomatic correctness must yield to those of common humanity."[34] They did not.

After Germany quit the League, the two offices for refugees—the International Nansen Office and the High Commissioner for Refugees from Germany—were consolidated into what became the fourth High Commissioner for Refugees, which functioned until after the end of World War II, in 1946. The powers of the new High Commissioner, Sir Herbert Emerson, were even more rigidly limited than they had been in the past. He was denied the power to enter into any legal commitment whatsoever on behalf of the League of Nations, and the League assumed no responsibility, legal or financial, for his activities. He had no power to engage in material assistance, and he was assisted only by a skeleton staff. The severe limits on the High Commissioner were also evident in the unwillingness of member states to assume greater responsibility for dealing with the rapidly worsening refugee crisis. Consequently, as political conditions deteriorated in the late 1930s and as an increasingly restrictionist political and economic environment emerged, the influence of Nansen's successors on government behavior and attitudes toward refugees evanesced.

## The Évian Conference

The only significant international effort to resolve the problem of Jewish refugees reflected and subsequently strengthened the restrictive attitudes and policies of governments that were already in force at the time. Under considerable pressure from Jewish groups and private voluntary agencies, Franklin Roosevelt called an international conference at Évian, France, in 1938 to consider ways of resettling Jews who fled Germany and Austria. Up to that time, the United States had taken little notice of the existing international refugee structures and refugee norms of the League of Nations. It had failed to ratify either refugee convention, and it had refused to modify its own immigration law, even to the extent of permitting the entry of Jewish refugee children.[35] At Évian, the United States made no new pledges for increased quotas, Other government delegates noted that the movement of Jewish refugees was "disturbing to the general economy," since those in flight were seeking refuge at a time of serious unemployment. Jewish refugees posed a "severe strain on the administrative facilities and absorptive capacities of the receiving nations," racial and religious problems were rendered more acute, international unrest increased, and "the processes of appeasement in international relations" might be hindered.[36] Although Germany had favored emigration as one way to rid itself of its minorities, the Évian Conference yielded no new resettlement places and merely reaffirmed the extreme reluctance of the United States and the rest of the world to offer a lifeline to Jewish refugees.

## The Intergovernmental Committee on Refugees (IGCR)

The only concrete measure taken at Évian was the creation of a new refugee mechanism outside the League of Nations structure—the Intergovernmental Committee on Refugees (IGCR)[37]—to negotiate with Germany about Jewish migration. For the next eight years (until 1946), the IGCR existed alongside the League of Nations' office of the High Commissioner for Refugees, and the two staffs shared common facilities.

Despite this augmentation of the institutional framework for dealing with the problem, the international community's response to the plight of Jews in Europe remained limited and ineffectual. The IGCR tried to work with Germany to achieve an orderly exodus of Jews, who would be allowed to take their property and possessions with them. Yet Germany would not agree to let Jews leave without sacrificing most of their possessions; Western states were not willing to finance a resettlement program or to increase immigration quotas; and the migration of Jews to Palestine was sharply curtailed by the British. Avenues of exit from Germany and entrance to Western countries were closed. Germany regarded Évian and the Western nations' policy of closing their doors against refugees as exonerating its policies and began to use more draconian measures to rid the Third Reich of its Jewish population. Thus, the subsequent mass murder of Jews by the Nazis was tacitly tolerated by most of the Western world until it was too late for effective counteraction. In 1943, the United States and Great Britain convened yet another conference in Bermuda to mollify voices of concern for European Jews, but no effective steps were taken to alter a Western policy toward refugees based on rigid barriers to immigration.

## The Breakdown of the International Refugee Regime

Unlike many earlier refugee movements, twentieth-century refugee problems defied quick solution. Most of these refugees could not simply return home; nor could they settle in Europe or travel across the Atlantic to a new home. A solution to their problems had to be found in the prevailing political, economic, and social climate of the interwar period in Europe. During the 1930s, the world's statesmen were essentially impotent in confronting Europe's dictators, and the response to the refugee problem by governments and international organizations was inevitably politicized and selective. Throughout the period, assistance and protection were temporary and limited to certain groups. As the League's political effectiveness and credibility declined—particularly after the withdrawal of Germany, Japan, and Italy from the League, and after its failure to resolve the Manchurian and Ethiopian conflicts—its competence to deal with refugee problems also decreased.

The institutions created to respond to refugee problems during the interwar period did leave one lasting and important legacy. Twenty years of organizational growth and interstate collaboration had firmly established the idea that refugees constituted victims of human rights abuses for whom the world had a special responsibility. Moreover, the first international cooperative efforts on behalf of refugees and the establishment and evolution of the international refugee agencies of the period provided the foundations on which successor institutions would build.

## The Postwar Crisis

By the end of World War II, millions of people were outside of their home country and in need of assistance.[38] A State Department report prepared in early 1945 described the situation in Europe at the end of the war as "[one] of the greatest population movements of history taking place before our eyes. As the German retreat has rolled westward before the oncoming Soviet troops and as the Allies have pushed eastward on the western front, millions of people have been uprooted and are fleeing toward the center of Germany."[39] The report estimated that this flow not only included the 20 to 30 million people uprooted during the war, but also "some $9\frac{1}{2}$ million displaced Germans returning from outside the Reich, and 4 million and probably more war fugitives who fled before the oncoming Soviet and Allied troops."[40]

As the concentration camps in Eastern Europe were liberated, some 60,000 gaunt, starved, and half-crazed Jewish survivors joined this huge group of homeless people.[41] Postwar conflicts and political changes in Eastern Europe generated millions of additional fugitives, most notably about 12 million ethnic Germans driven out of the countries of Eastern and Central Europe who surged westward into the British, French, and American zones of military occupation.[42] The bulk of Europe's displaced population was absorbed by Germany. Concurrently, tens of thousands of new refugees were being generated by the civil war in Greece between Communist partisans and the returning royal government, as well as by postliberation conflicts in Eastern and Southern Europe.

The influx of so many refugees and displaced people in such a short time into an area where most of the physical infrastructure had been destroyed put immense strains on Western European states, particularly Germany, and on the Allied military authorities responsible for administering significant areas of former enemy territory. Scores of private voluntary agencies[43] sprang up to relieve the misery of war victims, and new intergovernmental organizations came into existence.

## United Nations Relief and Rehabilitation Agency (UNRRA)

In November 1943, the Western powers set up the United Nations Relief and Rehabilitation Agency (UNRRA)[44] to provide immediate relief when the anticipated anti-Axis counteroffensive and liberation of Europe occurred. In 1944 and 1945, UNRRA provided temporary emergency assistance for millions of displaced persons (DPs) who fell into Allied hands, thus following the pattern set in the interwar period. UNRRA, however, was not strictly a refugee organization: it aided all who had been displaced by the war, and only incidently refugees with political fears.

Working directly under Allied military command, UNRRA was given a very limited mandate. It was to extend aid to civilian nationals of the Allied nations and to DPs in countries liberated by the Allied armies. UNRRA had no power to resettle refugees and displaced persons to third countries; the goal was simply to return home as soon as possible all the people who had been uprooted and displaced by the war. Relief and rehabilitation in Europe were to be for the short term only. Once people were repatriated and adequate resources for rebuilding were provided, planners widely assumed that Western European states would be able to stand on their own feet again and deal with their own problems.

Unlike in the interwar period, however, enormous amounts of money were donated by UNRRA's forty-four member states for relief purposes. From its inception in November 1943 until its disbandment in June 1947, UNRRA expended over $3.6 billion (of which the United States contributed $2.8 billion), and at the peak of its activity it employed 27,800 people. Because it was not strictly a refugee assistance agency, UNRRA's functions also included rehabilitation of agricultural and industrial production and support of basic social infrastructure, including public health, public education, and other social services.

One of UNRRA's principal functions was to promote and oversee repatriation. The great majority of the dislocated people under UNRRA care were anxious to go home and rebuild their lives. The overburdened countries of asylum—particularly Germany, but also Austria and Italy—were anxious that these people be repatriated quickly. At the Yalta Conference in February 1945, the big powers paved the way for large-scale repatriations to the Soviet Union;[45] and at the Potsdam Conference in August 1945, they provided for the return of the ethnic German minorities in Poland, Czechoslovakia, and Hungary.[46] The solution agreed on by the Allied powers was that all citizens of each of the powers would, without delay after their liberation, be separated from enemy prisoners of war and alien members of the national population until they were handed over to their national authorities. At this time authorities still generally

expected that refugees would voluntarily seek repatriation to and rehabilitation in their own countries; so this sensitive issue, later to play such
an important a role in United Nations debate, did not trouble UNRRA at
its inception. Thus, UNRRA devoted a substantial part of its efforts to
aiding Allied military forces in identifying displaced persons, separating
them into broad national categories, putting them into trucks and boxcars,
and shipping them back to the countries from which they had originally
come, without regard to their individual wishes. So successful were these
methods that in the first five months after the war, UNRRA and the
Allied military command managed to repatriate nearly three-quarters of
the displaced people in Europe.

Among those repatriated were large numbers of Soviet and East European citizens, many of whom ended up in Stalin's labor camps when
they returned to the East.[47] Baltic and Polish nationals whose territory
had been annexed by the Soviet Union, Ukranians who convinced the
Western authorities that they faced political persecution and possible exe-
cution if returned, and Jewish refugees were all considered ineligible for
immediate repatriation and were put into camps until decisions could be
reached about what to do with them. However, the Western powers initially yielded to the Soviet insistence that all its nationals be repatriated
and were slow to acknowledge that many of those who resisted being sent
back home faced possible persecution. Thus, the great majority of Soviets
and East Europeans were not the beneficiaries of even the limited protection of camps.[48] Before long, the fate of those who refused to return
became the focus of a sharp international political debate between East
and West.

## Refugees as an East–West Issue

After World War II, relations between the Western powers and the Soviet
Union rapidly deteriorated, and the problem of refugees in the West who
either did not want to return or were hesitant about returning home
erupted into a major East–West controversy. Several dramatic suicides in
the displaced persons camps and bloody confrontations between Western
military officials and Russians resisting forced repatriation finally convinced the United States military command that the fears of many of those
remaining in their custody were genuine. As the Western powers became
increasingly reluctant to return displaced persons to areas under Soviet
control, the mass repatriations of 1945 slowed and then came to almost a
complete halt by the end of 1946.[49] By this time, less than one-quarter of
the estimated 2.5 million Soviet nationals in the British, American, and
French zones had not been handed over to Soviet authorities, and over 1
million demoralized people remained in camps. They presented a relief
and security problem that UNRRA was not in a position to solve. Nonetheless, it had to continue to support them. The situation was exacerbated
by Soviet complaints that the Western powers were refusing to fulfill their

obligations under the Yalta agreements and were encouraging Soviet nationals to resist repatriation.

After the War, East and West quarreled bitterly over the issue of forcible repatriation and about what the international community's responsibility was for those who refused to go home. In the 1920s, it had been customary to regard refugees as persons who could not return home because their own governments were unwilling to have them back. In the mid-1940s, by contrast, many hundreds of thousands of persons were unwilling to return to their countries, although their governments were anxious to have them back.

The question of repatriation, colored by the emerging East–West conflict, also became a major political issue within the United Nations.[50] The status of refugees and displaced persons was among the most contentious of all the issues discussed at these early UN sessions, and on few subjects were more prolonged and exhaustive negotiations carried on between the Soviet Union and the Western countries.[51] Repatriation touched on the fundamental ideological conflicts dividing East and West. The core of the conflict concerned the rights of people to choose where they wanted to live, to flee from oppression, and to express their own opinions. Although Soviet representatives privately acknowledged that many of the displaced persons rejected the communist system and that it was unrealistic to force them all to go home, in public the Soviet Union and the Eastern European countries rejected outright the idea that citizens of Eastern European countries could have any valid reason for opposing return and maintained that those who resisted return were war criminals, quislings, and traitors.[52]

A major dispute arose over whether UNRRA was obligated to provide assistance to displaced persons who refused repatriation. The Eastern bloc asserted that assistance should be given only to displaced persons who returned home, while the Western countries insisted that each individual should be free to decide whether or not to return home, without prejudicing his right to assistance. An immediate blow-up was avoided when the Western and Eastern delegations agreed to a compromise plan that permitted such aid to continue for a maximum of six months, while acknowledging that UNRRA was entitled to repatriate displaced persons and would be prepared to do so in the future.[53]

## The International Refugee Organization (IRO)

The United States remained strongly critical of UNRRA operations, in particular its repatriation policies and its rehabilitation programs in Eastern bloc countries, which it felt only served to consolidate Russian political control over Eastern Europe. Toward the end of 1946, the United States, which provided 70 percent of UNRRA funds and much of its leadership, took action to kill UNRRA by refusing either to grant it additional aid or to extend its life beyond 1947.[54] In its place, and in the face of adamant opposition from the Eastern bloc, the United States worked to create a new International Refugee Organization (IRO), which had as its chief function not repatriation but the resettlement of refugees and displaced persons uprooted by World War II and its aftermath.

From the beginning of the UN General Assembly debates on the formation of IRO, it was apparent that the question of a new refugee organization would generate additional tension between East and West.[55] The Soviet bloc favored the retention of UNRRA, both because of the aid it channeled to Eastern Europe and because its limited mandate—which favored repatriation over resettlement—accorded well with the official Soviet view that all those resisting repatriation were criminals or traitors. The subsequent debates within the General Assembly on the mandate of IRO were embittered by the American desire to terminate UNRRA, which the Soviet Union regarded as a decision to deny Eastern Europe economic aid.

The debates covered various topics, including the length of term of the new organization, its method of selecting a director, and its means of raising funds. Yet the principal East–West split centered on the definition of the individuals who fell within the IRO's mandate and on the related issue of resettlement versus repatriation. The Western bloc insisted that the mandate of the IRO be broad enough to offer protection to individuals with "valid objections" to repatriation, including objections based on "persecution, or fear, based on reasonable grounds, of persecution because of race, religion, nationality or political opinions" and objections "of a political nature, judged by the organization to be valid."[56] Previously, international organizations had dealt only with specific groups of refugees, such as Russian or German refugees; and governments had never attempted to formulate a general definition of the term *refugee*. For the first time, therefore, the international community made refugee eligibility depend on the individual rather than on the group and accepted the individual's right to flee from political persecution and to choose where he wanted to live.

As a gesture to assuage communist bloc objections, the IRO constitution included the assertion that its principal objective was "to encourage and assist in every way possible early return [of refugees and displaced persons] to their countries of origin," and that "no international assistance should be given to traitors, quislings and war criminals, and that nothing should be done in any way to prevent their surrender and punishment."[57] Despite this concessionary statement, the Soviet Union saw the IRO as a tool of the West and criticized the organization for preventing DPs from repatriating. The Eastern bloc reiterated its charges that "the refugee camps of the West had become centers of anti-communist propaganda; that the refugees were being used as forced laborers and as mercenaries; and that the West intended to enrich itself by resettling the so-called refugees to the countries of the world making the highest bid for their labor."[58] More plausibly, the Soviet Union claimed that the West used refugee organizations to recruit spies and anti-Soviet intelligence experts from the large numbers of pro-Nazi East Europeans who had fought against the Soviet Union during World War II.[59] Regarding the IRO as an "immigration bureau" and as an instrument of the U.S. bloc, the Soviet Union and its allies refused to join the new organization and made no contribution of any kind toward its operations.

Given the depth of East–West hostilities at the time, it is hardly surprising that the IRO's policies should have been caught up in the politics of the day. Initially, persons unwilling to return to their countries of origin became the concern of the IRO only if they could present a valid case against repatriation, on the grounds of racial, religious, or political persecution. But following the outflow of refugees from Czechoslovakia after the communist coup of 1948, the IRO's program was expanded beyond displaced persons from World War II to include escapees from East European communist regimes. Moreover, perceiving refugees to be of symbolic and instrumental use in the Cold War between East and West, Western governments—especially the United States—prevailed on the IRO to apply the refugee eligibility criteria more liberally, to accommodate larger numbers of escapees. The United States, which underwrote over two-thirds of its costs and controlled its leadership, played the key role in investing IRO's refugee protection with specific ideological content.

## Resettlement over Repatriation

Resettlement seemed the only practical policy option for resolving the refugee problem. Germany and the nations of Western Europe were in favor of it, since their chief interest was to minimize relief problems during a period of intensive reconstruction. Resettlement also served the broader political interests of the West by discrediting and embarrassing the newly established communist regimes.

With the opening up of a major resettlement program, the number of repatriations was reduced to a small trickle. During the four and one-half years of IRO's existence, no more than 54,000 people returned to Eastern and Central Europe. By 1949, all Eastern European repatriation missions were asked to leave the areas under Western control, and the IRO was requested by host governments to close offices in their capitals. Repatriation as a possible solution to refugee problems became entirely discredited in Western eyes, tainted by the forcible returns of the immediate postwar period.

Because the war-torn countries of Western Europe were incapable of accepting all the remaining displaced persons, pressure was put on the United States, Canada, Australia, and other overseas countries to make available at least some admissions slots. The United States admitted nearly 400,000 displaced persons during the next five years, through a series of ad hoc legislative and administrative measures collectively known as displaced persons legislation.[60] U.S. refugee admissions policy reflected intensive lobbying and constituency pressures from ethnic groups both to aid surviving victims of Nazi and fascist persecution and to open up new immigration channels from the Old World.[61] Even more importantly, foreign policy concerns, such as anticommunism and the need to restore stability to Western Europe, were employed by refugee advocates such as the Citizens Committee for Displaced Persons to overcome the restrictionist attitudes and policies of the American Congress. Labor recruitment programs enabled large numbers of displaced persons to emigrate to Canada, Australia, New Zealand, South America, and even parts of the Middle East and Africa.

The IRO resettled the majority of the refugee caseload it had inherited from UNRRA within the first year of its existence. It was able to accomplish this because Western European nations and the overseas resettlement countries saw practical advantages for themselves in alleviating labor shortages by recruiting from the camps.[62] Mainly single men, childless couples, and manual laborers could agree to several years' government-designated labor—mostly in coal mines, road building, and construction work—in return for being granted the opportunity to apply for citizenship. During the four and one-half years of IRO operations, the United States received 31.7 percent of the refugees resettled; Australia, 17.5; Israel, 12.7; Canada, 11.9; Britain, 8.3; Western Europe, 6.8; and the countries of Latin America, 6.5.[63]

After this initial surge of resettlement activity, the IRO encountered patterns of discrimination against certain groups of immigrants who, for one reason or another, were considered undesirable. Chile, Argentina, and Brazil, for example, refused to take Jews. European states by and large discriminated against intellectuals and members of professional classes; and no one wanted to take the unemployable, particularly the sick, the elderly, and the handicapped.[64] Thus, by the end of IRO's tenure, selective admissions policies left what became known as the "hard-core" cases. These totaled some 400,000 people, most of whom were still in camps scattered throughout Western Europe.[65] The scandal of these camps was to become the subject of criticism in the West and elsewhere for the next ten years or more. Beyond the "hard-core" group, the numbers of refugees continued to grow, with large numbers of persons fleeing Eastern European countries for resettlement in the West.

Despite the achievements of the IRO, refugee problems showed few signs of disappearing. Resettlement of the remaining wartime displaced persons had become more difficult, as European states that had once welcomed new arrivals now claimed that their economies could handle no more; and with the onset of the Cold War, new groups of refugees from the East began to make their way westward. A series of East–West crises—including the communist seizure of Czechoslovakia, the explosion of the first Soviet atomic bomb, the Berlin blockade and airlift, the victory of Mao Tse-tung in China, and the beginning of the Korean conflict in

1950—greatly increased political tensions between the two blocs. These events consequently brought about a series of reactions: the Truman Doctrine, which proclaimed that the United States would "support free peoples who are resisting attempted subjugation by armed minorities or by outside pressures";[66] the Marshall Plan; the North Atlantic Treaty Organization (NATO); and on the other side, Comecon as the central economic organization for East European communism, and the Warsaw Pact military alliance. Thus Europe became divided, and the opposition of each side to the other hardened considerably.[67] In this tense international environment, Europe was being pressed between the remains of one refugee problem and the emergence of another.

Recognizing the threat that the refugee problem posed to Europe, the IRO in one of its final reports to the UN General Assembly warned that the temporary problem it was assigned to deal with was rapidly becoming permanent. Despite the IRO's successes in resettlement, there remained a large camp population, mainly in Austria and Germany; an urgent caseload of some 5,000 European refugees, mainly White Russians, in Shanghai; groups in Turkey, Spain, Portugal, and the Middle East; and a tense international situation in Europe that was daily generating large numbers of new refugees.[68] It seemed, therefore, that the problem of refugees was almost as serious when IRO closed down as it had been when it came into existence. But the international community, particularly the United States,[69] was weary of the vast scale and cost of the refugee problem.

A widespread perception grew among governments that there were limits to the numbers of immigrants resettlement nations could accept. In addition, the U.S. government was concerned that continued reliance on the IRO would institutionalize the refugee problem as an indefinite responsibility of the overseas resettlement countries and of the United States, rather than of Western Europe. The United States thus turned decisively toward direct economic assistance of the European countries through the Marshall Plan, a strategy that Washington believed would make it easier for governments in Europe to absorb the remaining refugees. Implicitly, this policy shift assumed that the need for exceptional or urgent relief and resettlement measures for European refugees was past and that the remaining problems were temporary and could be dealt with by a small successor agency to the IRO.

The United Nations organization as a whole had not lived up to American expectations, and the IRO was a particular economic burden. In its brief period of existence, the IRO's expenditures totaled more than $400 million, a figure that greatly exceeded the combined operating budgets of the rest of the UN, and the United States had contributed over $250 million of this amount. Increasingly, U.S. authorities came to believe that American national interests could be served better by relying on their own refugee schemes—on bilateral, regional, or even international arrangements outside the United Nations system.

Against this background, discussions took place within the United

Nations General Assembly and the UN Economic and Social Council from 1948 through 1950 regarding the creation of a new international refugee organization—the office of the United Nations High Commissioner for Refugees (UNHCR)—and the drafting of the 1951 UN Convention on Refugees. In framing the functions and mandate of what was to become the heart of the post–World War II refugee regime, Western governments drew on the experience of a wide range of international efforts extending back to 1921. These debates over the refugee question were contentious and politicized, revealing problems that continue to this day.

# 3

# The Cold War and the Early Development of the UNHCR

The tense state of East–West relations in the postwar period virtually excluded the possibility of any significant cooperation between the two blocs over the refugee problem. The refugee question centered on the core of ideological opposition between capitalism and socialism. The Office of the United Nations High Commissioner for Refugees (UNHCR) was established at the height of these Cold War ideological tensions. Like its predecessors, it was intended as a temporary body with a three-year life, during which time it was to provide protection and assistance to refugees. But being supplied with financial resources for administrative costs only, it did not have the means to enforce the international legal norms for the world's refugees.

Both the United States and the Soviet Union resisted participation in this emerging UN refugee regime. As the dominant Western power, the United States established a refugee policy based on its own foreign policy priorities (which emphasized overseas resettlement), while the Soviet Union opposed all efforts whose prime goal was not repatriation. To the Russians, the UNHCR, like the Nansen office of the interwar period, was an instrument of the Western powers that they deeply distrusted. Thus the Soviet Union and Eastern Europe, as the source of most refugee movements during this period, would not participate in UN refugee programs, while the United States sought to implement an independent (and principally anticommunist) refugee policy through agencies created outside the UN system. It was inconceivable, therefore, that the UNHCR could act as a mediator between the Western countries of asylum and resettlement and the refugee-generating countries of Eastern Europe.

American attitudes toward the UNHCR changed fundamentally in the wake of the first major postwar refugee crisis in Central Europe. The UNHCR's management of the 1956 Hungarian refugee crisis demonstrated that it was the only international refugee agency capable of dealing with a complex humanitarian problem involving high politics between East and West. After 1956, when developments in the international political system shifted the spotlight of attention from Europe to the developing world, American foreign policymakers began to see the potential usefulness of the UNHCR to U.S. interests. As a result, the UNHCR was authorized to undertake tasks well beyond the scope of its original mandate and became the centerpiece of the emerging post–World War II international refugee regime.

## The Formation of the UNHCR

In the negotiations leading to establishment of a new UN refugee agency, serious differences surfaced among participating governments regarding the authority and financing of the successor to the IRO. The United States sought a temporary refugee agency with narrow authority and limited function. In particular, the United States sought to deny the UNHCR a relief role by depriving it of General Assembly assistance for operations and by denying it the right to seek any voluntary contributions. According to the United States, the sole function of the proposed office should be international protection. The European countries, led by France and Belgium, which were anxious to secure large-scale operational funds for the continued outflow from Eastern Europe, and non-European countries such as Pakistan and India, which faced significant refugee problems in their own region, thought that the UNHCR should be a strong, permanent organization, with the ability to raise funds for material assistance on a voluntary basis. American attempts to limit the mandate of the High Commissioner and to deny his office the authority and the funding to carry out material assistance operations were largely successful. In the end, the United States succeeded in making UN General Assembly approval a precondition of all appeals for voluntary contributions, and so the UNHCR became totally dependent on a small administrative budget granted by the UN General Assembly and on a small "emergency fund" to which the United States made no contributions at all until 1955, when the fund was made permanent. The net effect was the temporary reduction of the official UN role in refugee affairs to something close to the role assigned to earlier High Commissioners by the League of Nations.[1]

The decision to place severe limitations on UNHCR's original functions and authority were followed by interstate negotiations to determine the international legal obligations of states toward refugees.[2] These discussions were principally motivated by a desire on the part of states to create an international refugee convention that neither posed any threat to their national sovereignty nor imposed any new financial obligations on them. In the negotiations leading to the formulation of the 1951 Convention Relating to the Status of Refugees, Western governments were mainly interested in limiting their financial and legal obligations to refugees. As the International Refugee Organization had been an extremely expensive operation, the United States was opposed to establishing a new refugee agency that would be committed in advance to undertaking responsibility for all possible refugees that might appear in the future. Faced with events on the Indian subcontinent, the Korean Peninsula, China, and Palestine, American and other Western officials were beginning to believe that the world refugee problem would be virtually unending and were opposed to having the UN commit itself in advance to unspecified responsibilities.

The Statute of the UNHCR, adopted in 1950, and the Convention Relating to the Status of Refugees, promulgated the following year, defined a refugee as a person who had a "well-founded fear of being persecuted for reasons of race, religion, nationality, membership of a particular social group or political opinion."[3] The adoption of persecution as the central characteristic of the refugee was made to fit a Western interpretation of asylum seekers. The definition would include political refugees, mainly from Eastern Europe, and would stigmatize the fledgling communist regimes as persecutors. It was also perceived to be an appropriate way of dealing with the concerns of religious and ethnic minorities in Europe, especially the Jews, who were anxious to ensure that, in the event of future persecutions, international arrangements existed for facilitating departure and resettlement elsewhere.

Although governments agreed on a general, universally applicable definition of the term *refugee,* they were divided on whether the refugee convention should apply to refugees worldwide or whether it should be restricted to European refugees. The British, supported by the Scandinavian and Benelux countries, desired a broad definition of refugee. The United States and France, on the other hand, argued for limiting the responsibilities of states who were signatories to the refugee convention. In the end, the view that the refugee convention should serve mainly as an instrument for the reception and care of European refugees prevailed. Thus, whereas the Statute of the UNHCR placed no temporal or geographical limits on the High Commissioner's mandate, the UN Refugee Convention defined the obligations of signatory nations more narrowly. The Convention covered only individuals who were refugees as "a result of events occurring before January 1, 1951," and governments were given the discretion to apply it to those who were refugees "owing to events in Europe or owing to events in Europe and elsewhere."[4]

Given an annual budget of $300,000, and operating with temporal and geographic limits, the UNHCR was severely restricted and had a minimal impact on the situation of refugees in Europe in the immediate post–World War II period. Not until January 1954 were the accessions of six states obtained that were needed to bring the 1951 Refugee Convention into force. The United States did not sign it, and assumed no treaty obligations toward refugees until 1968.[5]

## Refugee Movements amid Escalating Cold War

For most of the 1950s, the refugee problem assumed an almost exclusively East–West dimension. Thousands of refugees from Eastern and Central Europe left their homes to seek asylum in the West. They emigrated illegally or in flagrant contravention of government policy and felt unable to return because of the likelihood that they would face persecution.

As large numbers sought to escape the persecution and regimentation of the East, Communist authorities in most Eastern European regimes quickly erected barriers to emigration and reacted with extraordinary harshness to anyone attempting to leave their countries without permission. Several East European governments were concerned about a "brain drain" and the loss of manpower needed to rebuild their economies. The crux of their opposition to emigration, however, was the fact that mass flight constituted a challenge to the ideological foundations of the new regimes, for which reason it came to be seen in several countries as a crime against the state. Unapproved emigration was punishable by imprisonment, heavy fines, and in some instances death. In addition, the fact that the police were responsible for enforcing migration policy and for holding the passports of persons not traveling greatly limited the numbers of people who could flee. A major exception to this pattern of closed borders and travel restrictions occurred in Bulgaria, where communist officials forcibly expelled some 170,000 members of the country's ethnic Turkish minority between 1949 and 1952 because they refused to integrate into the political and social life of the new socialist regime.

Political persecution in the Eastern bloc was accompanied by harsh economic conditions. After the establishment of communist regimes in Eastern Europe, Soviet-style economic plans were adopted throughout the region, deliberately emphasizing heavy industry at the expense of consumer goods, and imposing collectivized agriculture on an unwilling peasantry. Hardships were increased when the postwar reconstruction of Eastern Europe was subordinated to the central priority of strengthening the Soviet economy. In the West, however, economic reconstruction and recovery, aided by the $17 billion poured into the region under the Marshall Plan, was quick and provided a stark contrast to conditions in the East. The disparity in living conditions created further incentives for people trying to escape the grim Spartan life under communism.[6]

The new persecution-centered refugee definition accurately reflected the situation of many East European exiles, but it had serious drawbacks for the large-scale refugee movements that came to characterize the Third World situation after 1960. If the entire refugee problem were seen as one of persecution, the primary solution would inevitably be resettlement (the Western preference) rather than repatriation (the Eastern preference). It would also exclude the cooperation of the country of origin. This obliged the High Commissioner, in making a favorable determination of refugee eligibility, to make an adverse finding about the conduct of the country of origin in regard to its own nationals.

The recognition of East European emigrants as refugees stigmatized their countries of origin as willful violators of the human rights of their citizens. Reacting to international criticism of their domestic policies, communist authorities lashed out at the receiving states and refused to cooperate with the UNHCR. Indeed, Western governments encouraged the flow from East to West in order to weaken their rivals ideologically and to gain political legitimacy in their Cold War struggle. The Federal Republic of Germany, for example, offered automatic asylum, generous resettlement assistance, and citizenship to all East Germans. West German media, easily received in East Germany, emphasized the superior standard of living in the West. These inducements created a "pull factor" that resulted in the outflow of hundreds of thousands more people than might otherwise have migrated. But the number of refugees who required resettlement was not considered a problem, since it was a period of renewed European migration to the continents of North America and Australia.

For American policymakers, the acceptance of such migrants served clear ideological ends. A series of decisions made between 1949 and 1952 established an official (albeit unacknowledged) policy of exploiting the symbolic value of mass migration and defections. Eastern European exiles were employed in various propaganda exercises and covert military operations. Thus, special legislation approving the recruitment of up to 100 defectors each year was included in the 1949 act that created the Central Intelligence Agency.[7] In 1950, the State Department and the CIA launched the National Committee for a Free Europe, a nominally private organization dedicated to promoting the policy of "liberation" and the "rollback of communism." With the authority of the Mutual Security Act of 1951, President Truman set up the United States Escapee Program (USEP) to facilitate defections from the communist bloc. By 1952, the Psychological Strategy Board, charged with coordinating U.S. intelligence and propaganda activities, was actively monitoring the influx of East Europeans and was organizing the recruitment of a substantial number to become intelligence operatives or to staff U.S.-run clandestine radio stations.[8] In fact, United States policy until 1980 was that refugee admissions were limited by law to individuals fleeing communist countries or countries in the Middle East. Of the 233,436 refugees admitted between 1956 and 1968, all but 925 were from communist countries.[9] Thus, for political and ideological reasons, refugees from communism were welcomed, if not encouraged, to "vote with their feet," particularly at the height of the Cold War.

## Consequences of the Post–World War II
## Refugee Movements

The largest flow out of the Eastern bloc during the 1950s was created by the mass exodus of East Germans into West Germany. Until the early 1950s, the lines between the occupation zones in Germany could easily be crossed. In 1950, taking advantage of this route, some 197,000 East Europeans applied for political asylum in West Germany; in 1951, 165,000; in 1952, 182,000; and in 1953, 331,000.[10] Even after the Soviet Union instituted tight border controls around its zone in Germany, the door remained opened in Berlin, which continued to be administered jointly by the four powers. The mass emigration of East Germans to West Germany continued throughout the decade and created a serious labor shortage in East Germany. By the time the Berlin Wall was constructed in 1960 to staunch this East–West flow permanently, an estimated 3.5 million East Germans—about 20 percent of the population—had resettled in West Germany.

Although cultural similarities made for relatively easy integration of Eastern European refugees into the host West European countries, and although refugees provided labor for the expanding economies, not all were spontaneously welcomed. By 1952, nearly 200,000 were held in overcrowded camps and centers in West Berlin and the Federal Republic of Germany, "sometimes living in appalling conditions."[11] To relieve the pressures, the United States increased its resettlement admissions quotas[12] and granted the Attorney General the power to "parole" refugees—that is, to admit those outside the national origins quota system for "emergent reasons" and in cases where doing so was deemed to be in the "public interest."

The nature of the American commitment to refugees continued to evolve during the 1950s, becoming increasingly regional and unilateral. The United Nations became a very low foreign policy priority, particularly since, in the eyes of many Americans, the UN was too subject to communist influence. Rather, America chose to concentrate its resources heavily in its own military and economic programs, beginning with the Marshall Plan and followed by the Mutual Security Acts of 1951 through 1961. The Mutual Security legislation also provided funding for humanitarian programs, and refugee assistance came to be viewed within this framework. Special modifications were made in American immigration law to facilitate the admission of more Germans, primarily on the grounds that West Germany was afflicted with a "surplus population" problem that could destabilize that nation, and promote the spread of communism.[13] Provision was also made for admitting more "escapees" from Iron Curtain countries. It greatly suited the United States' interests that international attention remain firmly focused on refugees from communist countries. From the American perspective, UNHCR's programs and expenditures might benefit refugees who were of little political value to the United

States and might create more demands for their resettlement into the United States. Thus, as much as possible, the United States sought to support only refugee agencies created and maintained outside the UN, where the United States and its allies could be directly and exclusively involved.

## Creation of Parallel Refugee Organizations

In the period leading up to the declaration of the State of Israel by the Jewish community of Palestine in May 1948, and immediately following the subsequent invasion of the region by the armies of neighboring Arab countries, some 700,000 Palestinians fled or were expelled from areas under Jewish control. They arrived in miserable condition in the surrounding countries. In this case the United States supported the United Nations and helped establish the United Nations Relief for Palestine Refugees, soon to be replaced by the United Nations Relief and Works Agency for Palestine Refugees in the Near East (UNRWA). Its mandate was to provide aid—but no resettlement opportunities in Western countries—to Palestinian refugees. It was authorized to foster the economic integration of the refugees in their host countries, but it was not called upon to provide legal protection to Palestinians nor to seek a political solution to the Arab–Israeli conflict.[14] While some refugees were absorbed into Arab states and others were repatriated, the majority of Palestinians remained in camps in the region. This was necessitated by the foreign policy objectives of the Arab states, since the refugees' resettlement or assimilation would have made it difficult if not impossible for them to contest the legitimacy of the newly established Jewish state or to construct a Palestinian state in the future.

At the insistence of Arab states, Palestinians registered with UNRWA were purposely excluded from the competence of the UNHCR, both in its Statute and in the 1951 Refugee Convention. American support for a separate UN agency for Palestinians reinforced the anticommunist impulse behind U.S. refugee policy. UNRWA provided stability in a strategically important region by materially assisting the refugees and by preserving the internal security of the Arab states as a bulwark against communist subversion. This view was emphasized in testimony before Congress given by U.S. Assistant Secretary of State George McGhee:

> The political loss of the Middle East would be a major disaster . . . . the political strategic position of the Soviet Union would be immeasurably strengthened by the attainment of its objectives in the Near East, and the Cold War materially prolonged.
>
> Against this background, our solicitude for the Palestine refugees, partly based on humanitarian considerations, has additional justification. As long as the refugee problem remains unsolved . . . attainment of a political settlement in Palestine is delayed . . . [and] the refugees . . . will continue to serve as a

natural focal point for exploitation by communist disruptive elements which neither we nor the Near Eastern governments can afford to ignore.[15]

The second UN agency that received significant American funding was the United Nations Korean Reconstruction Agency (UNKRA). Along the same lines as UNRWA, UNKRA provided a limited service to the millions of people displaced by the Korean War, and it assisted South Korea in relocating refugees from communist North Korea and in repatriating Koreans from Japan.[16] Although the 1951 Refugee Convention only applied to Europeans and therefore excluded Koreans, Korean refugees nevertheless benefited from a massive UN relief effort. The provision of material assistance to those who had either fled from North Korea or been displaced by the war was considered integral to the anticommunist war effort by American forces who were fighting on the South Korean side under the UN flag. Like the Palestinian refugee situation in the Middle East, the plight of Korean refugees drew the foreign policy attention of the United States, and a special organization was created to administer to their needs. In both instances, the refugee assistance programs were viewed as supporting larger American interests in strategically important regions, and there was little risk that the activities of these agencies might generate demands for resettlement in the United States. Thus, the United States provided the bulk of financing for these organizations.

The massive displacement of peoples in other regions of Asia during the early post–World War II years did not generate any large-scale international response, and indeed these upheavals largely met with indifference from the United States and the Western powers. The partition of India in 1947, for example, unleashed an enormous outflow of peoples from both Pakistan and India.[17] About 14 million Hindus and Muslims fled from one country to the other, and the newly independent governments of India and Pakistan were left to deal with a huge resettlement problem on their own. Despite Indian and Pakistani appeals for material assistance from the UN, very little aid from the international community was forthcoming. Refugees on the Indian subcontinent clearly did not fall within the purview of the 1951 Refugee Convention, and unlike the Koreans and the Palestinians, they were not viewed by the United States and the West as geopolitically important refugee populations. Hence, the material needs of the displaced Hindu and Muslim communities were not recognized as placing a legitimate demand on the emerging international refugee regime, and no special international agency was created for them.

The United States was specifically interested in assisting European refugees, who continued to pour in from the East. To deal with overpopulation in Western Europe, in 1951 the United States launched the Intergovernmental Committee for European Migration (ICEM).[18] ICEM inherited the resettlement function of the IRO and was generously financed. It was established outside the United Nations, was administered almost exclusively by American directors, and was composed entirely of nations friendly to the United States.[19] ICEM salvaged some of the resettlement experience and machinery of the IRO.

At the time, it was widely believed that West Germany, Italy, Greece, and the Netherlands were overpopulated as a result of involuntary migrations and high birth rates. Fearful that a large, unemployable, and discontent population would threaten economic recovery and political stability in Europe and would be ripe for communist exploitation, the United States utilized ICEM to move refugees and other elements of "surplus population" out of Western Europe to final resettlement sites in skill-starved Latin America, Australia, and Canada, and in other less-populated parts of the world.

In 1952, the United States formally established the United States Escapee Program (USEP), essentially the national governmental arm of the U.S. effort to resettle communist bloc refugees. The statutory extension of a covert program that had existed at least since 1949, the USEP was regarded by its Congressional supporters as part of a "new American foreign policy" dedicated to the "liberation of Poland and other captive nations."[20] The United States allocated more than $4 million to establish better facilities for escapees and to facilitate their integration in the West. These programs and institutions also played a major role in shaping American refugee policy and investing it with specific ideological content. Escapees from the East were encouraged to flee and were used to gain intelligence and information about life on the other side of the Iron Curtain; to destabilize the regimes they fled; and to reveal the political, moral, and economic bankruptcy of life under communism.

## The UNHCR as a Sideshow

While creating and developing its own refugee institutions, the United States treated the UNHCR almost as a sideshow.[21] The first High Commissioner, G. J. van Heuven Goedhart, remained on poor terms with American officials throughout his tenure. West European governments supported the UNHCR, but they were not interested in expanding their financial commitments to refugees. In particular, European governments were reluctant to spend large sums of money on local refugee settlement, especially if it meant diverting any of the economic aid they were receiving from abroad. Moreover, local populations feared competition for jobs and services.

The Soviet Union's antagonism toward the emerging international refugee regime was chiefly attributable to its desire to stifle publicity about the grievous maltreatment it was inflicting on its nationals, to curb the exodus of skilled and scientific workers, and to deny the opportunity of escape to liberal political forces that had been overthrown in Eastern Europe and were still being subjected to persecution. Yet its hostility also reflected an awareness that refugees and the refugee issue were being used increasingly by the West—and particularly by the United States—as a means of discrediting and destabilizing the international communist system. The Soviet Union and its allies claimed that the UNHCR and the United States were working together to exploit refugee problems for political, economic, and military purposes; consequently they made no contribution of any kind toward the UNHCR's operations and refused to have anything to do with it.

Refugee problems in the developing nations were considered to be national problems that did not impose a legitimate demand on the emerging international refugee regime. Third World refugee populations located in areas of strategic interest to the United States were handled exclusively by specially created UN agencies and were therefore not within the mandate of the UNHCR. Thus, from the inception of his office in January 1951, the High Commissioner had to prove the worth of his agency and to fight constantly for more funds and political support to carry out his programs.

The refugee problems the UNHCR faced were enormous. Despite the considerable achievements of IRO, an estimated 400,000 "hard-core" displaced persons remained at the end of IRO's tenure, over a quarter of them still in camps scattered throughout Western Europe (mostly in Germany and Austria).[22] The UNHCR initially focused on these "leftovers." The High Commissioner repeatedly drew attention to the plight of refugees who had been passed over for resettlement because of poor health or economic nonproductivity and were still in camps many years after the end of the war.[23] He argued that in the future the UNHCR had no choice but to support local integration projects, emphasizing not only the financial cost to governments of maintaining unsettled refugees but also the political and security costs of not providing lasting solutions for them. He believed that, if governments were to be expected to offer long-term asylum, the international community had to provide material assistance to countries such as Germany, Austria, Greece, and Italy, where geopolitical circumstances had resulted in unusually heavy burdens. The UNHCR needed greater funds and more solid political support, particularly from the United States.

The lack of support from and frequent hostility of the United States were a major problem. The UNHCR's initial attempt to establish a definite role for itself and to implement its program occurred in 1952, when van Heuven Goedhart proposed establishing a limited relief fund of $3 million for IRO residuals and emergencies. Although the UN General Assembly authorized the UNHCR to launch its first appeal for government donations for emergency aid,[24] governments were initially almost totally unsupportive. The United Nations Refugee Emergency Fund (UNREF) was virtually a complete failure, principally because the United States refused to lend any diplomatic and financial support to it. According to Eleanor Roosevelt, the U.S. delegate to the United Nations at the time, the United States could not vote for a resolution authorizing the United Nations to administer relief because such a program would set a precedent of "authorizing a United Nations official to collect funds for a rather indefinite program in competition with other and more definite . . . programs."[25]

The U.S. government's public justification for not funding UNREF was that American contributions to European economic reconstruction through Marshall Plan aid and its own refugee programs more than supplemented the UNHCR's activities. Washington also felt that UNREF duplicated its own refugee programs, but in fact these programs—USEP in particular, and also ICEM—directly competed with the UNHCR. USEP operated in most of the same European countries and performed many of the same services, often for people who fell under the jurisdiction of the UNHCR. Yet the terms of reference and operating procedures of the USEP were far more exclusionary than were those of the UNHCR, and they were totally political in character. USEP only assisted anticommunist refugees, except those from Yugoslavia, and it didn't take anyone expelled from the western zones of Germany and Austria. Most importantly, USEP only aided refugees who had escaped after 1948, thereby excluding the "hard-core" IRO residuals.

ICEM's principal objective was to move people from the overpopulated countries of Germany, Austria, Greece, and Italy—the very countries for which the High Commissioner had requested permission to launch his international funding appeal. UNREF included local integration projects, but it also emphasized overseas resettlement, which was identical to the function of ICEM. At least part of the reason why the United States chose not to view the work of the two organizations as complementary and deserving of support was that they radically differed in political composition. As has been noted, the membership of ICEM was composed entirely of nations friendly to the United States, and its enabling statute forbade the participation of communist states.

Until the end of 1954, then, the United States opposed funding any part of the UNHCR's program. And although the UNHCR frequently conferred and collaborated on operational issues with the two American-funded organizations, their existence—parallel to and outside the United Nations—diverted resources from an agency that desperately needed American support to succeed. From 1952 to 1955, a period when the UNHCR was vainly trying to raise $3 million, the United States allocated $45 million to USEP and ICEM.

American opposition to the UNHCR was personal as well as political. Not only did many in Congress and the media believe that the UN was not the best forum to maximize American national interests, but Washington was also unhappy that its own candidate for UN High Commissioner (the former American director of IRO) had not been elected, and they remained convinced that van Heuven Goedhart was too independent-minded. Senior officials within the State Department personally disliked van Heuven Goedhart, and he was frequently attacked in the conservative American press.[26] The opposition to the High Commissioner, coupled with the fact that the United States perceived the UNHCR to be largely irrelevant to American interests, led the United States to pursue its own independent course. This negative attitude adversely affected the responses of practically all other potential donor governments. By March 1954, only slightly more than one-third of the $3 million had been collected, and only eleven of sixty UN members had contributed at all. While refusing to give a penny to the UNHCR, the United States became the principal donor supporting two other special UN refugee agencies: UNRWA, at a level of funding reaching over $150 million; and UNKRA, at around $75 million.

America's opposition toward UNHCR also had a deleterious effect on the willingness of the major voluntary agencies (many of them American) to cooperate with the UNHCR. According to the terms of its mandate, the UNHCR was not an operating agency and had to find voluntary agencies to implement its meager programs. Many U.S. voluntary agencies were reluctant to serve as implementing partners, particularly when ICEM and the USEP could provide them with lucrative refugee contracts.[27] Moreover, the U.S. government, fully recognizing the political significance of the refugee issue in the Cold War, encouraged voluntary agencies to act as its surrogate in the field. In this highly politicized environment, most agencies willingly utilized American government funds and implemented programs that, although undoubtedly humanitarian, chiefly benefited refugees of direct political interest to the United States.[28]

Faced with a void of governmental support, the High Commissioner turned to the private sector for help. Limited financial assistance for local integration programs came from a 1952 Ford Foundation grant of $2.9 million[29] to bring the "hard-core" refugees into the life of the domestic communities of West European asylum states.

## The American About-face

American opposition to funding the High Commissioner's programs was finally overcome when the United States cosponsored a UN General Assembly resolution in the fall of 1954 calling for a four-year plan for permanent solutions, known as the United Nations Refugee Fund. The resolution recognized that certain European countries were facing particularly heavy burdens due to their geographical situation and stated that "some complimentary aid" had been shown to be necessary.[30] This American about-face was partly due to a new "Soviet redefection campaign," which sought, with some success, to persuade recent escapees to abandon the West and to return to their homelands. Moscow granted general amnesties, rehabilitation, the release of political prisoners, and reforms of the judiciary and police in Eastern Europe. The United States perceived this campaign to be a direct threat to its own escapee program and consequently increased funding of its refugee programs in Europe. American foreign policy officials felt that the United States had to be more generous not only to recent escapees from East Europe but also to the IRO residuals who had been left behind in camps and who were now coming under increasing pressure from communist propaganda campaigns to return home.

Thus, for the first time, the UNHCR benefited from the ideological struggle between East and West. In an appeal to Congress for an American contribution to this new UN Refugee Fund, the State Department warned that the communists under the Soviet redefection campaign were "finding fairly fertile minds in those camps where these people have been festering for a very long time" and that the United States "cannot afford to have refugees returning to communist countries because, in view of their experience as refugees, they come to believe that conditions of living behind the Iron Curtain are better than in the free world. . . . "[31] It was only by emphasizing the UNHCR's contribution to U.S. security interests that the State Department was finally able to secure Congressional support for the High Commissioner's program. Thus, U.S. Congressmen were advised that the UN Refugee Fund would support refugee projects in "countries closely linked in interest to the United States—Germany, Austria, Italy and Greece," where "it is also in our own self-interest to encourage those countries to maintain liberal asylum policies."[32] Assured that the UN Refugee Fund constituted an important part of the American struggle against communism, the U.S. Congress in 1955 approved the first American financial contribution to the UNHCR, in the sum of $500,000.

While approving an initial American contribution to the United Nations Refugee Fund, the U.S. Congress also obtained assurances that the program would receive close intergovernmental supervision through a Refugee Fund Executive Committee, that the communist governments would be excluded from this committee, and that the fund would be carefully managed. When the United States initially cosponsored the Fund, it made its support contingent on several conditions, including definable limits to American contributions, adequate support from other governments, and assumption of responsibility for the refugees by the countries of asylum at the termination of the Fund in four years' time. By insisting on these preconditions, the United States was able to spread the financial burden and yet at the same time to assume some degree of international control over the use of funds, through its dominant position as the principal donor and most powerful government on the Executive Committee.

The American decision to contribute to the UN Refugee Fund had the predictable effect of encouraging other governments to become donors as well. In contrast to the earlier United Nations Refugee Emergency Fund, with its disastrous lack of contributions, the new fund quickly attracted government support and ultimately collected almost $14.5 million of its $16 million goal.[33] The successful establishment of the UN Refugee Fund represented the first major international recognition of the centrality and importance of the UNHCR to the resolution of refugee problems.

## Changes in the International Political System

The emergence of the UNHCR from the wings to center stage coincided with a major political transformation in the international system, particularly in the United Nations. The year 1956, by which time the United Nations had increased its membership to a total of eighty countries, marked the close of a period of absolute Western hegemony and the beginning of Third World preponderance in voting power within the General Assembly. The United Nations assumed growing political importance both for developing countries and the Soviet bloc, particularly as a forum for pressing their claims. Anticolonialism became a political weapon for the Soviet Union to use in its ideological conflict with the West, and the Soviet Union joined a number of African and Asian states to form an anticolonial coalition in the United Nations.

During this time, the dimensions of the Cold War and the location of U.S.–Soviet competition began to shift away from Europe and toward the Third World. As the East–West conflict extended to Asia and Africa, the struggle to end colonialism and to draw attention to the economic and political disparities between rich states and poor states gained importance within the international political system. The first Asian–African Conference was held in Bandung, Indonesia, in April 1955 to articulate Third World concerns and to lobby for a greater voice in international affairs.

The Soviets helped facilitate the admission of several developing countries to the United Nations, and these countries recognized the potential usefulness of the UNHCR to their own refugee problems. This was a determining factor in moving the Soviet bloc out of its rigid opposition to the office of the High Commissioner. Thus, in the autumn 1955 session of the United Nations, the Soviet Union abstained from, rather than opposed, a vote to extend the High Commissioner's activities. For the first time, the UN General Assembly passed a resolution concerning UNHCR activities without any opposing votes.

## The Hungarian Revolution and the Coming of Age of the UNHCR

The visibility and viability of the UNHCR within the international refugee regime were further strengthened by that agency's rapid response to a major Cold War refugee crisis that erupted with the 1956 Hungarian Revolution. The invasion of Hungary by the Soviet army on November 4, 1956, presented the UNHCR with a rare opportunity to demonstrate that it was the only agency capable of taking large-scale international action for refugees.

Within a few months of the outbreak of the Hungarian Revolution, approximately 180,000 Hungarians had entered Austria and another 20,000 had crossed over into Yugoslavia. Neither country had the physical infrastructure needed to deal with this mass influx, and they were initially hesitant to take action on behalf of the Hungarians for fear of provoking a hostile Soviet reaction.[34] Almost immediately, the UN General Assembly requested the UNHCR to intervene,[35] and UN Secretary-General Dag Hammarskjöld directed James Read, the Deputy High Commissioner, who was temporarily in charge after the death of Van Heuven Goedhart, to coordinate the international response to the Hungarian refugee crisis. The High Commissioner's office established a coordinating group that included ICEM, the International Committee of the Red Cross (ICRC), USEP, the League of Red Cross Societies, and a number of voluntary agencies. In both Austria and Yugoslavia, the High Commissioner's local representative chaired groups that administered the emergency aid.[36] For the first time in its history, the UNHCR directed a large-scale emergency operation for a group that was immediately determined to be eligible for refugee status.

UNHCR appeals to governments for the resettlement of Hungarians generated numerous offers from governments all over the world. A tremendous groundswell of sympathy and support for the Hungarians arose. Spurred by extensive television coverage of students hurling paving stones and Molotov cocktails at Soviet tanks, the Western public viewed the Hungarians as heroes who deserved their help. More than any other event of the 1950s, the Soviet suppression of the Hungarian Revolution symbolized the brutality of the Soviet Union and vindicated Western descriptions of life behind the Iron Curtain. Expressing guilt over its failure to back up its policy of the "rollback of communism" with direct assistance to the Hungarian "freedom fighters," the West felt that it owed these recent victims of communism safe haven and the opportunity to start afresh. Assisting refugees also alleviated the destabilizing potential of the exodus in Austria and elsewhere in Europe.

From the beginning of the crisis, it was assumed that all Hungarians were fleeing persecution and deserved asylum. At the height of the Cold War, Western policymakers did not seriously consider that Hungarians' motivations for leaving might have been influenced by a suddenly open border, an enticing image of the West as portrayed by Radio Free Europe, and the opportunity to pursue a better life elsewhere, as well as by a desire to escape genuine political persecution. Moreover, in a mass exodus situation, judging each individual's motive for flight was deemed to be physically impossible. The UNHCR therefore determined to grant all Hungarians in Austria and Yugoslavia prima facie group eligibility as refugees.[37]

One of the most striking aspects of this episode was the speed with which the process of resettlement was begun. In a remarkable demonstration of solidarity with the Hungarian refugees, governments all over the world lowered their immigration barriers and granted visas to entire families, including the ill and the disabled, without regard to quotas. Western Europe immediately began to provide resettlement opportunities. Great Britain took approximately 21,000 Hungarians; West Germany, 15,000;

Switzerland, 13,000; France, 13,000; Sweden, 7,000; and Belgium, 6,000. Similar generosity was displayed by some less heavily populated countries of Europe, such as Denmark and Norway, and was matched by the actions of a number of non-European nations. Canada accepted 37,000 refugees; Australia, 11,000; and Israel, 2,000. Several thousand more were brought to Latin America by the governments of Honduras, Guatemala, Venezuela, Argentina, and Brazil.[38] The United States, taking advantage of a small loophole in the law that gave the Attorney General authority to "parole" aliens temporarily into the U.S. "for emergent reasons or for reasons deemed strictly in the public interest,"[39] admitted approximately 38,000 Hungarians. Nearly 200,000 Hungarian refugees were permanently resettled in less than two years, at a global cost of more than $100 million—a sum that far surpassed the amount channeled through the UN Refugee Fund to postwar refugees.

In addition to reflecting international responsiveness to the anticommunist sentiment then prevalent in the West, the success in resettling so many refugees so quickly was also attributable in part to the personal qualifications of the Hungarians and to the favorable economic conditions that prevailed in their new home countries. In many ways, Hungarians were a model immigrant group. A large percentage of them were young, skilled, and educated, and they entered labor markets at a time when unemployment rates were low.

Another remarkable feature of this episode was that the new High Commissioner, Auguste Lindt, for the first time made the High Commissioner's Office directly useful to a communist state. Hungarian officials charged that many young people under 18 years of age had left the country during the crisis without their parents' knowledge or consent, and that some of the asylum and resettlement states were refusing to help determine whether any of these persons wanted to return home to rejoin their families. The issue of repatriation to a communist state, particularly during a period of heightened Cold War tensions and amid Western charges of a reign of terror in Budapest and mass deportations in Hungary, was highly contentious and politically divisive. Any action on the part of the UNHCR that even hinted at forced repatriation would have caused an immediate outraged response by the United States and other Western governments and would have been slapped down immediately. But by painstaking diplomacy, Lindt was able to gain the cooperation of both the Western asylum and resettlement countries and the Hungarian authorities in embarking on what became the first successful repatriation program to an East European communist state. More than 13,000 persons returned to Hungary during the first year; and by the end of the crisis, approximately 18,000—or ten percent of those resettled abroad—had gone home.

In its handling of the Hungarian refugee operation, the UNHCR convincingly showed itself to be the only international institution capable of dealing effectively with a political crisis and a refugee problem of major proportions. It had worked quickly to defuse the refugee crisis, and it had even earned the respect of some socialist governments. The office had clearly come of age and had won international acceptance and recognition.

The generous and rapid response of the international community to the Hungarian exodus stood in marked contrast to the attitude toward the displaced people within Europe who were still in need of resettlement. In the mid-1950s, more than 200 refugee camps remained in Austria, Italy, Germany, and Greece, and more than 80,000 "hard-core" refugees had been living in them since the late 1940s. Thousands more refugees lingered in China and the Middle East. The worldwide publicity given to the Hungarians drew international attention again to the shameful conditions in which these other, stateless people were still living. Consequently, the United Nations in 1959 gave its full backing to the establishment of a "World Refugee Year," during which member nations pledged to resolve the problem of Europe's remaining refugees by resettling them.

## Expansion Through "Good Offices"

By the late 1950s, the UNHCR faced political problems arising not only from the East–West nature of refugee flows but also from the South–North dimension of new refugee movements in the developing countries. In the past, when refugee problems were perceived exclusively in an East–West context, a political consensus among Western nations regarding international approaches was assured. In cases involving Third World refugees, the situations encountered in various poor countries differed considerably. In many instances, refugee situations directly involved the interests of Western colonial powers that were also among the founding members of the international refugee regime. In the end, a distinctly new way of responding to refugee problems emerged within the United Nations. Whenever refugee situations arose with political dynamics and problems that did not correspond with those of the European situation, that were not covered in the UNHCR Statute, or that involved one or more of the Western powers, the UN General Assembly simply granted the High Commissioner authority so that he could take action. Thus, for the next two decades, the United Nations was willing to turn to the UNHCR whenever its services could be usefully applied on behalf of new and different groups of refugees and displaced persons.

The limited scope of international legal instruments for dealing with refugees had been obvious from the very inception of the UNHCR. Soon after taking office, the High Commissioner was approached to provide limited material assistance to Chinese refugees who had flooded into Hong Kong after the Chinese communists' establishment of the People's Republic of China and their introduction of land reforms and revolutionary social and economic programs. The mass influx of 700,000 displaced persons put an enormous strain on Hong Kong authorities, but the UNHCR was initially prevented from assisting the arriving Chinese because Britain didn't consider them to fall within the purview of the UNHCR

Statute.[40] In addition, when the United Kingdom adhered to the international refugee instruments, it did not extend the application of the 1951 Refugee Convention to its colony, Hong Kong. Thus, the British were not obligated to treat the Chinese newcomers as refugees and did not welcome the possibility that the UNHCR might recognize them as such.[41]

More important, however, was the fact that the Chinese revolution had led to the creation of two Chinas. The Chiang Kai-shek government in Taiwan took the position that aid to refugees from "China" would constitute implicit recognition of the PRC. As long as the Chiang Kai-shek government remained China in the eyes of the United Nations, it could not very well recognize the new arrivals in Hong Kong as refugees without offending the government in Taiwan. Yet without a declaration that the Chinese in Hong Kong were within the UNHCR's mandate, the office had no authority to seek assistance for them.

The legal technicalities over contending recognition policies were finally sorted out in 1957, when the UN General Assembly made it possible for the UNHCR to assist Chinese refugees in Hong Kong without making an evaluation of the political conditions in either of the two Chinas and without seeming to take sides between the two competing governments. The UN General Assembly acknowledged that "the problem of Chinese refugees in Hong Kong . . . is such as to be of concern to the international community" and requested the High Commissioner to "use his good offices to encourage arrangements for contributions" to the Chinese refugees in Hong Kong.[42] In the end, only a small amount of international assistance was ever required, because most of the Chinese refugees were absorbed by the rapidly growing Hong Kong economy of the 1960s. Nevertheless, this UN resolution set an important precedent that led to a steady expansion of the High Commissioner's authority to mount assistance programs throughout the developing world during the next decade.

In 1958, the UNHCR was authorized by the UN General Assembly to assist refugees from the Algerian war of independence—the first African struggle against European colonial rule in the postwar period to produce significant numbers of refugees. This was also the first occasion on which UNHCR emergency assistance was requested in the Third World; thus it marked an important step in the development both of the political conditions under which the UNHCR had to act and of the functions it was permitted to perform. Morocco, with some 80,000 Algerian refugees, and Tunisia, with 85,000, both requested material assistance from the UNHCR. As in the Hong Kong crisis, the High Commissioner was almost paralyzed by the politics of interstate conflict, this time between France and Algeria.

The UNHCR felt that it had to grant assistance to Tunisia and Morocco, because failing to do so would estrange the organization from a growing bloc of developing nations. Yet the UNHCR found it politically impossible to declare the Algerians refugees, because such action would imply that France—one of the great powers within the United Nations, and a member of the High Commissioner's Executive Committee with a history of liberal asylum policies and support for international assistance to refugees—was persecuting some of its own subjects. To make matters more difficult, the French government denied the authority of the UN-HCR to give assistance in this case, claiming that Algeria was an integral part of the state of France and that the eventual solution had to be the return to Algeria of the people who had taken refuge in Tunisia and Morocco. Eventually, the French were persuaded to accept a compromise that enabled the UNHCR to provide assistance through its good offices to Tunisia and Morocco; and in 1958, the United Nations General Assembly approved the High Commissioner's assistance to Algerians in a text that deliberately avoided reference to their eligibility for refugee status.[43] Another important precedent for later expansion was established when the General Assembly approved assistance to Algerians who began to return home after the war in 1961.

Continued expansion of the UNHCR's authority came via a series of UN General Assembly resolutions. The High Commissioner was freed of the obligation to seek the approval of the General Assembly for each separate appeal for new groups of refugees.[44] He was given authority to finance and coordinate permanent solutions to all refugees under his mandate on a continuing basis; and a new Emergency Fund was established, with a $500,000 ceiling, to be used solely at his discretion.[45] In 1959, the UN General Assembly for the first time distinguished between refugees within the mandate of the UNHCR and "refugees who do not come within the competence of the United Nations," on whose behalf the High Commissioner was authorized to use his good offices to transmit contributions for their assistance.[46]

The new approach was both pragmatic and provisional. The concept of "good offices" enabled the UNHCR to avoid the undesirable political consequences of making refugee determinations in the Third World that might damage relations with some of the principal Western supporters of the international refugee regime. It also allowed the High Commissioner to extend limited financial and material assistance to people in need who were not statutory refugees. But at the same time, the UNHCR disclaimed any intention of seeking a long-term solution to these problems or of assuming ongoing protection for these groups. Thus, the de facto extension of international action to non-European refugees was confined, for political reasons, to categories of emergency relief and material assistance only.

At the same time, the Refugee Fund Executive Committee was replaced by a larger body, the Executive Committee, which gave advice about and directions to the agency's annual programs, known generally as the High Commissioner's Program. With these changes, the High Commissioner gained greater prominence, and the international community recognized that the task of material assistence had become more than a mere adjunct to international protection.

In six years, the UNHCR had grown from a strictly nonoperational agency with no authority to appeal for funds to carry out its limited programs into an international institution with a long-range program emphasizing housing, vocational and professional training, local integration, and resettlement. More importantly, it enjoyed nearly universal support for its activities, including the critical financial support of the United States. The newly independent nations generally approved of the office and sought to influence the nature of its programs. The Soviet Union and Eastern Europe tacitly approved specific projects of the agency, whose policies they had previously attacked consistently as instruments of Western imperialism. Moreover, after the failed uprising in Hungary, the U.S. view that refugee policy could play a significant role in the Cold War in Europe was shelved;[47] and indeed refugee movements did not reemerge as a force for fundamental change in East–West relations in Europe until 1989 when masses of East Germans brought down the Berlin Wall.

By the end of the 1950s, Westerners saw that the center of refugee attention was moving from Europe to Africa and Asia, and they took action to strengthen the UNHCR's capability to respond to these new movements. Existing international legal norms were not suitable for dealing with refugee issues in the Third World. The 1951 Refugee Convention had been developed to respond to a largely European refugee problem of the late 1940s and early 1950s. Clearly, the 1960s refugees did not fall within the classic definition in the Convention; that is, they had not fled as a result of conditions in Europe before 1951, nor could they meet the individual persecution criteria outlined in the international legal instruments. Fleeing violence and conflict associated with decolonization, national liberation struggles, and the establishment of nation-states in the Third World, large groups of destitute people were in need of numerous special kinds of emergency assistance. In response, the High Commissioner had to reorient the programs and priorities of his office from Europe to the Third World.

# 4

# The International
# Refugee Regime and
# Third World Refugees

At the beginning of the 1960s, the attention of the international refugee regime passed to the Third World, where millions of displaced people posed a serious challenge to international stability. In Europe, the era of refugees (except for waves of Czechs in 1968 and Poles in 1980) was mostly finished, and the problem would not reappear until the late 1980s. Although political repression in Eastern Europe and the Soviet Union continued to produce more refugees, fewer and fewer Eastern Europeans were able to flee to the West, especially once the countries behind the Iron Curtain consolidated their rule, imposed exit controls, and closed their borders. It was assumed that the continuing process of overseas resettlement, as well as residual local integration, would dispose of the remaining European refugee problem.[1] By the early 1960s, the westward flow of Eastern Europeans had rapidly been eclipsed by new refugee movements in the Third World.

The 1960s and 1970s marked a second phase in the global refugee crisis. In Africa and Asia, anticolonial insurgency and postindependence civil strife and warfare generated vast numbers of refugees.[2] With the major exception of refugees admitted from Indochina and the Southern Cone of Latin America, nearly all Third World refugees remained in their regions of origin, either returning home after independence or being given long-term asylum in neighboring communities. With rapid decolonization, the character of refugee problems changed. South–South movements predominated, and the international community came under mounting pressure to adapt its programs and policies to give greater priority to refugees in developing countries.

African and Asian governments mounted impressive efforts on behalf of refugees from nearby countries, but in most cases host countries were extremely poor. External assistance was still needed from Western governments, who continued to determine international refugee policy and action through their control of the UNHCR. And with the exception of anti-Castro Cubans and (later) anticommunist Vietnamese, the new refugees were generally not seen as serving the political or ideological interests of the United States or the other major Western powers.

It was also clear that the possibility of overseas resettlement, which underpinned the entire international approach to the European refugee problem, essentially did not exist in relation to the refugee problem in the developing countries. Most of those fleeing conflict in Africa had no wish to settle in Europe or North America. Instead they fled across borders to stay with closely related ethnic groups until they could return home. The majority of these people clearly did not fall within the classic refugee definition enunciated in the 1951 Refugee Convention; in particular, few could meet the individual persecution criteria outlined in the international legal instruments. Most refugees were participants in mass movements.

During the 1960s, the UNHCR focused on emergency assistance; during the 1970s, on repatriation. For refugees who could not return home, the UNHCR attempted to upgrade its assistance to those who stood some chance of integrating into the local populations of host states. Naturalization in countries of first asylum, however, proved almost impossible to obtain. During the 1960s and 1970s, therefore, the UNHCR underwent a period of sustained growth; and its functions, operations, and geographical outreach expanded to meet the increasing demands being placed on it in Africa, Asia, and Latin America.

The 1980s saw the beginning of yet another phase in the refugee crisis, coinciding with the dramatic rise in the number of internal and regional conflicts in which external powers were directly or indirectly involved. As a result, the developing world produced an increasing number of refugees, the majority of whom faced long-term stays in camps, while the UNHCR's energies were completely occupied in helping people who had fled from regional conflicts from Afghanistan to the Horn of Africa to stay alive.

During much of the 1980s, when the superpowers and their Third World clients were locked in conflicts, Western donor states were reluctant to open dialogue with refugee-producing nations that were typically their political enemies and strategic adversaries. In the absence of political negotiations, voluntary repatriation programs that had been used successfully in the past became difficult to broker, and the burden of the refugee problem fell on neighboring host countries or resettlement nations overseas. Moreover, the sheer size of many refugee movements, as well as the political and security implications of hosting refugees from adjoining countries, made permanent local settlement difficult in and even unacceptable to many countries. Apart from a costly and prolonged program for Vietnamese refugees, overseas resettlement became distinctly unpopular in the 1980s, and a growing number of refugees appeared destined to remain indefinitely in exile.

At the beginning of the 1990s, the reduction in tension between the erstwhile superpowers and their disengagement from some of the major internal and regional conflicts that had generated so many refugees in the past seemed to open up opportunities in all regions of the world for terminating conflicts, arresting refugee flows, and creating conditions that might allow large-scale repatriations. But the "new world order" proved increasingly elusive. Many long-standing conflicts continued unresolved, and new refugee crises emerged as a result of national disintegration and ethnic and communal fragmentation in such countries as the former Yugoslavia, the ex–Soviet Union, and Somalia.

In the 1990s, internal wars are fought not only by military means but by preventing international aid from reaching people living in conflict areas. Frequently, the international community is unable to assist or intervene, and the willingness of governments and international organizations to influence behavior in such situations is often lacking. Massive displacement of people is the inevitable result. In the 1990s, therefore, traditional solutions to refugee problems are clearly no longer adequate, and the search for more effective alternative approaches has become pertinent and pressing.

## Violent Decolonization and Political Conflict in Africa

During the 1960s most of the world's refugees were located in Africa. According to one authoritative account, the numbers grew from about 400,000 in 1964 to 625,000 in 1966 to about 1 million by the end of the decade.[3] There were at least two distinct categories: refugees from territories under Portuguese colonial administration (and later from Zimbabwe and southern Africa); and refugees produced by internal strife, political instability, ethnic conflict, and repression in several countries that had already gained independence.

About two-thirds of the present member states of the Organization of African Unity (OAU) won their independence in the 1960s. Although independence in sub-Saharan Africa was achieved in a more peaceful and orderly way than it was in any other major region of the world, constant and often violent resistance to the end of colonial rule occurred in certain places. Portugal, in particular, vigorously opposed political independence for its African colonies, and the armed repression it inflicted on its colonial subjects resulted in masses of refugees, especially from Angola.

In 1961, Portugal embarked on a campaign of terror in Angola.[4] The resulting protracted national liberation struggle provoked confrontation between the major world powers, each of which supported its own client political movement inside Angola, and caused thousands to flee to Zaire and Zambia. The struggle against Portuguese rule in Mozambique produced yet more refugees, especially when Portugal outlawed most African organizations in Mozambique and instituted a scorched-earth policy, forcibly relocating people into fortified villages. As a result, Mozambiquans fled into Tanzania, Zambia, and Malawi, where they numbered nearly 80,000 in 1974.[5] Under similar conditions, the anticolonial struggle in Guinea-Bissau generated some 80,000 refugees who fled to Senegal and Equatorial Guinea.[6]

In Rhodesia, the numbers of refugees greatly increased after the colony of Southern Rhodesia unilaterally declared independence from British rule in 1965 and an armed independence struggle was initiated by two black political organizations, ZAPU and ZANU. By the end of the 1970s, a total of 250,000 blacks from Rhodesia lived in exile in Mozambique, Zambia, and Botswana.[7] By this time, too, increasing numbers of Namibian and South African refugees had appeared in Angola, Zambia, Botswana, Lesotho, and Swaziland.

Although resistance to foreign domination and wars of national liberation accounted for many African refugee problems, colonial suppression was not the sole cause of mass movements. Refugees also fled political repression and ethnic conflict in newly independent, African-ruled states. Many of these states had extremely weak civil societies, vulnerable economies, and governments that were unrepresentative and ineffective. More often than not, the former colonial powers had established the borders between African countries arbitrarily. As a result, tribes and ethnic groups were split up across state boundaries, creating dual loyalties and building centrifugal forces into the systems of most of the newly independent countries. Internal heterogeneity, political repression, and economic deprivation made many states potential powder kegs. The tensions generated by these unstable conditions took varied, usually violent forms. Communal conflict—based on ethnic, sectarian, or tribal affiliation—became a basic characteristic of most African societies and created large numbers of refugees throughout the continent.

In the early 1960s, over 100,000 refugees fled Rwanda when the subjected Hutu majority, which gained control of the government through a general election, set out to destroy the power of the Tutsi minority. This conflict initiated an exodus of Tutsi to Uganda, Burundi, Tanzania, and Zaire, where their numbers swelled to approximately 150,000.[8] Internal conflict in the newly independent state of Zaire resulted in movements of refugees to Burundi, the Central African Republic, Sudan, Uganda, and Tanzania. By 1966 their numbers had reached more than 80,000.[9]

Major waves of refugees from Sudan after it gained independence in 1956 resulted from the policies adopted by successive Islamic regimes in Khartoum to incorporate the mainly Christian and animist southern region. As widespread resistance to northern rule developed, the south became engulfed in civil war. Conflict between Sudanese government forces and southern rebels, such as the guerrilla force known as Anya-nya, resulted in major refugee flows into the Central African Republic, Uganda, and Zaire and smaller flows into Ethiopia and Kenya.[10] By the end of the first Sudanese civil war in 1972, well over 500,000 Sudanese had been internally displaced, and at least 170,000 southerners had taken refuge abroad. In turn, Sudan became one of the largest refugee-receiving states in Africa.[11] Beginning in 1967, an influx of Eritrean refugees striving for political independence from Ethiopia poured into Sudan, followed by other groups of Ethiopian refugees.

Although the conclusion of the first civil war in Sudan in 1972 and the attainment of independence in 1975 by Portugal's African colonies took more than half of Africa's refugees off of the UNHCR's rolls, within a few years new ones arose to take their place. Masses of people fled brutal tyrants who seized power in the Central African Republic, Uganda, and Equatorial Guinea. In Burundi, with a tribal makeup resembling that of neighboring Rwanda, the Tutsi embarked on a genocidal massacre of Hutus, thereby generating a huge outflow of refugees. As in the Sudan, Chad became involved in a protracted conflict between Muslim and non-Muslim populations that resulted in the flight of Chadians to Sudan, the Central African Republic, Cameroon, and Nigeria. In northern Africa, war between the Polisario Front, a movement fighting for the independence of the Western Sahara and the combined armies of Morocco and Mauritania, subjected the Saharawi people to military attack and precipitated their mass flight to nearby Algeria.[12] By the end of the 1970s, Africa's refugee population stood at several million. The expansion and internationalization of the conflicts in southern Africa and the Horn during the 1980s and 1990s generated further flows, making Africa a continent of uprooted people.

## Responses to African Refugee Movements

The majority of Africa's refugees in the 1960s were self-settled and widely dispersed,[13] making their impact less dramatic than that of their counterparts today. The UNHCR provided some emergency relief and established programs to support organized rural settlements and urban refugees, but most refugees had to fend for themselves.[14] Where land was relatively abundant, refugees were often welcomed. However, while there were many positive instances of refugees spontaneously integrating with their host population, they were not equally welcome everywhere, particularly not when they put strains on food supplies and other local resources.[15] Therefore, lasting settlement, including naturalization, was not a real possibility for most.

Political problems compounded the difficulties. Portugal objected to calling Angolans refugees, because this implied that Lisbon was sanction-

ing the persecution of its colonial subjects. The High Commissioner
wanted to avoid any dispute about the refugee character of these new
groups and any question about his competence to deal with these problems.[16] Felix Schnyder, who became High Commissioner in 1961, thus
sought greater authority from the UN General Assembly so that in future,
the UNHCR could respond fully to these situations.

In 1961 the United Nations gave the UNHCR authority to assist
both "refugees within his mandate and those for whom he extends his
good offices."[17] This measure allowed the UNHCR to consider Angolans
and other Africans as prima facie eligible for assistance, without accusing
Portugal or any of the newly independent states of persecuting their subjects. In effect, the resolution obviated the need to make individual determinations of eligibility.[18]

The distinction between mandate refugees and good offices refugees
was completely abandoned in 1965, when the General Assembly requested the High Commissioner to provide protection and permanent
solutions to all groups within his competence.[19] Humanitarian assistance
thus became the primary consideration of UNHCR; protection became
secondary.

As new refugee groups emerged in the 1960s (particularly in Africa)
whose circumstances could not be related to events prior to 1951, the
Refugee Convention's time limitation became a growing handicap for the
High Commissioner. While General Assembly resolutions made many
new refugee groups the concern of the UNHCR, the measures were recommendations only and could not impose fresh or greater obligations on
sovereign states. Consequently, Schnyder and his Executive Committee
sought to delete the geographic and time limitation provisions from the
1951 Convention by means of a "protocol." In 1967, after Schnyder had
been succeeded by Sadruddin Aga Khan, such a protocol was signed by
many nations, including some that were not parties to the original Convention.[20] Rather than simply amending the Convention, the new Protocol Relating to the Status of Refugees was drafted in such a way that a
government signing it would in effect agree to undertake all the obligations of the original Convention. The High Commissioner was thus able
to secure ratification by a number of governments, including the United
States, that had not signed the original Convention. And in contrast to the
slow pace with which states accepted the 1951 Convention, the Protocol
was quickly ratified by a large number of governments.[21] The most important effect of the 1967 Protocol was that it brought the 1951 Convention
on Refugees into line with the universal mandate of the Statute of the
UNHCR.

The High Commissioner's interest in seeking rapid adoption of the
Protocol was at least partly stimulated by efforts of the Organization of
African Unity (OAU) to draft its own regional convention on refugees,
which the UNHCR feared might supersede or compete with the 1951
Convention.[22] Although African states viewed their efforts on behalf of

refugees as an expression of political solidarity with those groups struggling against white colonial rule in southern Africa, the importance they
attached to their own regional refugee convention grew primarily out of a
desire to have the legal instruments reflect more adequately the situation
of Africans and to minimize the security threat posed to states by refugees.
Hence, in 1969 the OAU extended the definition of *refugee* in its convention to include "every person who, owing to external aggression, occupation, foreign domination or events seriously disturbing public order . . . is
compelled to leave his place of habitual residence."[23] By covering individuals seeking refuge from the violence and devastation of war, the OAU
offered a significantly broader interpretation of *refugee* than did the Convention and the Protocol.

During a time when the majority of the world's refugees were originating in the Third World, most states had little difficulty accepting the
extension of the UNHCR's mandate to include war victims and other
externally displaced persons. Some argued that UN General Assembly
resolutions had given the UNHCR a competence comparable to that
contained in the expanded definition of the OAU Convention. The Western states at that time, however, were not faced with masses of Third
World arrivals into their own countries; therefore, they could avoid coming to grips with the question of whether these people were formally
within the High Commissioner's mandate. Moreover, until the oil crisis
of 1973, Western countries enjoyed an economic boom and a need for
cheap labor. This meant that Third World migrants who did come to
Europe were almost certain to be admitted as immigrants if they were
rejected as refugees.

No consensus on a single definition of *refugee* existed among states.
Indeed, many governments believed that the situation required multiple
definitions for multiple purposes. At least two definitions were being
applied by the early 1960s.[24] Among Western countries, the term *refugee*
was restricted to persons who fulfilled the criteria of the UNHCR Statute
and the 1951 Convention; among non-Western countries, the UNHCR
offered assistance but only limited protection to persons who did not
easily meet the Convention definition, according to a series of specific
General Assembly resolutions. During the next two decades, this pragmatic and principally nonlegalistic approach served the interests of most states
and the vast majority of the world's refugees.

The inadequacies of the prevailing system did not become apparent
until the 1980s, when deteriorating political conditions, increasing ethnic
and religious tensions, proliferating internal conflicts, and growing East–
West tensions in the Third World generated massive outpourings of refugees who sought political asylum in the industrialized nations. The problem confronting governments in the 1990s is how to accommodate these
many thousands of people, including many who do not meet the strict
criteria of the 1951 Refugee Convention, but who are nevertheless in need
of humanitarian assistance and protection.

## Expansion into Assistance

As the categories of migrants and refugees expanded, the UNHCR's program in the Third World dramatically increased. In particular, the UNHCR's decision to assume responsibility for populations displaced by wars of national liberation and by civil and ethnic strife under the "good offices" mechanism led to its direct involvement in large-scale assistance programs throughout Africa.

A major thrust of the UNHCR's policy toward Africa during the late 1960s and the 1970s was to create refugee resettlement schemes. In sharp contrast to the approach that had been adopted to deal with the postwar European refugee problem, overseas resettlement was rarely offered to Africans.

The UNHCR hoped that, within organized rural resettlement schemes, rural refugees would be able to reestablish themselves in their accustomed way of life and simultaneously contribute to their host country's economy. Settlements were planned and services were provided so that refugees could become self-sufficient at a standard of living comparable to—but not markedly better than—that of the surrounding local population. Rural settlements were to be managed in such a way that they could be handed over to the host government without imposing any undue burden on its limited resources.

In collaboration with various other international agencies,[25] the UNHCR sought to integrate these schemes into broader national rural development strategies throughout the continent. The strategy of "zonal development" was tried in Zaire, Burundi, and Uganda in the 1960s. There was great interest in local integration, and most international assistance was directed toward supporting the development of organized rural settlements. During the 1960s and 1970s, more than 100 rural refugee settlements were established.[26]

In addition, small and scattered groups of urban refugees—individuals with some intellectual or professional background—began to congregate in Africa's capital cities. Given the pressing economic conditions there, many of these young and educated migrants had difficulty obtaining employment and had to be given counseling and relatively expensive maintenance grants.

During the 1970s, then, the preferred solution, in Africa and elsewhere, was repatriation. An estimated 15 million people returned home during the decade, including 10 million Bangladeshis; 200,000 Burmese; 300,000 Cambodians; 250,000 Nicaraguans; large numbers of Spaniards, Portuguese, and Greeks, following the restoration of democratic governments in their countries; and millions of Africans.[27] In Africa, most of the refugee problems from Angola, Mozambique, Guinea-Bissau, and later in the newly formed Zimbabwe were resolved by extensive repatriations. At the end of these national liberation struggles in the mid- and late 1970s, large numbers of people returned home,[28] as did most of the refugees from bloody internal wars in Nigeria, Zaire, and Sudan. For example,

170,000 Sudanese streamed home from the Central African Republic, Zaire, Uganda, and Ethiopia after a settlement in Addis Ababa in 1972 between the Sudanese government and southern rebels.

While many Africans returned home without UNHCR assistance or involvement, the High Commissioner was frequently involved. In Sudan, for example, grim economic conditions required not only emergency relief supplies but considerable reconstruction work as well. The UN Secretary-General designated the High Commissioner to coordinate a major UN relief and rehabilitation effort, called the South Sudan Operation,[29] which established several important precedents. As in the case of Algeria, it involved assistance within the country to which refugees returned—this time, however, on a much larger scale.[30] In addition, the UNHCR attempted to assist all the people who had been uprooted during the war in Sudan, whether they had actually left the country or not, thus officially aiding internally displaced persons for the first time. When the Portuguese territories achieved independence in 1975, the UNHCR embarked on similar repatriation and reconstruction programs.[31]

The sums of money required to administer and finance these programs were reflected in a sizable expansion of the UNHCR's budget and personnel. In the first twenty years of its existence, the office grew from a staff of 33 officers at headquarters in Geneva, with no field officers and a budget of $300,000 in 1951, to a staff of 350 at headquarters and in the field, with scores of branch offices and a budget of nearly $9 million in 1971.[32]

The bulk of UNHCR expenditures shifted from Europe to Africa. During the late 1950s and early 1960s, European operations had accounted for half of the UNHCR's annual expenditure. Patterns of assistance changed radically from the mid-1960s on: in every year from 1967 to 1973, postcolonial African countries received more than 50 percent of all international refugee aid.[33] Until 1971, UNHCR assistance in Africa was primarily targeted for the development of rural settlements. From 1972 on, the UNHCR's African expenditures increased significantly to cover the Sudanese repatriation program and the needs of urban refugees, especially from southern Africa.[34]

This reorientation toward the developing world included Asia as well as Africa. By 1970 more than half of the UNHCR's staff was assigned to oversee the daily management of field projects,[35] and the material assistance function of the UNHCR enjoyed higher priority than did its legal protection function.

## Seeds of the 1980s Refugee Movements: Aiding the Victims of Conflict in the Third World

From its expansion in the 1960s, the UNHCR rapidly evolved into a truly global organization during the next decade. It embarked on ambitious assistance programs in a number of "refugee-like" situations around the world, beginning with the Bangladesh operation in 1971, the South Sudan Operation in 1972, and the UN Humanitarian Assistance Program for Cyprus in 1974.

The Bangladesh operation occurred in response to the 1971 war between West Pakistan and secessionist East Pakistan, and the subsequent flight of East Bengalis to India. Almost overnight, 10 million refugees flooded into the Indian states of West Bengal, Tripura, and Assam. This was the largest single population movement since the formation of the UNHCR; and the costs of mounting a relief effort of this size dwarfed its already stretched budget. In response, the UN Secretary-General set up a separate international relief apparatus under a special coordination organization. Sadruddin Aga Khan was appointed to head this operation.[36] His tasks included coordinating of the work of all the UN agencies involved (including WHO, WFP, and UNICEF, among others), and mobilizing UN assistance totaling $185 million. Fortunately, after the defeat of Pakistani forces, the 10 million people who had taken refuge in India quickly returned home to the newly independent Bangladesh.

As a result of the UNHCR's success, Sadruddin was called on to coordinate both the UN relief effort in southern Sudan in 1972 and the administration of UN humanitarian assistance to Cyprus in 1974. Thus, during the 1970s, assistance to people displaced by conflict—including those who did not cross national borders—became an integral part of the High Commissioner's programs. For example, in authorizing the UNHCR to coordinate the repatriation and resettlement of displaced Sudanese, the United Nations placed refugees and internally displaced persons side by side for the first time in a General Assembly resolution.[37] By 1979, the High Commissioner had been unequivocally requested to "promote durable and speedy solutions to problems of refugees and displaced persons wherever they occur."[38] The objective in almost every case was repatriation.

## Overseas Resettlement of Latin Americans and Indochinese

The major exceptions to the emphasis on repatriation occurred in Latin America and in Indochina, where overseas resettlement was used as almost the sole solution. In the 1970s, Latin America, a region renowned for its long-standing tradition of asylum, underwent a series of internal crises. Political and civil unrest resulted in widespread political repression; between 1973 and 1976, military juntas took power from civilian regimes in Chile, Uruguay, and Argentina.[39] The military and police then exercised absolute power under states of emergency. Arbitrary detentions, lack of due process, systematic use of torture, physical disappearance of opponents, prohibition of political parties and unions, and censorship of the press became the norm.[40] These policies produced major waves of refugees; more than 1 million people are estimated to have departed these three countries during the 1970s.[41]

## Latin America

The first wave of Latin American refugees included those who fled violence during and after the overthrow of the Allende government in Chile in 1973. Some 15,000 refugees who had previously escaped from Brazil, Argentina, Uruguay, Paraguay, and other authoritarian regimes in Latin America and had been granted asylum in Chile during Salvador Allende's presidency were immediately targeted for persecution by the new military junta. Many were detained and tortured; others were forced to seek political asylum in foreign embassies in Santiago or to go underground. Large numbers were executed. In addition, thousands of Allende supporters were summarily imprisoned, tortured, or shot. The acute refugee problem that surfaced in Chile necessitated an emergency response.[42]

Most Latin American governments responded by filling their embassies to capacity with refugees seeking diplomatic asylum. Many Western governments, with the notable exception of the United States, also provided asylum in their Santiago embassies. Virtually all of these refugees, as well as others who were then in hiding or in prison, had to be resettled overseas.

The resettlement effort was led by the UNHCR, ICEM, and the International Committee of the Red Cross (ICRC). Within days of the coup, the UNHCR established an emergency office in Santiago and arranged with the Chilean government to establish a National Committee for Aid to Refugees. The UNHCR initially concentrated on foreign refugees stranded in Chile and on Chileans who had left the country, but not on Chilean nationals who remained at home. ICEM and ICRC negotiated to help move the thousands of Chileans held in prisons and in detention centers who wanted to leave the country.

The High Commissioner's appeals to foreign governments to accept Chileans for resettlement were highly successful. The Federal Republic of Germany, France, Great Britain, Italy, the Netherlands, Spain, and Sweden, as well as the German Democratic Republic, Hungary, Romania, and Yugoslavia all took large numbers. Intensive media coverage of the atrocities and of massive human rights violations surrounding the Chilean coup aroused the widespread attention and sympathy of Western publics. Labor unions and the European left campaigned vigorously to get their governments to react positively.

In sharp contrast to its European allies, the United States remained singularly unresponsive to the plight of Chilean refugees. It ignored appeals for resettlement, and it refused to provide any funding to support ICEM programs to finance resettlement. Fearing that a generous refugee admissions policy would result in the admission of "leftist radicals" into the United States, the Nixon and Ford administrations and the U.S. Congress resisted establishing a comprehensive parole program for Chilean refugees.[43]

The military coup in Chile, along with the military takeovers in ‌

Uruguay in 1972 and in Argentina in 1976, increased the involvement of the international refugee regime in the affairs of the Western Hemisphere. The Latin American crises spawned a worldwide diaspora, as the exiles were resettled in forty-four different countries with the assistance of the UNHCR, which rapidly expanded its presence on the continent in order to respond to these developments. Prior to 1973, a single UNHCR regional office in Buenos Aires covered all refugee problems south of the Rio Grande; by the end of the decade, the UNHCR had offices in Brazil, Chile, Costa Rica, Honduras, Mexico, and Peru.

## *Indochina*

The largest overseas resettlement program since World War II was organized in Indochina. The refugee crisis in that region, more than any other recent refugee movement, captured the attention and sympathy of the world. This was at least partly because of America's long-standing involvement in Vietnam and its subsequent leadership in forging an international response. During the Vietnam War, an estimated half of South Vietnam's 20 million population was uprooted. Millions of Laotians and Cambodians, caught up in violent and indiscriminate warfare, fled from the countryside into the cities and refugee camps.[44] The population of Saigon swelled from 1.8 million to 3.8 million; and by the war's end, the majority of the rural population of the three Indochinese countries had moved into the cities for safety. The economic and social effects of these forced migrations were devastating to the rural economies; massive relief assistance was required just to keep people alive.

Before 1975 the conflict in Indochina resulted in relatively few cross-border population movements, and the UNHCR had only small programs in place to provide aid to large numbers of displaced persons in Vietnamese and Laotian territories under both communist and government control. Although Sadruddin expected the UNHCR to play a major role in the reconstruction and development of Indochina during the postwar era, he did not anticipate the huge outflows of refugees that were to follow the rapid fall of the governments in Saigon, Phnom Penh, and Vientiane during 1975.[45] In the wake of the subsequent mass evacuations, the UNHCR expanded its presence by opening up offices in Bangkok and other Southeast Asia capitals and by developing resettlement machinery to deal with these population movements.

From the beginning, regional responses to the outflows were conditioned by different strategic, political, social, and economic interests. Neighboring states perceived the refugee influxes as constituting a threat to their national security, political and social stability, and economic development. Consequently, when tens of thousands of people crossed into their territories or landed on their shores, the refugees were met with hostility. First-asylum states declared that they were willing to provide temporary refuge only if the West would make firm commitments to resettle the Indochinese outside the region. Malaysia and Thailand warned that they would forcibly turn away refugees if they did not receive such prior commitments, and they did indeed push away boatloads of refugees, causing great loss of life. The UNHCR was powerless to act because neither Malaysia nor Thailand had ratified the 1951 Convention, and they were under no legal obligation to abide by its provisions.

In July 1979, with the crisis reaching alarming proportions, the United Nations held a conference in Geneva at which Vietnam agreed to impose a "moratorium" on illegal departures. Simultaneously, Malaysia and Thailand were persuaded to respect the refugees' right to asylum after the United States, Canada, Australia, France, and some thirty other nations embarked on a huge and costly resettlement program that was to continue into the 1990s.

Over time, the generous assistance and preferential treatment for Indochinese refugees had a magnet effect, attracting large numbers of people out of the embattled and impoverished countries of Indochina. It became extremely difficult to stem the flow. By the early 1980s, the impetus for Western countries to sustain their large resettlement programs diminished. In the United States, for example, the arrival of large numbers of Indochinese coincided with the Mariel boatlift from Cuba and a huge influx from Haiti. From 1975 to 1980, the United States accepted as many refugees as did the entire rest of the world, and hundreds of thousands of new arrivals were pouring in. Such large admissions inevitably led to a backlash from local communities and eventually to reductions in the numbers of overall quotas.[46] Australia, Canada, and other resettlement countries soon followed suit.[47]

"Compassion fatigue" hit Hong Kong and the ASEAN countries particularly hard. Western resettlement countries not only cut back their admissions quotas but also passed over certain Vietnamese, known as "long-stayers," who did not fit their immigration criteria. The backlog, plus frustration over the protractedness of the problem and concern at being left with tens of thousands of unwanted Indochinese, led Hong Kong and the ASEAN countries to initiate a series of deterrent measures to discourage new and future arrivals.[48] Initially implemented against Cambodian refugees by Thailand, "humane deterrence" became the policy adopted against all Indochinese refugees throughout Southeast Asia and in Hong Kong. As a steady stream of refugees continued to flow from Vietnam and Laos, the ASEAN governments took even more severe steps, including detention in closed camps, forcible repatriation, push-offs, and more drownings at sea.

The UNHCR was powerless to act; the United States was implacably opposed to repatriation and refused even to consider discussing this option with Vietnamese authorities in Hanoi. Vietnam was equally adamant in refusing to accept the return of those who had fled the country.

Between the crises in Africa and in Indochina, the UNHCR had developed an enormous agenda. Between 1975 and 1980, the number of

UNHCR field offices increased from fewer than fifty to more than eighty, and the total staff rose from 380 to 1,700. Annual expenditures rose from approximately $12 million in 1972 to more than $500 million in 1980—an extraordinary increase by any standard.[49] Despite this phenomenal growth, the international refugee regime proved inadequate to deal with the problems it was to confront in the 1980s.

## The 1980s: East–West Conflict and Internal Wars in the Third World

What distinguished Third World conflicts in the 1980s from the wars of previous decades was the major political involvement of external powers. Throughout the decade, the superpowers played an important role—whether "by proxy," in an attempt to find regional allies, or by expanding local conflicts into "internationalized" civil wars. Backing either the established regimes in the countries of origin or (more typically) the exile warriors seeking to overthrow those regimes, the superpowers exploited local conflicts to their own advantage and accelerated local arms races.[50]

The civil wars in Afghanistan, Angola, Cambodia, and Nicaragua offer examples of conflicts where the flow of external support to the warring parties altered the balance of forces in the field, and so made a decisive resolution even more difficult to achieve. Refugees themselves were increasingly used as so-called "freedom fighters" or guerrillas to intimidate revolutionary regimes into altering their political orientation and foreign policies.[51] In regions of intense superpower conflict and competition, such as in Afghanistan, Indochina, Central America, the Horn of Africa, and southern Africa, refugees were armed and their military struggles were supported both materially and ideologically. Indeed, the competitive sale and provision of arms to Third World clients increased tensions, exacerbated regional conflicts, and enlarged the flow of victims of violence.

The military use of refugees also served the strategic and political interests of the West, and particularly of the United States. The demonstrable existence of "freedom fighters" symbolized popular rejection of communist governments in these regions and served to legitimate the resistance movements. Thus, humanitarian support for refugees coincided with long-term Western objectives.

The 3 million Afghan refugees who fled to Pakistan after 1979 formed a base for mujaheddin resistance to Soviet-backed control of Afghanistan. Military assistance to the insurgents came from the United States, the Arab states, and China; it was channeled through Pakistan, where a large international relief assistance program run by the Pakistani government and the UNHCR (and largely financed by the United States) had been set up to aid the mujaheddin and their supporters. By distributing food through local Afghan middlemen, the UNHCR and the World Food Program had no way of ensuring that food went exclusively to noncombatants, since the camps were used by the mujaheddin as headquarters between military raids.

Relief for the Cambodians along the Thai–Cambodian border was initially provided by UNICEF and the ICRC. In 1982, the United Nations recognized the coalition of resistance movements on the border as the Cambodian government; and a new agency, the UN Border Relief Operation (UNBRO) was set up. UNBRO did not provide protection, and the UNHCR (until it took over UNBRO in late 1991) was unwilling to exert its influence on behalf of Cambodians along the border. Thus, as in Afghanistan, humanitarian aid from the West sustained the rebel forces. China, the United States, and the ASEAN nations supported the Khmer resistance front and the Khmer Rouge as a way of maintaining pressure on the Soviet Union's client, the Vietnamese government, and its client, the unrecognized but de facto government of Cambodia. Refugee camps provided sanctuary for the Khmer Rouge and the noncommunist forces; refugees were sources of new military recruits and were pawns in the larger geopolitical struggle.

While the situations along the Pakistani and Thai borders constituted blatant political uses of humanitarian aid, refugee programs in Central America also had a political dimension. The United States supported Nicaraguan contras and refugee groups to wage a war of resistance in Nicaragua from bases in Honduras and Costa Rica. Salvadoran refugees, on the other hand, were viewed by the U.S. and Honduran governments as supporters of the leftist Salvadoran rebels. Accordingly, in Honduras, refugee camps for Nicaraguan refugees remained relatively open throughout the 1980s, while those for Salvadorans remained closed and ringed by hostile Honduran armed forces. The fact that Honduras, like Thailand, had not ratified the 1951 Convention (and did not do so until 1992) limited the UNHCR's formal protection role there.

While many of the armed conflicts and secessionist movements in the Horn of Africa during the 1980s could be traced to long-standing religious and ethnic rivalries and other internal factors, the regional tension there must also be seen within a broader international context. Because the Horn was perceived as having geopolitical significance, the superpowers and various Middle Eastern states became involved in these regional struggles by supporting one faction or one government over another. As in other regional conflicts, humanitarian assistance was used for political purposes both by host governments and by guerrilla groups.[52] In Somalia, for example, the Barre government inflated its country's refugee figures in the hope of obtaining more assistance from the international community. The UNHCR could do little but try to keep refugees alive by providing assistance to camps in remote regions, even as the camps themselves came under armed attack and some of their inhabitants were forcibly conscripted into government or rebel armies.

Apart from the meddling of the two superpowers, military intervention in local Third World conflicts by other outside powers increased as well—specifically by South Africa, Cuba, Israel, Vietnam, China, Syria, Iraq, Iran, Saudi Arabia, and India, among others. In attempting to preserve and establish their own regional security interests and objectives, even developing countries became heavily involved in internal conflicts, from Pakistani support of Afghan mujaheddin to Nicaraguan arms supplies for Salvadoran insurgents to the Vietnamese occupation in Cambodia to Indian intervention in Sri Lanka. The South African military used proxies against its frontline states in southern Africa—especially Angola and Mozambique—to destabilize these neighboring countries, resulting in the creation of large-scale refugee movements. Sudan assisted guerrilla groups in northern Ethiopia; and Ethiopia and Libya, in turn, supported the Sudan People's Liberation Army's insurgency in southern Sudan. Libya, Egypt, and Sudan became involved on different sides in Chad; and Somalia supported the guerrilla activities of Ethiopian liberation movements and allowed them considerable freedom of movement within its borders. Such interventions transformed local wars into complex and intransigent international confrontations, with direct implications for refugee flows.

Third World conflicts became extremely difficult to resolve quickly, not only because of external involvements, but also because governments and opposition movements frequently saw themselves locked in life-or-death struggles with each other. In the eyes of most governments, secessionist struggles threatened the physical survival of the state and presented serious risks to the central government. For example, successive regimes in Ethiopia believed that according self-government to the Eritreans would cut off its access to the Red Sea. Similarly, Iraq opposed granting autonomy to its Kurds for fear of losing control over the country's oil reserves and causing tensions with neighboring Iran and Turkey.

Religious issues also contributed to the violence and civil conflict in many parts of the developing world. Islamic fundamentalism reasserted itself not only in the Middle East but in regions as far apart as Southeast Asia, Southwest Asia, and North Africa. Religious revivalism was the direct cause of several major refugee movements during the decade. In Sudan, for instance, demands by northerners for the adoption of Islamic laws alarmed southern Sudanese Christians and animists and fueled the insurgency led by the Sudanese People's Liberation Army. More recently, the rise of Hindu fundamentalism in India has complicated the Indian government's efforts to deal with Muslim dissent in Kashmir and has severely damaged Indo-Pakistani relations.

## Long-term Exile

The politicization of refugee problems during the 1980s precluded any easy solution to the refugee dilemma. The magnitude of the problem expanded so dramatically that the institutional constraints on repatriation, local settlement, and resettlement were quickly revealed. There were no compelling political or ideological reasons for Western states to resettle large numbers of Third World refugees. Even the Indochinese were discovering that the doors to overseas resettlement were rapidly closing. Moreover, outside Central America and Indochina, there was no evidence that any sizable number of refugees ever wanted to abandon their countries and settle permanently elsewhere. Local settlement leading to naturalization was perceived by most countries of first asylum to be politically and economically infeasible. Given the volatile security situation and lack of social stability and cohesion in most host societies, successful local settlement was very much the exception, not the rule. And repatriation to countries where conflicts had dragged on for nearly ten years was extremely difficult to negotiate, as well as being dangerous for refugees. The repatriations of Tamils to Sri Lanka, of Salvadorans to El Salvador, of Cambodians to Cambodia, and of Afghans to Afghanistan, for example, posed considerable risks for returnees because those who went home were returning to extremely violent civil wars. As a result, the majority of the world's refugees were given temporary asylum in camps, with no prospect of effective long-term solutions.

The 1990s has ushered in a new era for refugees. In a time of growing disparity between countries of the developing and developed worlds, as well as of rising nationalism and the consequent violent fragmentation of existing states and formation of new national entities, the tension between the rich and poor worlds may prove to be even more destabilizing and destructive than was the old East–West division. At present, refugee movements are likely to be the result of ethnic, communal, and religious conflicts. The most common form of warfare in the developing world and in Eastern Europe in the 1990s is internal conflict, fueled by the increasing availability of modern weaponry, sharp socioeconomic inequalities, and human rights abuses. One unanticipated consequence of the demise of superpower interests in the Third World is that conflicts there have become harder to mediate, and national resistance forces have the potential to create internal anarchy and to disrupt interstate relations.

Current political, diplomatic, and economic strategies and mechanisms are not sufficiently developed to cope with the increasingly complex and volatile refugee movements of the post–Cold War period. The most difficult political issues confronting the international community in the 1990s are how governments and international organizations can intervene to prevent refugee flights within countries or across international borders, and how they can provide assistance and protection to internally displaced people when their governments object to intervention or when (as in Somalia, Liberia, or Bosnia) it is impossible to determine the legitimate government or authority in the country. The more immediate short-term problem for governments and international agencies at present is to determine when and how repatriation and reintegration are most appropriate. These tasks will inevitably depend not only on the efforts of traditional refugee and relief organizations but also on the more active involvement of development agencies, human rights networks, and peacekeeping and conflict-resolution mechanisms.

While the contemporary situation is characterized by the emergence of new mass population movements as a result of violent ethnic conflict, as well as of the possible return home of large numbers of long-staying refugees in the Third World, the advanced industrialized states are increasingly reluctant to allow people to enter their countries and apply for political asylum. During recent years, refugee-producing countries have experienced a succession of crises, including political instability, armed conflict, ethnic tension, drought, famine, economic collapse, mounting indebtedness, and deterioration of civil society. Viewed from the perspective of the industrialized West, there seems to be no limit to the number of refugees and asylum seekers the developing countries, including those from the former Soviet Union, could produce. Consequently, Western governments, whose domestic economies and social welfare systems are under great strain, have adopted a far less welcoming attitude to refugees.

# 5

## Asylum Crises in the Industrialized World

As the global refugee crisis intensified during the 1980s, greater numbers of people traveled to Western Europe and North America to claim political asylum. Western governments never envisaged such large-scale population movements. Political asylum was an exceptional event before the 1980s. The developed world was simply too distant, and jet-age travel too uncommon, for most Third World nationals to reach it.

The 1980s rudely shook the industrialized countries out of their old notions of insularity. The asylum caseloads in all Western countries grew rapidly, as most asylum applicants came from places where a mixture of political chaos and economic hardship prevailed. Most of these new arrivals did not even fit the image of refugees for most Westerners: asylum seekers arrived from all over the world; they generally had few political and cultural links with the industrialized countries; their religions were often foreign; and their ways of life were completely alien.

### In Search of a Safe Haven

Particularly disturbing to Western governments is the fact that, in contrast to the past, today's asylum applicants increasingly bypass established refugee-processing channels. Unlike the millions who endure the rigors of camp life throughout the Third World, the new refugees either independently take the initiative to secure safety in the West or turn to immigrant-trafficking organizations to purchase false documents that enable them to travel to industrialized countries to apply for asylum.

Western governments regard such activities as illegal and have been quick to brand these people as opportunists, "bogus refugees," and queue jumpers. But although some asylum applications are clear attempts to enter the West by subterfuge, most asylum applicants are fleeing mixed situations involving violent conflict, economic hardship, and political uncertainty. In reality, many do move north in search of a safe haven. Two examples should suffice. Throughout the 1980s, Salvadorans whose close relatives had "disappeared" streamed northward toward the U.S. border, where they were joined by others who had been threatened by roaming "death squads" or terrified by the violence of the protracted civil war in El Salvador.[1] Early in the decade, the UNHCR had established camps for Salvadoran refugees in Honduras, Costa Rica, and Nicaragua, but these camps were small, understaffed, remote, and unable to take more than a tiny fraction of the hundreds of thousands of people who fled.[2] Moreover, protection in the region was precarious; many refugees were the target of periodic attacks, forced recruitment, harassment, and abuse.[3] In response to such conditions, as early as 1980, many began to enter the United States, further swelling both the illegal immigration population and the number of asylum applicants. As of mid-1992, it was estimated that in excess of 500,000 Salvadorans lived in the United States, of which some 190,000 had recently received temporary protected status.

A similar situation existed with respect to Iranian asylum seekers in Europe. Following the accession to power of fundamentalist Islamic leaders in Iran in 1979, thousands of Iranians were executed after summary trials, and thousands more were imprisoned and tortured for political offenses.[4] Throughout the 1980s, vast numbers of people (especially young men) were killed and maimed in the Iran–Iraq War. To escape such brutality, hundreds of thousands of Iranians poured into neighboring Turkey and Pakistan, where they eked out a marginal existence and lived under the constant surveillance of radical Iranian groups allied to the ruling regime in Tehran. Despite the presence of the UNHCR in both places, neither Turkey nor Pakistan offered dissident Iranians satisfactory legal protection or a safe refuge.[5] In both countries hundreds of Iranians were forcibly repatriated to Iran, and some of these returnees were reportedly executed upon return. It was extremely difficult for Iranians to study, work, or otherwise settle into any semblance of a normal life. Consequently, tens of thousands of Iranians sought asylum in Europe during the 1980s.

Where no local protection exists, people escape however they can, and they will resort to desperate measures to seek refuge in Western countries. The lack of any real opportunity to apply for resettlement has made such measures necessary. For example, during the last decade, there was practically no possibility for Iranians to leave Turkey by obtaining a visa from a West European embassy or consulate; and opportunities for official reemigration to third countries were extremely limited.[6] Similarly, no real third-country refugee resettlement processing to the United States existed for

Central Americans within their own region.[7] Since 1982, not one Guatemalan has been admitted to the United States as a refugee through the U.S. resettlement program. With the exception of a group of ninety-three Salvadoran political prisoners who were admitted directly from El Salvador in 1984, only fifty-four Salvadorans were admitted between 1982 and 1990.

Even if more opportunities to emigrate directly from countries of origin were available, not all threatened individuals would be helped through these procedures. Overseas refugee admissions procedures are usually slow and discretionary. Most people in fear of their lives risk being arrested or persecuted if they stay at home. Real refugees simply cannot afford the luxury of waiting for their applications for refugee status and visas to be processed by Western officials. Moreover, Western governments are under no obligation to admit desperate people from countries of origin and can designate anyone they want as refugees. For example, in 1992 the U.S. government introduced a program of in-country refugee processing within Haiti. Haitian applicants had to appear at the U.S. Embassy in Port-au-Prince to apply for refugee status. On later occasions they had to return for interviews—first with State Department consular officials, and then with Immigration and Naturalization officers. Successful applicants then had to wait again while their visas were processed. In the first eight months of the program, some 15,500 Haitians applied for refugee processing, yet fewer than 2,500 cases were adjudicated, and fewer than 60 individuals were admitted to the United States.[8] Such procedures are unlikely to offer real protection to the multitude of people claiming to be living in fear. Rather than making use of these procedures, refugees will take all kinds of risks and resort to paying bribes and obtaining false identification documents to assist their escape. Thus, in-country refugee processing cannot be a substitute for the right to seek asylum outside the country of persecution.

As long ago as 1985, the Executive Committee of the UNHCR took notice of governments that were voicing alarm about "irregular" asylum seekers, stating that these individuals are in fact only persons who have failed to comply with "structured international efforts to provide appropriate solutions. . . ." They are people who, sensing themselves to be in jeopardy, dare to take their fate into their own hands and move on "without the proper consent of . . . national authorities."[9] Indeed, as international legal scholars have noted, nothing in the international refugee instruments indicates that asylum seekers who find neither security nor means of subsistence in the country where they first arrive should not be allowed to proceed to another country where their situation might be more secure.[10]

Western governments perceive this spontaneous movement to the industrialized countries as threatening, and they often fail to understand the complex and varied motives these refugees have for moving and for claiming asylum. Although many can point to conditions of general violence and repression in their home countries, most cannot clearly document that they are individually threatened with persecution. The UNHCR has long advised governments to exercise fairness and a consistent and reasonable judgment when determining refugee status. Asylum seekers rarely arrive with substantive documentation to support their claims of persecution, and the UNHCR has urged governments to give applicants the benefit of the doubt. Yet increasing demands are being made on asylum seekers today to prove their credibility beyond a reasonable doubt, and governments frequently issue generalized blanket rejections to nationals of certain countries or to members of particular ethnic groups on the grounds that they are all "economic" migrants, not political refugees.

## Migration Pressures on Asylum Systems

The unexpected arrival in the West of large numbers of people with various claims to asylum has severely jolted existing practices and has overtaxed the procedural systems for handling refugee determinations. Once in the West, the majority of asylum seekers stay, sometimes for several years, working their way through appeals procedures up to and including judicial review. In Germany, for example, despite the introduction of accelerated procedures for some applicants, it can take many years for a final determination to be made. In other countries it takes 18 months or longer. And because of the substantial backlog of claims, claimants remain even longer in Western countries and require additional material assistance, thus putting a considerable strain on reception and integration facilities. In addition, the more than 80 percent of asylum applicants who are finally rejected frequently are not expelled, because Western governments are reluctant to return people to countries undergoing brutal civil wars.

The reality is that the present increase in the number of asylum seekers, refugees, and migrants is neither a temporary phenomenon nor a random product of chance events. It is the predictable consequence of fundamental (and often interrelated) political, demographic, economic, and ecological crises occurring throughout the Third World. The refugee problem is part of the emerging global crisis of mass migration generated by structural economic, political, and social changes in the world—particularly in large parts of the Third World, but also in Central Europe, the Balkans, and the former Soviet Union.

Western immigration officials increasingly view all requests for political asylum against this backdrop of ongoing international migration. Because some countries have been sources of significant illegal immigration or labor migration in the past, border officials in the West tend to control (and oppose) all population movements from these countries. Thus, when large numbers of people from Haiti, El Salvador, or Turkey began to apply legitimately for asylum in the 1980s, they were often not taken seriously by the immigration bureaucracy.[11] Clearly, Western officials have become increasingly skeptical of the genuineness of many of today's claims, and they see the influx of refugees as part of a mass attempt by foreigners to enter their societies illegally in search of employment and social welfare. Furthermore, they believe that foreigners are simply taking advantage of the work permits and social service benefits that have been provided to asylum applicants in the past. They argue that most asylum claims are spurious, thinly disguising economic migrants as political refugees.

Public opinion too tends to categorize aliens as undesirable. The confusion over classifications has led some people to view refugees, terrorists, and drug dealers more or less as one and the same, equating victims of political persecution with common criminals. Not surprisingly, the assumption that most asylum seekers are law-dodgers masquerading as genuine refugees undermines public support for a generous asylum policy. The unexpected arrival of increasing numbers of people and the difficulties of evaluating various claims to asylum have added to this climate of confusion, putting the governments of Europe and North America under severe pressure.

As the numbers of asylum seekers grow, the problems of defining and selecting refugees, determining what kinds of assistance and protection should be provided, deciding whether and when refugees should be repatriated or resettled, and identifying which international, regional, or domestic institutions should play a role become ever more important. Strategies are needed that anticipate as well as react and that deal with the root causes of problems that make it impossible for people to remain at home. Resolving the asylum problem for Western nations, therefore, requires a comprehensive approach, embracing prevention as well as cure and extending beyond the shores of Europe and North America.

## The Limitations of Restrictionism

Rather than adopting a comprehensive approach to meet intensifying migration pressures, states are racing to close doors to asylum seekers. During recent years, the West has been building barriers, first by revising immigration laws and asylum regulations and procedures to make them more stringent, and second by adopting restrictive practices and deterrent measures (such as imposing visa requirements, intercepting boats on the high seas, and making on-the-spot eligibility decisions at the border) to curb new arrivals.[12]

Government officials believe that the deterrents will lead to fewer applicants, thus avoiding xenophobic, racial, and political tensions that might otherwise arise from the unregulated arrival of unwanted foreigners. The result of such measures is that, besides being difficult to obtain asylum, it is now becoming increasingly difficult even to reach a point at which an application can be made.

Yet despite deterrent measures, the number of asylum applications in Europe, North America, and Australia rose more than sevenfold from an estimated 100,000 in 1983 to about 715,900 in 1991 (see Table 5-1).

*Table 5-1*  Estimates on Asylum Applications in Europe, North America, and Australia, 1983–1991 (rounded figures)

| | 1983 | 1984 | 1985 | 1986 | 1987 | 1988 | 1989 | 1990 | 1991 | 1983–1991 |
|---|---|---|---|---|---|---|---|---|---|---|
| Europe | 75,000 | 110,000 | 178,500 | 214,700 | 203,150 | 243,950 | 321,900 | 461,100 | 599,400 | 2,407,700 |
| IGC countries | 65,400 | 98,300 | 164,400 | 194,200 | 172,250 | 220,450 | 306,900 | 426,100 | 544,400 | 2,192,400 |
| Central Eastern and Southern Europe | 9,600 | 11,700 | 14,100 | 20,500 | 30,900 | 23,500 | 15,000 | 35,000 | 55,000 | 215,300 |
| North America | 25,000 | 31,400 | 28,400 | 41,900 | 61,100 | 102,000 | 122,000 | 109,600 | 100,500 | 621,900 |
| Canada | 5,000 | 7,100 | 8,400 | 23,000 | 35,000 | 45,000 | 22,000 | 36,000 | 30,500 | 212,000 |
| USA | 20,000 | 24,300 | 20,000 | 18,900 | 26,100 | 57,000 | 100,000 | 73,600 | 70,000 | 409,900 |
| Australia | — | — | — | — | — | — | 500 | 3,600 | 16,000 | 20,100 |
| Total | 100,000 | 141,400 | 206,900 | 256,600 | 264,250 | 345,950 | 444,400 | 574,300 | 715,900 | 3,049,700 |

SOURCE: Secretariat for Intergovernmental Consultations, Geneva.

Indeed, between 1983 and mid-1992, over 3 million people sought asylum in the industrialized states. Furthermore, repeated changes in laws, procedures and structures have failed to eliminate backlogs or to reduce waiting periods in many countries. Deterrence not only does not seem to work, it undermines the entire international refugee regime and has serious repercussions for the maintenance of asylum principles and practice in the West.

Simply building new barriers around Western countries will not make the refugee problem go away. Restrictive measures taken unilaterally by Western states do not solve the problem but merely pass it on to some other country to resolve, thus contributing to interstate tensions, protectionism, and a breakdown in the international refugee regime. Furthermore, restrictive measures fall indiscriminately and with equal weight on illegal aliens and "bonafide" refugees. Detention, crowded and austere living conditions, and the total lack of employment opportunity must be endured by refugee and illegal alien alike. Many are isolated and deprived of any reorientation and adjustment to a new environment. In most Western countries, where it can take months or even years before claims to asylum are determined, by the time applicants are recognized as refugees, many have been rendered totally unfit for integration into their new societies.

## The United States: Confronting the Pressures of Asylum

Many of the new restrictive measures were first introduced in the United States in reaction to mounting requests for political asylum from Caribbean and Central American migrants during the early 1980s. Until then, when the so-called Mariel Cubans arrived in Florida, the United States had been one of the most generous Western nations both in the overall numbers of refugees admitted and in the amount of refugee assistance given overseas. This generosity, however, was nearly always tempered by political calculation,[13] so that admissions policy favored refugees escaping from communist regimes and those belonging to nationalities or ethnic and religious groups of special concern to various domestic constituencies. It was not commonly extended to individuals fleeing repressive regimes that were diplomatically tied to the United States. The reason for the admission of some 400,000 displaced persons from post–World War II Europe, of 38,000 Hungarians from Austria between 1956 and 1958, and of nearly 500,000 Indochinese from Southeast Asia from 1975 to 1980 was American concern over the destabilizing effect of large refugee populations in parts of the world deemed vital to its national security.

Apart from refugees who were admitted to the United States under special legislation,[14] the Attorney General was authorized to "parole" persons outside the normal immigration system into the United States for "emergent reasons" or for reasons deemed to be in the "public interest." Ideological considerations dominated these decisions.[15] According to the

U.S. Committee for Refugees, only 2,700 (less than 0.3 percent) of the 1,027,407 refugees paroled into the United States between 1956 and 1979 originated from noncommunist countries.[16]

## The Cuban and Haitian Influxes

The United States was confronted with major asylum decisions for the first time in the late 1950s, when it admitted Cubans fleeing the establishment of a communist regime in Havana and Haitians fleeing repression at the hands of "Papa Doc" Duvalier. The U.S. policy toward Caribbean refugees was shaped by the Cold War politics it learned in other parts of the world. Accordingly, from the time of Fidel Castro's accession to power until the 1980 Mariel boatlift, special welcome was extended to over 800,000 Cubans who were "voting with their feet" against communism.[17]

Although never the beneficiaries of the same strong public support as the Cubans, the Haitians who arrived in the United States between 1957 and 1971 were generally tolerated, even though they were denied the virtually certain asylum granted to Cubans. Haitians were never characterized as voting with their feet against an oppressive regime, nor was there any significant American effort to expose the Duvalier regime as one of the most abusive in the world. After the death of "Papa Doc" and the normalization of U.S.–Haitian relations under "Baby Doc" Duvalier in 1971, Haitian asylum claimants were treated harshly and were almost inevitably designated for deportation.[18]

Similarly, no "open arms" were ever extended to refugees who had supported President Salvador Allende, following General Augusto Pinochet's successful coup d' état in 1973, which ousted the democratically elected but avowedly Marxist Chilean government.[19] Opponents of other Third World authoritarian leaders such as President Marcos of the Philippines or the Shah of Iran, who were close allies of the United States, were routinely denied political asylum. Furthermore, since the large-scale refugee flows in Africa that punctuated the 1960s and 1970s were regarded by the United States as essentially local phenomena with few Cold War implications, virtually no African refugees were resettled in the United States.

Before the late 1970s, the number of asylum requests submitted in the United States was very small—only a few hundred applications each year. Cubans were classified as refugees, not as asylum seekers, and the vast majority of Haitians did not apply formally for political asylum. But even during the late 1970s, when a growing number of asylum seekers (along with hundreds of thousands of Indochinese and tens of thousands of Soviet Jews) sought entry into the country via the resettlement channel, the United States was still able to regulate the flow of entrants and avoid unacceptable levels of domestic backlash.

Then two events in the spring of 1980 profoundly affected the flow of refugees into the United States, as well as the government's ability to control that flow. The first was the passage of a new Refugee Act in March;

the second was the beginning of the Cuban boatlift in April. Together, they created practical and political difficulties that made continuation of the customary U.S. refugee admissions system almost impossible.

The 1980 Refugee Act incorporated into domestic law a definition of *refugee* that was neither ideologically nor geographically limited. By adopting the definition outlined in the 1951 Refugee Convention and removing all reference to communism, it afforded protection to any migrant from any country who was able to demonstrate a personal "well-founded fear of persecution on account of race, religion, nationality, membership in a particular social group or political opinion." When Congress passed the act, it apparently believed that no more than 5,000 aliens per year with potentially valid asylum claims would enter the United States. Within a month of the new law's passage, however, it became graphically clear that this figure was woefully inadequate. When the first wave of boats, which were eventually to bring 130,000 Cubans to Florida over a five-month period, hit American shores, the asylum system was totally swamped. By the end of 1980, these Cubans had been joined by over 11,000 Haitian boat people and an indeterminate number of Iranians, Nicaraguans, and Ethiopians seeking political asylum. Perhaps 150,000 to 160,000 aliens with potential asylum claims entered the United States in 1980; and according to a high Immigration and Naturalization Service (INS) official at the time, "within six months after the passage of the Refugee Act, more than 100,000 individual claims for asylum had been filed."[20]

The domestic backlash and public resentment resulting from the sudden and chaotic arrival of Cubans in Florida jeopardized the principle of asylum and the tradition of refugee welcome in the United States. Initially, the United States responded favorably to the Cuban influx. The press briefly dubbed the boatlift a "freedom flotilla,"[21] and two weeks before the Mariel crisis began, the mayor of Miami was quoted as saying that "either we welcome [the Cubans] or we take down the Statue of Liberty."[22] However, as the Marielitos continued to stream ashore, the public perception of the boatlift and the official U.S. response quickly shifted toward considerable antagonism. After the arrival of approximately 85,000 Cubans in south Florida in May of 1980 alone, Cubans, no longer welcomed by high American officials with "open heart and open arms,"[23] were viewed "as bullets aimed at this country."[24]

The U.S. government agencies that were responsible for regulating refugee flow and determining asylum claims were completely overwhelmed. The INS lacked the personnel to interview and evaluate each applicant properly. During the height of the Cuban influx, the Department of State, charged with issuing an "advisory opinion" as to the probable good faith of each applicant's "well-founded fear of persecution" had one officer assigned full-time to handling asylum claims.[25] According to the Assistant Director of the INS at the time, "overnight the U.S. had become a country of first asylum. No machinery had been assembled to handle this workload. And no serious thinking or planning had been done to analyze the implications of the U.S. as a country of both first asylum and resettlement."[26]

The arrival of Cubans and Haitians reached crisis proportions at the same time that the refugee flow from Indochina peaked at nearly 200,000. In 1980 alone, 800,000 immigrants and refugees—more than the total number entering all other countries in the world combined—entered the United States legally; simultaneously, hundreds of thousands of Mexicans and other aliens entered illegally. The problem of asylum seekers and refugees came to be linked in the public mind with the problem of illegal aliens, fanning public fears of inundation by hordes of uncontrolled illegal immigrants crossing U.S. borders at will.

## The Reagan Response

As the asylum system became hopelessly bottlenecked and as resettlement problems grew, the mood of the American public shifted, first in Florida and then in the nation as a whole. The government was widely perceived as being totally unable to control its borders, and the asylum process was viewed as "a dagger pointed at the throat of the American immigration process."[27] This belief was impressed indelibly on the public mind and figured critically in the shape of the policy responses formulated by the Reagan administration, which assumed office in 1981.

In reaction to domestic pressures to gain control over the national borders, the Reagan administration "managed down" overseas refugee admissions numbers. For example, admissions declined from over 200,000 in 1980 to an average of less than one-third of that in 1988, even though the world's refugee population nearly tripled in the decade between 1978 and 1988—from 4.6 million to 13.3 million.[28] As in the past, geopolitical and ideological considerations dominated refugee admissions decisionmaking, despite the fact that the 1980 Refugee Act was intended to remove that bias from U.S. policy. Thus, the United States admitted 731,647 refugees in the period from October 1981 to September 1990, about 95 percent of whom were from communist countries.[29] Meanwhile, many refugees from other parts of the world where persecution was at least as widespread and life-threatening were not granted entry.[30]

Many critics of U.S. policy expressed concern that the United States was primarily assisting individuals from communist countries when these persons were often in less need of physical protection from their governments and had less compelling claims than did many others. Indeed, an empirical study comparing the level of human rights violations in various countries and the refugee response of the United States showed virtually no relationship between the two.[31] To the contrary, individuals fleeing from various countries notable for gross violations of human rights generally were not offered safe refuge in the United States.

Not only did the Reagan administration "manage down" overseas refugee admissions numbers, but, in order to reduce the number of asylum claims from the Caribbean and Central America, it also adopted a number of restrictive measures and deterrents, including interdiction, widespread use of detention, denial of due process, and swift deportation—all of which were discriminatory and inhumane.

## Asylum Discrimination

An interdiction campaign was launched in September 1981 against Haitian boatpeople, who were accosted in international waters by the U.S. Coast Guard, towed back to Haiti, and delivered to Haitian authorities.[32] From the inception of this program until the end of 1990, out of more than 23,000 Haitians who were given asylum hearings aboard a U.S. cutter, only 8 were allowed to enter the United States to pursue their claims.[33] In this way, the United States drastically reduced the number of Haitian asylum claims. Those few who managed to evade the U.S. Coast Guard and reach the United States were subject to a general detention policy that fell, according to a U.S. federal court, with "vastly disproportionate impact . . . on Haitian, as opposed to non-Haitian, immigrants."[34]

The detention of Haitians was described as demonstrating "a stark pattern of discrimination,"[35] including automatic sequestration in prisonlike camps, while most other undocumented aliens were permitted to remain free; removal to locations remote from Miami, "a city with a substantial immigration bar as well as volunteer lawyers . . . interest[ed] in representing these refugees";[36] and the conducting of exclusion proceedings "at mass hearings behind closed doors with inadequate translators."[37] The same officials who systematically detained Haitians determined their asylum claims, rejecting all but a handful of applicants during the 1980s.

Salvadorans were treated much as Haitians were. A general determination was made in the Department of State that almost all Salvadorans who entered the United States did so either because they feared "generalized violence," rather than "persecution," or for economic motives.[38] This determination was made despite the fact that, from 1979 to 1990, about 50,000 civilians were killed in El Salvador and over 1 million people (about one-quarter of the population) were displaced from their homes. In addition, the International Commission of Jurists, Amnesty International, the U.S. Commission on Civil Rights, and the UNHCR argued that Salvadorans should have a prima facie right to political asylum; but to no avail: many were turned back at the border.

Salvadorans not physically turned back were detained in holding facilities a few miles from the Mexican border. Legal representation was discouraged; and INS officials frequently coerced Salvadorans into leaving the country "voluntarily" within hours after their arrival, thereby avoiding the necessity of protracted asylum and deportation hearings.[39] Until passage of the 1990 Immigration Act, "extended voluntary departure"—a kind of humanitarian or de facto refugee status, offering temporary safe haven in the United States until conditions were safe for people to return home—was withheld, despite urging from church groups, voluntary agencies, many congressional offices, and the UNHCR.[40] Asylum requests were processed slowly and in the end almost always turned down.

Throughout the 1980s, asylum adjudications clearly showed that an applicant's country of origin and the relationship of that country to the United States government were the primary factors determining the granting of asylum. For example, a 1987 U.S. General Accounting Office study of asylum compared the treatment of four nationalities—Salvadorans, Nicaraguans, Poles, and Iranians. The study found that "aliens who stated on their application forms that they were arrested, imprisoned, had their life threatened, or were tortured had much lower approval rates if they were from El Salvador and Nicaragua than if they were from Poland and Iran."[41] Among asylum seekers making such claims, the approval rates were: Iranians, 64 percent; Poles, 55 percent; Nicaraguans, 7 percent; and Salvadorans, 3 percent.[42] Only Haitians (1.8 percent) and Guatemalans (0.9 percent) fared worse.[43] Moreover, of the four groups examined in the GAO study, only Salvadorans were deported to their home country after having been denied asylum (at the rate of 300 per month).[44]

During the latter part of the Reagan administration's second term of office, the admissions figures for Central Americans, with the notable exception of Nicaraguans, changed little. By mid-1987, American policymakers had reverted to traditional ideological biases—favoritism toward those fleeing communist regimes and discrimination against those escaping right-wing governments. Following Attorney General Edwin Meese's July 1987 announcement that Nicaraguans with a well-founded fear of persecution would not be deported and that qualified Nicaraguans would receive authorization to work, the asylum approval rate for Nicaraguans jumped to 84.6 percent by the end of 1987. In contrast, Salvadoran asylum claims were only being approved at a rate of 3.6 percent, and Guatemalans at 3.8 percent.[45] As a result of these extremely low approval rates and fearing deportation, the great majority of Salvadorans and Guatemalans in the United States remained underground and did not bother to make claims for political asylum at all.

The Reagan administration also gave priority to new legislation to make it unlawful for illegal immigrants to work in the United States. The Immigration Reform and Control Act of 1986 had adverse consequences for Salvadorans and Guatemalans, most of whom had arrived in the United States after the legalization cutoff date of January 1, 1982. Many of these people joined a new underclass of undocumented aliens who could not or would not come forward to legalize their residence status under the new immigration law.[46] White House officials and the Attorney General called for aggressive immigration enforcement at the border and substantial new resources for the INS, even as most domestic agencies were facing significant cutbacks. New holding facilities were established in New York, in Louisiana, and in the Southwestern states where most asylum seekers and illegal immigrants entered the country.

Despite these measures, Central Americans kept coming; the number rose from about 7,000 in 1985 to more than 50,000 in 1988. More than half of these were from Nicaragua. By early 1989, 2,000 Central Americans per week were arriving in southern Texas. After registering with the INS, these migrants moved on to Hispanic communities in Miami, New York City, and Los Angeles where many simply vanished.

## The Bush Administration

In response to pressure from local communities that had to bear the brunt of the rising tide of immigrants,[47] one early action on asylum policy taken by the Bush administration was to reinstitute a policy of expedited asylum hearings and mass detention of asylum seekers—a policy that had been employed by the previous two U.S. administrations but was declared illegal by the U.S. courts.[48]

In its first year, the Bush administration did not pursue a more even-handed refugee policy than had its predecessor. An INS/State Department Refugee Report published at the end of 1989 showed that the overall approval rate for asylum seekers had dropped from 25 to 18 percent, and that individuals from the Soviet Union, Romania, Iran, and Czechoslovakia still had a far greater chance of obtaining asylum in the United States than did nationals of Guatemala, Haiti, Sri Lanka, Honduras, or El Salvador. More than 81 percent of Soviet applications and more than 90 percent of Romanian cases gained approval, compared with less than 2 percent of Guatemalans, 3.5 percent of Haitians, 1.3 percent of Hondurans, and 2.3 percent of Salvadorans—despite serious and well-documented human rights abuses and political violence in recent years in all of these countries.

At the beginning of the 1990s, several important developments raised hopes that the Bush administration's asylum policy might soon become more even-handed and responsive. In July 1990, the INS issued regulations that provided for a more professional corps of asylum adjudicators, a less adversarial first stage of interviewing, more extensive training of immigration officers, and better documentation about human rights conditions in countries of origin. In addition, certain provisions of the 1990 Immigration Law signed by President Bush in November 1990 give Salvadorans already living illegally in the United States a temporary protected status for 18 months—a measure for which refugee advocates had been fighting for nearly a decade. Moreover, this legislation gave the Attorney General the discretion to extend similar status to other specific groups in the future. In a landmark legal settlement as a result of a class action suit—

*American Baptist Churches* v. *Thornburgh*—the INS agreed in December 1990 to suspend deportations of both Salvadorans and Guatemalans and to rehear all previously denied asylum claims.

But while the beginning of the 1990s saw a significant restructuring of the way the United States adjudicates asylum claims, these reforms were accompanied by renewed efforts to prevent or deter the arrival of new refugee claimants. The United States was especially harsh and unwelcoming toward Haitian boat people fleeing their homeland in the aftermath of the military overthrow of the elected government of President Jean-Bertrand Aristide in September 1991.

The initial U.S. response to the Haitian refugee crisis was to interdict and forcibly return the boat people to Haiti. As political conditions in Haiti deteriorated, however, the policy of forced returns was halted by various district court injunctions. More than 38,000 Haitians were intercepted by the U.S. Coast Guard between the September 1991 coup d' état and the end of 1992. Nonetheless, despite widespread violence and well-documented persecution in Haiti,[49] the Bush Administration refused to grant Haitians temporary protected status, as provided for in the Immigration Act of 1990. For several months the U.S. Coast Guard brought interdicted Haitians to the U.S. naval base at Guantanamo Bay, Cuba, where INS asylum officers interviewed and screened them to see whether they had a credible basis for their asylum claims. Subsequently, a legal challenge was mounted, claiming that the U.S. screening procedures were deeply flawed and raising questions as to whether some people genuinely and justifiably fearful of persecution were being wrongly "screened out." In testimony before Congress, the lead attorney Ira Kurzban offered the following observations:

> INS officers readily admitted that they had interviewed hundreds of Haitians without receiving any information about the political conditions in Haiti. They also candidly acknowledged that they had received no training on interviewing Haitian asylum applicants. . . . Immigration officers were also applying incorrect standards. One officer could not even name all the grounds necessary to obtain asylum.[50]

Despite these flaws in the screening procedure, the Bush administration successfully petitioned the U.S. Supreme Court to lift the injunction against forced repatriation; and in early 1992, Haitians who had been "screened out" at Guantanamo Bay were forcibly repatriated to Haiti without access to legal counsel or the right to appeal negative decisions. In May 1992 the Bush Administration dropped screening entirely and ordered the U.S. Coast Guard to interdict and return all Haitian boat people. Although the policy of summary return may eventually be overturned by court action or by Congressional legislation to allow Haitians some form of temporary protection, the incoming Clinton administration indicated that it intended to continue at least temporarily the previous American policy of forcibly preventing Haitians from reaching U.S. territory to apply for asylum.

In recent years, the INS and the U.S. Border Patrol have also sought to block the transit by land of Central Americans, by closely cooperating with and encouraging their Mexican counterpart—the Directorate of Migration Services—to interdict Central Americans before they ever reach the U.S. border.[51] According to human rights and refugee protection agencies, the numbers of apprehensions and of deportations across the Guatemalan border carried out by the Directorate of Migration Services, primarily of people not permitted to register asylum claims, have increased steadily in recent years.[52]

## Resurgence of American Nativism

In the early 1990s, a growing sentiment was evident among some sectors of the population that too many foreigners had been allowed to immigrate to the United States in recent years. Immigration is now at its highest levels since the beginning of this century. More than 8 million newcomers entered the United States during the 1980s, which ranks these years second only to the years from 1901 to 1910 as the highest immigration decade in U.S. history. Currently, in addition to the approximately 125,000 refugees and 700,000 immigrants the United States officially admits every year, several hundred thousand illegal immigrants are believed to enter annually.

Immigration to the United States has not only accelerated rapidly in recent decades; it has also become significantly more diverse in terms of national origin and ethnic and cultural background of the immigrant population. As a result of the Immigration Act of 1965, immigration shifted from Europe—the origin of about 70 percent of legal immigrants before that year—to Asia and Latin America, which now account for well over 80 percent of the newcomers. As a result, immigration has assumed a visibility and prominence in the life of the United States not evident since the early 1900s. The effects of the new immigration are felt most immediately at the local level, particularly in schools, neighborhoods, and the workplace. In the late 1980s, more than 70 percent of immigrants and refugees settled in just six states, over 45 percent in California and New York alone.[53] In both California and Texas, whites are expected to become a minority of the population by early in the next century. If present trends continue, whites in the United States as a whole will be outnumbered by members of other ethnic groups by the middle of the next century. By the year 2000, barely half of the people entering the workforce will be native-born and of European stock. White retirees will thus find that their pension benefits depend heavily on the social security contributions of an increasingly brown workforce.

Even in a society as open and diverse as the United States, local impact of the new immigration is rapidly becoming an important political issue. The new immigration presents a challenge to the educational, health-care, and other social welfare institutions that are trying to absorb immigrant workers into the labor force and to promote social integration. In recent years interethnic conflict and economic competition among different minority groups have gained public attention. Bitter tensions and feuds exist between blacks and recently arrived immigrants and refugees, such as Koreans, other Asians, and Hispanics; and in some communities, immigrants and refugees are used as scapegoats for economic and social problems. Outbreaks of violence involving these groups have occurred in some cities and neighborhoods in California and in other states. There appears to be noisy, if not widespread, concern that continued large-scale immigration will threaten America's social cohesion and national identity. The Republican primary elections in 1992 included candidates who blamed America's social ills on the influx of recent immigrants, and the Governor of California accused refugees and illegal immigrants of abusing the welfare system and of costing American taxpayers unnecessary expenses.[54]

Thus, while recent changes in legislation and asylum procedures hold out the promise of a more even-handed and generous U.S. policy toward refugees, domestic politics and concern among some sectors of the population that immigration poses a threat to national stability and the economic welfare of native-born Americans have become increasingly important forces shaping U.S. refugee acceptance. A resurgence of American nativism could well result in the imposition of new restrictionist policies and curbs on immigration flows and in new threats to the practice of asylum in the United States in the years ahead.

## Canada's Asylum Policy

To the north of the United States, the Canadian government's asylum system has faced similar pressures but in recent years has managed to maintain procedures that are relatively nondiscriminatory and fair.[55] As recently as the late 1970s, Canada received only 200 to 400 spontaneous arrivals annually; by 1982–1986, that number had increased to between 2,500 and 4,000 claims per year.

The Canadian asylum system came under serious pressure when President Reagan signed the Immigration Control Reform Act in November 1986. As the new law's employer sanctions began to take hold, Central Americans who did not meet the law's residence requirements began to lose their jobs, and a growing stream of them, anticipating their deportation, crossed northward from the United States into Canada. The number of Salvadorans appearing at the Canadian border in the month of January 1987 nearly equaled the total number of Salvadoran asylum applicants during the entire previous year. In February, the Canadian government enacted a series of new restrictions on entry that caused large numbers of asylum seekers to pile up on the U.S.–Canadian border.

In May 1987, bill C-55 was introduced in the Canadian Parliament to bring about major changes in the refugee determination system and to create a new, independent Immigration and Refugee Board. Catalyzed by highly publicized landings of boatloads of Tamils and Sikhs along the east coast of the country in 1986 and 1987 and fearing "floodtides" of asylum seekers, the Canadian government called Parliament into emergency session in August 1987 to consider even more restrictive legislation, bill C-84. Bill C-84 introduced strict detention and deterrence measures, including criminal penalties for people who assisted undocumented aliens; authorization to exclude asylum seekers from the hearing process and to return them to an intermediary country judged to be "safe," notwithstanding any fear of persecution the claimant might have; and new powers to interdict at sea and to turn away ships carrying undocumented aliens, without determining any claims to refugee status. During 1988, the numbers of asylum applicants shot up to over 40,000, another tenfold increase. In the face of fierce opposition from the Canadian Bar, the major Canadian churches, Amnesty International, other prominent voluntary agencies, and the UNHCR, both government bills were approved in July 1988 and went into effect in January 1989.

Despite fears that the new laws would significantly curtail entry into Canada, many of the restrictionist measures introduced in Bill C-84 were in fact either allowed to expire or were never implemented by the government. As a result, mainly the positive aspects of the reform legislation survived. In 1989, the government established the Convention Refugee Determination Division of the Immigration and Refugee Board, which is the sole authority charged with protecting refugees in Canada. To support the activities of the board and to ensure informed and impartial decision-making on asylum cases, a Documentation Center with extensive information on human rights conditions in countries of origin was also established. After three years, the new system has produced some of the highest acceptance rates anywhere in the world. For displaced persons from each of the six largest source countries in 1990 (Sri Lanka, Somalia, China,[56] Iran, El Salvador, and Lebanon), approval rates were well over 70 percent. By and large, the approval rates reflect human rights conditions in countries of origin. For the three "worst" countries (Iran, Somalia, and Sri Lanka), the approval rate was over 90 percent.[57] For Eastern European applicants, on the other hand, admission declined significantly, reflecting improving political conditions. In 1991, 64 percent of asylum applicants were granted refugee status; and during the first six months of 1992, 57 percent were approved, reflecting a gradual downward trend in acceptance rates since the new system was instituted in 1989.

The Canadian system is not without flaws.[58] Like other Western countries, Canada continues to employ deterrent measures such as visa controls on refugee-sending countries, resulting in the screening out of many genuine Convention refugees. Large backlogs still bog down the system, and critics fear that any future rise in the number of spontaneous arrivals will lead to vigorous implementation of some of the more restrictive provisions of the new legislation, such as returning asylum seekers to so-called "safe" third countries. In June 1992, the Canadian government introduced Bill C-86 into Parliament, which proposes to streamline the asylum procedure by eliminating the initial hearing in which an asylum applicant's eligibility and credibility for a full hearing is determined.

Perhaps the most serious threat to future asylum protection in Canada involves the possibility that Canada will join with West European governments and the United States in a process of collective deterrence.[59] As of mid-1992, some 80 percent of asylum applicants appearing in Canada originated outside the Western Hemisphere. The majority, therefore, appeared to be people who had bypassed European countries or the United States to come to Canada, where they were likely to receive a more sympathetic hearing. In order to stem these flows, Canada has entered into negotiations with the United States and Europe to permit Canadian officials to send directly back to the United States and Europe refugees seeking asylum in Canada who passed through these countries on their way to Canada.

Faced with rising demands for asylum, Canada will come under heavier pressure to adopt a more restrictive policy. In the future, Canada will continue to struggle with the task of maintaining a refugee policy that balances fairness and adequate protection with efficiency and effectiveness.

## "Fortress Europe": Asylum Policy in the European Community

Racism and xenophobia have always been a part of European society; but until the 1980s, Western Europe demonstrated a generally liberal attitude toward asylum seekers. A series of measures—including work permits, social welfare benefits, and language training—promulgated during the 1960s and 1970s were relatively generous and fair. Relatively liberal asylum policies were also facilitated by the fact that, until the early 1960s, nearly all refugees who sought asylum in Western Europe were generated by political repression and harsh economic conditions accompanying the transformation of Eastern European states into communist regimes. Throughout this period, communist bloc refugees—Hungarians, Czechs, and East Germans among others—were accepted into the West with little scrutiny into their motives for departure. By the early 1960s, this influx largely subsided, however, as fewer people were able to flee from behind the Iron Curtain.[60] Others who sought asylum were primarily from areas where West European countries had earlier maintained political and cultural links.[61]

Pressure for resettling Third World refugees was relieved by improved economic conditions in the 1950s and 1960s. During their period of rapid economic expansion, Western European nations needed labor and easily absorbed not only thousands of asylum seekers from Eastern Europe, but also millions of actively recruited manual laborers—the so-called "guest workers"—from former colonies in Africa, Asia, and the Caribbean and from Southern Europe.

As long as the economic situation remained generally buoyant and labor migration was clearly in the interest of the industrialized states, refugees and migrant workers tended to be well received. However, with the oil price shock of 1973 and the subsequent economic recession, this welcoming attitude changed. European governments had never intended the guest worker programs of the 1960s to lead to long-term resettlement; and with the onset of labor surpluses during the 1970s, they expected most of the guest workers to return home. But despite the withdrawal of the welcome mat and the offer of material inducements to leave, the majority of such workers stayed.[62] Immigration levels actually increased during the rest of the decade, as immediate family members were brought over to join those who had entered as guest workers.

## New Asylum and Migration Pressures on Europe

The 1980s put additional pressures on the political asylum systems of Western Europe, as they did in the case of United States. The number of applicants in European countries suddenly rose from approximately 20,000 in 1976 to 158,500 in 1980.[63] The steep rise in European unemployment, combined with high immigration levels, led to increasing concern and fear among indigenous Europeans of being inundated by foreigners. Governments reacted by tightening their border controls, but such deterrent measures did not work for long. As was shown earlier in Table 5-1, the numbers reached almost 545,000 per annum by 1991.[64]

From 1983 to 1989, some 60 percent of the 1.3 million asylum seekers in Europe came from the Third World, driven by political crises and armed conflicts in Africa, Asia, and the Middle East.[65] (One-third originated from the Middle East; 15 percent from the Indian subcontinent; 10 percent from Africa; and over 20 percent from Eastern Europe.) The protracted war between Iran and Iraq during the 1980s generated 150,000 asylum applicants, and civil wars in Sri Lanka and Lebanon brought another 100,000 Tamils and some 50,000 Lebanese to Europe.[66] Following the collapse of communist regimes in Eastern Europe and in the Soviet Union in 1989, asylum seekers from the Balkans and Central Europe have increased considerably and now constitute a significantly higher proportion of displaced persons than they did in previous years (see Table 5-2). During 1992, asylum seekers from former Yugoslavia constituted the largest group, due mainly to the brutal interethnic war there.

*Table 5-2*   East European Asylum Seekers in the Whole of Europe
(Bulgarians to Turkey excluded)

| Country | 1987 | 1988 | 1989 | 1990 | 1991 | Total |
|---|---|---|---|---|---|---|
| Albania | 206 | 205 | 226 | 5,391 | 26,788 | 32,816 |
| Bulgaria | 369 | 587 | 7,981 | 13,167 | 16,739 | 38,840 |
| Czechoslovakia | 5,129 | 4,619 | 7,441 | 1,713 | 1,958 | 20,860 |
| Hungary | 6,990 | 5,967 | 3,393 | 967 | 701 | 18,018 |
| Poland | 21,099 | 44,309 | 33,820 | 15,687 | 8,053 | 122,968 |
| Romania | 6,738 | 10,677 | 47,048 | 80,309 | 64,349 | 209,121 |
| USSR | 171 | 505 | 1,252 | 5,471 | 10,814 | 18,213 |
| Yugoslavia | 7,710 | 24,055 | 26,038 | 33,229 | 115,152 | 206,184 |
| Total | 48,412 | 90,924 | 127,199 | 155,934 | 244,554 | 667,023 |

SOURCE: Secretariat for Intergovernmental Consultations, Geneva.

Otherwise, Romanians, Turks, Sri Lankans, Somalis, Iranians, Zairians, Iraqis, Bulgarians, Albanians, and Lebanese were by far the most numerous asylum seekers in Europe. (see Table 5-3).

The growing influx includes many people who, although they cannot safely return to their countries of origin, do not meet the criteria of the 1951 Convention. Growing numbers of economic migrants are also trying to use the asylum system to enter Europe.

### Resurgence of East–West Flows

With the disintegration of communist regimes at the end of the decade, citizens from former Eastern bloc countries arriving in Western Europe represented the biggest population movement the continent had seen since the late 1940s.[67] In 1989, over 1.3 million people left Eastern Europe and the Soviet Union for the West: 720,000 ethnic Germans (*Aussiedler* and *Ubersiedler*); about 320,000 Bulgarian Turks, half of whom later returned to Bulgaria; 71,000 Soviet Jews; and 127,000 asylum seekers, mostly from Poland and Yugoslavia. During the next two years, the East-to-West flow moderated, with 923,000 moving westward in 1990 and 800,000 in 1991 (see Table 5-4). During this period, 220,000 Jews in 1990 and 173,000 in 1991 emigrated from the ex–Soviet Union, mostly to Israel; 397,000 ethnic Germans in 1990 and 222,000 in 1991 poured into Germany; and the number of Eastern European nationalities who sought asylum in the West increased from 156,000 in 1990 to 245,000 in 1991, as detailed in Table 5-2. Most of the emigrants have been members of ethnic minority or religious groups with close links to receiving countries such as Germany, Hungary, Turkey, the United States, Israel, and Greece. But there have also been unanticipated outflows of war refugees

***Table 5-3***  Estimates of Asylum Applications in Participating States,
January–May 1992

| State | Asylum Applicants | | Top Nationalities |
|---|---|---|---|
| Australia | 1,942 | | China, Fiji, Pakistan, Sri Lanka, Bangladesh |
| Austria | 10,047 | | new Yugoslav Federation, Romania, Turkey, Iraq, Nigeria, Iran |
| Belgium | 5,580 | | Zaire, Romania, ex-Yugoslavia, India, Turkey, Ghana |
| Canada | 15,673 | (projected) | Sri Lanka, Somalia, CIS, ex-Yugoslavia, China |
| Denmark | 2,254 | | new Yugoslav Federation, Iraq, Somalia, stateless Palestinians, Sri Lanka |
| Finland | 649 | | CIS, ex-Yugoslavia, Somalia, Zaire, Turkey |
| France | 10,497 | | Sri Lanka, Zaire, China, Turkey, ex-Yugoslavia (without Croatia and Slovenia), Romania |
| Germany | 156,440 | | ex-Yugoslavia (without Croatia and Slovenia), Romania, Turkey, Nigeria, Vietnam, Bulgaria |
| Italy | 1,181 | | Romania, Ethiopia, Bulgaria, Somalia, Albania |
| Netherlands | 5,890 | | ex-Yugoslavia (without Croatia and Slovenia), Iran, Romania, Somalia, Sri Lanka, Turkey |
| Norway | 1,500 | | new Yugoslav Federation, Somalia, Sri Lanka, Iran, Lebanon |
| Spain | 4,610 | | Peru, Poland, Senegal, Iraq, Romania, Bulgaria |
| Sweden | 22,346 | (projected) | ex-Yugoslavia, Iraq, Somalia, Peru, Iran |
| Switzerland | 8,948 | | ex-Yugoslavia (without Croatia and Slovenia), Sri Lanka, Turkey, Somalia, Zaire |

(*continued*)

**Table 5-3**   *(Continued)*

| State | Asylum Applicants | | Top Nationalities |
|---|---|---|---|
| UK | 7,997 | (excluding dependents) | Sri Lanka, Turkey, India, Pakistan, ex-Yugoslavia |
| USA | 103,000 | (10/91–5/92) | |
| Total (excluding USA) | 255,554 | | |

SOURCE: Secretariat for Intergovernmental Consultations, Geneva.

from the former republics of Yugoslavia, of boat people from Albania, and of Gypsies and other minorities from Romania.

In the early 1990s, emigration from Croatia, Serbia, Bosnia-Herzegovina, and Kosovo to other European countries increased dramatically as a result of ethnically motivated violence and prolonged and brutal civil war among Yugoslavia's erstwhile republics. By late 1992, more than 2.5 million had been displaced in the former Yugoslavia, and several hundred thousand had taken refuge in Germany, Hungary, Austria, Italy, and Sweden. Any extension of the war into Macedonia or Kosovo, with an attendant and massive spillover of ethnic co-nationals into Albania, Greece, Turkey, or Bulgaria, could internationalize the conflict and increase the likelihood of further refugee outflows.

## A Disintegrating Ex-Soviet Union

In addition to being directed toward the refugee crisis in ex-Yugoslavia, West European attention has been riveted on the political and economic disintegration of the former USSR. A number of forecasters have expressed fears that the dismantling of this vast multinational empire, with the resultant conflict and economic dislocation within and between successor republics, could generate millions of emigrants and refugees. These mass outflows have so far not occurred. During the past few years, out-migration from the ex–Soviet Union has followed historical patterns.[68] Between 300,000 and 400,000 people are now leaving the former Soviet Union annually. Almost all are ethnically distinct groups—Germans, Jews, Armenians, and Greeks—with fixed destinations, and informal networks in the West are instrumental in facilitating their continuing emigration (see Tables 5-5 and 5-6). These emigrations have been subject to quotas, and for the most part they have taken place under bilateral agreements with Germany, Israel, the United States, and other governments; consequently, they have been affected in the past by fluctuations in international politics, particularly U.S.–Soviet relations. Apart from these large minorities, most of the people of the fifteen new independent states of the old

**Table 5-4** Exodus from Eastern Europe, 1984–1991

| Type of Migrant | 1984 | 1985 | 1986 | 1987 | 1988 | 1989 | 1990 | 1991 |
|---|---|---|---|---|---|---|---|---|
| Asylum seekers | 25,000 | 30,000 | 41,000 | 48,000 | 91,000 | 127,000 | 156,000 | 245,000 |
| Jews from USSR | 1,000 | 1,000 | 4,000 | 6,000 | 30,000 | 71,000 | 220,000 | 173,000 |
| German settlers | 77,000 | 64,000 | 69,000 | 98,000 | 240,000 | 720,000 | 397,000 | 222,000 |
| Bulgarian Turks | — | — | — | — | — | 320,000 | — | — |
| Others (estimate) | 6,000 | 6,000 | 10,000 | 25,000 | 50,000 | 100,000 | 150,000 | 160,000 |
| Total | 109,000 | 101,000 | 124,000 | 177,000 | 411,000 | 1,338,000 | 923,000 | 800,000 |

SOURCE: Secretariat for Intergovernmental Consultations, Geneva.

Table 5-5  Soviet Emigration, 1948–1990[a]

| Period | Jews | Germans | Armenians | Greeks | Evangelicals & Pentacostals | Others[b] | Totals |
|---|---|---|---|---|---|---|---|
| 1948–1970 | 25,200 | 22,400 | 12,000 | — | — | — | 59,600 |
| 1971–1980 | 248,900 | 64,300 | 34,100 | — | — | — | 347,300 |
| 1981–1986 | 16,900 | 19,500 | 6,300 | 1,300 | — | — | 44,000 |
| 1987–1989 | 100,000 | 160,200 | 24,900 | 8,700 | 14,200 | 200 | 308,200 |
| Subtotals | 391,000 | 266,400 | 77,300 | 10,000 | 14,200 | 200 | 759,100 |
| 1990[c] | 201,300 | 148,000 | 6,800 | 14,300 | 4,200 | 2,600 | 377,200 |
| Totals | 592,300 | 414,400 | 84,100 | 24,300 | 18,400 | 2,800 | 1,136,300 |
| Proportion of total(%) | 52.1 | 36.5 | 7.4 | 2.1 | 1.6 | .03 | 100.0 |

[a]Figures may not add up, due to rounding.
[b]Others consist of Soviet citizens of various identities.
[c]Precise figures are: Jews 201,344; Germans, 147,950; Armenians, 6,821; Greeks, 14,300 (est.); Evangelicals and Pentecostals, 4,150; and others, 2,649.

SOURCES: U.S. Department of State; Israeli Embassy, Washington, D.C.: German Ministry of Interior; Internationale Gesellshaft für Menschenrechte, Frankfurt/Main; Hebrew Immigrant Aid Society (HIAS); and Armenian informants. Cited in Mikk Titma, "An Assessment of Recent and Current Empirical Research on Prospective Emigration," (Institute of Sociology and Law, Estonia Academy of Science, 1991).

**Table 5-6** Destinations of Soviet Emigrants by Nationality, 1948–1990[a]

| Years | Jews | | | Germans | Armenians | | | Greeks | Evangelicals & Pentecostals | | Others |
|---|---|---|---|---|---|---|---|---|---|---|---|
| | Israel | U.S. | Other[b] | Germany[c] | U.S. | France | Other[d] | Greece | U.S. | Canada | U.S. |
| 1948–89 | 191,900 | 170,800 | 28,300 | 266,400 | 63,800 | 12,000 | 1,500 | 10,000 | 14,000 | 200 | 200 |
| 1990 | 181,800 | 6,500 | 13,000[e] | 148,000 | 6,500 | — | 300 | 14,300 | 4,100 | 100 | 2,600 |
| Totals | 373,700 | 177,300 | 41,300 | 414,400 | 70,300 | 12,000 | 1,800 | 24,300 | 18,100 | 300 | 2,800 |

[a]Totals may not add up due to rounding.
[b]Other places where Jews have resettled include Canada, Europe, Latin America, and Oceania.
[c]Figures for Germany include emigrants who settled in both the FRG and the GDR.
[d]Other places where Armenians resettled include the Middle East, Greece, and the Netherlands.
[e]This figure is composed of 6,000 Jews who resettled in Germany and 7,000 who went to other countries; see note b.

SOURCES: See Table 5-5.

Soviet Union have few links to the Western world and therefore at this time cannot be considered strong potential emigrants.

While it is impossible to predict with certainty how great the future outflow will be, there is a serious prospect of mass migration at least from western parts of the former Soviet Union.[69] If the internal situation deteriorates badly, the urge to flee to the more prosperous West European states while conditions still permit may prove irresistible to many. According to public opinion surveys conducted in the former USSR in 1991, anywhere from 10 to 16 percent of the population want to emigrate.[70] For over 60 years, the state police were responsible for enforcing migration policy, and Soviet citizens were not allowed to travel freely to the outside world. The loosening of state controls on emigration in the 1990s has made exit less risky than before. Moreover, because of greater access to the West, large numbers of ex-Soviet citizens are becoming increasingly aware of the huge economic disparities between Western societies and their own. Although practical considerations such as the visa and entry requirements of Western governments and the incapacity of the internal transportation system to move large numbers of people (particularly from remote republics in the East), as well as severe shortages in convertible currency and prohibitively expensive foreign travel, will undoubtedly limit the numbers able to leave,[71] people of the ex–Soviet Union have considerable pent-up desire to work and to visit abroad.

Economic reform itself is a push factor, causing rising rates of unemployment, hyperinflation, acute shortages, and grave dislocation in the domestic economy. Only the most rudimentary social safety net exists to cushion the people from the social and political instability that are likely to follow from mass unemployment. A large percentage of industrial production in the ex–Soviet Union was concentrated in the military-industrial complex. As this sector is further disbanded, entire defense plants and factories will be shut down; and there is little chance that this sector will be converted to civilian use or that many former employees will be retrained or relocated in other industries. Hundreds of thousands of people with marketable skills, such as scientific and technical workers, may feel compelled to seek attractive job opportunities in other countries and try to emigrate.

Finally, in recent years, ethnic conflicts fueled by ancient hatreds and grievances have torn the former USSR apart, creating an estimated 2 to 3 million internally displaced people.[72] Since 120 different nationalities live within the boundaries of the ex–Soviet Union, and since more than 65 million people currently reside—forcibly or voluntarily—outside their "ethnic homelands" (including perhaps 25 million Russians), the potential for mass internal migration is staggering. Should large numbers of these people decide to emigrate, many might qualify as political refugees, thereby putting pressure on Western countries—which now label all emigrants as economic migrants—to accept them as legitimate refugees. Such a situation may evolve, for instance, as a result of the conflict between

Armenia and Azerbaijan or as a result of conflicts in South and North Ossetia, in the Dniester region of Moldova, or in Belarus, Ukraine, or the Baltic states over the fate of Russian minorities. Thus, although the flow of permanent departures from the former USSR will depend very much on the evolution of its internal political situation, the ex–Soviet Union's emigration potential seems immense.

## Central and Eastern Europe as Host and Sending States

It is generally acknowledged that large-scale population movements from the East could pose a risk to regional stability, and long-term East–West relations will inevitably be affected if ethnic conflict and internal displacement spill over into neighboring countries. For the first time since the inception of communist rule, a number of Eastern European countries feel endangered by immigration rather than by emigration. In particular, a mass exodus from the Soviet Union would present major security problems for the newly democratizing Central European states. Poland, the Czech and Slovak Republics, and Hungary are undergoing major structural changes that leave them with little capacity to admit, house, and feed large numbers of immigrants without undermining their own attempts at economic and political reform. It is unlikely that these states could absorb large numbers of people, although they might be able to integrate some citizens from the former USSR who share ethnic or religious ties or other close connections.

Poland, in particular, faces the danger of a mass influx from the former Soviet Union's western republics. Some 2 to 3 million ethnic Poles, currently living as more or less well-tolerated minorities in Lithuania, Belarus, and Ukraine, could be confronted with increased discrimination at the hands of highly ethnocentric governments and publics. Any such maltreatment of Poles might well give rise to serious bilateral tensions between Poland and the Soviet successor states, perhaps culminating in a mass exodus of ethnic Poles to their ancestral homeland across the 600-mile border it shares with the former USSR.

Central and Eastern European states are also receiving refugees from the countries of the South as well as from their neighbors to the East. A number of Third World migrants are trying to use Central and Eastern Europe as a transit route to the more prosperous western part of the continent; but as West Europe continues to tighten its borders, larger numbers of asylum seekers are trapped in Central Europe. In Hungary, for example, which has become a transit country for Arabs, Africans, Romanians, and former Soviet citizens, there were already an estimated 100,000 illegal immigrants in the country as of mid-1992, due to Western restrictions on entry.[73] By that time, Hungary had also received over 50,000 ex-Yugoslavs. In addition, Hungary is potentially a country of resettlement for the 3.5 million ethnic Hungarians who now live in neighboring countries, particularly in Transylvania, Slovakia, Vojvodina, and Ukraine. As a result of these new pressures, and in search of international assistance, Hungary and a number of other postcommunist states, have joined the international refugee regime.

In the event of mass migration from the Balkan states or from the former USSR, Central European states will emphasize that the migration problem must be seen as an all-European concern and will demand burden-sharing agreements with the West. This already has occurred with respect to those fleeing the former Yugoslavia. While modest financial help for the front-line receiving countries was offered, Western governments were unwilling to resettle the majority of Yugoslav nationals who sought refuge and stipulated that would-be refugees should remain in their country of origin. It is unlikely that Western states will be any more generous in the event of a mass exodus from the ex–Soviet Union.

Besides being countries of asylum, many East European states are also sources of emigration to the West. Yet the potential for mass exodus from the region varies greatly from country to country.[74] First of all, one must distinguish between the countries of Central Europe, which are relatively stable and advanced, and the Balkans, which are still highly unstable and impoverished. Moreover, Poland and Romania, the countries most affected by emigration pressures, together account for almost two-thirds of the total population of Eastern Europe and share between them over 80 percent of the population growth recorded in the region over the past twenty years.[75] Because the dislocation caused by the transition from centrally planned to market economies in these countries is likely to produce a continuing escalation in prices and further unemployment, particularly among the young, emigration on a large scale is likely unless it is forestalled by positive action. For example, in the early 1990s, a Polish construction worker active on the Western black market can earn as much in one or two months as he can in four years in Poland.[76] Neighboring countries have adopted a fairly liberal entry regime toward Poles, but they have not done so toward Romanians. Poles also have a long-standing tradition of emigration; and since the abolition of exit permit requirements in 1988, about 1 million Poles (mostly German *Aussiedler*) have left their homeland and chosen not to return. In Romania, great uncertainty about the country's political and economic future has dramatically increased the number of emigrants, particularly among Gypsies and ethnic Hungarians in Transylvania.[77]

Reports by international banks and agencies indicate that unemployment could reach 21 percent of the working population in Eastern Europe by 1994.[78] If economic conditions do not improve markedly and quickly, Eastern Europeans are likely to become increasingly disaffected and may opt to leave their homelands. During 1991, over 100,000 people escaped from Albania, the least developed nation in the region, and fled principally to Italy and Greece. These departures herald further migrations that are already beginning, particularly among Albania's sizable ethnic Greek community in northern Epirus. In neighboring Bulgaria, hundreds of thousands of people—most of them young, highly educated, and skilled—have left since 1989 because of the country's worsening economic plight and its still feeble and uncertain movement toward political reform. This movement is in addition to the exodus of 320,000 members of its Turkish minority in 1989 (many of whom have since returned).

A surge westward of large numbers of disaffected people would undermine political and economic stability within Eastern Europe and might adversely affect the future course of political and security relations between East and West. In fact, a sizable brain drain is already underway from Bulgaria, the former Soviet Union, and Poland; and it could become a mass phenomenon. The mass out-migration of East Europe's best-educated and best-trained people would hinder these states' developmental capacity and undermine their attempts to establish more liberal economic and social institutions. Western policymakers may soon be confronted with the necessity of determining the limits (if any) beyond which these states cannot permit the hemorrhaging of their skilled manpower, as well as of assessing the implications of the limits on future domestic stability and regional security.

Western governments no longer regard Central and East Europe as an area that generates asylum seekers on the basis of wholesale violations of human rights by its rulers. Accordingly, most West European countries are imposing stricter conditions for granting asylum to former socialist countries and are offering less material assistance, to deter new arrivals from the East. By late 1992, Germany had indicated its intention to revise its generous constitutional provisions on asylum and to introduce a list of countries where political persecution is no longer judged to be a feature of national life. This list was expected to cover all Central and East European countries and effectively to close political immigration from these states to Germany. Austria, which had served as a major country of transit for nearly 2 million refugees since the end of World War II, returned asylum seekers to third countries, imposed visas for nationals from neighboring East European states, and stationed soldiers on its eastern border to stop the entry of undocumented asylum seekers.[79]

In the early post–Cold War era, the United States did not see the strategic necessity of dramatically increasing its annual intake of immigrants and refugees to accommodate East Europeans and to relieve pressure on host states in Eastern or Western Europe. For example, the United States no longer automatically admitted large numbers of refugees transiting through Austria. Moreover, the United States reduced its fiscal year 1993 East European refugee admissions ceiling to 1,500, the lowest level since 1980.[80] And although the Immigration Act of 1990 raised the ceiling on immigration to the United States from 540,000 to 700,000 people per year, the number of immigrant visas issued to East Europeans is not expected to rise significantly. Canada, with its large ethnic Ukrainian community, is likely to take immigrants from Ukraine, but it is unlikely to admit huge numbers of other Eastern Europeans.

## Strains on Host Nations

The unexpected emergence of significant East–West movements within the continent, combined with the continuing unplanned arrival of Third World nationals in Western Europe, has placed new strains on governments and local communities and has necessitated additional governmental expenses for social assistance. The cost of these programs—currently estimated at more than $7 billion a year—is roughly seven times greater than the annual worldwide expenditures of the UNHCR and nearly one-seventh the size of total annual development aid made available to the Third World from the West, an imbalance that suggests the misallocation of resources to address the problem.

Cost alone does not explain the restrictive European attitudes; nor do abstract figures reveal the extent of the impact felt by the governments of Western Europe. Clearly, some countries have been more heavily affected than others. For example, Germany accounted for 44 percent of the asylum applications in Europe from 1983 to 1990, France for 16 percent, Sweden for 10 percent, and Switzerland for 7 percent. From 1987 to 1991, asylum applications in Germany nearly quintupled, from 57,400 to 256,100 (47 percent of Europe's 1991 total), as detailed in Table 5-7. During 1992, that may again have almost doubled, given that 450,000 persons were expected to apply for political asylum during 1992.[81]

The refugee burden cannot be measured by costs and numbers alone. The limits of a country's reception capacity is related to the adaptability of its population to multicultural change, the conditions of its labor market and the overall performance of its national economy. Most European governments have serious reservations about the ability of the new arrivals to adjust to life in Europe and are greatly concerned about the willingness of their own people to tolerate aliens in their midst. In contrast to many of the newly arriving Eastern Europeans, Third World asylum seekers often arrive without readily transferable skills, and with the stigma of belonging to a different race and religion. The rise of Islamic fundamentalism and other ethnoreligious political movements within Western Europe introduces a new element internally and externally and is seen to present a security threat and to complicate Europe's relations with other countries, particularly in the wake of the 1991 Gulf War. France is concerned that the growth of Islamic fundamentalism in Algeria might lead to a large-scale refugee influx into France by secularists. In the face of these perceived risks, xenophobic and racist attitudes are increasingly evident among some segments of the Western public. Recession and unemployment have pushed immigration to the top of the political agenda in France and have triggered sporadic violence in suburban ghettoes across the country. In Germany, brutal physical attacks on foreigners and asylum seekers by skinheads and neo-Nazis, sometimes abetted by local populations, have caused politicians in Bonn to redraft their country's asylum provisions. On top of this, according to OECD figures, the rate of unemployment among for-

*Table 5-7*  Estimates on Asylum Applications in European Participating States, 1983–1991 (rounded figures)

| Country | 1983 | 1984 | 1985 | 1986 | 1987 | 1988 | 1989 | 1990 | 1991 | 1983–1990 |
|---|---|---|---|---|---|---|---|---|---|---|
| Austria | 5,900 | 7,200 | 6,700 | 8,700 | 11,400 | 15,800 | 21,900 | 22,800 | 27,300 | 127,700 |
| Belgium | 2,900. | 3,700 | 5,300 | 7,700 | 6,000 | 5,100 | 8,100 | 13,000 | 15,200 | 67,000 |
| Denmark | 800 | 4,300 | 8,700 | 9,300 | 2,800 | 4,700 | 4,600 | 5,300 | 4,600 | 45,100 |
| Finland | — | — | — | — | 50 | 50 | 200 | 2,500 | 2,100 | 4,900 |
| France | 14,300 | 15,900 | 25,800 | 23,400 | 24,800 | 31,600 | 60,000 | 56,000 | 46,500 | 298,300 |
| FRG | 19,700 | 35,300 | 73,900 | 99,700 | 57,400 | 103,100 | 121,000 | 193,000 | 256,100 | 959,200 |
| Italy | 3,000 | 4,500 | 5,400 | 6,500 | 11,000 | 1,300 | 2,200 | 4,700 | 31,700 | 70,300 |
| Netherlands | 2,000 | 2,600 | 5,700 | 5,900 | 13,500 | 7,500 | 14,000 | 21,200 | 21,600 | 94,000 |
| Norway | 200 | 300 | 900 | 2,700 | 8,600 | 6,600 | 4,400 | 4,000 | 4,600 | 32,300 |
| Spain | 1,400 | 1,100 | 2,300 | 2,300 | 2,500 | 3,300 | 4,000 | 8,600 | 8,100 | 33,600 |
| Sweden | 3,000 | 12,000 | 14,500 | 14,600 | 18,100 | 19,600 | 32,000 | 29,000 | 27,300 | 170,100 |
| Switzerland | 7,900 | 7,500 | 9,700 | 8,600 | 10,900 | 16,700 | 24,500 | 36,000 | 41,600 | 163,400 |
| United Kingdom | 4,300 | 3,900 | 5,500 | 4,800 | 5,200 | 5,100 | 10,000 | 30,000 | 57,700 | 126,500 |
| Total | 65,400 | 98,300 | 164,400 | 194,200 | 172,250 | 220,450 | 306,900 | 426,100 | 544,400 | 2,192,400 |

SOURCE: Secretariat for Intergovernmental Consultations, Geneva.

123

eign workers in France, Germany, and the Netherlands has increased in recent years, thereby placing additional pressure on the integration process.[82] Throughout Europe, antirefugee feeling is being exploited by extreme right-wing political parties, which advocate stricter immigration and naturalization legislation as a prominent plank in their platforms.

## Overburdened Asylum Systems

The complex claims and large influxes of the new asylum seekers overload the existing procedures and mechanisms, which were established to deal with much smaller numbers of applicants. As a consequence, large backlogs of asylum applications have arisen, placing a severe strain on reception facilities and public and private relief efforts. Moreover, sending home unsuccessful applicants has proved to be extremely difficult. Human rights and religious groups strongly object to such deportation, and few Western countries feel comfortable about forcibly expelling large numbers of people who must return to situations of poverty and insecurity. Thus, the great majority of denied asylum applicants are not deported. For example, in the 1980s, most West European governments denied many Tamils, Iranians, and Turks refugee status on the grounds that they had not been targeted for individual persecution in their home countries. Although their requests were thus formally rejected, most have not been expelled or forcibly returned to their home countries. Rather, they typically have been treated as de facto refugees and have been accorded a form of humanitarian or non-Convention status. They enjoy only the minimum of legal protection and social care in most European countries[83] and remain in something of a legal limbo, not benefiting from international legal guarantees and subject to unpredictable political fluctuations. But so far most have been allowed to remain.

## Erecting Barriers to Entry

These developments spark concerns and raise questions among some sections of the European public, and they cast doubt on the host governments' ability to retain a reasonable measure of deliberate control over the entry and stay of foreigners. Responding to these pressures, European governments, like other Western governments, have increasingly turned to erecting barriers to prevent asylum seekers from ever reaching their territories.

By the early 1990s, most European nations had already begun to require visas for citizens from all the major asylum-producing countries. They began to use the staff of airlines and shipping companies to police their passengers' return tickets and documentation, and they fined carriers that brought in foreigners who either lacked documentation or carried false documentation.

Government officials also adopted a stricter interpretation of the refugee definition when examining asylum claims. Authorities widely recognize that the background of many of today's asylum seekers is varied and
complex and cannot be satisfactorily described by the "persecution" criterion in the UN Refugee Convention. Nevertheless, in recent years governments have refused to award refugee status if they find that an applicant's
claim is not justified on the basis of a strict reading of the definition
outlined in the 1951 Refugee Convention. The proportion of those considered genuine refugees, therefore, declined from about 50 percent in the
early 1980s to less than 20 percent by the end of the 1980s.[84] In the early
1990s, on average, only 10 percent or fewer of asylum applicants in Europe were granted refugee status.

## Europe-wide Cooperation on Asylum

In addition to making individual efforts to stem the influx of asylum
seekers, by the mid-1980s European states had also adopted informal
common policies to control their borders. Even before formal discussions
about steps for controlling large-scale influxes of refugees and irregular
movements within the European Community began in 1985, the Dutch
and Swiss governments, for example, had formulated a joint policy on the
handling of displaced Tamils.[85]

Europe-wide cooperation on asylum greatly increased after the decision by European Community heads of state to create a "Single Europe."
The removal of internal borders and the creation of a common external
border have considerable bearing on refugee and asylum policy and constitute important components in the establishment of a unified internal market in Europe. In recent years, several regional and intergovernmental
groups have focused on this issue;[86] most of the meetings, however, have
been closed to outside observers, including the UNHCR, reflecting the
growing restrictionism in the region.

In December 1988, an intergovernmental group of coordinators was
established within the European Community to draw up plans for dealing
with asylum seekers. A program was drawn up that included two conventions. The first, approved at the Dublin summit of EC heads of state in
June 1990, identified procedures for determining which state was responsible for examining an asylum request. The Dublin Asylum Convention
does not attempt to harmonize the different national laws on asylum. A
draft external Frontiers Convention deals with procedures for enforcing
the future external border of the European Community, including provisions on visas and sanctions against transport companies; in late 1992, this
convention was deadlocked by a dispute between the United Kingdom
and Spain over the status of Gibraltar.

Parallel to these EC initiatives, the five countries at the center of
Europe—Germany, France, and the Benelux countries—signed the

Schengen agreement, which contains provisions establishing uniform principles for controlling their common borders and for harmonizing conditions of entry and visa requirements. In an effort to prevent unsuccessful applicants from lodging successive asylum claims in the same or other countries, the Schengen agreement also includes a formula for determining which country is responsible for receiving an asylum request. Finally, the agreement specifies that a permanent information system, known as the Schengen Information System, is to be set up and computerized, listing the personal details of all asylum seekers. When the agreement eventually comes into force, it is likely that other EC states will join the Schengen agreement; Italy, Spain, and Portugal have already become parties to it.

These agreements are to be supplemented by parallel conventions extending many of these rules to countries that are not currently members of the EC, with the intention of extending a *cordon sanitaire* around the European Community. If fully implemented, the plan may make it impossible for asylum seekers to arrive in an EC state to present a request for asylum. Already, by the end of 1992, EC government ministers had proposed sending prospective asylum seekers back to the first "safe" country they transited on their way to Western Europe. Germany has separately negotiated agreements with Romania and Bulgaria to return rejected asylum seekers in exchange for financial incentives and has indicated its intention to reach similar agreements with Poland, Czechoslovakia, and Hungary.

Despite these considerable steps toward greater cooperation on asylum and migration policies, serious differences of interests and approaches remain among European Community members. Immigration and asylum policies are closely linked to national security and the exercise of sovereignty and touch on politically sensitive areas. Southern European states, including Italy, Spain, Portugal, and Greece, have been key points of entry and transit for nationals from the Third World, who then traditionally moved on to the more prosperous northern European states for permanent settlement. Germany, the Scandinavian states, and others in the North want their southern neighbors to take primary responsibility for those who arrive on their territories. But the Mediterranean states, who already host large numbers of North African migrants (many of them illegal), fear that in the future they may find themselves with too great a refugee burden.

Other geographical factors among EC countries also play a role in determining different approaches. For example, with the advent of the Single Europe after January 1, 1993, frontier controls on individuals who cross internal community borders should disappear, while controls should be maintained and strengthened at the community's external borders. Great Britain, Ireland, and Denmark contest this and insist on retaining strong border controls at ports of entry; in contrast, Italy, with its long sea frontiers, advocates after-entry control, which requires national identity cards and greater police power. By late 1992, it was unclear whether an agreement could be reached among all EC states regarding the lifting of internal border controls.

## Asylum Policy at a Crossroads

Asylum in the West is at a crossroads. Governments seem reluctant to open their doors to asylum seekers when they are unsure how many will seek to benefit from their hospitality and for how long. Thus, every Western government is having difficulty reconciling the rights of refugees to a fair determination of their claims to asylum with its own need to maintain an effective immigrant control mechanism.

Although immigration controls are necessary and must be part of the overall response to growing migration pressures, evidence suggests that enforcement measures alone are insufficient to deal with the problem. Barriers to entry can be only partially effective, particularly along the Mexican–U.S. border and the porous southern and eastern borders of Europe. Thus, despite redoubled border-control efforts and a 1986 program by the United States to legalize more than 3 million undocumented persons, most observers estimate that already there are once again about 3 million illegal migrants in the United States.[87] The U.S. experience has been repeated throughout Europe and East Asia. Moreover, even if control mechanisms were sufficient, it is unlikely that democratic industrial states could engage in measures harsh enough to have a lasting effect, as these would breed unacceptably deep social tensions. Rigid policies adopted by receiving countries to prevent entry and halt the flow of illegal migrants would also have significant international repercussions, creating conflicts between sending and receiving countries and damaging the attempted economic and political liberalization of newly democratizing countries in the South and the East.

There is no magical "international" solution to the problem of uncontrolled refugee flows, and concerted international political action on these multifaceted and complex issues is not easy. Migratory pressures in the South and the East are likely to intensify in the 1990s, and Western countries will not be able to shut themselves completely off from these migrations by instituting policies aimed at restricting movements. Simply building barriers will not make the problem go away, nor will it ensure a stable political base for East–West and South–North relations. The way forward in this difficult situation is to resolve or prevent the problems of displacement by adopting an integrated approach in which foreign policy, human rights policy, and relief and development policies are formulated to address the underlying causes of the problem while at the same time preserving the practice of asylum.

Until recently, the UNHCR has been slow to appreciate the significance and complexity of developments in Western Europe and in other parts of the world. During the 1990s, the UNHCR has been confronted with one refugee emergency following another in rapid, sometimes over-lapping succession. Refugee crises in Iraq, Bosnia, Kenya, Bangladesh, Nepal, the Caucasus, Tajikistan, Benin, Ghana, and Rwanda have strained the capacities of the UNHCR almost to the breaking point. At the same time, UNHCR is trying to resolve the long-standing refugee problems of the previous decade primarily through repatriation in a context of continuing instability and insecurity. In the post–Cold War era, the UNHCR is becoming increasingly involved in providing assistance and protection to displaced people in situations of internal conflict. The current refugee crisis raises questions about the viability of the UNHCR and about the capacity of existing organized structures to cope with (much less resolve) today's refugee problems. The UNHCR is the organization mandated by the international community to protect and assist refugees. Does it have the infrastructure and resources to do the job? What can it do to alleviate the current refugee stalemate, to help resolve the global problem of refugees, and to prepare for the almost inevitable refugee burdens of tomorrow?

# 6

## The Limitations of the International Refugee Regime

The international refugee regime is rapidly being overwhelmed by the unprecedented refugee crises that began during the past decade, and it is ill equipped to address either the causes or the consequences of the problems involved. Host and resettlement countries feel that the economic, social, and political costs of dealing with refugee problems have become too high. The traditional hospitality of many Third World countries has been replaced by intolerance and restrictionist policies. Industrialized countries have become increasingly reluctant to finance international refugee aid, to resettle refugees from the Third World, or to admit asylum seekers and to consider their claims fully. Any humanitarian consensus seems to have vanished; the international cooperation that helped resolve the postwar refugee problem in Europe and alleviate refugee crises in Africa, Asia, and Latin America during the 1960s and 1970s is more difficult to obtain.

Many observers feel that the international refugee regime, and in particular the UNHCR, is not doing enough to contain a deteriorating situation. Yet in reality the major responsibility for providing protection, assistance, and long-term solutions lies with states. Governments have traditionally sought to preserve their territorial sovereignty by controlling their borders. And in no area do they more jealously guard their sovereignty than in immigration affairs. Yet in the aftermath of the massive dislocations of World Wars I and II, governments recognized that, although in a legal and political sense they retained absolute power over immigration and refugee matters, their effective power to limit transnational population movements was limited and that the global refugee problem far outstripped their individual capacities to manage. Thus, the international refugee regime was established to serve the interests of governments and to facilitate both burden sharing and the coordination of policies regarding the treatment of refugees. Although refugee policy has always tended to be restrictive, the history of the interwar and contemporary refugee regimes provides many examples of governmental flexibility that is sorely needed today.

The task now for the UNHCR is to demonstrate how multilateral cooperation can continue to be a more effective means of coping with refugee problems than unilateral alternatives. The High Commissioner must first persuade policymakers that the global refugee problem is not a humanitarian problem requiring charity, but a political problem requiring political solutions; moreover, it cannot be separated from such other areas of international concern as migration, human rights, international security, and development assistance. Such an approach raises complex questions of harmonization of efforts, determination of institutional responsibilities, coordination, and allocation of resources.

In this situation, the UNHCR can continue to play a major role, either by providing emergency aid and technical support or by offering legal protection to asylum seekers. The UNHCR can also serve as a catalyst to bring together affected governments and international agencies to consult on appropriate international responses, such as long-term development assistance, and to provide the administrative medium for more effective cooperation on refugee issues.

But the High Commissioner, acting alone, is unlikely to be effective in the long term, because she cannot resolve the political causes of refugee problems. Thus, the challenge of the 1990s for the international community is to respond not only to the immediate humanitarian problems of refugees and displaced people, but in the long run to confront the conditions that lead to these dislocations. These are political tasks that require a more active role from national policymakers and a greater willingness to utilize fully the UN and regional mechanisms on security, peacekeeping and peacemaking, and human rights to anticipate and react effectively to refugee incidents around the world.

## The UNHCR: Organizational and Structural Limits

A number of international agencies exist to respond to refugee crises. Among these are the UNHCR, whose mandate is to protect and assist refugees; the International Committee for the Red Cross, which assists people caught in conflicts; the World Food Program, which coordinates food aid to refugees; and UNICEF, which aids children. Elsewhere, the United Nations Relief and Works Administration for Palestinian Refugees (UNRWA) aids Palestinians in the Middle East, and the International Organization for Migration arranges for the transportation of refugees resettling overseas and for the safe and humane repatriation of refugees and migrants from countries unable or unwilling to absorb them.

The international community also relies on a vast network of non-governmental organizations (NGOs), ranging from large international agencies to small organizations working in one particular country, to offer assistance programs. As implementing partners for the UNHCR, NGOs bear the brunt of delivering food and providing shelter, water, sanitation, and health care to refugees. Where funding is available, they also provide community outreach services, and educational and skills programs.

More than two-thirds of all international assistance is channeled through the UNHCR, the principal international organization servicing the needs of refugees. This specialized UN agency, with a staff of over 2,700, representatives in over 80 countries, and annual expenditures well over $1 billion, protects and assists refugees and works toward one of three durable solutions: voluntary repatriation, local integration, or third-country resettlement.

Notwithstanding its central position, the UNHCR suffers from several structural and organizational problems. These involve resources and planning, the ambiguity of international law and norms, the restricted base of its state membership, and the chronic tension that exists between the humanitarian tasks of UNHCR and the political context in which it has to work.

## Resource Constraints

The most significant institutional weakness of the UNHCR is its dependence on voluntary contributions to carry out its programs. Less than 5 percent of the UNHCR's annual expenditures are covered by the UN Regular Budget; the remainder of the UNHCR's funding and resources comes from voluntary contributions, mainly from national governments. Its assistance activities are divided broadly into General and Special Programs. Each year, the High Commissioner's Executive Committee approves a General Program budget, comprising activities financed through the annual program, the Emergency Fund, and appeals to all UN members for the resources needed to cover the program year. The primary allocation of these resources goes to the traditional areas of the High Commissioner's competence: emergency relief, voluntary repatriation, integration into host societies, and resettlement.

In addition to its General Program budget, the UNHCR, at the request of the Secretary-General or the UN General Assembly, undertakes Special Programs; these include major new and unforeseen emergency operations and transportation and rehabilitation assistance to refugees and displaced people who have returned to their homes. Special Programs are the subject of specific fundraising appeals to interested governments and are financed from trust funds framed by particular purposes and conditions. Thus, the UNHCR must raise funds for each new refugee problem.

The level of annual UNHCR expenditures has increased progressively over the years. Until the mid-1970s, the UNHCR spent only modest sums, the annual average remaining less than $10 million during the

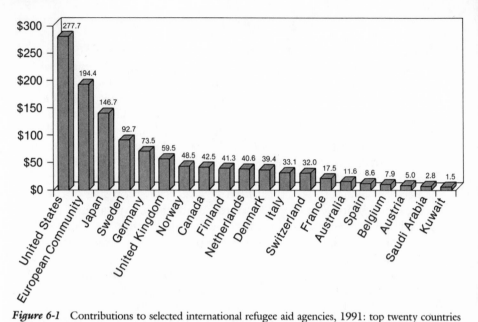

**Figure 6-1** Contributions to selected international refugee aid agencies, 1991: top twenty countries (in millions of dollars). This graph reports the amounts of financial assistance provided to international agencies by countries. The relative significance of contributions should be considered not only in terms of absolute size, but also in relation to population and gross national product. Included are estimated 1991 contributions to UNHCR, IOM, and UNRWA. Each country's contributions to the European Community are not reflected. Bilateral aid, some forms of aid that are not exclusively or even primarily designated for refugees, and aid through such agencies as the World Bank, which may benefit refugees, are also not reflected. (SOURCE: *World Refugee Survey 1992* [Washington, D.C.: U.S. Committee for Refugees, 1992].)

1960s and just exceeding $20 million during the early 1970s. Between 1971 and 1978, however, annual expenditures rose from $9 million to $135 million; then they jumped to $270 million in 1979 and shot up to nearly $500 million in 1980. These dramatic leaps in expenditure came in response to major refugee emergencies in Indochina, Africa, and Afghanistan. During the 1980s, the annual spending of UNHCR remained over $400 million. Thus, even allowing for inflation, the level of expenditures amounted to a fifteenfold increase over that of the early 1970s.[1]

The 1990s have presented the UNHCR with several new refugee emergencies, and its expenditures for Special Programs have increased dramatically. In 1991, as a result of emergency relief operations in northern Iraq and the Horn of Africa, the total voluntary funds expenditure amounted to $862.5 million, an increase of almost 60 percent over 1990.[2] In 1992, new refugee and humanitarian crises in the former Yugoslavia, Bangladesh, the Horn of Africa, and southern Africa, as well as continued responsibilities in northern Iraq and new repatriation programs in Cambodia, Ethiopia, and Angola, are estimated to have pushed UNHCR expenditures for the year over $1 billion.[3]

As noted, the geographical distribution of UNHCR assistance has changed considerably since the agency's inception, reflecting the shift of the refugee problem from being a European problem to becoming a global crisis. During the 1950s and 1960s, the majority of UNHCR expenditures were directed toward Europe. In 1963, for example, European states received approximately 51 percent of total UNHCR expenditures, but by 1970 the European percentage had dropped to 7 percent, and it had fallen to less than 5 percent by 1990. During the early 1960s, assistance programs for African refugees accounted for 24 percent of UNHCR expenditures, a figure that had climbed to 68 percent by 1970. During the late 1970s and early 1980s, the mass exoduses in Indochina and Afghanistan consumed some 60 percent of UNHCR finances. With prolonged emergencies in the Horn of Africa and southern Africa in the mid- to late 1980s, Africa again accounted for 50 percent of expenditures. Recent conflicts and refugee crises in Central America have taken 10 percent of UNHCR resources.[4] In the early 1990s, a large proportion of expenditures went toward UNHCR Special Programs in the Persian Gulf, ex-Yugoslavia, and the Horn of Africa. In general, UNHCR expenditures have tracked the shifts in geographic distribution of refugees around the world, and continue to grow as refugee numbers increase.

The vast majority of the UNHCR's annual spending is covered by donations from industrialized nations: the United States, Western European countries, Japan, Canada, and Australia (see Figure 6-1). In 1991, the top twenty contributors to the UNHCR provided 97 percent of total contributions. The Soviet Union and its allies traditionally offered no support. Among donor countries, the contributions have varied considerably. In total contributions to the three principal international refugee agencies (the UNHCR, UNRWA, and the International Organization for

Migration), the United States has consistently given the highest amounts ($277.7 million in 1991), followed by Japan ($146.7 million), Sweden ($92.7 million), Germany ($73.5 million), Great Britain ($59.5 million), Norway ($48.5 million), and Canada ($42.5 million).

Up until the mid-1980s, U.S. contributions for humanitarian assistance generally kept pace with the explosive growth in refugee numbers. Then, during 1985–1989, U.S. financial support declined consistently. Its share of the UNHCR's total expenditures dropped from 30 percent in 1982 to 22 percent in 1989, during a period when the number of refugees under UNHCR protection increased by 50 percent. American financial support for ICRC, another important refugee agency, dropped from 30 percent to 15 percent of the agency's total expenditures, from 1985 to 1988.[5] The Bush administration did little to rectify the situation, proposing marginal increases in its spending on refugee assistance.

On a per capita basis, the level of U.S. contributions is also not very impressive (see Table 6-1). In 1991, Norway ($11.28), Sweden ($10.78),

*Table 6-1*   1991 Contributions to International Refugee Aid Agencies, Top 20 Countries (ranked by contribution per capita)

| Country | Contribution per Capita | Population (in millions) | Contribution (in millions) | GNP per Capita |
|---|---|---|---|---|
| Norway | $11.28 | 4.3 | $48.51 | $21,850 |
| Sweden | 10.78 | 8.6 | 92.72 | 21,710 |
| Finland | 8.27 | 5.0 | 41.34 | 22,060 |
| Denmark | 7.72 | 5.1 | 39.38 | 20,510 |
| Switzerland | 4.71 | 6.8 | 31.99 | 30,270 |
| Luxembourg | 3.38 | 0.4 | 1.35 | 24,860 |
| Netherlands | 2.71 | 15.0 | 40.59 | 16,010 |
| Canada | 1.59 | 26.8 | 42.50 | 19,020 |
| Japan | 1.19 | 123.8 | 146.73 | 23,730 |
| United States | 1.10 | 252.8 | 277.73 | 21,100 |
| Kuwait | 1.08 | 1.4 | 1.52 | N/A |
| United Kingdom | 1.03 | 57.5 | 59.51 | 14,750 |
| Germany | 0.92 | 79.5 | 73.47 | 16,200 |
| Belgium | 0.80 | 9.9 | 7.90 | 16,390 |
| Australia | 0.66 | 17.5 | 11.56 | 14,440 |
| Austria | 0.64 | 7.7 | 4.95 | 17,360 |
| Italy | 0.57 | 57.7 | 33.07 | 15,150 |
| France | 0.31 | 56.7 | 17.54 | 17,830 |
| Spain | 0.22 | 39.0 | 8.55 | 9,150 |
| New Zealand | 0.20 | 3.5 | 0.70 | 11,800 |

SOURCE: *World Refugee Survey 1992* (Washington, D.C.: U.S. Committee for Refugees, 1992).

**Table 6-2** Refugees Resettled and Persons Granted Asylum in Relation to Local Population (in order of refugees-to-population ratio)

| Resettlement Country | 1975–1990 Cumulative | 1990 Only | Local Population | Ratio of Refugee-to-Population |
|---|---|---|---|---|
| Sweden | 121,154 | 12,839 | 8.6 | 1/71 |
| Canada | 325,045 | 37,820 | 26.8 | 1/82 |
| Australia | 183,104 | 10,281 | 17.5 | 1/96 |
| United States | 1,478,184 | 122,326 | 252.8 | 1/171 |
| Denmark | 29,480 | 747 | 5.1 | 1/173 |
| Norway[a] | 21,708 | 3,767 | 4.3 | 1/198 |
| New Zealand | 11,428 | 440 | 3.5 | 1/306 |
| France | 200,030 | 13,073 | 56.7 | 1/283 |
| Switzerland | 22,295 | 808 | 6.8 | 1/305 |
| Austria | 24,249 | 3,678 | 7.7 | 1/318 |
| Netherlands | 21,880 | 1,709 | 15.0 | 1/686 |
| Germany[b] | 91,478 | 6,518 | 79.5 | 1/869 |
| Spain | 38,713 | 527 | 39.0 | 1/1,007 |
| United Kingdom[a] | 14,897 | 1,100 | 57.5 | 1/3,860 |

NOTE: The primary source for numbers of refugees resettled or granted asylum was the U.S. State Department. Countries that have established resettlement programs generally provide particularly precise data, but data were not available for all countries for all years.

[a] Statistics were unavailable for 1975–1981.

[b] Does not include 222,000 ethnic Germans from the Soviet Union, Poland, and Romania.

SOURCE: *World Refugee Survey 1992* (Washington, D.C.: U.S. Committee for Refugees, 1992).

Finland ($8.27), and Denmark ($7.72) provided the largest contributions per capita to the three principal refugee agencies; Japan ranked ninth ($1.19), and the United States tenth ($1.10).

The generosity of the industrialized states can also be measured by the number of refugees resettled and granted asylum in relation to domestic population (see Table 6-2). During the years 1975 to 1990, Sweden had the highest ratio (1 in 71), followed by Canada (1 in 82), Australia (1 in 96), the United States (1 in 171), Denmark (1 in 173), and Norway (1 in 198). Overall, in terms of both financial aid and resettlement of refugees, the Scandinavian countries are the most generous of the industrialized nations; southern European countries are the least generous; and the traditional resettlement countries—the United States, Canada, and Australia—are in the middle. Although Japan has substantially increased its financial contributions in recent years, it stands out as a rich country that provides mid-level assistance but admits practically no refugees—a record that could clearly stand continued improvement.

Although the financial support offered to the UNHCR is significant, it usually falls short of the UNHCR's real needs. Accurate prediction of resource requirements is inherently difficult, and UNHCR programs often require rapid adjustment by field and headquarters staff in the course of their implementation. Because the problems faced by refugees are often unpredictable and usually urgent, response cannot be postponed to some future program cycle if resources are not immediately available. Although the High Commissioner has available an emergency fund of $25 million, a single refugee emergency can easily swallow this up. The Kurdish refugee emergencies in Turkey and Iran in 1991 and the crisis in the former Yugoslavia in 1992, for instance, required the immediate expenditure of hundreds of millions of dollars. The UNHCR must constantly request additional contributions in order to meet chronic shortfalls. Efforts by the international community to deal with displacements of ex-Yugoslavs in Europe, of Kurds and other war victims in the Persian Gulf, of Burmese Muslims in Bangladesh, and of Sudanese, Somalis, Ethiopians, Liberians, Mozambicans, and others in Africa have exacerbated both the resource and the mandate limitations constraining the UNHCR. The current complexity of refugee flows and the exponential growth in numbers of displaced people in recent years have presented enormous challenges to the UNHCR with regard to planning, managing, and funding its worldwide network of protection and relief programs. More than ever, a more comprehensive approach is needed to meet these contingencies.

The UNHCR is increasingly being asked by the United Nations to bear more responsibility and leadership in a growing number of international crises, but with diminishing resources. Although the UNHCR serves twice the number of refugees it did a decade ago, the financial support levels for General Programs of the UNHCR have remained virtually unchanged. The overall lack of funds has threatened to reduce and postpone repatriation programs, cancel needed improvements in refugee facilities, and stem efforts to avert new flows of refugees. It has also forced the UNHCR to make cuts in some nutrition and education programs.

According to one report, in 1980 the UNHCR had approximately $60 for each refugee under its care and protection; by 1990 this had fallen to $38 each.[6] Moreover, some refugee groups receive even less than this small sum per capita. According to one researcher, during the 1980s, individual refugees from the Ogaden, Cambodia, and Afghanistan received a sum of perhaps $10 to 20 per year; Angolan and Eritrean refugees received only about half this amount. On average, a Third World refugee received around 5 cents a day through the UNHCR during the last decade.[7] In most cases this meager sum was supposed to cover not only food, water, and shelter, but also transport, logistical support, and medium- to long-term development assistance for both refugees and the host population. These sums are clearly insufficient, a fact admitted by the UNHCR and many concerned governments.

## The UNHCR's Dual Role

The problems facing the UNHCR are not exclusively economic. They also have to do with the contradictory role it plays in refugee affairs today. The High Commissioner has the dual mandate of protecting refugees and overseeing relief operations. Yet governments largely determine the rules and procedures by which the UNHCR must operate. To initiate relief operations, the UNHCR must solicit funds from the industrialized countries and must obtain approval or acquiescence from the governments of both developing and developed nations to operate within their states. Thus the UNHCR must confront states on politically sensitive protection issues at the same time that it asks them to contribute to its budget and to permit aid programs to operate within their territories.

Increasingly, the UNHCR is required to operate in the midst of ongoing conflicts, where even its most humanitarian activities are perceived as "political." In situations where fight is conflict-generated, conditions are often life-threatening because of the inability of relief workers to reach those in need. In Somalia, for example, where all government collapsed in the early 1990s and where an extremely vicious interclan war generated massive numbers of famine victims, the United Nations was unable for a long time to intervene or to offer assistance. In the newly independent republics of former Yugoslavia, United Nations influence on the behavior of combatant forces was extremely limited, and even the delivery of humanitarian assistance to war victims was fraught with danger and uncertainty.

The UNHCR's dependence on voluntary contributions forces it to adopt policies that reflect the interests and priorities of the major donor countries. Politics and foreign policy priorities cause donor governments to favor some refugee groups over others. During the 1980s, for example, international aid levels per Afghan refugee in pro-Western Pakistan were more than three times higher than those allocated to Afghan refugees in anti-Western Iran. Similarly, during the 1991 Gulf crisis, international aid to Iraqi refugees in Iran was substantially less than that to Kurds who fled to Turkey and other areas. And now that repatriation to Afghanistan has begun from both Pakistan and Iran, international aid is directed almost exclusively to refugees repatriating from Pakistan.

Because the UNHCR relies on new donations for each new situation as it arises, its independence is restricted. Additional funds come from the emergency or relief budgets of the industrialized governments, which often explicitly earmark funds or exert direct and indirect political pressure to guide their use.[8] During the 1980s, for example, the UNHCR objected to the U.S. policy of returning Salvadorans to their homelands and criticized the substandard conditions of collective accommodation centers for asylum seekers within the Federal Republic of Germany; but in both instances the High Commissioner could exercise only very limited influence, because American and German donations form an essential portion of the UNHCR budget. Criticism was met with threats to cut off funding. In the 1990s, the United States and West European governments have continued to override UNHCR protests and disregard widespread criticism of their forcible repatriation of thousands of Haitians and Albanians.

In such situations in the past, the UNHCR has often either become subservient to the policies of powerful donors or become immobilized, thereby damaging its credibility as an effective and impartial advocate for refugees. The High Commissioner simply lacks the financial independence and institutional strength to challenge benefactors or to embark on programs without the cooperation of host governments. As a result, the world's principal refugee protection agency is prevented from unduly criticizing either donor or host governments' policies.

Governments have the power, whatever their legal obligations, to turn a blind eye to violations of the rights of refugees. Asylum countries may be unwilling to receive or provide protection to particular groups of refugees lest they risk becoming party to conflicts involving their neighbors, damage diplomatic relations with nearby countries, or encourage a mass influx of people seeking refuge. The UNHCR has limited leverage in persuading host nations such as Thailand and Honduras to protect refugees, given that it needs these governments' permission to maintain camps in their territories. Effective protection requires operational independence; but setting up camps, generating assistance efforts, and raising money necessitate dependence on national governments.

This places the UNHCR in a situation of structural disharmony. One analyst has noted that the better the High Commissioner performs the agency's protection function, the more seriously effective oversight of relief is jeopardized, since such action risks alienating the governments on which UNHCR depends for its budget and its permission to operate.[9] The better funded and more expansive the UNHCR's organization of physical care becomes, the more heavily it relies on national governments for money and authorization to advance assistance efforts and the weaker its position becomes in the disinterested pursuit of protection. No refugee agency can simultaneously be independent for the purpose of protection and dependent for the purpose of relief.

As a first step toward improving effectiveness, therefore, the High Commissioner must be given a resource base that will permit more autonomous operations. Donor governments must resist earmarking funds to promote their political priorities. Refugees, as a persistent feature of international life, require sustained financial allocations and sustained attention by the international community. Consideration should be given to funding the UNHCR by assessed rather than voluntary contributions, thereby acknowledging the permanent character of the refugee problem and the need to deal with the issue systematically.

## International Refugee Law and the Obligations of States

The High Commissioner's activities on behalf of refugees are generally limited to providing material assistance, citing violations of international law, and publicly condemning those violations. Because the office has no power to force countries to provide refugees with even minimal humanitarian treatment, the High Commissioner's major weapons for urging nations to abide by international refugee law are diplomatic pressure and moral suasion.

International refugee law provides a set of standards against which the actions of states can be measured, and it places some pressure (especially on nations that have acceded to international instruments) to meet the obligations these impose.[10] The UNHCR's strategy is to measure state actions against international standards. Unfortunately, the obligations international refugee law imposes lend themselves to a variety of interpretations. Therefore, considerable scope exists for governments to perceive their obligations in ways that suit their policy goals. Moreover, no supranational authority exists to enforce the rules of the international refugee regime, and few if any safeguards are built into the law itself to prevent abuse by states or to compel governments to administer international refugee law in a consistent and fair manner.

While most states agree that refugees ought to be protected and that the principles of the international refugee instruments ought to be observed, the extent of compliance should not be overstated. Most governments have in recent years circumvented several major provisions and have exploited areas left unregulated. For example, there is no mandate to provide protection and assistance to refugees; almost all aid is voluntary and discretionary. Thus, in order to limit the increasing numbers of asylum seekers, governments have employed a number of technically permissible measures, including placing refugees in harsh, austere camps and even deporting them to countries other than their place of origin. Such deterrents are consistent with the letter, if not the spirit, of international refugee law.[11] The UNHCR can do little but protest such actions. Recalcitrant governments can only be persuaded—not compelled—to conform to international standards regarding refugees.

Considerable controversy surrounds the question of who should determine when a person is a refugee. The major problem is that granting asylum is not specifically dealt with in either the 1951 Convention or the 1967 Protocol, although it is recognized in the Universal Declaration of Human Rights, which states that every individual has "the right to seek and enjoy asylum" when in danger. While refugees have a right to seek asylum, states do not necessarily agree that they have an obligation to grant it. In drafting the 1951 Refugee Convention, Western governments rejected a provision that would have guaranteed a right to asylum. Although there have been some efforts in recent decades to move toward recognition of an individual's right to apply for asylum, such a right is far from being recognized by the international community. In 1977, an attempt to draft an internationally binding convention on the right to asylum failed when it became apparent that any changes in legal standards that countries would be willing to endorse would effectively narrow, rather than expand, their protection responsibilities.[12] In the realm of asylum, states remain the final arbiters of refugees' fates. They retain the power to grant and to deny asylum.

Furthermore, the international refugee instruments leave it up to governments to tailor refugee determination procedures to their administrative, judicial, and constitutional provisions. States regard these procedures as aspects of their national sovereignty and have been unwilling to transfer this authority to the UNHCR or to any other intergovernmental body. The role of the UNHCR is restricted to advising and assisting applicants for refugee status and participating in an advisory or voting role in the decision-making process.

Nevertheless, the UNHCR has a more active role in some countries than in others. France and Belgium, for example, allow a formal institutionalized role for the UNHCR; and Germany, Great Britain, and Canada offer it informal access to government decisionmakers. In the United States, apart from the possibility of contacting government authorities to express its views, the UNHCR has no role at all in the refugee determination process. For the past twelve years, UNHCR pressure on the United States to make its policy toward asylum seekers accord with international standards has had little visible effect.

The past U.S. policy of interdicting boats carrying Haitians bound for Florida is a clear example of the lack of UNHCR influence on state behavior. From the program's inception in 1981 until the end of 1990, Haitians interdicted at sea had less than five minutes to answer questions posed by an official of the Immigration and Naturalization Service (INS).[13] These interviews were often conducted on a U.S. Coast Guard cutter's deck, without regard to privacy and without legal representation or outside observers, such as the UNHCR.

The UNHCR argued that the interdiction measures deprived asylum seekers at sea of access to counsel and of the appeal possibilities that they would have been entitled to had they entered the United States. In 1990, human and civil rights groups filed a petition with the Inter-American Commission on Human Rights of the Organization of American States, claiming that American practice violated internationally accepted standards of providing fair hearings for claimants to refugee status.[14] In May 1992, the United States stopped conducting asylum hearings on Coast Guard cutters altogether and reverted to a policy of mass return of Haitians. The UNHCR protested, to very little visible effect.

## Definitional Problems

International law is also ambiguous in defining the term *refugees,* and there is widespread disagreement within and between countries on the appropriate criteria for conferring refugee status on an individual. The determination of refugee status is left exclusively in the hands of states. The definition of refugee incorporated in the 1951 Convention and the 1967 Protocol is limited to persons fearing a narrow spectrum of human rights violations—persecution for reasons of race, religion, nationality, membership of a particular social group, or political opinion.

Policy debates focus on the difficulty of separating political reasons for flight, which qualify people for refugee status, from economic motives, which do not. Frequently, the choice is not between a spurious claim without any merit and a clear-cut case of a well-founded fear of persecution. In fact it is extremely difficult to distinguish between migration-inducing events that are political and ones that are not. In many refugee situations today, the economic and political causes of the migrations are inextricably mixed. Many developing countries have few resources, weak government structures, and poorly designed development programs. In such places, economic hardships are generally exacerbated by political violence. Thus, in the cases of boat refugees from desperately poor countries like Haiti and Albania, Western immigration officials are confronted with having to decide whether people who are driven abroad by impoverishment that is directly attributable to unequal land tenure systems maintained by brutal state force or to their governments' inability or willful refusal to meet subsistence or protection needs are in fact refugees according to the 1951 Convention. Under such circumstances, it is difficult to determine whether the sending government's conduct constitutes a form of persecution.

The debate over definition has placed the UNHCR in frequent opposition to governments. The UNHCR and a number of international legal experts and refugee advocates urge a more generous reading of the qualifications for refugee status. They argue that the definition of *refugee* has been widened in practice to cover various people in diverse situations who need assistance and protection. The most notable of these expansions is found in the Convention on Refugee Problems in Africa, a regional instrument adopted by the Organization of African Unity in 1969, which includes people fleeing "external aggression, internal civil strife, or events seriously disturbing public order" in African countries.[15] The Cartagena Declaration of 1984 covering Central American refugees also goes beyond the 1951 UN Convention, by including "persons who have fled their country because their lives, safety or freedom have been threatened by generalized violence, foreign aggression, internal conflicts, massive violation of human rights or other circumstances which have seriously disturbed public order."[16]

These regional legal norms are in fact much more inclusive and consistent with the actual causes of flight in Africa and Central America and throughout the rest of the Third World than are the UN norms. Accordingly, in practice, over the past several decades the UNHCR has interpreted its mandate to cover people who have been forcibly displaced from their countries because of internal upheavals, armed conflicts, or massive violations of human rights. Western governments routinely contribute to UNHCR programs designed to assist and protect these broadly defined refugees in their regions of origin. In recent years, however, great resistance has emerged in the West to this pragmatic expansion of the *refugee* definition and of the UNHCR's mandate to asylum seekers and refugees who seek protection in the industrialized countries. In most industrialized nations, the 1951 definition—with its focus on individuals and on persecution—is used for resettlement and asylum purposes, although groups of people who are at risk of death or grave harm from violence if returned home are often given temporary protection by some governments.

Western states, therefore, have denied that the UNHCR's competence has been expanded in practice to include people other than Convention refugees in the North and have opposed efforts to persuade them to be more generous in their interpretation of refugee criteria. Indeed, to the contrary, they have moved toward a more narrow definition of refugee in recent years and have applied the criteria for refugee status more restrictively, as a means of excluding unwanted arrivals. In many Western countries onerous demands are made on applicants to prove beyond a reasonable doubt the authenticity of their claims, and even then only for a narrow range of causes.

During most of the 1980s, the United States maintained that asylum seekers must establish a "clear probability" of persecution rather than the lesser standard of a "well-founded fear of persecution," as specified in the 1980 Refugee Act and the 1951 U.N. Refugee Convention.[17] Thus, despite their fears of persecution and violence at the hands of death squads, Salvadorans throughout the 1980s were regularly returned to El Salvador by U.S. authorities on the grounds that they were victims of a "generalized climate of violence" rather than of individual persecution. There existed no neutral body to which refugees who were not accepted could appeal.

Today, asylum seekers in the United States not only have to establish their own motivations for flight, but the intentions of their persecutors as well. In a January 1992 case, *INS* v. *Jairo Jonathan Elias Zacarias,* the U.S. Supreme Court ruled that an 18-year-old Guatemalan, who had fled his country to seek asylum in the United States after refusing to join masked armed guerrillas who came several times to his home demanding that he join them, was not a refugee because he did not fear persecution on account of his political opinion.[18] In defending its refusal to grant asylum, the Bush administration had argued that Elias Zacarias's situation "was wholly unlike that of Christians under the Romans, the Jews under the Nazis, or any other people who were made to suffer for their race, nationality or beliefs."[19] Furthermore, the administration had maintained that the guerrillas intended to field an army and had argued that "even evidence that Guatemalan guerrillas kill people who do not join them . . . would not make [the] respondent eligible for asylum because such retaliation would not be 'on account of' [the] respondent's political opinion—it would be intended to terrorize prospective recruits into joining."[20]

Similarly, asylum applicants in Great Britain are required not only to demonstrate a subjective fear of persecution on returning to their home countries but to satisfy British authorities that their fear is "reasonable." Thus, Tamil asylum seekers are frequently denied refugee status because the British government considers the domestic situation in Sri Lanka to be safe enough to justify their return. (Several Tamils, forcibly returned in the past, have been tortured or otherwise treated inhumanely by Sri Lankan authorities.)

In Germany, the subjective view of persecution is completely discounted. German courts have even ruled in the past that, in the case of Turkish asylum applicants, the fear of torture is not sufficient for claiming fear of persecution, since torture in commonly inflicted on all prisoners in Turkey and not just on political prisoners.[21]

International rules regarding the treatment of refugees leave considerable room for flexibility; states can choose to interpret their obligations broadly or narrowly. Historically, state actions have depended not so much on an understanding of their legal responsibility or on humanitarian considerations as on advancing their own policy objectives. In recent years, states' perceived self-interest has elicited a restrictive reading of their protection functions.

## Protection of Refugees

In theory, asylum seekers are supposed to be protected by international protocols as soon as they cross national frontiers to seek refuge in another country. The primary protection found in the international legal instruments is contained in Article 33 of the Refugee Convention, which provides for *non-refoulement* of refugees: no state "shall expel or return [*refouler*] a refugee . . . to the frontiers of territories where his life or freedom would be threatened."[22] Therefore, asylum seekers cannot be sent back home against their will, at least until their cases are examined. While refugees reside in host countries, the UNHCR's mandate is to protect them against forcible repatriation, military attacks from the armed forces of their home countries, and legal and economic exploitation by the host nation. In practice, the UNHCR is rarely able to provide full protection.

Asylum countries are supposed to provide the same legal, police, and military protection to displaced aliens that they extend to their own citizens. But today's host countries often are too poor and too deficient in the requisite legal and security institutions to provide satisfactory protection even to their own citizens. As was noted earlier, the 1980s and 1990s are rife with incidents of governments sending their armies or unofficial forces across borders to attack refugees in UNHCR camps and settlements.

Governments disagree over the exact obligation that the principle of *non-refoulement* imposes on states. In the current restrictionist climate, many national policymakers say that it does not apply to groups seeking asylum if these are encountered before they actually enter a state's territory. Thus, regarding Haitian boat people, for example, the U.S. government took the position that "the U.N. Refugee Convention does not pose an obligation on a state with respect to refugees outside of its own territory,"[23] and therefore that the United States was not contravening Article 33 of the Convention regarding *non-refoulement*.

Governments have also taken measures to prevent refugees from arriving in their countries in the first place. Thus, visa restrictions and sanctions against airlines that carry undocumented passengers ensure that many would-be refugees never leave their home countries. For example, despite the forcible displacement of some 2.5 million inhabitants of the former Yugoslavia, caused by a policy of "ethnic cleansing," practically all Western European governments imposed visas on people fleeing conflict in this region in an attempt to bar their entry and to prevent them from being able to apply for political asylum. In early 1993, the U.S. imposed a blockade of Coast Guard cutters, patrol boats, and monitoring aircraft in the waters north of Haiti to block an expected wave of refugees seeking to reach the United States. Such actions violate the most fundamental principle of refugee protection: the right of refugees to flee their own countries and seek asylum from persecution in other countries.

Deterrence has become official policy for a number of states. Mexican officials stop the flow of Central Americans by capturing potential refugees before they cross Mexico's border with Guatemala; Malaysia and Thailand push off Vietnamese boatpeople; Thailand has on occasion forcibly turned back both Laotian refugees, as they have tried to cross the Mekong River, and Burmese refugees in the north; Honduras has regularly seized and forced back Salvadoran refugees attempting to cross the heavily patrolled border with El Salvador; and Western European border police sometimes enter airplanes at international airports, checking documents, automatically refusing asylum seekers entry, and expelling them either to neighboring countries or to their countries of origin, without considering the merits of their claims. Thus, large numbers of potential refugees in the world today never have the opportunity to file an asylum claim.

The principle of *non-refoulement* is interpreted by the United States and many other Western governments to apply only to persons who meet the Convention persecution standard. Accordingly, people fleeing generalized violence from civil war and intercommunal strife—such as Salvadorans, Guatemalans, and Haitians— have customarily not been protected by *non-refoulement,* despite the fact that the UNHCR and many international legal authorities contend that they should be.[24]

It is also the states' own business just how much material assistance, administrative attention, and legal aid they provide to refugees. The UNHCR can call attention to a country's legal obligations according to the UN Convention, but it has virtually no direct means to affect the course of action.

Governments are the decisive actors in refugee affairs. As long as states are the sole arbiters of status and protection and remain unwilling to accord autonomy to the UNHCR, it is difficult to see how international standards can be applied more even-handedly. Strengthening refugee protection requires adopting strategies that recognize the uses and limits of international instruments and legal norms and that go beyond them. Genuine refugee protection can only be accomplished through more active political intervention by states and intergovernmental organizations, both internationally and regionally.

## The Refugee Regime's Limited State Membership

Despite the fact that over 110 governments are signatories to the Convention, many major asylum countries have not yet signed the basic instruments. As of mid-1992, the only Asian signatories were Japan, the Republic of Korea, the People's Republic of China, Fiji, Papua New Guinea, and the Philippines; and the only Middle East signatories were Israel, Iran, and Yemen. Until only very recently, no Eastern European state except the former Yugoslavia had signed the Convention,[25] and as of late 1992 important refugee-generating countries such as Albania, Bulgaria, and the Russian Federation are not yet signatories. During the 1980s, neither Honduras nor Mexico had signed the Refugee Convention. Many of the world's largest and most urgent refugee situations have arisen in these regions. For over a decade, Pakistan hosted the largest refugee population of any country in the world; Thailand and Malaysia bore the burden of hundreds of thousands of Indochinese; Mexico continues to host large numbers of Guatemalans, Salvadorans, and Hondurans; and huge refugee populations have fled to other nonsignatory nations such as Bangladesh, Lebanon, and Jordan. While many of these nonsignatories have offered asylum seekers at least temporary refuge, they have done so on the basis of their own policy decisions rather than from an incurred responsibility to international legal instruments.

It is unclear what legal obligations actually apply to states that have not signed the refugee documents. Some scholars maintain that the basic principles of protection apply to all countries, and that certain minimum standards of treatment—including observance of the principles of *non-refoulement* and temporary refuge—are rooted in fundamental international law and are obligatory on all nations.[26] The UNHCR handbook on procedures states, "A person who meets the criteria of the UNHCR Statute qualifies for the protection of the United Nations provided by the High Commissioner regardless of whether or not he is in a country that is party to the 1951 Convention or 1967 Protocol."[27]

Nevertheless, the legal obligations of nonsignatories are not altogether clear to many nations. Thailand, for example, has consistently refused to ratify the conventions because, in the face of large influxes of refugees from Burma, Laos, Cambodia, and Vietnam, it does not want to undertake any new responsibilities. Thai authorities alternate between providing temporary refuge to Indochinese and Burmese refugees and pushing back unwanted new arrivals. Thailand sees itself as having no legal obligation to recognize the rights of potential refugees, except when doing so advances its national interest.

## Effectiveness of the UNHCR

It is extremely difficult to measure the effectiveness of the UNHCR, particularly since the agency often must work within a highly politicized environment. Certain large-scale operations in the past, such as the aid and repatriation programs involving East Bengali refugees in 1971, Burmese refugees in 1978–1979, and Namibian refugees in 1989, have been regarded as unequivocal successes. In other instances, the UNHCR has been criticized by humanitarian agencies, as well as by representatives of some governments that finance UNHCR programs, for its inability to provide protection for all groups of refugees and to offer quick and effective assistance. Critics cite the past UNHCR refusal to assume an active protection role on the Thai–Cambodian border; on the safety of forced returnees to Vietnam from Hong Kong and other Southeast Asian nations, of Haitian boat people to Port-au-Prince, and of Albanians to Tirana; on the risks confronting returnees to conflict zones in El Salvador, Cambodia, and Afghanistan; on the incompetent and often negligent treatment of refugees throughout southern Africa, the Horn of Africa, and Liberia; and on the abuse of asylum standards with respect to certain national groups of asylum seekers throughout much of Western Europe and the United States. They are concerned at the lack of an absolutely clear definition of the UNHCR's responsibility for protection on all levels; at the lack of a clear, consistent response to specific refugee situations; and at the lack of accountability for its programs and policies.

In the absence of clear and effective UNHCR human rights monitoring, NGOs are called upon to record human rights violations of refugees and to report these to regional and international bodies, which, in turn, can try to pressure offending governments to stop the abuses. But NGOs, like the UNHCR, are severely constrained in their activities by the desire of states to protect their sovereignty. Most relief and development agencies, moreover, prefer to remain neutral; and because they frequently fear expulsion from the countries in which they are working, they are reluctant to involve themselves in human rights advocacy and reporting. Human rights organizations, such as Amnesty International and the Lawyers' Committee for International Human Rights, fill some of this gap. Yet most of these organizations have their headquarters in the West, where their constituency base and funding are strongest. There is an urgent need to support NGO efforts to train and place independent human rights monitors in regions where they can provide liaison with local organizations interested in the problem, and to assess the protection needs of refugees, asylum seekers, and the internally displaced. These Refugee Watch organizations could record and publicize human rights violations without jeopardizing operational agency relief services.

The UNHCR has also been criticized frequently in the past for its slow response to large-scale and rapidly evolving humanitarian emergencies and for its lack of coordination with other international agencies and NGOs. Such deficiencies were graphically displayed, for example, in the UNHCR's initial response to the Kurdish exodus from Iraq after the Gulf War and in its response to some dire refugee situations in the Horn of Africa—in particular, in Somalia, Sudan, Ethiopia, and Kenya. In a number of countries, basic needs of refugees have not been met, leading to unacceptably high levels of malnutrition and mortality, as well as to damaging public criticism of the UNHCR's performance. The UNHCR clearly has a very limited capacity to procure, transport, store, and distribute large amounts of assistance within a short time frame,[28] and it has often proceeded without adequate assessment of relief needs, appropriate staffing, or clear coordination with other actors.

In an effort to rationalize international humanitarian relief efforts, the United Nations established a single Emergency Relief Coordinator in late 1991[29] and strengthened the ability of relief officials to provide aid to the needy when governments resist. Recently, the UNHCR also improved its overall emergency relief preparedness and response mechanisms by bolstering its standby capacity in emergency staffing, relief supplies, needs assessment, and emergency program implementation. Five Preparedness and Response Officers and attendant regional emergency response teams have been established. Stockpiles of commodities for use in emergencies have been amassed, and a roster of standby technical experts and relief workers for deployment in relief situations has been established. The UNHCR has signed an agreement with the World Food Program that is intended to clarify and simplify the coordination of all food relief. At the same time, UNHCR Emergency Management Training Programs, which have been carried out since 1985, have introduced a component on early warning for emergency response. Moreover, the UNHCR is in the process of institutionalizing a Refugee Emergency Alert system designed to forewarn the UNHCR of the likely scope, nature, and needs of refugee emergencies.

While the UNHCR and other humanitarian agencies have made a promising start in strengthening their capabilities to respond quickly to future mass exoduses, it is too early to assess the effectiveness of the new measures. Other major problems also exist—in particular, concerning the importance of increased involvement of refugees and local NGOs in decisionmaking and training, the psycho-social needs of refugees, the implementation of gender-specific programs with particular emphasis and sensitivity to the needs of female refugees, the need for developing institutional expertise in logistics (especially in accessing vulnerable populations in civil strife situations), and the timely provision of the right kinds of food and relief rations to refugees.[30]

Some of the UNHCR's problems derive from lack of adequate personnel and funding. To deal effectively with complex problems in a rapidly changing world, the UNHCR needs to enable managers to think strategically. For this to occur, the UNHCR must develop the capability to generate creative policy analyses, and the senior managers must take decisions on the basis of this information and advice. However, it is extremely difficult to undertake long-range planning, policy analysis, and multisector programming when personnel assigned to these tasks must constantly be redeployed from their normal functions to emergency operations in the former Yugoslavia, Iraq, Somalia, or Bangladesh.

One major weakness of the UNHCR and of the UN system as a whole is the lack of accountability for their programs. In addition, the experience gained in past operations is inadequately exploited. Although some UNHCR operations are now evaluated by a small central evaluation unit, high priority should be given to ensuring that subsequent policy planning systematically takes past lessons into account. Furthermore, the UNHCR should routinely subject its programs and policies to independent assessment and evaluation, with a view toward becoming institutionally accountable for its performance. Personnel should be recruited and selected on the basis of their potential for performance, particularly for working in internal conflicts, and adequate training should be given to staff to ensure more effective and more professional work.

But regardless of how one evaluates the effectiveness of the UNHCR, many millions of refugees throughout the world need it to survive. Despite its considerable limitations, its existence does have an effect on the conscience of most governments. The principal problems that the UNHCR and the UN system encounter stem from political constraints and from lack of sufficient resources. Therefore, rather than attempting a detailed assessment of the organizational effectiveness of the UNHCR, it is necessary to identify the factors that advance or complicate its mission.

## Protracted Relief at the Expense of Long-term Solutions

In recent years, the dearth of long-term solutions to refugee problems has given rise to questions about the capacity of the UNHCR and the international refugee regime to respond to the ongoing crises. During the 1980s, the UNHCR had been concerned primarily with meeting the immediate needs of refugees in camps; in the 1990s, UNHCR is bogged down in providing emergency assistance in internal wars.

The priority given to extended relief aid has swallowed up most of the UNHCR's resources, and it has also made achieving the traditional "durable" solutions—resettlement, local integration, and repatriation—increasingly difficult. Third-country resettlement is offered to no more than one percent of the world's refugees; and faced with economic difficulties and growing popular xenophobia, Western nations are much more reluctant to admit large numbers of people who are not easily assimilable.

Another preferred solution, local integration, is also difficult in today's circumstances, as most first-asylum countries are very poor and unstable. A sudden influx of refugees can disrupt a fragile economy, exacerbate unemployment, and heighten ethnic tensions. Many countries of asylum are unwilling to settle refugees close to border areas if their presence is likely to raise diplomatic or security problems, or provoke popular resentment and domestic conflict. Few countries are willing to offer citizenship to refugees, although this would greatly facilitate their long-term integration into host societies.

The third traditional durable solution, repatriation, depends for its legitimacy and effectiveness on conditions in the home countries and on the refugees' willingness to return.[31] In past decades, large numbers were repatriated following the successful conclusion of wars for national independence against Western colonial powers. The reduced tension between the two erstwhile superpowers during the 1990s and their disengagement from several major internal and regional conflicts that generated huge numbers of refugees in the past have opened up opportunities for the termination of conflicts and for the arresting of refugee flows.

Yet the prospect for resolving many of the long-standing refugee problems in the South is complicated by the revival of deep-rooted nationalist, religious, and ethnic conflicts. The end of the contest between the superpowers has only revealed more specific local tensions around the world. Ethnic antagonisms between Armenians and Azeris, Somali and Amhara, Tamils and Sinhalese, Serbs and Croats and Muslims, and Palestinians and Israelis illustrate the local roots of many refugee exoduses. The domestic roots of many regional rivalries, especially in the Middle East, South Asia, and Eastern Europe are so deep that the disengagement of the United States and the former USSR will do little to ameliorate them. In particular, the intensity of conflicts in such places as Kashmir and Sri Lanka testify to the irrelevance of changes in East–West relations to many local wars. Thus, although 2.5 million returned home in 1992, the prospects for large-scale repatriation amid many of the protracted struggles that have engulfed entire regions for the past ten or more years are not very good.[32]

Failure to achieve appropriate solutions has meant that refugees by the millions remain in camps and settlements. Designed as temporary accommodations, they have, by default, become permanent. In many instances, the basic necessities are well provided in UNHCR camps. In a few places, the refugees enjoy more plentiful and more nutritious food, cleaner water, and better medical treatment than do many local residents. Physically, some refugees may be better off than they were in their home countries. In other locations, conditions are horrific, and refugees are dying for lack of adequate political attention. Whatever the local conditions, authorities and observers are beginning to recognize that prolonged stays in closed camp environments can have extremely damaging psychological effects and are totally unsatisfactory as a long-term solution.

At a minimum, the UNHCR and host governments must act on the supposition that many refugees either are going to be permanent settlers in the host country or will be in need of long-term assistance in reintegrating into their home societies. This necessitates giving them land, legal protection, and residency rights, and perhaps altering national development plans to accommodate them. Most refugees are not offered durable solutions of this kind, however, but are instead provided with extended temporary asylum in UNHCR-administered camps or short-term assistance to see them through the initial repatriation phase. By allowing camps to become semipermanent, governments force refugees to become wards of international welfare. By not offering returning refugees adequate development assistance, they increase the likelihood that returnees will contribute to internal instability and will ultimately become refugees once again. The major problems are not logistical but political.

## Restrictions on Dealing with the Political Causes of Refugee Flows

Many critics assert that existing international approaches cannot resolve the world refugee problem because they treat only the symptoms and not the causes. Yet there are considerable limits to the actions that the UNHCR can take: the High Commissioner cannot intervene politically against governments that violate human rights and thus preempt the need to flee. The international refugee regime was designed to seem nonpolitical and strictly humanitarian in order to help it gain permission to work in host countries and secure funding from donor governments. UNHCR officials avoid raising political questions for fear of overstepping their mandate or damaging relations with sensitive governments, many of whom would view such intervention as an interference in their internal affairs.

In addition, the international community and individual governments find it difficult to take preventive action in countries of origin, because the root causes of contemporary refugee situations frequently require political intervention against governments that violate human rights—preferably before people need to flee. For the most part, UN institutions have been unable or unwilling either to prevent human rights violations or to punish those responsible. In some measure, this is because preventing human rights abuses depends on overcoming the barrier of national sovereignty, something no international organization has yet managed to accomplish consistently.

While refugee flows often occur as the result of persecution at the hands of brutal rulers or because of indiscriminate violence, external powers can significantly influence the factors that generate refugee flows by arming or refusing to arm violent past and present Third World dictators like Saddam Hussein of Iraq, Slobodan Milosevic of Serbia, Pol Pot of Cambodia, Mohammed Siad Barre of Somalia, and Mengistu Haile Mariam of Ethiopia. Outside powers help prolong instability, exacerbate nationality and other conflicts, divert scarce resources into militaristic activities, increase repression, and thereby multiply the numbers of refugees.

Until the international dimensions of the causes of refugee flows are fully acknowledged, little headway will be made toward resolving the problem.

Concerted international political action on these issues is not easy, but recognition is growing that the only effective way to reduce outflows of refugees is to address concretely the conditions that create them. Present refugee crises are complex emergencies, combining political instability, ethnic tensions, armed conflict, economic collapse, and the disintegration of civil society. Refugee movements frequently spill over borders and aggravate existing problems, such as environmental damage or food shortages. Refugee emergencies are seldom confined to single countries but often affect entire regions, such as the Balkans or the Horn of Africa. In the former Yugoslavia, UNHCR staff not only distribute relief but also try to restrain ethnic cleansing and protect human rights. In the face of cynical manipulation by the protagonists, these humanitarian efforts have been stop-gap measures only. To deal with political problems requires efforts that well exceed the scope of humanitarian organizations. International and regional peace, security, human rights, and economic structures must be strengthened with broader mandates and financial support, if they are to become more constructive interlocuters. The humanitarian mandate of the UNHCR cannot be viewed as a satisfactory substitute for wider-ranging political solutions.

One problem that makes the task of dealing with refugee issues particularly difficult is the general sense of pessimism and defeatism that characterizes so much of the discussion on human rights and displacement in the contemporary world. While pictures of misery and neglect in conflict areas and in refugee camps arouse sympathy and concern around the globe, people often assume that nothing much can be done to remedy these awful situations, at least in the short run.

In reality, there is little factual basis for such pessimism and no grounds at all for assuming that nothing can be done. Pessimism concerning the refugee problem is not new and only promotes despair and forestalls preventive action. Clearly, there is no easy solution, and virtually all responses are problematic in some way. Nevertheless, a range of short- and long-term measures and institutional reforms are possible that, if adopted, would go a long way toward resolving many of the refugee problems likely to confront the international community during the remainder of this century. The challenge is to reshape current concepts and institutions, without abandoning traditional commitments to humanitarian principles.

# 7

## Resolving Refugee Problems: Asylum and Development Assistance Policies

It has never been easy for international institutions dealing with refugees to respond to major political, economic, and social shifts in international politics. Over seventy years ago, Western leaders committed themselves to creating an international refugee regime to help both refugees and host countries and to promote regional and international stability. The need is still there, but the practices of individual governments have had only limited success in managing an increasingly difficult refugee situation. It is now generally recognized that the complex cooperative tasks required to deal with the global refugee problem require a strengthened international regime.

Refugees present a particularly vexing international problem, not only because of their large numbers but also because their situations defy quick solutions. Essentially the problem is political, and in the long run the international community needs to address the political conditions that lead to refugee movements in the first place. But several policy actions need to be taken immediately, to improve the management of refugee problems and to prevent further deterioration in the international protection of refugees. In particular, it is necessary to improve asylum procedures in Western countries, to create mechanisms that respond to various migration pressures, and to provide support for Third World countries of first asylum that do offer refuge.

International cooperation is a chain that is only as strong as its weakest link. Governments rarely act in isolation when developing refugee policies; rather they generally react to actions taken by other governments.

The generosity of Western nations can be a powerful incentive in getting other countries to act humanely; but conversely, the withdrawal of this generosity can be quite devastating. In recent years, restrictionist asylum policies in the West (most notably reflected in current U.S. policies toward Haitians and in West European policies toward Albanians, ex-Yugoslavs, and other national groups) have seriously affected the willingness of first-asylum countries in the Third World to receive displaced persons or to grant them refugee status. Thus, the capacity of the West to improve refugee prospects in the Third World depends on what initiatives are undertaken by the industrialized democracies, which hold the power and which also profess humanitarian concern. Such a cooperative approach demands exceptionally committed leadership from the United States, Japan, and several of the stronger West European countries, as well as unprecedented cooperation between developing and developed countries.

## Refugee Admissions and Asylum Policies in the United States

The United States must establish and properly fund a fair procedure for choosing refugees for admission and for determining refugee status. The 1980 Refugee Act clearly defines who may be admitted as a political refugee, but it offers no guidelines for choosing among the many who qualify. Instead, the act provides that the President should annually report to the Congress the foreseeable number of refugees who will be in need of resettlement and the anticipated allocation of refugee admissions for the coming year. In practice, the President has assigned the State Department this task; and as a result, foreign policy factors determine the allocation of refugee numbers.[1] Thus, for the eight years between 1980 and 1988, the United States resettled approximately 700,000 refugees—as many as the rest of the world combined—but over 650,000 of that number came from only ten countries (all but one of which were communist): Vietnam, Cambodia, Laos, the USSR, Poland, Romania, Afghanistan, Ethiopia, Iran, and Cuba. Citizens from countries where a great deal of persecution in the form of massive killings, torture, and political disappearances occurred—such as Guatemala and El Salvador—were not offered official refuge in the United States during the 1980s.

Even more remarkably, despite recent profound changes in the international political system and the virtual collapse of communism throughout Eastern Europe and the former Soviet Union, the composition of the flows of refugees to the United States has changed very little. In Fiscal Year 1993, the United States will admit 132,000 refugees. Two national groups—the Vietnamese and the ex-Soviets—will account for more than 75 percent of that number (see Table 7-1).[2] Many observers and international officials have long held that most Vietnamese and Soviet Jews no longer have a "well-founded fear of persecution," but simply want to join their relatives or make a new start in life. While convincing cases can be

*Table 7-1*  Refugee Admissions to the United States, FY 75–93

| | FY 75–78 | FY 80 | FY 81 | FY 82 | FY 83[a] | FY 84[b] | FY 85[b] |
|---|---|---|---|---|---|---|---|
| Africa (actual admissions) | | 955 | 2,119 | 3,326 | 2,645 | 2,747 | 1,953 |
| (ceilings) | | 1,500 | 3,000 | 3,500 | 3,000 | 2,750 | 3,000 |
| East Asia[c] | 254,095 | 163,799 | 131,139 | 73,522 | 39,406 | 51,960 | 49,970 |
| | | 169,200 | 163,000 | 96,000 | 64,000 | 52,000 | 50,000 |
| Eastern Europe | 11,096 | 5,025 | 6,704 | 10,760 | 12,083 | 10,285 | 9,350 |
| | | 5,000 | 4,500 | 11,000 | | | |
| Soviet Union | 56,989 | 28,444 | 13,444 | 2,766 | 1,409 | 715 | 640 |
| | | 33,000 | 33,000 | 20,000 | 15,000 | 11,000 | 10,000 |
| Latin America | 19,000 | 6,662 | 2,017 | 602 | 668 | 160 | 138 |
| | | 20,500 | 4,000 | 3,000 | 2,000 | 1,000 | 3,000 |
| Near East and South Asia | | 2,231 | 3,829 | 6,369 | 5,465 | 5,246 | 5,994 |
| | | 2,500 | 4,500 | 6,500 | 6,000 | 5,260 | 6,000 |
| Unallocated Funded Reserve | | | | | | | |
| Privately Funded (unallocated) | | | | | | | |
| Total | 341,180 | 207,116 | 159,252 | 97,355 | 61,681 | 71,113 | 68,045 |
| | | 231,700 | 217,000 | 140,000 | 90,000 | 72,000 | 70,000 |

[a]From FY 83 to FY 90, the Eastern Europe ceiling was combined with ceiling for the Soviet Union.

[b]This chart shows the adjusted regional ceilings that were established at mid-year consultations in FY 84, FY 85, FY 87, FY 88, FY 89, FY 90, FY 91, and FY 92. The overall annual ceilings did not change, except in FY 88, FY 89, and FY 92.

[c]Ceilings and actual admissions figures for Asia include both first asylum resettlement and the Orderly Departure Program (ODP) from Vietnam, ODP numbers include Amerasian immigrants.

[d]For the first time, the FY 92 admission numbers included an unallocated, federally funded reserve for 1,000 "high risk" cases. These unallocated places were incorporated into the adjusted regional ceilings for FY 92, maintaining the overall ceiling of 132,000 funded admissions.

SOURCE: U.S. Department of State, Bureau for Refugees Programs. Tabulated by the U.S. Committee for Refugees.

*Table 7-1* (*Continued*)

| FY 86 | FY 87[b] | FY 88[b] | FY 89[b] | FY 90[b] | FY 91[b] | FY 92[b] | FY 93 | Total |
|---|---|---|---|---|---|---|---|---|
| 1,315 | 1,994 | 1,588 | 1,922 | 3,493 | 4,424 | 5,491 | | 33,976 |
| 3,500 | 2,000 | 3,000 | 2,000 | 3,600 | 4,900 | 6,000 | 7,000 | |
| 45,454 | 40,112 | 35,015 | 45,680 | 51,611 | 53,484 | 51,848 | | 1,087,097 |
| 45,500 | 40,500 | 38,000 | 50,000 | 51,600 | 53,500 | 51,850 | 52,000 | |
| 8,713 | 8,606 | 7,816 | 8,948 | 6,196 | 6,855 | 2,886 | | 115,345 |
| | | | | | 7,000 | 2,900 | 1,500 | |
| 787 | 3,694 | 20,421 | 39,553 | 50,716 | 38,661 | 61,298 | | 319,527 |
| 9,500 | 12,300 | 30,000 | 50,000 | 58,300 | 46,500 | 61,400 | 50,000 | |
| 173 | 315 | 2,497 | 2,605 | 2,309 | 2,237 | 2,924 | | 42,307 |
| 3,000 | 1,000 | 3,500 | 3,500 | 2,400 | 3,100 | 3,000 | 3,500 | |
| 5,998 | 10,107 | 8,415 | 6,980 | 4,991 | 5,359 | 6,844 | | 77,828 |
| 6,000 | 10,200 | 9,000 | 7,000 | 5,000 | 6,000 | 6,850 | 7,000 | |
| | | | | | | 1,000[d] | 1,000 | |
| | 0 | 733 | 1,550 | 3,009 | 1,789 | 853 | | 7,934 |
| | 4,000 | 4,000 | 4,000 | 4,000 | 10,000 | 10,000 | 10,000 | |
| 62,440 | 64,828 | 76,487 | 107,238 | 122,326 | 112,809 | 132,144 | | 1,684,014 |
| 67,000 | 70,000 | 87,500 | 116,500 | 125,000 | 131,000 | 142,000 | 132,000 | |

made for individual applicants from Vietnam and the former USSR, al-
locating the great majority of refugee slots to these groups deprives other,
often more deserving individuals in other parts of the world the opportunity for resettlement. For example, few, if any, places are allocated for the
many ex-Yugoslavs and Africans fleeing brutal ethnic conflicts; for Guatemalans, Salvadorans, Tibetans, East Timorese, and Burmese fleeing persecution; or for Iraqis and Palestinians in desperate situations in Saudi
Arabia, Kuwait, and Turkey. Virtually no relationship exists between human rights abuses and the overseas U.S. refugee admissions program.
Thus, the United States admits very few refugees fleeing from the most
repressive countries in the world.

Realistically, domestic politics and foreign policy considerations, as
well as humanitarian sentiment, will continue to shape American responses to refugees in the future. However, the end of the communist
threat to American security interests offers the United States an opportunity to move beyond politics and programs that reflect the East–West
tensions of the past four decades and promote policies designed for the
post–Cold War era. Major new security threats are already arising from
political and social instability in the Third World and in Eastern Europe,
as a result of ethnic, intercommunity, or religious tensions, or because of
economic upheaval. A consequence of this instability is a rise in the number of refugee and migration movements. Containing forced population
movements in regions of conflict is impossible, nor is it likely that such
policies will promote stability in the Third World or the postcommunist
states of Europe. An important component of a new comprehensive strategy to defuse ethnic tension, contain violence, and contribute to the stabi-
lization of state formation will consist of opening up at least some opportunities for emigration and refugee resettlement in the advanced industrial
democracies, particularly to those fleeing political terror and ethnic cleansing. Thus, establishing a generous refugee admissions policy is not just a
matter of adhering to international human rights standards; it is also an
increasingly important foreign policy instrument in the post–Cold War
era to advance international stability.

The 1990s present the United States with a new opportunity to abide
by humanitarian standards that conform to the nation's image of itself.
The United States perceives itself as having responded positively throughout its history to the world's "tempest-tossed." Indeed the country became
a great power by welcoming a continuous stream of immigrants and refugees. In recent years, however, this self-image of the United States as a
land that welcomes indiscriminately the "huddled masses yearning to
breathe free" has been increasingly challenged by resettlement programs
that respond more to political and ethnic group pressures than to the need
for protection of persecuted individuals around the world.

Refugee admissions constitute one of the few opportunities the
United States has to demonstrate concretely its commitment to international human rights. Indeed, more than a decade ago, Congress clearly

outlined the direction that U.S. refugee policy should take: "the plight of the refugees themselves, as opposed to national origins or political considerations, should be paramount in determining which refugees are to be admitted to the United States."[3] In a first step toward recognizing the need to protect the most vulnerable, the 1992 refugee admissions numbers included provision for 1,000 "high risk" cases. This special category needs to be greatly expanded to protect refugees who face the greatest danger, regardless of their ethnicity, politics, or national origin.

If the intention to offer assistance and protection to a greater number of victims of oppression is to be a major force shaping the U.S. response to refugee movements overseas in the post–Cold War era, one of the most meaningful short-term actions the United States could take would be to provide adequate aid in overseas relief to ameliorate deteriorating conditions in UNHCR camps and settlements. In recent years, increasing competition for resources has occurred between refugee admissions and overseas refugee assistance. The great majority of U.S. funds have been used for domestic resettlement and emergency-oriented overseas assistance. Meanwhile, the sums devoted to local settlement assistance, repatriation programs, and extensive care and maintenance efforts for long-staying refugees in Africa and large parts of Asia have been progressively declining. While huge amounts of money were raised and expended on the people displaced in the Gulf War and in ex-Yugoslavia, the United States and many other donor countries continued to regress on basic care and maintenance for the remainder of refugees worldwide. As a consequence, many refugee camps are plagued by widespread child malnutrition (even starvation in extreme cases), disease, and absence of basic education for children and vocational training for adults. In addition, the United States should bolster its refugee-related development assistance. Improving conditions in host countries in the developing world enhances their capacity to cope with the stress of assisting and absorbing newcomers and makes them a more hospitable place for refugees to settle, thus to a certain extent diminishing pressures for third-country resettlement.

## Full Support for an Independent Authority for Asylum Decisions

Foreign policy and immigration control considerations have traditionally played an important role in U.S. asylum policy. In refugee determination procedures, the Immigration and Naturalization Service (INS) always sought an "advisory" opinion from the State Department on each individual applicant's claim to asylum.[4] Cases were typically reviewed by the appropriate country desk officers, whose primary task was to advance the foreign policy interests of the United States and maintain good working relations with countries of refugee origin. The assessment of conditions in the asylum seeker's home country was therefore frequently not the crucial factor in INS asylum decisions.

For most of the past decade, many analysts, scholars, and the refugee rights network advocated creating an independent refugee authority to make asylum decisions.[5] Composed of individuals specially trained in human rights and refugee conditions and law, the agency would ensure less intrusion of foreign and domestic policy concerns into the determination process and would develop the appropriate sensitivity and knowledge needed to make asylum decisions more fairly. Such an initiative would also simplify the complicated refugee admissions decisionmaking machinery, in which the INS and several State Department bureaus currently have active (and sometimes conflicting) roles.

Responding to calls for reform, the Attorney General issued new asylum regulations at the beginning of the 1990s that were intended to make the asylum process fairer and more consistent. In April 1991, a specialized corps of asylum officers, familiar with human rights law and political conditions in countries of origin, supervised by the INS central office, and intended to be supported eventually by a human rights documentation center, took over from local INS district directors the responsibility for initial hearings of asylum claims. In this way, it was intended that foreign policy and immigration enforcement concerns would no longer exert a major influence on asylum decisions.[6] The State Department would no longer be the sole source of documentary evidence regarding the internal situation in countries of refugee origin, including detailed information about specific groups likely to be targeted for persecution. As a result of these changes, the approval rate for asylum applications to the United States improved considerably for most groups during 1992 (see Table 7-2).

Although the new asylum adjudication system is a marked improvement over past procedures, questions remain about the financial resources available for it to maintain a credible status determination system and about how it will handle a growing backlog of cases. Financial constraints and staff shortages have plagued the new asylum system from the time it was initially implemented. As of late 1992, the documentation center was still not fully operational; there was insufficient staff to compile and distribute information on human rights conditions in refugee-generating countries; and materials from prominent human rights organizations were not available in some offices.

Furthermore, the number of asylum officers allocated to implement the new system was clearly inadequate for the task. When the new asylum officer corps assumed their responsibilities in April 1991, approximately 114,000 asylum applications were pending. Lack of sufficient funding and the 1991–1992 Haitian boat exodus quickly overwhelmed the new system, and a backlog of cases developed. By October 1991, the backlog had grown to 141,000 and by December 1991 to over 177,000. By the end of 1992, approximately 216,000 cases were pending.[7]

Not only do questions remain about whether the asylum adjudication system is capable of achieving a fair and efficient procedure, but the new temporary protected status set forth in the Immigration Act of 1990 is evidently being unevenly applied. Although Congress mandated that temporary protected status apply to Salvadorans, the Bush administration repeatedly refused to extend this protection to Haitians after the coup of 1991. Neither did the United States apply this status to other vulnerable groups, such as Palestinians in Lebanon and Kuwait, and nationals of Sri Lanka and Sudan—despite the fact that the Immigration Act of 1990 sets forth criteria, including "ongoing armed conflict," that enable the Attorney General to postpone deportation of certain nationals whose return would "pose a serious threat to their personal safety."[8]

## An Active Monitoring Role for the UNHCR

It is encouraging that the U.S. government has sought the assistance of the UNHCR in designing the new asylum system, including its training component and the resource and documentation center. Even greater involvement by the UNHCR would provide an additional structural safeguard for fairness in the review of refugee determinations.

Unlike some other countries with formal procedures for determining refugee status, the United States gives the UNHCR no role, advisory or otherwise, in its formal procedures. Until recently, the UNHCR could only intervene informally with U.S. government officials or formally through the courts by submitting *amicus curiae* briefs. In asylum cases, these briefs point out the relevant international legal rules on particular asylum issues, describe the international legal obligations that provide the background for municipal law and practice, and attempt to influence U.S. courts to observe international standards more fully. These measures have only limited effectiveness, however, thus pointing up the need for more formal UNHCR involvement in procedures to help depoliticize the refugee screening process.

The UNHCR must also pursue a more assertive role in the United States by upgrading its presence and assuming greater responsibility for offering protection to asylum seekers. At a minimum, it should closely monitor interdiction exercises against Haitian boat people and mount more on-site missions to detention centers at the U.S.–Mexican border. In light of the continuing violence in Haiti, the UNHCR should also monitor the subsequent treatment of refugees who are forcibly returned there.

## The European Community and Asylum

The asylum systems in greatest need of overhaul are those in Western Europe, where public controversy has mounted over the treatment and processing of asylum applicants. The issue is assuming greater policy significance not only because of an increase in numbers of applicants, but more importantly because of the movement to create a unified Europe. Free population movements across national borders within the European

**Table 7-2**  Asylum Cases Filed with the Immigration and Naturalization Service (approved and denied, by selected nationalities)

| Country | Cases Decided by District Directors (June 1983–March 1991) | | |
| --- | --- | --- | --- |
| | Approval Rate for Cases Decided | Cases Granted | Cases Denied |
| Total[a] | 23.6% | 41,227 | 133,178 |
| USSR[b] | 74.5 | 624 | 213 |
| China | 69.0 | 970 | 434 |
| Romania | 62.6 | 1,676 | 999 |
| Iran | 61.0 | 13,411 | 8,550 |
| Bulgaria | 49.2 | 92 | 95 |
| Somalia | 49.1 | 546 | 565 |
| Ethiopia | 47.4 | 2,422 | 2,680 |
| Syria | 43.6 | 267 | 344 |
| Czechoslovakia | 41.9 | 189 | 262 |
| South Africa | 40.1 | 73 | 109 |
| Afghanistan | 37.7 | 468 | 773 |
| Vietnam | 34.5 | 87 | 165 |
| Poland | 33.1 | 3,013 | 6,073 |
| Peru | 26.8 | 48 | 179 |
| Hungary | 26.0 | 219 | 622 |
| Uganda | 26.0 | 104 | 295 |
| Nicaragua | 24.8 | 12,684 | 38,270 |
| Iraq | 22.9 | 165 | 721 |
| Cuba | 18.5 | 630 | 2,773 |
| Pakistan | 16.4 | 89 | 451 |
| Liberia | 15.3 | 72 | 470 |
| Philippines | 14.9 | 91 | 517 |
| Lebanon | 13.8 | 279 | 1,732 |
| Yugoslavia[b] | 10.5 | 66 | 560 |
| Sri Lanka | 6.7 | 12 | 166 |
| India | 3.4 | 14 | 411 |
| El Salvador | 2.8 | 1,365 | 46,712 |
| Honduras | 2.1 | 41 | 1,899 |
| Guatemala | 2.0 | 204 | 9,593 |
| Haiti | 1.8 | 42 | 2,259 |

NOTE: Prior to June 1983, INS asylum figures were for actual number of individuals, not for cases, which can represent more than one individual. For consistency, this chart begins with June 1983. In April 1991, the responsibility for adjudicating asylum claims was moved from INS district directors to a new corps of asylum officers. No statistics are available on asylum approval rates for the period April through September 1991. This chart is based on data for asylum cases filed with district directors and asylum officers only. Many applications for asylum are filed with immigration judges, particularly in the context of deportation proceedings.

*Table 7-2*   (*Continued*)

|  | Cases Decided by Asylum Officers (FY 92) | | |
|---|---|---|---|
| *Approval Rate for Cases Decided* | *Cases Granted* | *Cases Denied* | *Cases Pending as of 9/30/92* |
| 36.8% | 4,019 | 6,904 | 215,772 |
| 48.7 | 308 | 324 | 9,273 |
| 84.9 | 241 | 43 | 4,266 |
| 26.5 | 120 | 333 | 4,414 |
| 72.8 | 193 | 72 | 2,349 |
| 17.7 | 35 | 163 | 1,579 |
| 89.9 | 107 | 12 | 563 |
| 74.8 | 299 | 101 | 2,935 |
| 27.9 | 12 | 31 | 832 |
| 10.0 | 1 | 9 | 175 |
| 57.1 | 4 | 3 | 65 |
| 75.0 | 48 | 16 | 659 |
| 66.7 | 4 | 2 | 63 |
| 1.3 | 3 | 233 | 2,166 |
| 37.5 | 57 | 95 | 1,503 |
| 13.6 | 3 | 19 | 342 |
| 56.3 | 9 | 7 | 116 |
| 15.5 | 212 | 1,156 | 21,496 |
| 64.5 | 40 | 22 | 437 |
| 47.0 | 156 | 176 | 4,097 |
| 52.0 | 40 | 37 | 3,525 |
| 51.8 | 131 | 122 | 4,016 |
| 7.4 | 11 | 138 | 4,867 |
| 29.2 | 50 | 121 | 1,326 |
| 40.6 | 43 | 63 | 3,398 |
| 80.0 | 32 | 8 | 394 |
| 41.7 | 63 | 88 | 3,380 |
| 28.0 | 90 | 231 | 44,982 |
| 17.3 | 18 | 86 | 2,346 |
| 21.1 | 62 | 232 | 69,359 |
| 30.6 | 82 | 186 | 5,243 |

[a]The total includes all nationalities, not just those listed here.
[b]FY 92 figures for USSR include all former republics. FY 92 figures for Yugloslavia include all former republics.

SOURCE: U.S. Department of Justice, Immigration and Naturalization Service (INS). Tabulated by the U.S. Committee for Refugees.

Community is central to the realization of a unified Europe; that much is almost axiomatic. Less widely appreciated is the fact that eliminating internal frontiers will necessitate strengthening external borders—a move that will inevitably have major implications for refugee and asylum policy. West European governments have met in a number of different regional forums in an attempt to harmonize future European Community policies and practices toward asylum seekers.

Many of the parties traditionally involved in protecting the interests of refugees in Europe have looked upon these efforts with grave suspicion and even hostility. The UNHCR, voluntary agencies, churches, and some parliamentarians fear that West European governments intend to control the influx of asylum seekers by restricting access, and that in their attempt to forge a regional policy on asylum, they will adopt the policies of the most restrictive states as the standard for the entire continent.[9]

By the beginning of the 1990s, the regional responses were still being formulated, since significant differences still existed among EC governments. The Schengen group (Germany, France, and the Benelux countries) signed an agreement for controlling their external borders, which Italy, Portugal, and Spain subsequently co-signed. In addition, the twelve European Community states have drawn up two conventions that establish criteria for determining state jurisdiction over examinations of asylum requests and procedures for entering the European Community. The challenge for European states in the 1990s is how to develop a system that fairly distinguishes between migrants and refugees in order to benefit the groups most in need of support, while simultaneously protecting the receiving country from large, uncontrolled population movements from the Third World and Eastern Europe.

Whatever final shape the West European response eventually assumes, accelerating, streamlining, and professionalizing the existing procedures would go a long way toward alleviating the financial and human problems and costs associated with protracted delays, and would restore confidence in the various asylum systems. Canada, for example, has streamlined its procedures so that asylum claimants from major refugee-sending countries are given expedited hearings, thereby reducing costs and processing time for individuals from states known for strife or serious human rights abuses.[10] Similarly, in Europe, if individual refugees are recognized quickly, they can begin the integration process without delay, and governments will not be burdened by long-term maintenance costs. At the same time, migrants who simply seek a "back-door" entry into Europe will be discouraged from applying. The personnel and resources needed to determine refugee status would cost considerably less than is currently being paid for assistance to asylum seekers who wait years before their cases are determined.

## A Regional Refugee Regime for Europe

The growing scale and complexity of Europe's refugee problem, as well as the changed international context, clearly reveal the inadequacy of asylum as the only response in the region. Europe needs a refugee regime of its own, both to address its regional refugee and asylum problems and to help ameliorate the global refugee problem. To be effective, a European refugee strategy must go beyond traditional immigration control and humanitarian measures; it must make managing refugee and migration pressures a part of Europe's central economic, political, and security objectives.

At present, two general kinds of South–North and East–West refugee and migration situations confront Europe in the short term: first, mass exoduses (which consist of victims of conflict and persecution); and second, intensifying South–North and East–West migration pressures (of which refugees and asylum-seekers form an important but not exclusive part). Because these two categories of movement have different causes, the most appropriate responses are necessarily also different.

An effective and comprehensive refugee strategy must include several lines of endeavor:

> Development of a set of approaches that mirror the complex nature and causes of today's population movements
>
> Development of regional instruments and burden-sharing mechanisms for providing temporary protection and assistance to victims of civil war and ethnic violence
>
> Extension of assistance to border states in the East and to host states in the South that face large-scale population movements, particularly of war victims and others forced out of their home countries
>
> Reform of existing asylum systems to expedite decision-making, to return people who can be returned in safety and dignity, and to better help those who will be remaining to become part of their new societies
>
> Development of policies to address the political and economic causes of emigration, including support for economic development, the establishment of a protection regime for national minorities, and more effective in-country assistance to the internally displaced so that they do not need to emigrate.

## A New Humanitarian Admissions Status

Asylum policy will continue to pose difficult political and moral choices for European governments. This is so because increasing numbers of people who apply for asylum cannot demonstrate that they are victims of persecution per se, even though their motives for leaving their homelands may have been politically generated and their circumstances may have been life-threatening. Fleeing armed conflict or political violence, often in combination with economic deprivation, ecological disasters, and other compelling circumstances, many of these people are moving out of necessity to countries that can provide them with life-sustaining conditions. Many are not moving simply to improve their standard of living or for greater economic opportunity. Most refugee flows today (as in past) are the result of political repression combined with economic hardship.

The basic international instruments of refugee protection offer neither a comprehensive nor a sufficiently flexible response to the diverse forced population movements taking place today. For those who cannot demonstrate a well-founded fear of persecution, Western European nations provide few formal mechanisms for admission or protection, either on temporary or permanent grounds. Faced with the disparity between an asylum system limited to narrowly defined victims of persecution and the need for a humanitarian response to forced migrants who cannot prove that they are refugees, West European governments have granted temporary protection to members of some nationalities, usually on a discretionary basis. Other people have been allowed to remain illegally because governments do not make an effort to find and deport them. However, these recurring practices do not amount to coherent, consistent policies.[11] The existing process is costly for governments, and the long delays it entails are demoralizing for asylum seekers who do meet the requirements of the 1951 refugee definition.

New concepts of protection must be devised for the kinds of large-scale refugee flows the West is witnessing today. Refugee movements stemming from nationality and ethnic minority tensions are already well underway in ex-Yugoslavia and the former Soviet Union, and instances of this phenomenon are likely to increase dramatically in the years ahead. Neither traditional immigration nor refugee mechanisms are well equipped to handle victims of civil wars and deteriorating states. In lieu of more effective mechanisms to deal with mass movements, European governments have resorted to strict interpretation of the 1951 U.N. Convention definition of *refugee,* to erection of barriers to entry, and to containment of forced migration in countries or regions of origin. But for those uprooted in ex-Yugoslavia and in other brutal internal wars, the consequences of these restrictive policies can be lethal.

By sealing all escape routes and means of refuge, European governments are trapping refugees and displaced people in besieged cities and regions and placing them in the crossfire between warring forces. The consequences of the ethnic conflicts unfolding in ex-Yugoslavia and in parts of the former Soviet Union, where expulsion and "ethnic cleansing" are the central objectives of the conflicts, have brought home the urgency and importance both of providing temporary safety and of keeping alive the notion of return. A new European refugee regime should allow for temporary sanctuary, followed by voluntary return in safety and dignity.

In the future, states must go beyond the limited refugee standard codified in international instruments, to respond to people who clearly are not refugees according to the 1951 Convention but who are nevertheless in need of some form of coordinated international protection. At the end of 1990, the U.S. Congress passed a new immigration law that took the first steps toward recognizing the need to respond to these crises by creating a new "temporary protected status" class. Similarly, West European states should collectively adopt a new humanitarian admissions status that offers temporary protection to victims of protracted civil war, ethnic conflict, arbitrary violence, and radical regime changes, who cannot return home safely. The time has come to give broader recognition to temporary protection as a legitimate tool of international protection.

Adoption of a new humanitarian status by European Community governments would reduce the current need to select from among the many deserving and urgent asylum claimants and would reduce the risk of returning people to genuinely dangerous situations. Such a mechanism would also result in a considerable savings in resources. Those who seek only temporary protection would no longer overload the asylum system, and those with legitimate claims would obtain refugee status more quickly. Finally, if a generous humanitarian admissions category in EC states were applied to those fleeing conflicts outside the European states, it would probably strengthen the willingness of Third World countries of asylum, like Pakistan, Turkey, and Malawi, to continue to provide safe haven for thousands, if not millions, of individuals from neighboring countries.

As a result of the refugee outflows from the war in former Yugoslavia, burden-sharing has emerged as an area of major disagreement and tension between EC member states. In the future, this issue will undoubtedly gain greater prominence, particularly if ethnic conflict and internal displacement within the former Soviet Union spill over into neighboring Central European countries. At the end of 1992, in an effort to protect themselves from unwanted flows of refugees and migrants, West European governments were formulating new procedures to return home or to so-called "safe countries" all asylum seekers who were not specifically targeted for persecution, thereby excluding the great mass of refugees driven from their homes by war. Since the collapse of communism in 1989, all Central European states have been declared "safe countries"—that is, free from persecution. Thus, Hungary, Poland, and the Czech and Slovak republics—countries that are the first ports of call for many potential refugees—are in danger of becoming the dumping ground for Western Europe's unwanted foreigners.[12]

It is unlikely that Central European states could absorb large numbers of people indefinitely, without creating domestic and regional instability and undermining their own attempts at economic and political reform. They have neither the resources nor the institutions to cope with these new arrivals. At present, few EC governments seem prepared to consider a joint approach to help neighboring countries sustain the burden of new population flows and to strengthen their capacity to continue granting temporary protection.

## Addressing Migration Pressures

The real problem is that large numbers of people in developing countries and in Eastern Europe see no prospect of improving their circumstances at home. Because they have no opportunity to emigrate through recognized channels, many such people are tempted to move to the more prosperous European countries and to submit requests for asylum there. But asylum cannot and should not be used to resolve the problem of poverty. That issue must be tackled through effective development and assistance policies.

In the future, the numbers of foreigners wishing to migrate to Europe can only increase. Markedly unequal rates of population and economic growth between countries of the North and the South are creating pressures for migrant flows into Europe that exceed politically tolerable levels. For example, current demographic projections put the populations of Turkey and Egypt in the year 2025 at over 100 million each and the population of the five states of the Maghreb Union (Algeria, Morocco, Tunisia, Libya, and Mauritania) at a total of 127 million (up from a total of 61 million in 1989).[13] Thus, these seven countries combined will have a population comparable to that of the existing European Community. All of these countries have faced worsening economic problems and high unemployment levels in recent years, and their economies are highly unlikely to expand rapidly enough to absorb the huge projected increase in their labor force. Moreover, the 1.5 million Turks already living in Germany and the estimated 6 million North Africans living in other parts of Western Europe will act as a significant bridgehead for further migration. Thus, intensified out-migration pressures in North Africa and the Eastern Mediterranean, combined with recent political and economic changes in Eastern and Central Europe, threatens to produce large numbers of new migrants and has presented Europe with a major immigration crisis.

To date, the focus of government action in addressing intensifying migration and asylum pressures has been on domestic and unilateral responses that by necessity dwell on controls. But policymakers need to refocus their efforts away from controls and toward the much more difficult task of developing concerted bilateral and multilateral responses that address the root causes of migration.[14] Much greater attention must be paid to conditions within the migration- and refugee-producing countries, particularly conditions that are amenable to influence by receiving countries. This requires, on the one hand, greater North–South and East–West cooperation in trade liberalization and development assistance and, on the other hand, greater observance of human rights conditions in a number of countries, especially with respect to the treatment of ethnic minorities.

Numerous studies of South–North migration[15] have pointed to the developing countries' need to pursue more job-creating economic growth as the only long-term solution to the problem. No single international development is likely to be more successful in improving economic growth in the less developed countries and thereby reducing economic incentives for emigration than trade liberalization combined with foreign investment. In this sense, successfully concluding the current negotiating round of the General Agreement on Tariffs and Trade (GATT) and negotiating regional trade agreements that include the developing world may hold greater promise for narrowing the economic disparities between North and South and reducing unauthorized migration than any imaginable development assistance scheme. Similarly, only by providing adequate levels of assistance and investment, and by embarking on job creation, management training, and income generation projects aimed at promoting effective development in Third World and East European countries of origin, can Western industrial democracies provide hope to disheartened young people there who see the short-term economic costs of staying at home and the chance of better opportunities abroad.

During the early 1990s, a number of intergovernmental meetings were held under the auspices of the Council of Europe, the International Labor Organization, the Organization for Economic Cooperation and Development, the International Organization for Migration, and the UNHCR. These meetings stressed the necessity of adopting a coordinated policy approach to East–West and South–North migration that enlists the efforts of receiving states, sending states, and regional and international institutions. There have also been limited attempts to give some order to existing and potential migration flows. For example, Germany and other West European governments have signed bilateral agreements with some East European states for limited labor exchange programs; Germany is carrying out development policy projects with a view toward controlling the migration of ethnic Germans from Eastern Europe and the ex–Soviet Union; various European programs of targeted employment and training opportunities have been designed to facilitate economic reform in the East; Italy provides food aid to Albania in order to stabilize the situation there and prevent outflows of boat people; the International Organization for Migration and the UNHCR have initiated information campaigns in Romania and Albania that provide realistic assessments of the circumstances in which people leaving these countries would find themselves in the West; and the UNHCR has opened offices throughout the region to offer training and advice in implementing immigration and refugee laws.

For the most part, however, the receiving countries in Western Europe are not prepared for large-scale movements; and in the future, migration and refugee pressures must be addressed with policies of far greater scope and ambition than those encompassed by the framework of traditional humanitarian and immigration control policies. Unfortunately, if the Association Agreements that were rather grudgingly negotiated between the European Community and the Central European states in December 1991 are any indication of future West European policy in accommodating Europe's newly democratizing countries, the prospects for alleviating the causes of economic migration are not good. Rather than generously helping their Eastern neighbors to enlarge their economies by opening Western markets to Eastern products, EC governments have maintained barriers to trade in agricultural goods, textiles, and iron and steel. According to some estimates, these items account for one-third of Czech and Slovak exports, more than 40 percent of Polish exports, and half of Hungarian exports. As long as Central Europe's trading opportunities remain restricted, the region's economies will be hard-pressed to provide sufficient jobs to help deter out-migration, at least in the short term. Failure to accommodate East Europe's postcommunist states will clearly inhibit the region's progress toward establishing market economies and democratic institutions—a development that presents significant security implications for Europe.

The European Community has been similarly shortsighted regarding opening up trading opportunities for migration-sending countries along its southern periphery. With the development of the Single European Market in 1993, North African industrial products became subject to new nontariff barriers, and North African agricultural products became subject to new quota restrictions designed to hinder competition with similar products from Spain and Portugal. As a result of the Schengen and EC agreements, migration from all Maghreb states except Libya became subject to strict new migrant controls. Yet as with Eastern Europe, access to the EC market remains the single most important factor in any effort to strengthen the economies of the North African states and to deter future migration flows. The efficacy of a transfer of resources from North to South in the form of investment, technology transfer, aid, and loans will be sharply curtailed if the Maghreb states are unable to sell their products to the European Community.

Moreover, while it seems clear that free trade, economic development, and human rights protection are essential parts of any long-term strategy, the nexus between migration and these economic, political, and diplomatic tools is poorly understood. Numerous questions about the relationship between migration flows and the policies that receiving states might adopt to stabilize population movements and reduce these flows remain unanswered. For example, under what conditions can free trade increase employment and thereby reduce the economic incentives for emigration? By promoting human rights in some countries—especially with respect to the treatment of ethnic minorities—can Western democracies influence the political conditions that induce people to leave these countries? For the most part, there is insufficient understanding about the conditions in sending countries in relation to migration and little attention to what policies might change the conditions leading to emigration.

It is also important to note that every policy option creates political and economic trade-offs and raises new questions and dilemmas for Western countries. For example, will free trade lead to declining employment in the receiving country? In the short run, will migration increase or decrease as a result of free trade agreements? In some instances, policies may have unintended and undesirable consequences. For instance, will promoting the rights of ethnic minorities and supporting democratic forces embroil states in other countries' internal affairs and encourage movements for self-determination that in turn generate more refugee exoduses? Will regime changes toward democracy and market economies result in greater rather than less emigration?

Some evidence indicates that economic development may actually exacerbate the problem of migration during the early to middle stages of economic transition. Indeed, there appears to be a contradiction between the short-term and long-term effects of development on migration. In the long term, economic development in the Third World and Eastern Europe would reduce the pressures that produce outmigration. However, a U.S. commission[16] appointed in the late 1980s to study the nexus between migration and development concluded that the effects of rapid development are profoundly destabilizing and in the short term often lead to increased internal and eventually international migration. The commission contended that, in the early to middle stages of economic transition, development forces workers out of subsistence jobs and into new areas of economic activity, thus opening up a new awareness of opportunities to embark on unauthorized migration.[17] Short of a mammoth injection of resources over a considerable period of time, any pro-development policy is unlikely to discourage mass departures from the South and the East in the near future.

However, the findings of the U.S. commission were limited to South–North migration in the Western Hemisphere, principally from Mexico to the United States; consequently, they are not necessarily applicable to other migration flows, such as from the Maghreb to Southern Europe or from Eastern to Western Europe. In general, little research has been done on the conditions in sending countries in relation to migration, and little attention has been paid to the question of what economic policies might change the conditions that lead to emigration. A greater understanding of the relationships between trade, development, and human rights policies and migration is essential to the success of a future targeted and structured policy to reduce economic and political emigration pressure.

The advanced industrialized democracies must develop a multifaceted long-term strategy, not only to relieve migration pressures but also to promote political stability in the South. This overall strategy should include foreign policies that place greater stress on the need for political reforms in countries of emigration. In particular, Western governments must address the conditions that create these mass movements, by conditioning aid to increased political pluralism and greater observance of human rights—including those of minority groups—and by curbing arms sales programs and supporting regional peace systems. However, a foreign policy that supports democratic forces and promotes the rights of ethnic minorities is not without risks for the West. Such policy initiatives can involve states in other countries' domestic affairs and can contribute to internal unrest that may generate new refugee crises. At a minimum, however, Western democracies should ensure that their policies do not foster the growth of repressive dictatorships. For example, Western states should curb their involvement in arming and training military forces of governments that persecute their citizens or of rebel groups that commit human rights abuses.

Many responses that states could adopt to deal with intensifying migration pressures would be simplified if Western governments (particularly West European states) expanded their existing immigration programs, guest-worker agreements, and migration quotas to relieve pressures on their overburdened asylum systems. Immigration quotas have the advantage of being subject to public determination, control, and variation; and this fact would help reassure the public that the government was in control of its borders. Clearly, with eventual economic recovery and with low birthrates and aging populations, most industrialized states will find it necessary to import labor in the future anyway. Most West European states are experiencing fairly widespread sectoral or occupational shortages, particularly in agriculture, the construction industry, the hotel and catering sector, nursing, and cleaning services both for businesses and private households. Many economists and demographers argue that migration has been beneficial not only to the migrants but also to the host countries, and greater immigration from the East and the South could help the West deal with its emerging shortage of young workers. Such a mix of asylum and immigration policies may give European governments greater flexibility to deal with the various population movements that exist today, while at the same time protecting asylum procedures from abusive claims.

While the issues that immigration raises for advanced industrial democracies obviously require a long-term perspective and a systematic approach, successfully managing these problems also requires unprecedented cooperation between North, South, East, and West. In particular, countries of origin have a duty to their own citizens to prevent situations that give rise to refugee and migrant flows, and national sovereignty should not be used to shield governments from their responsibilities. In this regard, the countries of the South and the East must refrain from political repression and persecution of their ethnic and religious minorities. The international human rights machinery, which was long paralyzed by ideological confrontation, must now be used to greater effect to hold governments accountable for abuses.

One of the biggest challenges confronting policymakers in the non-Western world and in postcommunist Europe is how to reconcile the claims of ethnic groups to self-determination with the asserted right of states to maintain their national borders intact. Not only must governments reach accommodation with their ethnic and religious minorities, but they must also devise creative solutions to achieve decentralization and regional self-government without redrawing international boundaries. A minority rights protection regime—established at the international and regional levels—should safeguard the existence and exercise of group rights, mediate between governments and national minorities, and enforce the decisions of courts and human rights bodies regarding minority rights abuses. Without directly addressing the root cause of refugee flows, countries have no realistic prospect of regulating emigration pressures.

Rapid population growth in the Third World threatens to swamp any progress achieved in economic development and human rights. Of the projected doubling of the world's total population between now and the middle of the next century, some 95 percent will take place in developing countries. Transnational refugee and migration flows cannot be curbed until the South, with appropriate international assistance, manages to control its population growth.

## European Nations as "Countries of Immigration"

West European nations must also come to terms with being "countries of immigration," even if their leaders and people do not see themselves in this way. Admissions to Western Europe now stand at historically high levels: since the mid-1980s, an average of 900,000 new immigrants have arrived there annually. The European intake is now comparable to that of the three traditional overseas immigrant countries (the United States, Canada, and Australia) combined.[18] France, Germany, Great Britain, and most of the smaller European countries have a higher percentage of foreign-born residents than does the best known "immigration country," the United States.[19]

Despite this ongoing multicultural influx, immigration is not central to the West European national experience in the way that it is to that of the United States, Australia, or Canada. Moreover, most European countries have experienced serious problems in integrating immigrant and ethnic minority populations, as well as in responding to the challenge that these communities pose for European national identities. For example, many governments continue to assume that most migrants are only temporary residents in the host country; and integration policies tend to be ad hoc, partial, and incoherent. But failure to integrate minorities has resulted in long-term adverse social consequences, including the rise of increasingly assertive and alienated immigrant communities, and the creation of large underclasses of illegal and semilegal migrants.

High unemployment and working-class insecurity have exacerbated the situation and have eroded public confidence in politicians and political institutions. In many areas, interethnic hostility is more pronounced now than at any time in the past several decades, and violent racist and xenophobic attacks against refugees occur regularly throughout the European Community. In several large West European states, including France, Germany, and Austria, political parties—and not only those on the far right—are competing for votes with slogans and platforms hostile to foreigners.

Despite the political difficulty of doing so, the way forward for European governments is to develop programs to achieve better integration, reduce racial discrimination, and uphold the principle of equality of opportunity and treatment. Immigrant communities, on the other hand, have some responsibility to adapt to the values and customs of their host communities. In many cases, the desire to integrate depends crucially on whether immigrants feel secure about their residence status. For instance, long-term Turkish residents in Germany are denied political rights and citizenship, while Russian-speaking immigrants who can prove German ancestry are automatically granted citizenship. There appears to be little chance of integrating foreigners into German society until the government reforms its naturalization and citizenship laws.

Immigrants are rapidly becoming a large proportion of the younger, working population of West European societies, and providing for their successful integration is one of the most important social policy issues confronting European policymakers in the 1990s. European integration programs and adaptations by immigrant communities to their new societies will promote domestic stability, restore public confidence, and deny fuel to right-wing extremists who seek to exploit anti-immigrant feelings and tensions.

## Rethinking Assistance to Refugees in the Third World

Asylum seekers are symptoms of chronic political and economic problems in the Third World and in post-Communist states in the East. In their search for appropriate policies, Western decisionmakers must realize that the asylum problem cannot be successfully dealt with by stricter eligibility requirements or stronger immigration controls. Rather, policies must constitute an independent but integral part of a comprehensive international approach toward greater protection of refugees outside the West and toward addressing the underlying causes of refugee movements.

The reformulation of Western asylum policy makes no sense unless industrialized countries also extend financial assistance to nations that provide safe haven, frequently with extremely meager resources. In this regard it is important to remember that, although resettlement and asylum in the West are important programs, only a few percent of the world's nearly 18 million refugees are taken care of in this way. Most refugees remain in very dire situations—often in regions of widespread conflict—desperately in need of assistance and protection. Moreover, the majority of the Third World's uprooted people remain outside UNHCR camps and have settled among local populations, where they try to find employment and share the health, education, and other services intended for nationals. In Africa, for example, researchers estimate that no more than 25 percent of the continent's refugees live in settlements or camps.[20] However, current aid programs are designed primarily for the benefit of refugees or returnees located in camps or settlements, and they are only geared in a limited way toward assisting the host or home country to cope with the extra burden. In the future, if aid is to reach all refugees—whether they are in camps and settlements or not—refugee assistance must be directed at host and home countries as well as at refugees.

The provision of greater resources to host countries should be accompanied by a shift in the emphasis of assistance away from short-term emergency relief and toward long-term development purposes.[21] In addition, refugees should become part of the solution to development problems. Ample research indicates that they are often more receptive to development initiatives and new technology than are local residents.[22] Refugees are survivors and often arrive in their new countries with skills, education, work practices, and personal resourcefulness that can have a highly positive impact on economic growth. They constitute a ready supply of labor; and they settle on empty lands and turn bush into farms and villages, thus raising the standard of living of the locality.

In southern Sudan, for example, Ugandan refugees, arriving in the early 1980s, brought new crops and agricultural techniques, as well as their labor, to an area struggling to recover from a debilitating civil war. In the space of two years, the area was transformed into one that exported agricultural produce to other parts of the country.[23] Other examples of countries that put the creative energies of refugees to work include Cyprus, where, focusing on labor-intensive policies and the need for housing, the government used the refugee situation as a catalyst for reconstructing its economy, and Nepal, where Tibetan refugees were allowed to use their carpetmaking skills and were paid a wage rather than receiving food aid, with the result that "30 years on, having created employment for thousands of others, carpet making is the largest manufacturing industry in Nepal, with foreign currency earnings of $50 million annually."[24]

Unfortunately, these examples are the exception rather than the norm. All too often, current practice forces refugees to live in camps and to rely on the distribution of food and health supplies rather than encouraging them to contribute to their host's economies. Numerous refugee situations around the world demonstrate that refugees tend to be less resentful when they mingle with the rest of the population, paying their own way, than when they are kept as a separate embittered community. There is an urgent need to tap the economic potential of refugees. Far too many are virtually warehoused in camps, in a state of near total dependence, until the day when they might be able to return home.

## Linking Development and Refugee Assistance

The ultimate goal for refugees should obviously be to become self-sufficient. International assistance should encourage self-reliance and productivity so that refugees begin to become assets rather than liabilities to their community.

The challenge is to provide resources in a way that enables refugees and locals alike to participate and to contribute to national economic output. This can be accomplished, in the first place, by directing development funds to local communities to improve their infrastructure and their employment possibilities, in order to meet the new demands created by a refugee and returnee influx. Development projects are more likely to be successful if the local communities involved participate in designing and implementing them. Local organizations are more cost-effective than outside agencies and have a better understanding of local needs and opportunities. Moreover, strengthening the local infrastructure equips a country to cope better with future emergencies.

While it is essential to address refugee problems from a developmental perspective, not all problems associated with uprooted people can be resolved through long-term economic assistance programs. In some regions, no amount of economic assistance to host countries will make the permanent settlement of refugees either desirable or possible. Political, social, and security factors, at least as much as economic conditions, often predominate in forming national attitudes. For example, countries like Malaysia and Turkey, with acute problems of ethnic heterogeneity, will not under any circumstances undermine their social and political order by adopting a policy of unrestricted access for refugees from Vietnam or Iraqi Kurdistan. In such places, the admission of foreigners is attractive only if it reinforces the status quo or the power of the dominant ethnic group. For fear of becoming a party to conflicts involving its neighbors, Honduras resisted permanently accepting Salvadorans and Guatemalans; and for similar reasons, Thailand will not take in Vietnamese, Cambodians, or Burmese on a permanent basis. Thus, because of political, cultural, and security factors, some countries of asylum will always consider refugees to be alien intruders.

Although there is a limit to what development assistance can accomplish, it could be tried in many more places than it has been. Ideally, refugee assistance should function as a kind of preinvestment for eventual development of a refugee- or returnee-settled region, inviting early bilateral participation and follow-up investment to maximize the early contributions. It should concentrate on agriculture and essential services, as well as on infrastructural development such as roads and transportation. Without such an agenda, it is difficult to see how refugees will ever be able to escape the confinement of permanent camps or how returnees will avoid having to seek refuge once more across national borders when local conditions again deteriorate.

## Overcoming Institutional Constraints to Cooperation

Considerable institutional constraints hinder linking development and refugee assistance. In many donor countries, refugee funding is budgeted and programmed separately from long-term economic assistance to developing countries. Similarly, in most host countries, refugees are not included in national or local planning through education, health, agricultural, labor, and other ministries. Instead, separate offices exist for refugee affairs, and these depend on international humanitarian agencies for international aid to maintain themselves as well as to assist refugees. Thus, in both donor and host countries, "humanitarian" or "emergency relief" aid is administratively and programatically divorced from "developmental" concerns.

An additional problem relates to the proliferation of aid agencies in developing countries. A typical Third World host state may have scores of different foreign aid agencies at work on its economy, plus twice as many voluntary agencies assisting refugees. The capacity of these nations to absorb and manage inputs of assistance is limited, yet failure to coordinate their activities almost inevitably leads to an inequitable distribution of scarce resources between different refugee settlements and between refugee and indigenous populations.

Institutional constraints between intergovernmental organizations also inhibit cooperation on development projects. The UNHCR is not a development agency. Although the UNHCR can be a catalyst in initiating development-oriented assistance, other organizations, such as the United Nations Development Program (UNDP), are more suited to the task. Unfortunately, coordination between the UNHCR and other agencies has been difficult to arrange because each has specialized functions that require it to proceed in different time and policy frameworks. The planning and implementation machinery of the World Bank and the UNDP are geared toward long-term development, and projects funded by them are subject to laborious scrutiny before being implemented. Refugee influxes, on the other hand, are often sudden, unexpected, and unplanned and require rapid responses on the part of the international community and the UNHCR in particular.[25] Unlike development agencies, the UNHCR operates on an annual program basis, even in administering long-term solutions.

These divergences in priorities and operational calendars have inhibited progress in assimilating refugees into host communities. It is especially difficult for UNDP to fund refugee development projects because developing countries decide for themselves how to allocate UNDP resources, and most are reluctant to assign any portion of the limited UNDP funds they receive to refugee efforts not related to national development priorities. Not surprisingly, these funds are used for the benefit of the host country's nationals rather than for refugees, whose presence is often unwelcome anyway.

For many less developed countries, the UNHCR remains the sole instrument within the UN system for dealing with refugees. Yet even the UNHCR faces resistance. Many host nations reject local development projects on the grounds that refugees alone will be the primary beneficiaries of the economic assistance—perhaps even at the expense of nationals. These countries have increasingly called for implementation of "additionality," under which refugee aid or aid derived from the presence of refugees would be provided supplementarily to the assistance levels that the country would receive if it harbored no refugees.

During the past decade, a number of international initiatives have tried to make funds available to incorporate refugees into national development plans. Both the International Conference on Assistance to Refugees (ICARA I and II) and the International Conference on Central American Refugees (CIREFCA) argued for infrastructural development assistance to both asylum and home countries.[26] The European Community attempted to stimulate a similar approach by establishing a special fund for development projects, to be implemented in areas affected by refugees or returnees, within the Lome Agreement.[27] Both the UNHCR and the International Council of Voluntary Agencies (ICVA) formulated recommendations for translating the development-oriented approach into action.[28] In the 1980s, interagency joint projects involving the UNHCR and the World Bank were undertaken in Pakistan and Sudan—in afforestation, irrigation, and road-building—that benefited both refugees and host governments.[29] While the concept of development-directed refugee assistance put forward at ICARA II and CIREFCA makes sense, these initiatives have not significantly changed international policy toward refugees, because of insufficient funds, a lack of political will, and the continuing absence of close collaboration between international agencies.

Despite these difficulties, a consensus exists that coordinated development represents a key solution to refugee problems.[30] Recently, the UNHCR and UNDP have increased their efforts to coordinate their actions.[31] Among other things, they have agreed to collaborate on management training for refugee aid and development and to set up a common database on displaced persons. At the same time, UNDP has established a Humanitarian Programs section and has set up emergency units in Africa in an attempt to make in-country emergency responses more timely. UNDP and the UNHCR have also agreed to try to coordinate their actions in Central America, southern Africa, and the Horn (where mass displacements coincide with structural development problems), to collaborate on quick-impact projects in water, health, and farming aid in settings involving mass returns such as in Nicaragua, Cambodia, and Mozambique, and to establish joint management structures to create preventive zones and cross-mandate programs to stabilize and prevent displacement in border areas in the Horn of Africa.

Although relationships between the UNHCR and UNDP have improved in recent years, a pressing need remains for far more effective interagency planning, consultation, and implementation. The roles and responsibilities of the main UN institutions in such efforts continue to be determined on an ad hoc, situation-by-situation basis. To create adequate mechanisms to accommodate a development approach, structural changes and a clarification of mandates are needed within the United Nations, within the host countries, and in the national budgets of donor countries.

Especially urgent is the need to rationalize the mandates of various UN organizations involved in refugee and development assistance.[32] UNDP, in particular, must be encouraged to view refugees as a development resource and to include refugee-affected areas in its country development planning. The creation of the UN Department of Humanitarian Affairs (DHA) has added new potential for bringing the UN's development and emergency capacities together. The UN General Assembly resolution that created the new office emphasized the need to bridge the gap between relief and development. The DHA should act quickly to clarify the roles and responsibilities of the UN agencies and to translate the linkages between relief and development into concrete programs.

Likewise, local NGOs and host governments should be encouraged to take responsibility for managing refugee programs from the outset. The traditional pattern of assistance has been for the UN agencies and international NGOs to design and implement the bulk of refugee aid and development programs, relying only modestly on the involvement of local NGOs and the refugees themselves. But local NGOs are often already present; and with adequate resources, they are more adept both at identifying those in greatest need and at responding effectively and quickly than are overseas agencies.

Similarly, donor countries need to rationalize their mandates and programs. In the United States, for instance, principal responsibility for overseas refugee assistance could easily be assigned to A.I.D. rather than to the State Department. A.I.D. personnel have much more direct practical experience in dealing with mass influxes of refugees than do officials of the State Department Bureau of Refugee Programs. A.I.D. missions in refugee-producing and refugee-receiving countries have long experience in designing, managing, and monitoring relief activities. Moreover, as the development arm of the U.S. government, A.I.D. will more than likely play a significant role in future reconstruction following the repatriations to Afghanistan, Angola, Cambodia, Guatemala, and other places that are likely in the years ahead.[33]

Without more funding, however, structural changes will not enable the development approach to refugee problems to work. Most host countries simply lack the financial resources to manage the increasing influx of people. In particular, there is a need to bridge the institutional gap in the UN system where development falls outside the UNHCR's mandate and UNDP's resources focus almost exclusively on a country's own nationals.

## International Development Fund for Refugee Programs

The gap in UN programs can be addressed by the creation of a new international fund to support a development approach to refugee programs. This is not a new idea.[34] In 1979 the United States envisaged the creation of a United Nations Fund for Durable Solutions[35] whose main purpose was to help developing countries that wished to accept refugees for permanent resettlement, thereby relieving pressures on countries of first asylum and providing the human capital for development projects. The principle was approved by the UNHCR Executive Committee in 1979, but the program remained unfunded and untested, largely because increased demands were made on the donor governments in the early 1980s to assist with refugee crises in Indochina and Africa.

The need for such a fund is even more urgent today. It would fill the gap in the current UN structure, and it would encourage industrialized countries to share the refugee burden with countries of asylum by participating in developing or rehabilitating refugee and returnee areas. Most importantly, it would, in the long term, spare refugees from spending years in nonproductive camp life, and it would prevent returnees from becoming refugees again because of desperate conditions in their home countries.

A vehicle such as an international development fund ought to benefit more than just people who qualify as refugees as defined in the 1951 Convention; it should provide for internally displaced people and for local populations in need who fall between the cracks. Most mass displacements today occur under circumstances of internal conflicts and national disintegration where refugees, internally displaced people, and the rest of the population in the affected areas are inextricably commingled. In these conditions, it is impossible in practice to provide assistance to some of the groups and deny it to others. In certain situations in the Horn of Africa, the UNHCR has already reached beyond its mandate to assist entire communities, including both refugees and nonrefugees, on the basis of need. An international development fund should also bolster efforts to develop comprehensive preventive strategies that address the root causes of refugee outflows in countries of origin. By establishing a development approach to which industrialized nations contribute money and expertise, and poorer countries contribute hospitality and local assistance, the system would allow the double problems of helping refugees reestablish themselves and helping poorer countries develop their resources to be tackled more effectively than these are at present. It might also provide some incentive for refugees and migrants to stay put rather than to move on to the industrialized countries.

Linking refugee assistance with development is strongly advocated by the UNHCR and by prominent NGOs. Coordination between the various agencies is much talked about, and the ways to bring this into effect have been generally agreed on. What is required now is action. Governments must put the issue on the agenda of the governing and coordinating bodies of the UNDP, the World Bank, and other development agencies; and firm decisions and follow-up actions must be taken by the UN Undersecretary General of Humanitarian Assistance regarding the assignment of specific responsibilities for the agencies concerned. Whatever administrative arrangements emerge, additional financing that allows host governments to initiate a development process from the very early stages of a refugee situation will be an essential element of a comprehensive approach that preserves the right of political asylum and makes greater efforts to address the causes of refugee movements. Moreover, as the international refugee regime embarks on the post–Cold War era, the refugee problem must increasingly be addressed in the context of a broad-ranging, transnational diplomatic and political strategy.

# 8

# Resolving Refugee Problems: Addressing Political Causes

Throughout most of the twentieth century, international responses to refugee movements have been motivated by the political self-interest of states as well as by humanitarian interests. In the Nansen era, because refugees were seen as an irritant in interstate relations and as conflicting with the formation and consolidation of new states, governments established an international framework for regularizing the status and control of stateless people in Europe. In the post–World War II era, East–West ideological rivalry and geopolitical considerations provided a sufficient basis in self-interest for Western governments to fund and assist the emerging international refugee regime. The Cold War is finally over, and much has been said about the emergence of a new world order. Refugee movements played a key role both in bringing down the Berlin Wall, the most sinister symbol of the old era, and in ushering in the post–Cold War period by precipitating UN-approved intervention in the internal affairs of Iraq in the aftermath of the Gulf War.

There remains great uncertainty about what will replace the old international order. Local wars and civil unrest continue in many regions of Africa, the Balkans, Southeast Asia, and the ex—Soviet Union. Several countries have lapsed into virtual anarchy, for various reasons, but principally because one ethnic or political group exerts its power over another, often against a historical background of hatred and competition for scarce resources. The potential for violence in such situations has increased because of arms proliferation, population growth, and bankrupt economies;

and the result of this breakdown in governance and escalation of violence has been large-scale forced displacement.

Chapter 7 discussed the need to reform Western asylum policies and to provide significantly more development-oriented assistance. Refugees need assistance to become more self-sufficient in the long term, and impoverished host governments need help to cope with mass influxes of displaced persons. Similarly, countries receiving returning refugees after years of civil war need help in reconstructing their societies. But however important these measures are, they are no more than temporary and expedient policies designed primarily to help the receiving states and only secondarily to help refugees.

The real refugee problem is that political, economic, and security conditions in the home country are so bad that citizens feel compelled to leave. People become refugees because governments persecute citizens, violate human rights, or fail to accommodate competing interests of national minorities or communal or religious groups.

To deal more effectively with post–Cold War refugee movements, the international community must move beyond policies that reflect the thinking of the last four decades. It must promote policies and programs that are designed for the problems of today. While most international attention in the past understandably focused on refugee relief and conditions in host and resettlement countries, only a concerted effort by the United Nations, regional organizations, and governments to deal with the conditions that create refugees holds much prospect of restoring a decent way of life to the victims and of preventing mass buildups of refugees in the future.

The end of the Cold War loosened the logjam of East–West rivalry that once debilitated the efforts of the UN and of regional organizations to promote peacekeeping and to undertake peace enforcement. Consequently, in recent years the UN has taken a number of initiatives across the world that involve wider use of civilian and military observers, UN guards, and peacekeeping forces. While these initiatives have given new importance and visibility to humanitarian issues, the UN operates with considerable handicaps. The UN Secretariat and the Security Council are simply not well suited to coping with internal conflicts. In Angola, Cambodia, Somalia, Sudan, and the former Yugoslavia, the UN is presented with bitter civil wars, in circumstances where political systems and (in many cases) borders lack legitimacy.

While the UN has had some important recent successes in El Salvador, Namibia, and Nicaragua, where it has helped disarm contending forces, monitor elections, and end long-standing conflicts of a partly internal character, it is not likely to succeed in resolving all civil wars. Armed intervention even for simple humanitarian purposes, will always be carried out selectively, and in some cases it will stand no chance of success. Moreover, international political support for intervening in such situations is difficult to obtain. States remain reluctant to commit their soldiers to costly UN missions that seem distant and of little direct relevance to their own immediate national security concerns. However optimistic one may be about the future peacemaking capabilities of the international community, international organizations as presently constituted are highly constrained in their activities by the desire of governments to control both their commitment of armed forces and their financial expenditures.

Thus, given the nature, size, and complexity of today's refugee problem and the limitations of the existing international institutions to deal with these issues, no overall permanent solution or "quick fix" can be expected. On the other hand, neither individual governments nor international organizations can walk away from problems just because they are difficult to tackle. To do so would only increase the risk of having internal conflicts spill over borders and create further regional instability and refugee movements. Much more can be done to promote and improve collaborative actions on the refugee issue and to provide for a more action-oriented multilateral system. In particular, capabilities for quick and effective reaction to ethnic conflicts and refugee problems need to be built up. The aim of this concluding chapter is to indicate directions for more effective political and diplomatic approaches to refugee situations now and in the future.

## Dealing with Mass Exodus and Humanitarian Emergencies

Examples of mass population movements during the past few years— Kurds massing on the tops of mountains along national borders; Muslims, Croats, and Serbs forcibly expelled from their homes in deliberate attempts to "cleanse" land of certain ethnic groups; Rohingya Muslims fleeing Burma's war of attrition and persecution against them; emaciated Liberians, Sudanese, Ethiopians, and Somalis fleeing incredibly brutal civil wars—have raised new questions about the sanctity of borders, the nature of sovereignty, the right of external intervention, and the international protection of ethnic groups. They have also fostered intense debate regarding what operational and political changes are required in the international system to deal with these issues more effectively in the future.

Until recently, the international community has been utterly unable to respond to massive violations of human rights, because states resisted humanitarian intervention within their borders, claiming that their national sovereignty was at stake.[1] During the Cold War, the UN became involved in situations involving massive human rights violations or in internal conflicts only when invited to do so by the government of the state concerned. The impediments to action were both political and legal: Article 2 of the UN Charter prohibits the UN from intervening in matters that fall essentially within the domestic jurisdiction of any state.

While sovereignty is still recognized as a cardinal feature of the contemporary international political and legal systems, the legal and political arguments against UN intervention in internal conflicts are no longer unassailable. Recent events may be effecting a change in practice and in law. Certain internal actions and policies—especially those that result in mass expulsions or refugee movements—are increasingly regarded as threats to others, particularly by their neighbors. For example, internal wars frequently result in the spillover of conflict or of internal human rights crises into nearby countries, resulting not only in the outflow of refugees, incursions by rebel armies, and the loss of crucial materials and markets, but also in the exacerbation of interstate tensions and the destabilization and overthrow of governments. From this perspective, grievous human rights abuses are not solely an internal matter, particularly when neighboring countries must bear the cost of repression by having refugees forced on them.

The most notorious recent example is Iraq's brutal treatment of its Kurdish population. Resolution 688 condemned Iraq's repression of its civilian population and argued that the consequences of this repression— the massive flow of refugees across international frontiers—threatened "peace and security in the region". The ensuing military intervention by the allies in northern Iraq and the subsequent emplacement of UN guards constitute an example of collective action authorized by the Security Council under Chapter 7 of the UN Charter to maintain and restore "international peace and security."

Similarly, the international community's response to widespread suffering and famine in Somalia marked yet another major shift in practice. The UN resolution authorizing the dispatch of U.S. and other troops to Somalia to deliver humanitarian assistance broke new ground because the intervention did not require the prior consent of an established government or national authority in the country of destination for the troops. While it is still unlikely that the international community would be prepared to intervene in all cases with humanitarian aid to civilians against the express wishes of a government, the previously held notion of inviolable state sovereignty is increasingly called into question.

The grounds for humanitarian intervention to provide relief and protection are also bolstered by the greater recognition that is given to the notion that sovereignty carries with it certain responsibilities of states toward their own citizens. Sovereignty does not mean that a state can behave in any way it wants toward its own citizens without consequence; in fact, the most elementary justification for the modern state is its ability to provide reasonable security for its citizens. Thus, "states that abandon their principal *raison d'être*—protection of citizens—in the interests of *raison d'état*, chip away at the legitimacy that insulates them from external influence."[2]

In addition, there is now greater revulsion among members of the international community toward using the term *sovereignty* to shield dictators from outside interference. Indeed, in many cases, what is threatened by outside intervention is not the sovereignty of states, but only the license of violent men and lawless governments to abuse their people. The end of the Cold War makes it easier for the West to abandon the notion that Western aid to dictators is necessitated by considerations of anticommunism and other security interests. While the level of international concern regarding humanitarian crises continues to depend in part on international public opinion and the influence of particular states, governments are being pressed to become more accountable to their own citizens. In the post–Cold War era, human rights and good governance have moved from the wings to center stage and are increasingly viewed as matters of international political significance.

The international attention directed at human rights abuses and mass exodus emergencies is aided by the advent of global satellite communications. Television coverage of young children starving in Somalia and other African countries, of people being bombed and attacked in the Kurdish and Shiite regions of Iraq, and of people being forced out of their homes and herded into detention centers in Bosnia have made citizens of the advanced industrialized states increasingly aware of human rights worldwide and of their impact on regional and global stability. Western politicians have begun to realize that public opinion can be mobilized quickly by the media and that their populations now see them as having a new kind of international responsibility. As a result, refugee and migration matters appear increasingly on the agendas of the UN Security Council; the Group of Seven; the Group of Twenty-four; regional organizations such as the EC, OAU, OAS, and ASEAN; and collective security councils such as NATO and the Western European Union (WEU). There is also a growing realization that assistance and political efforts must extend far beyond charitable and humanitarian concern, and that strategies and anticipatory foreign policies that deal with the root causes of the refugee problem have become a necessary part of the search for long-term stability in the world today.

## A Comprehensive Strategy

Strong and sustained political commitment to preventive action is the attribute most required when dealing with mass exodus emergencies. Combating the causes of forced migration can no longer proceed solely within the confines of the UNHCR and international humanitarian organizations. A preventive strategy must involve practically the entire UN system, as well as regional organizations and NGOs, and requires enhancing these organizations' capacities to defuse, to deter, and to mediate incipient crises before they may need more serious and costly transsovereign intervention. At a minimum, therefore, the following measures need to be undertaken.

## The Establishment of an Independent
## UN Monitoring Body

Effective prevention depends on good intelligence, yet the UN has little means to gather information or to analyze it. Establishing an independent monitoring body within the UN that would alert the Secretary-General, the UN Emergency Relief Coordinator, and the Security Council to potential refugee emergencies could provide an early warning mechanism.[3] The UN system should be broadly mobilized to provide timely warnings, and members of the monitoring body could include UN officials, NGO representatives, and governments.[4]

For example, the capability and mandate of the UN Center for Human Rights needs to be strengthened to enable it to monitor and collect accurate and up-to-date human rights information, identify situations that have the potential to produce mass refugee flows, and bring these to the attention of the international community.[5] Furthermore, the UN Commission on Human Rights could assign its Sub-Commission on Prevention of Discrimination and Protection of Minorities to monitor the treatment of ethnic and religious minorities and to alert the Secretary-General when action is needed. Similarly, the early warning capabilities of the UNHCR and UNDP should be bolstered, and an annual review of the root causes of refugee flows should be prepared for review at the annual UN Human Rights Commission meetings.

Potentially among the most important new instruments added to the UN's capacities is the organization's ability to send UN fact-finding missions to defuse disputes and prevent major crises from expanding.[6] In addition, many human rights NGOs now monitor and report human rights violations, but there is little coordination among them and almost no realization of the connection between human rights abuses and refugee movements. Similarly, political analysts and independent research institutes could assist policymakers by identifying potential conflicts and risks to political and social stability and advising them about the sorts of situations against which the UN and regional organizations could take preemptive action. The time has arrived for the establishment of effective monitoring networks that can place both the United Nations and regional organizations in a better position to rationalize their efforts to plan more effective counteraction that addresses the causes of displacement.

No matter how advanced the early warning system, political obstacles frequently must be overcome to enable the interested international organizations to react quickly enough to minimize suffering and problems of insecurity. Moreover, early warning programs need to be connected to decision-making and response strategies both in governments and in relief, development, and human rights organizations. In many recent refugee crises, information about impending conflicts and mass migrations was available and well known in advance but was routinely ignored. In ex-Yugoslavia and in Somalia, for example, international agencies and an-

alysts had accurately predicted what would happen well before the disasters unfolded; but there existed no mechanisms and institutions for
averting conflicts or for dealing effectively and rapidly with these crises at a
time when they were still manageable.

It is critical to focus efforts on staving off refugee flows, not by forcing
people to stay and risk death but by helping them before they feel it
necessary to move. This requires reinforcing existing tools of diplomacy,
human rights monitoring, and assistance. Unless sufficient political will to
resolve conflicts and refugee problems is in place, any measures that might
be taken to prepare for future refugee flows—such as the institution of an
effective early warning system—are likely to be of limited use. The value of
such measures depends largely on the willingness of states and international organizations to take the necessary concerted preventive action.

### Greater Use of the UN Security Council
### in Human Rights and Refugee Emergencies

The international community has called on the UN repeatedly in recent
years to deal more actively with the consequences of many conflicts, including refugee movements. It is increasingly obvious that diplomatic and
international relief efforts also need to address the causes of displacement
before people are forced to flee to another country—not as a substitute for
asylum, but as a way of enabling people to remain in their own countries
in safety. Yet significant remaining obstacles prevent the UN from mobilizing an active anticipatory strategy for refugee movements.

Many governments, particularly in the developing world, continue to
resist a more assertive international organization, fearing that any Security
Council–sanctioned intervention would simply be a cover for more powerful nation-states to use in pursuing their own interests and in wielding
their international influence. Moreover, the Security Council appears to
be reluctant to support structural reforms that would give the Secretary-
General real power to engage in effective preventive diplomacy. Finally, the
ability of the UN to play a major role in peacekeeping and peacemaking is
sharply limited by financial constraints. The UN is starved for funds because many countries, most notably the United States, have been slow to
make up their long-standing deficits and to supply additional funds.

Notwithstanding these constraints, the upsurge of UN peacekeeping
and enforcement activities has demonstrated the indispensibility of international organizations in the post–Cold War period. The UN has a repu-
tation for impartiality that no other body can equal, and it possesses skills
in peacekeeping and mediation that no other source can offer. Only the
UN can muster the resources to respond and the legitimacy to override
sovereignty when necessary. But in order for the UN to realize its full
potential and to become more proactive, the Security Council must undertake a number of vital reforms.

The key to future UN effectiveness in preventive diplomacy depends on the UN's ability and willingness to move at the very earliest stage of a crisis. For this purpose the Secretary-General needs to have at hand a permanent standby military capacity, to prevent the escalation of conflicts, to enforce ceasefires among warring parties, and to undertake humanitarian interventions to feed and protect civil war victims.[7]

In responding to future refugee-generating conflicts, the Security Council does not face an "all or nothing" choice between authorizing a full-scale military intervention or doing nothing at all. Much can be done short of embroiling the international community in armed action every time an internal conflict threatens to erupt out of control and generate huge numbers of refugees and internally displaced people. Currently, UN personnel protect minorities and refugees threatened by communal violence, oversee disengagement agreements in civil wars, protect and deliver humanitarian relief, monitor human rights violations, supervise and observe elections, provide development assistance, help build civil and legal institutions, and enforce arms and economic sanctions.

Unfortunately, the mandates of the UN agencies carrying out these tasks are often unclear, and their activities are usually uncoordinated. As a first priority, the UN should rationalize and clarify responsibilities, improve interagency coordination, and establish guidelines for graduated responses to humanitarian crises. But preparing for a more comprehensive and effective UN response requires adequate funding and resources, which have to be available at short notice. The Secretary-General and the Security Council cannot fulfill their potential unless the United States and other major donor states are prepared to bear a greater financial burden—albeit one that, when compared to the monies spent on defense during the Cold War, is hardly significant.

### Full Support for the UN Department of Humanitarian Affairs

Another prerequisite is full political and financial support for the UN Emergency Relief Coordinator, in order to strengthen and expedite international action in humanitarian emergencies, especially in cases where governments refuse to cooperate.

Numerous contemporary conflicts—the 1991 Gulf War and its aftermath, interclan conflict in Somalia, and ethnic war in ex-Yugoslavia—highlight the plight of people in other countries around the world whom the international community has had difficulty in reaching. Existing human rights law does not stipulate that victims of massive displacements have a right to humanitarian assistance and access. Generally, providing assistance to refugees and internally displaced people has been contingent on approval by host or home governments; and in many cases, international organizations and NGOs have delayed assistance to people whose lives were at risk, either because governments have not given their consent or because no central authority exists to request and authorize outside aid.

Recent internal wars also highlight the problems of coordinating a rapid and effective humanitarian operation, especially in the opening days of an emergency.[8] The problem goes beyond the capacity of any one agency. What is needed is a coordinated and concerted response from the UN system and from the NGOs. Although several UN agencies and NGOs, including the UNHCR, are regularly involved in emergency refugee operations, no strong international structures exist for consultation and action on the global refugee problem.[9] UN agencies have a very limited capacity to procure, store, transport, and distribute large amounts of assistance within a short time frame. Insufficient resources are available to build and maintain the emergency preparedness and response capacities of agencies.

The new UN office is an important first step toward integrating the activities of the wide array of UN agencies and imposing a structural approach that would include long-term strategies for dealing with refugee problems, where only short-term ad hoc humanitarian efforts now exist. The Coordinator will facilitate the relief work of the different UN agencies, make contact with outside organizations, and negotiate access for such agencies in an emergency, without waiting for a formal government request.

The UN resolution establishing the Department of Humanitarian Affairs (DHA) allows humanitarian aid to be provided, with "the consent of the affected country,"[10] rather than at its request, as was the case in the past. Thus, while governments have not fully endorsed humanitarian intervention, the resolution gives political backing to practical strategies that are part of an emerging humanitarian diplomacy. Various actions are now available to give the international community access to intervene on behalf of refugees and displaced people.[11] "Corridors of tranquility," through which relief convoys are allowed to pass without interference, and "humanitarian ceasefires," "zones of peace," and "safe havens," which allow humanitarian assistance to be provided to those in need in conflict zones, are pragmatic mechanisms that have been used by the UN and by NGOs in recent years in such places as Angola, Ethiopia, Iraq, Sri Lanka, Sudan, Somalia, and ex-Yugoslavia. The UN Coordinator can build on these precedents to create modalities for protecting and assisting vulnerable populations and can devise further mechanisms to ensure freer humanitarian access.

In order for the establishment of DHA to lead to some improvements in the response capacity of the United Nations, the coordinating role of DHA needs to be recognized by other UN agencies, and the department needs to be fully supplied with political and financial support so that it can effectively undertake the tasks assigned to it. The international community also needs to go beyond simply coordinating humanitarian aspects of relief to address humanitarian, security, and political problems as a whole. In post–Cold War situations like those in Somalia and the former Yugoslavia, humanitarian agencies certainly need coordination, but greater efforts have to be made to prevent the manipulation by warring factions of international humanitarian aid.

Greater attention must also be given to bolstering the capability of the organization to intervene politically in internal and ethnic conflicts. For example, no provisions for conflict resolution are included in the UN resolution authorizing the new office, despite the fact that this is one of the primary ingredients needed to ameliorate the causes of displacement. In addition to developing a concerted response to refugee emergencies, the United Nations should concentrate on solving the underlying political problems, whether this involves developing capabilities for early warning or creating frameworks for prevention and conflict resolution. At a minimum, the DHA's activities must closely interface with the political and peacekeeping arm of the UN Secretariat. This will require that governments not only strengthen the capacity of the UN to engage in preventive diplomacy and reinforce regular UN peacekeeping operations by ensuring adequate financial and political support for these missions, but also support efforts to establish a UN humanitarian rapid deployment force to protect humanitarian relief operations, to monitor and report on ceasefire and human rights violations, and to create confidence and a measure of security in civil conflicts.[12]

Not all humanitarian emergencies and problems of international security will be amenable to UN solutions, however. As has previously been noted, the UN is overstretched in its commitments, particularly with regard to internal conflicts. While governments are likely to continue to turn to the UN for help in conflict resolution (given that as many peacekeeping operations have been launched since 1988 as in the previous 42 years), current expectations may be outstripping institutional capacities and political realities. Without structural changes and far greater resources and political backing, the UN will necessarily be limited in its response capabilities and will appear weak and ineffective in many situations.

### *The Establishment and Strengthening at the Regional Level of Emergency Relief and Conflict Resolution Machinery*

Regional structures of cooperation and intervention do exist, but their mandates and capabilities need to be strengthened and given financial and political support if regional organizations are to be used to modify refugee-producing situations and deal with local instabilities.

A regional approach to ethnic and minority disputes and displacement is a necessary supplement to a global-level effort. In some instances, governments are readier to cooperate with neighboring states or regional organizations than to tolerate intervention under direct UN auspices. In many situations, regional organizations may be better suited to resolving local conflicts than either the UN or outside powers, provided that they have the resources and political will to act. They may better understand the basis for local conflicts, and they are more likely to have a direct interest in resolving the problems. Regarding refugee movements, regional organizations typically develop standards that are more comprehensive than the relatively narrow UN definition of a refugee. Comprehensive regional plans have also attempted to address the causes of refugee outflows. The 1989 International Conference on Central American Refugees (CIREFCA) and the Comprehensive Plan of Action (CPA) adopted by the 1989 International Conference on Indochinese Refugees are significant examples of this trend.

The difficulty with a regional approach is that regional organizations are often poorly equipped to respond effectively to conflicts and to humanitarian emergencies. Generally, regional mechanisms and infrastructure for intervening in an anticipatory way to settle disputes are inadequate or nonexistent, and regional organizations have insufficient logistical capacities to engage in peacekeeping operations. An important task for the UN, therefore, is to offer regional organizations technical assistance and training to build their competence and operational capacity in these new functions.

Independent monitoring could also be greatly strengthened at the regional level. Regional organizations have traditionally not criticized member governments involved in internal conflicts that generated mass refugee flows and have demonstrated even more deference to state sovereignty than has the United Nations. As the UN increases its emphasis on the responsibility of regional organizations to assume leadership within their regions in areas such as conflict resolution and peacekeeping, so too might the UN emphasize the need for greater human rights monitoring and humanitarian aid within each region. African, Latin American, and Asian versions of the International Committee of the Red Cross (ICRC) could be established to ensure the neutral delivery of humanitarian aid to victims of conflict. Similarly, Refugee Watch organizations could be established within each refugee-producing region to monitor the protection needs of refugees, asylum seekers, and the internally displaced. Creating such organizations could provide a basis for consciousness-raising regarding humanitarian norms and democratic principles within regions, and it could enable local organizations to assume responsibility for monitoring, intervening, and managing humanitarian programs without major external involvement or infringement of concepts of national sovereignty.

### Europe

In Europe, the failure of the international community to prevent conflict in the former Yugoslavia and the threat of further instability in the Balkans, the ex–Soviet Union, and North Africa have made it imperative that West European organizations pay greater attention to prevention, early warning, and conflict management. To deal with these emerging problems, organizations such as the Conference on Security and Cooperation in Europe (CSCE) must become much more competent in arbitrating minority disputes, including promoting the establishment of democratic governments and fostering respect for human rights and the rights of minorities.

Some new form of security system for Europe is desperately needed to deal with European crises of the type that have recently occurred in former Yugoslavia. No single institution is likely to be able to deal quickly and effectively with internal conflicts in the new Europe. The CSCE, the European Community, NATO, the West European Union, and the Council of Europe will have to cooperate with and complement each other more closely in the future. The CSCE, with its crisis prevention center, could be strengthened to play a significant role in helping to defuse or discourage future military confrontations between ethnic groups and member states in the Baltics, the Caucasus, Moldova, Ukraine, and Central Asia, and to act as a crisis manager in Europe. Although the CSCE has great potential for humanitarian and preventive intervention in the region, the organization at present lacks teeth to implement its decisions.

In addition, the current absence of a regional military force to back up peacemaking efforts has limited Europe's ability to cope with ethnic conflict. Western peace enforcement interventions in the region would be greatly strengthened if they could take advantage of NATO's planning and logistical apparatus, as well as of its integrated command structure and forces. While NATO, the West European Union (WEU), and the Commonwealth of Independent States (CIS) have all pledged support for regional peacekeeping efforts, numerous practical and political issues make collective military action difficult to organize. Western political and military leaders consider military intervention in the region's ethnic conflicts to be not only too costly in human life and financial expenditure, but also operationally difficult to implement. They are reluctant to initiate military action in countries where ceasefires are not strictly observed and where conflicts continue unabated. Moreover, the CSCE, because of its unwieldy size (52 members in late 1992) and existing procedural limitations (including its rule—until recently—of taking decisions by consensus only), cannot be counted on to be successful in every case. Other smaller and more cohesive European institutions, such as the Council of Europe or WEU, may have to assume a larger role in minority rights and conflict resolution. Thus, the establishment of new regional arrangements that include encouraging more representative forms of government, offering explicit protection of minorities, providing arbitration measures between ethnic groups and states, and delineating the grounds for intervention are indispensible in dealing with Europe's future refugee and migration flows.

## Africa

Governments in Africa and other Third World regions may, because of their colonial history, be more ready to cooperate with regional organizations than with international ones to resolve their internal conflicts. Since its inception, the Organization of African Unity (OAU) has been prevented by African dictators from responding strongly against regimes that violated human rights and generated refugees. If the new democracies emerging on the continent survive and begin to take root, the capacity of the OAU and of African governments to enforce the observance of human rights, to resolve conflicts, and to deal more fully and effectively with refugee problems will be strengthened.

Democratization in Africa does not mean that ethnic conflicts and refugee movements will end. Indeed, the political changes now underway will probably result in increased conflicts, as groups contend for control of political systems after the demise of one-party states and military rule. In addition, most of Africa, which already hosts a large proportion of the world's refugees, is in the midst of a severe economic crisis, manifested by a drastic decline in per capita income, low or negative rates of economic growth, a collapsing social and physical infrastructure, high rates of population increase, declining terms of trade of primary commodities, and problems of indebtedness. To prepare for the predicted increase in refugee flows, the UNHCR, ICRC, the Federation of Red Cross and Red Crescent Societies, and human rights bodies should train OAU staff and African-based agencies in the areas of refugee assistance, international conventions pertaining to the legal rights of refugees, and the range of responsibilities that must be assumed by countries of first asylum.

Independent monitoring also could enhance the OAU's capability to play a more effective role in humanitarian emergencies. The OAU has already proposed to create both a regional ombuds panel, consisting of eminent mediators to serve the organization's Secretary-General as investigators, monitors, and negotiators, and a regional peacekeeping force for humanitarian intervention. An Africa Refugee Watch Group could monitor and report refugee protection problems and alert the OAU and the international community to emerging crises, without incurring the same degree of criticism that outside agencies might.

Regional conflict prevention machinery should also be bolstered to mediate ethnic disputes within African countries. Unfortunately, the history of African involvement is not very encouraging. Traditionally, the OAU has protected the interests of its state members by rigorously insisting that its members respect the territorial integrity of other states and by denying national minorities the right to secede. In addition, the OAU took few, if any, steps to try to resolve any of the major civil wars in the Horn of Africa or southern Africa during the 1980s. In the early 1990s, OAU action has been similarly lacking or ineffective. Although regional and U.N. initiatives were taken to negotiate peace in Somalia in 1991 and 1992, African leaders took insufficient action either to avert full-scale civil war after the overthrow of Siad Barre or to press the international community to intervene politically in the crisis when the danger of widespread famine was known.

The only case in which an African organization has intervened in an attempt to end a civil war on the continent was in Liberia beginning in 1990, when the Economic Community of West African States (ECOWAS) undertook a limited intervention in Liberia with a regional peacekeeping force to try to restore order after the Doe government in Monrovia had collapsed. Continued fighting threatened security in the region, both through creation of a huge refugee outflow into neighboring countries ill-equipped to handle such influxes and through the risk of a direct spillover of fighting from Liberia into adjoining West African states. Unfortunately, this regional force was unable to restore order and stability, and in subsequent years has itself become party to the internal conflict. In late 1992, the UN Security Council imposed an embargo on arms sales to the contending Liberian forces and supported ECOWAS's efforts to broker peace accords and enforce a ceasefire. While the willingness of ECOWAS to become involved in the civil war in Liberia indicates recognition by many African governments of the link between regional security and population displacements and thus points to new possibilities for finding regional solutions to internal conflicts and refugee problems in Africa, the region's leaders need to demonstrate greater responsibility for resolving their own problems.

*Latin America*

In the Americas, the Organization of American States (OAS) recently broke a forty-year tradition of nonintervention by forging a campaign of diplomatic and economic pressure to isolate the military junta in Haiti and tried to mediate between the contending parties to restore the elected government of President Jean-Bertrand Aristide. Political leaders in the Western Hemisphere were concerned that the failure of democracy in Haiti could embolden the militaries in their own countries to seize power, as well as setting off a civil war in Haiti and a quickening outmigration of refugees. While regional states were willing to address the root causes of the Haitian exodus, the diplomatic effort was undermined when the United States refused to provide temporary asylum for the large numbers of boat people who fled persecution and the already desperate economic conditions made worse by the embargo. A successful resolution of the Haitian refugee problem will require both a more active effort to mediate the overall political problem in Haiti and a more effective exercise of external leverage to ensure that human rights conditions improve in Haiti.

The election of constitutional governments in Latin America and the lessening of ideological polarities and tensions in the region do not spell the end to instability and refugee movements. Most people still live in poverty[13] and on the margins of the democratic process; and the growing inequalities of wealth, the lack of public facilities in housing, health care, and education, widespread corruption and mismanagement, the continuing mistrust and hatred between former enemies after years of civil strife,

and the underlying ethnic divisions between Indians and people of Spanish origin could produce violent confrontations and refugee exoduses. The
OAS has formally declared that it will support democratically elected governments against coups d'état and other antidemocratic attacks,[14] and it
has dispatched election monitors to Nicaragua, El Salvador, and Peru; but
the OAS needs to create stronger mechanisms and exert greater political
will to preserve fragile democracies and prevent refugee flows—in particular by bolstering the powers of the Inter-American Human Rights Commission and by establishing a regional rapid reaction force and peacekeeping capability.

The United Nations can provide important support to initiatives taken
by regional organizations to deal with the root causes of refugee flows. Two
examples are the UN Observer Mission in El Salvador (ONUSAL),
which has been set up to monitor the human rights situation in El Salvador, and the UN Transitional Authority in Cambodia (UNTAC), which
is charged with overseeing human rights protection during the period
leading up to national elections.

For more than a decade, prospects for a negotiated settlement of El
Salvador's civil war were bogged down by the intractability of the political
and military struggle for power and the inability of moderate and democratic forces to control or contain the actions of the army or the opposition
FMLN. Massive human rights violations and indiscriminate warfare drove
over 1 million people out of the country. UN-sponsored negotiations
seem finally to have broken this violent stalemate. Both sides agreed not
only to accept UN verification of the negotiated agreement, but to oversee
human rights practices and constitutional reforms designed to make Salvadoran political life more democratic. As part of ONUSAL, a special
human rights component was created to provide active monitoring of the
human rights situation in El Salvador, to investigate specific cases of
alleged violations of human rights, to promote human rights through
judicial and police reforms, and to make periodic reports to the UN
Secretary-General. While ONUSAL has been criticized for not being
more forceful in investigating allegations of human rights abuses, the
presence of independent observers has led to a general reduction in human
rights violations in El Salvador. Since the end of the war, the UNHCR has
worked closely with ONUSAL in monitoring the safety of returning refugees in El Salvador.

UNTAC in Cambodia exercises an even more ambitious mandate than
does ONUSAL in El Salvador. UNTAC's authority is vast: not only is it
responsible for demobilizing warring factions and protecting the return
home of hundreds of thousands of refugees, but it has an extensive mandate over the civil administration of the country. It is actively engaged in
human rights monitoring and in organizing and conducting national elections. Despite continuing tension in Cambodia, UNTAC has helped to
stabilize the situation of the returning refugees and of the internally displaced after more than 10 years of bitter civil conflict and horrendous

human rights violations. By early 1993, almost all Cambodian refugees had returned home from the Thai-Cambodian border.

The establishment of UNTAC and ONUSAL may point the way toward expanded roles for the UN in restoring order to other states riven by violence, anarchy, and economic collapse. The inclusion of human rights and humanitarian action in the mandates of UN peacekeeping and peacemaking operations is a viable and practical way of tackling the root causes of displacement and may provide useful lessons for dealing with similar situations in other regions of the world. It may also encourage both the UN and regional human rights regimes to focus more on the protection of returning refugees.[15]

## Political Leadership

In the final analysis, solving refugee problems depends on political leadership and on the exercise of political will. In the past, progress was made when an individual High Commissioner or political leader was prepared to seize the initiative to establish a program or to influence governments to be generous in providing assistance and protection to refugees. However, the problems of virulent nationalisms destroying societies and producing millions of refugees go beyond anything recent leaders have had to deal with and require Western governments, acting through the UN or in partnership with regional bodies, to confront instances of aggression and persecution conducted against civilian populations. Never more than now has it been so appropriate to launch a series of bold initiatives to deal with national and international policies and practices toward refugees.

Although the leadership of the UN High Commissioner for Refugees is crucial, it is not enough. The President of the United States and other political leaders also hold key assets in any serious effort to strengthen the UN refugee system; and the new UN Secretary-General, Boutros Boutros-Ghali, must be prepared to proceed with imagination and political courage to invigorate multilateral mechanisms. These initiatives would draw attention to the serious deterioration in norms and proper conduct that has occurred in some states with respect to the treatment of citizens and refugees. It would attempt to deal with the causes of refugee flows, rather than with the consequences.

The United Nations is still the only body capable of managing many of the complex global problems of the post–Cold War era. The international community needs to take advantage of both the structural and technical reforms that have occurred within the UN system and the higher expectations for the UN that now exist. But events in Iraq, in ex-Yugoslavia, and in Somalia have demonstrated that the UN is not a separate entity capable of imposing order by itself, nor is it capable of achieving success in every endeavor. The UN is the sum of its member states, and U.S. and Western leadership in invigorating multilateral programs is a key factor if the UN is to achieve optimum results.

The United States is still the only nation whose leadership most other nations are willing to follow, and it is the country most capable of setting up various measures to direct international efforts toward a constructive goal. Therefore, American leadership is vital in galvanizing collective efforts to resolve many of the complex humanitarian problems of the post–Cold War era. While addressing American domestic needs is important, governmental willingness to deal with regional and international instabilities, such as ethnic conflicts and mass refugee movements, is critical to America's prospects—particularly if the United States wants to play an effective role internationally. Moreover, without active American involvement, the international community will be limited to reactive, damage-control measures in response to humanitarian crises. As we move toward the twenty-first century, the United States, along with other donor countries, must make every effort to provide the financing, commodities, and other resources that alone can enable the UN to meet the expectations invested in it.

Western Europe and (especially) Japan must exert more initiative. Japan and Germany should be encouraged to take on roles commensurate with their economic stature, including more international responsibilities in humanitarian and peacekeeping activities. German and European concerns will by necessity be focused largely on humanitarian and political problems in Central Europe, the Balkans, and the former Soviet Union. Japanese efforts, on the other hand, will have a more global scope but undoubtedly will center on Indochina, Afghanistan, and other Asian locales with special political and humanitarian needs. The United States should recognize Japan's and Germany's new status by supporting non-veto, nonpermanent seats in the Security Council for these governments, along with seats for a number of representative Third World states.

A failure by the United States and its allies to increase the capacities of the UN at this time will almost surely lead to a breakdown in international security and to needless drains on future aid programs in order to deal with new war-caused famines or refugee movements. Not since 1945 has the international community been presented with such an opportunity to make substantial progress on many political and humanitarian issues. That opportunity should now be seized.

## An Action Program

The end of the Cold War gives the international community a unique opportunity to lay the foundations of an action program that includes the following elements.

### *Establishing a Basis for Collective Intervention in Internal Conflicts*

It is time for a major debate about how the UN, regional bodies, and states can effectively intervene in internal conflicts. In particular, the international community needs to find ways to deter the growing use by some governments of mass expulsion of national communities perceived to be political or economic liabilities. The democratic states must maintain the principle that territorial aggression and policies of forced expulsion are totally unacceptable, in the Balkans, in the former Soviet Union, and elsewhere. The international community must establish a basis for taking sanctions against such governments.

One approach would be for the international community to agree that national sovereignty is a privilege of government contingent on satisfying certain minimum standards of treatment of the country's own residents. Under this conception, when national minorities are subjected to violence or when a state is indifferent to the starvation of its citizens, the government loses its right to claim that it is pursuing a purely internal policy that lies within its authority to undertake, without external interference, as a matter of national sovereignty. Amending Chapter 7 of the UN Charter so that the UN could take action not only when a threat to international peace and security arises but also when a gross violation of human rights occurs would underline this fundamental change in the understanding of sovereignty.

However, many states—including some members of the Security Council—would be strongly opposed to changing the UN Charter in such a way. Another more politically feasible approach would be to establish a framework of general principles that would guide the international community in deciding when a domestic situation warrants international action, either by the Security Council or by regional organizations. By clearly articulating the principles on behalf of which the international community may need to intervene, as well as the practical considerations that might restrain such action, the UN would strengthen its capacity to respond to growing international instability and human misery.

Armed intervention would be only one of a set of possible policy options. In the first instance, oppressive regimes should be denied certain important benefits of the international system, such as access to the facilities of the World Bank and the International Monetary Fund. These institutions are beginning to scrutinize military expenditures by potential borrowers and in some cases are demanding cutbacks in military expenditures as a precondition for issuing loans. This conditioning of aid on reduced military expenditures discourages arms sales to abusive regimes and encourages recipient governments to spend more of their national budgets on human needs and social programs. The intended end result is the development of civil societies that are more prone to respect the rights of individuals and national minorities, thus making them safer places for people to remain at home.

A forceful human rights policy, linked to economic and diplomatic actions and collective sanctions, provides an appropriate basis for responding to regimes that maintain brutal policies and thereby force expulsion to neighboring countries. Under such circumstances, mass expulsions of people are analogous to military invasions, and UN or regional police or even military action should be seen as reasonable responses, particularly when other means of deterrence have failed.

The UN's capability to respond to mass expulsions would be strengthened further if UN and regional human rights machinery were designed to address the protection of minorities. At present, the UN human rights program is understaffed and underfunded, and it has neglected the politically contentious issue of national minorities. If the UN hopes to respond more effectively to the global problems of the 1990s, it should greatly strengthen its capacity to monitor developments in this field.

The UN human rights system demonstrated its potential capability to respond quickly to such emergencies when it called an extraordinary meeting of the UN Commission for Human Rights and appointed a special rapporteur to investigate human rights abuses of minority populations in Bosnia and to report his recommendations to the Security Council. Similarly, the establishment of an air exclusion zone over southern Iraq (although politically inspired) was given humanitarian justification by a stinging report by the UN rapporteur on human rights in Iraq, which alleged enforced deportation, murder, and burning of the Shiite population by the Iraqi Army.

These actions underscore the increasing involvement of the Security Council in humanitarian matters and the growing recognition that promotion and protection of human rights are an integral part of UN peacemaking. Without an enhanced capacity to collect information, intercede with governments, and develop recommendations for action by the Security Council and the Secretary-General, the UN's ability to focus international attention on human rights crises and to avert future mass expulsions will be severely limited.

### Ensuring International Access to Areas Experiencing Humanitarian Crises

It is essential to find ways to encourage governments to allow international access to victims in humanitarian emergencies. "Humanitarian corridors," "safe havens," and other such devices have thus far proceeded with the "acquiescence" of governments such as Sudan and Iraq; but in agreeing to them, these governments have in effect temporarily ceded their sovereignty over the parts of their national territory where the UN is present. The UN General Assembly adopted resolutions on humanitarian access (in 1988) and relief corridors (in 1990) to enable the safe passage of humanitarian aid, giving further legitimacy to these measures.[16] The deterioration of the security situation in Somalia in 1992 prompted the Security Council to approve the dispatch of UN military observers to monitor a ceasefire in Somalia and an armed humanitarian escort of UN guards to protect agency personnel and equipment and to escort humanitarian supplies inland to distribution centers.[17] When these efforts proved totally ineffective and insufficient for the task, the United States dispatched over 22,000 troops to Somalia in a UN-sanctioned intervention in late 1992.

The United Nations must build upon these precedents, declaring an international right to humanitarian access and including endorsement of cross-border relief operations.[18] Bernard Kouchner, France's minister for humanitarian affairs, has called for recognition of a right of humanitarian intervention to enable the international community to take action within another state for humanitarian purposes. The UN should also draft a convention that would commit governments to providing food in emergencies and would prohibit them from withholding food supplies in times of conflict. It should further outline sanctions to be targeted against states and insurgent movements that deliberately produce famines by obstructing the right to produce or acquire food in emergency situations.

### Encouraging Governments to Accord First Asylum Rights to Refugees

The refugee crises in ex-Yugoslavia, Somalia, Haiti, and numerous other places—and the reluctance of states to open their borders to people who are forcibly driven from their homes and subjected to murder, physical abuse, and starvation—illustrate the vital importance of maintaining the principle of asylum. The major lesson we can learn from past efforts to deal with refugee problems is that building walls is no answer to those who feel compelled to move. The need to assure asylum to refugees is critically important to maintaining human rights protection worldwide. The capacity of Western countries to improve prospects for granting asylum in the Third World depend on the fairness and generosity of their own policies in the heart of Europe and in the Caribbean, and on the assistance they provide to others.

A generous commitment to asylum is not simply a matter of charity or burden sharing; it is also a way of regularizing and controlling large numbers of people whose irregular situation creates interstate tensions and regional instability. The success of economic liberalism and political pluralism in the new democracies of Africa, Latin America, Eastern Europe, and the former Soviet Union is of decisive importance, not only in averting future refugee and migrant flows but also in the political realm. Liberalizing domestic regimes and economic systems is scarcely possible without free movement of people, goods, and ideas. Unduly restrictionist Western policies lead to more isolation and deprivation in countries forced to play host to rejected refugees and migrants. An angry, excluded world outside the West will inevitably give rise to conditions in which extremist and aggressive groups and governments can emerge and pose new political and security threats. Dealing effectively with refugee movements both at home and abroad through a combination of generous asylum policies and preventive programs in aid, trade, and human rights is, therefore, in the interest of the industrialized states and coincides with their search for long-term global stability.

Yet the right to asylum is under attack everywhere—perhaps most alarmingly so in Western Europe, where racism and xenophobia against foreigners and minorities, combined with economic difficulties, have provoked social instability and unrest. In this steadily deteriorating climate, political leaders in the West have a special responsibility to speak out forcefully against racism and against violent attacks against asylum seekers and foreigners. If political leaders do not speak out for tolerance and integration, they implicitly offer support to the forces of intolerance and violence. Lack of respect for minority rights and political inaction by Western leaders also set a dangerous precedent for nationalist leaders in neighboring countries in Eastern Europe and the former Soviet Union, where disaffected minorities and ethnic conflict could erupt into further violence and forced displacement.

The situation calls for political courage and creative thinking. Asylum procedures have to be speeded up, and provisions have to be made for the safe and humane return home of rejected asylum seekers; but amending these procedures in unduly restrictive ways will change little on its own. Unless the West treats asylum seekers fairly and accepts a share of the world's refugees, it is unlikely to succeed in encouraging better treatment of asylum seekers elsewhere. The industrialized democracies cannot insist that weak states in the Third World and Eastern Europe improve their human rights records and continue to provide refuge, on the one hand, and claim that they do not have the means to provide asylum themselves, on the other. In the post–Cold War era, showing a willingness to provide asylum is one of the few meaningful ways in which the West can demonstrate its direct commitment to international human rights.

## Resolving the Problem of Long-staying Refugee Populations

During the 1980s, the global refugee relief situation was characterized by long-term care and maintenance in enclosed camps for the majority of refugees fleeing regional conflicts in Africa, Asia, and Central America and by the failure of the international community to provide any alternatives to prolonged camp existence. In the 1990s, even as new refugee crises dominate places as far apart as Burma, Somalia, and ex-Yugoslavia, the international community is still caring for many of these long-standing refugee populations. Nevertheless, much greater attention is focused today on voluntary return and even on returns involving some coercion.[19]

In the early 1990s, observers hoped that the political transformations occurring in the developing nations after the end of the Cold War would give the international community an unprecedented opportunity to empty many of the world's refugee camps. UN and regional peace negotiations took place. Efforts were made to terminate hostilities and to deal with continuing political conflicts in many of the major refugee-producing regions—Afghanistan, Angola, Cambodia, Central America, and the Western Sahara. Following ceasefires and political settlements, many refugees and displaced people who had been in exile for years started to go home. Indeed, in late 1991, the UNHCR requested funding for twenty possible

*Table 8-1*    1992 Projected Repatriation Populations

| Country of Origin | Number | Country of Asylum |
| --- | --- | --- |
| Afghanistan | 200,000 | Iran, Pakistan |
| Angola | 300,000 | Zaire, Zambia |
| Burundi | 100,000 | Tanzania, Zaire |
| Cambodia | 350,000 | Thailand |
| Chad | 20,000 | Sudan |
| El Salvador | 3,000 | Belize, Costa Rica, Honduras, Nicaragua, Panama |
| Ethiopia | 425,000 | (returnees) |
|  | 12,000 | Djibouti, Kenya |
| Ethiopia/Eritrea | 250,000 | Sudan |
| Guatemala | 10,000 | Mexico |
| Laos | 8,000 | Thailand |
| Liberia | 430,000 | Ghana, Guinea, Ivory Coast, Nigeria, Sierra Leone |
| Mozambique | 135,000 | Malawi, Swaziland, Tanzania, Zambia, Zimbabwe |
| Nicaragua | 5,500 | Costa Rica, other |
| Rwanda | 55,000 | Burundi, Kenya, Tanzania, Uganda, Zaire |
| Sierra Leone | 170,000 | Guinea |
| Somalia | 400,000 | Ethiopia, Djibouti, Kenya, other |
| South Africa | 20,000 | Tanzania, Zambia, other |
| Suriname | 6,600 | French Guyana |
| Vietnam | 20,000 | Hong Kong, Indonesia, Thailand, other |
| Zaire | 2,000 | Angola |
| Western Sahara | 80,000 | Algeria, Mauritania |
| Total | 3,002,100 |  |

SOURCE: Office of the United Nations High Commissioner for Refugees.

repatriations worldwide that it foresaw might occur in the years ahead (see Table 8-1). Some 2.5 million people were returned home in 1992.

Many countries to which refugees have returned or will return have been devastated by years—sometimes decades—of war.[20] They already have large numbers of internally displaced people and possess little or no capacity to reintegrate those who left. Entire villages have been leveled; irrigation systems and other infrastructure have been destroyed; people have lost their homes and land; economies have been brought to a virtual standstill; and vast tracts of territory have been mined. It is unlikely that these countries can achieve political stability while their economies lie in ruins.

The emergence of regional peace processes has not meant the end of exile for many refugees. Some local conflicts have been aggravated rather than mitigated by the end of the Cold War and the withdrawal of the former superpowers from developing countries. During the early post–Cold War period, internal wars became prolonged and bloody as regional states, competing for influence and political advantage, sought to influence the course of neighbors' internal conflicts by backing local governments or opposition groups. In addition, well-armed local military and paramilitary groups contributed to rapid social fragmentation and sometimes anarchy in these countries.

As of late 1992, political uncertainty shrouded the fate of several of the more important regional settlements that had been concluded in the early post-Cold War period. Despite major political changes in Somalia, Sudan, and Ethiopia, the Horn of Africa remained locked in conflicts rooted in territorial disputes and demands for self-determination. Several Middle Eastern countries, including Egypt, Iran, Iraq, Israel, Saudi Arabia, Syria, and Yemen played out their rivalry in the region by buttressing the governments of Ethiopia and Sudan. In Afghanistan, an internal struggle for power between Hezb-i-Islam, backed by Pakistan and Saudi Arabia, and the Tajiks and Uzbeks supported by Iran threatened to reduce the country to a series of tribal and factional fiefdoms. In Cambodia, continued Khmer Rouge obstruction of the Cambodia Peace Accords threatened to disrupt national elections set for mid-1993 and to force a return to civil war. In Angola, renewed fighting broke out after UN-monitored elections were held in late 1992. Morocco's refusal to renounce title to the Western Sahara, which is also claimed by the Polisario Front, effectively torpedoed the UN Peace Plan for the Western Sahara.

If international and regional mediation initiatives finally take hold and reconciliation among competing ethnic and communal groups occurs, larger numbers of refugees will be returning home in the coming years. The focus of international concern must inevitably shift from repatriation to more long-standing reintegration. It is becoming increasingly evident that, in countries such as Cambodia, Afghanistan, and Ethiopia, one precondition for successful returns is development aid and reintegration assistance aimed at alleviating poverty in countries of origin. Without outside help and improved economic prospects, political instability and new displacements are likely to occur. The UNHCR's short-term relief aid to returnees must be complemented by and integrated with national development efforts for the entire population. Without careful reintegration and reconciliation, returning refugees will find themselves competing for scarce developmental resources; and this, in turn, may well result in fierce political and economic competition with indigenous populations that did not flee.

The immensity of the task of returning people safely to their homelands and of reconstructing war-torn regions clearly goes beyond the mandate or resources of the UNHCR. The cost of administering the UN Peace Plan in Cambodia—a nation of 8 million people—is estimated to be over $2 billion. The requirements of Afghanistan, Central America, the Horn of Africa, southern Africa, Liberia, and Western Sahara will also be sub-stantial. Furthermore, the funds for UN peacekeeping in these countries represent "overhead expenses," with little of the money being channeled to the local economies.

Although there is an urgent need for major international commit-ment, the international humanitarian system is ill-prepared to respond to repatriation and reintegration issues in the post–Cold War era. The UN and the UNHCR are experiencing fiscal crises, and the end of the Cold War means that many countries in Africa, Asia, and Central America are no longer as strategically important to the industrialized countries as they once were. There is increasing danger that refugee situations in the Third World will be perceived as local or regional problems of little, if any, foreign policy or security concern to the major donor countries. Donors are reluctant to give aid in unstable situations. However, this view is extremely short-sighted on the part of the West, since failure to deal with repatriation and reconstruction issues will encourage renewed conflict and will lead to a worsening of the global refugee situation.

If future negotiations are to succeed and current peace agreements are to stick, funds must also include resources for reconstruction and develop-ment to create proper conditions for return. One group of policy analysts has already called for establishing an international fund for reconstruction that would channel funds to war-torn areas in the Third World through an already existing multilateral mechanism such as the G-24, the World Bank, or UNDP.[21] This new funding mechanism could be used to support regional initiatives such as the International Conference for Central Amer-ican Refugees (CIREFCA) and the international fund for reconstruction in Cambodia, which are now financed by separate appeals; and it should concentrate on rural reconstruction, training, and education, and on de-veloping infrastructure such as roads and transportation. It could also be tied to local compliance with ceasefire and peace accords—particularly those on the verge of collapsing—and to observance of human rights and minority rights guarantees.[22]

## Human Rights Protection for Returning Refugees

Greater development assistance alone is not enough to create safe condi-tions for those returning home; international intervention must also en-sure democratization and respect for human rights. However, neither good governance nor respect for human rights fall within the UNHCR's domain. If a repatriation agreement neglects to deal with human rights conditions in the refugee-producing country, the safety of the refugees cannot be assured; yet human rights groups are generally not included in the repatriation process, and the UNHCR has only a minimal monitoring apparatus to ensure the safe reintegration of returnees. In addition, the large numbers of people who return without UNHCR assistance remain outside even this rudimentary system of protection. This situation must change, because the success of the international community in linking human rights and refugee concerns will likely determine the future capacity of the UNHCR to carry out the massive repatriation programs it is likely to confront in the future.

Going beyond traditional refugee emergency assistance to facilitating safe reintegration of returnees into countries of origin requires the development of improved collaboration on the part of international agencies and an enhancement and sharing of the resources available to them. Focusing on safety of the return and reintegration involves rethinking the roles and mandates of international organizations and NGOs; shifting their operational priorities from receiving countries to countries of return; training agency staff to work in conditions that require development and human rights protection as well as relief assistance; and closer cooperation and coordination between development and refugee agencies and between human rights and refugee agencies than has hitherto been the case.

In instances of mass returns, the UNHCR cannot respond to the human rights and protection requirements of returnees on an individual basis. Ongoing international operations, such as UNTAC in Cambodia or ONUSAL in El Salvador, may well provide models—or at least lessons—for improved protection and solutions in the future. Additional activities aimed at developing adequate protective mechanisms to ensure safety of return, including maintaining appropriate information about conditions in countries of origin, enhancing UN or regional human rights monitors, and strengthening indigenous NGOs, are urgently required.[23] Therefore, establishing effective national and international guarantees (and related facilities for monitoring and human rights reporting) constitutes an essential prerequisite for the return home of refugees.

The success of many repatriations will also depend on resolving the residual problems of these long-standing internal and regional conflicts. In Ethiopia, Cambodia, Afghanistan, Angola, Mozambique, and elsewhere, large numbers of people have been soldiers or "refugee warriors" for ten or more years. Former soldiers and their families need to be reintegrated into civilian society. An international effort should be mounted to develop the capacity to deal quickly and effectively with the massive number of landmines planted during the course of these wars.

## Beyond Charity

When we speak of refugees as representing a global problem, we are referring to a concern that transcends ideology and national borders—a problem whose resolution is in the clear interest of all humanity. The global refugee problem is not going to disappear soon; in fact, it is assuming new characteristics that require a new and different approach. In the past, refugee policy has been associated with charity on a worldwide scale. The international response to refugee problems focused on relief and rescue, and relied essentially on voluntary contributions. Yet it has long been apparent that the existing system of ad hoc international solutions is inadequate, nor have repeated appeals for additional funds, more resettlement places, and greater compassion resolved the problem. Charity, in the form of humanitarian aid, is insufficient to deal with today's global refugee crisis. The time cannot be too distant when people and governments in the West will become profoundly tired of refugee emergencies, and the consequences of our compassion fatigue will be dehumanizing to us all.

Refugee problems are essentially born out of political conflict, and they directly engage the interests of states all over the world. Resolving these problems requires intelligence, patience, and strong and sustained political commitment and economic support by all governments. Generosity and humanitarian action alone are not enough, but they are still essential. Short-term policies and draconian border controls will impede the long-term initiatives needed to deal with these complex and contentious issues. Failure to insist on the observance of international human rights and refugee norms—or to provide Third World countries either with adequate resources to respond generously to mass influxes from neighboring countries or to reintegrate those returning home after years of bitter civil wars—will have direct or indirect repercussion for the Western countries themselves. In countries where no local protection for human rights victims exists, people will seek safe haven elsewhere, and many will come knocking on our doors.

The time has come to move beyond charity and to broaden the scope of approach to the refugee problem. International cooperation to resolve the humanitarian and political problems of refugees and more active diplomatic intervention by the UN and regional organizations is in the long-term interest of all governments. Stability and growth in all parts of the world depend on controlling disruptive forced migrations. There have never been easy answers to the plight of the world's refugees. But given the inescapable reality that the global refugee crisis is here to stay, the time is undoubtedly right for a new, comprehensive, and humane approach. The world has responded with imagination and effectiveness before; it can do so again.

# Notes

## Introduction: The Global Refugee Crisis

1. The number of refugees in Africa rose from 1.2 million in 1976 to 5.6 million in 1990. Asia's increase over the period was more rapid—from 180,000 to 8 million. In the Americas the numbers trebled, from 770,000 to 2.7 million. Europe saw the smallest increase, from 570,000 to 894,000.

2. "The 1951 United Nations Convention Relating to the Status of Refugees" (July 28, 1951), *United Nations Treaty,* vol. 189, no. 2545, p. 137.

3. As many as 70 million people, mostly from developing countries, are working legally or illegally in other countries (Reginald Appleyard, *International Migration: Challenges for the Nineties* [Geneva: International Organization for Migration, 1991], p. 5).

4. In fact, this category of migrant comprises by far the largest number of legal immigrants from the Third World in both the United States and Europe today.

5. See Astri Suhrke, "Global Refugee Movements and Strategies of Response," in Mary Kritz, ed., *U.S. Immigration and Refugee Policy* (Lexington, Mass.: D. C. Heath, 1983), pp. 157–74.

6. Guy Goodwin-Gill, *The Refugee in International Law* (Oxford: Clarendon Press, 1983).

7. Atle Grahl-Madsen. *The Status of Refugees in International Law* (Leiden: A. W. Sijthoff, 1966), p. 97.

## Chapter 1. Refugee Movements: Causes and Consequences

1. For general background, see Yezid Sayigh, *"Confronting the 1990s: Security in the Developing Countries,* Adelphi Paper 251 (London: Brassey's, for Interna-

tional Institute for Strategic Studies, Summer 1990); Barry Buzan, "People, States and Fear: The National Security Problem in the Third World," in Edward Azar and Chung-in Moon, eds., *National Security in the Third World: The Management of Internal and External Threats* (Aldershot, England: Edward Elgar, 1988), pp. 14–43; and Mohammed Ayoob, "The Third World in the System of States: Acute Schizophrenia or Growing Pains?" *International Studies Quarterly* 33 (1989): 67–79. For a seminal work on the linkage between long-term social and political transformation and the generation of refugee flows, see Aristide Zolberg, Astri Suhrke, and Sergio Aguayo, *Escape from Violence: Conflict and the Refugee Crisis in the Developing World* (New York: Oxford University Press, 1989).

2. Yezid Sayigh, op. cit.; and Klaus Knorr, "Military Trends and Future World Order," *Jerusalem Journal of International Relations* 11 (1989): 68–95.

3. Recent research on conflict in the Third World demonstrates that nearly half of the world's refugees are fleeing from civil wars and repression arising out of communal conflicts. Ted Robert Gurr, "Ethnic Warfare and the Changing Priorities of Global Security," *Mediterranean Quarterly* 1 (1990): 82–98; and Robert Harkavy and Stephanie Neuman, eds., *The Lessons of Recent Wars in the Third World*, vol. 1 (Lexington, Mass.: Lexington Books, 1985).

4. Independent Commission on International Humanitarian Issues, *Modern Wars: The Humanitarian Challenge* (London: Zed Books, 1986), p. 25.

5. This conclusion is drawn from a comparison of the annual data provided in Amnesty International's and the U.S. Committee for Refugees' yearly reports and from the work of Ted Robert Gurr.

6. For background, see Ted Robert Gurr, op. cit.; James Scarritt and Ted Robert Gurr, "Minority Rights at Risk: A Global Survey," *Human Rights Quarterly* 11 (1989): 375–405; James Mayall, *Nationalism and International Society* (Cambridge: Cambridge University Press, 1990); Anthony Smith, *Theories of Nationalism* (London: Duckworth, 1983); and Anthony Smith, *Nationalism in the Twentieth Century* (Oxford: Martin Robinson, 1979).

7. Leo Kuper, *Genocide: Its Political Uses in the Twentieth Century* (New Haven, Conn.: Yale University Press, 1985); and Patrick Thornberry, *Ethnic Minorities and International Law* (Oxford: Clarendon Press, 1990).

8. The term "refugee warriors" was first termed by Zolberg, Suhrke, and Aguayo, op. cit.

9. According to recent human rights research, the share of ethnic wars in the total number of internal wars increased from 14 percent in the 1944–1955 period to 37.5 percent in the 1966–1975 period, and it increased even more in the 1980s. See Alex P. Schmid, *Research on Gross Human Rights Violations: A Programme* (Leiden: Interdisciplinary Research Project on Root Causes of Human Rights Violations [PIOOM], Center for the Study of Social Conflicts, 1989), p. 57. See also James Scarritt and Ted Robert Gurr, op. cit.

10. Ted Robert Gurr, "Ethnic Warfare," op. cit.

11. Samuel Makinda, *Security in the Horn of Africa,* Adelphi Paper 269 (London: Brassey's, for International Institute for Strategic Studies, 1992).

12. Richard Shulz, Robert Pfaltzgraff, Uri Ra'anan, William Olson, and Igor Lukes, eds., *Guerrilla Warfare and Counterinsurgency: U.S.–Soviet Policy in the Third World* (Lexington, Mass.: Lexington Books, 1989).

13. For data, see those provided by the U.S. Committee for Refugees in its annual reports; and by Barbara Harff and Ted Robert Gurr, "Toward Empirical Theory of Genocides and Politicides: Identification and Measurement of Cases

since 1945," *International Studies Quarterly* 32 (1988): 359–71; and by Zolberg, Suhrke, and Aguayo, op. cit.

14. William McNeill and Ruth Adams, *Human Migrations: Patterns and Policies* (Bloomington, Ind.: Indiana University Press, 1978); and Zolberg, Suhrke, and Aguayo, op. cit.

15. Particularly useful field research on causative factors and state responses to refugee flows from Vietnam has been carried out by Linda Hitchcox, *Vietnamese Asylum Seekers* (Oxford: St. Antony's College, 1990); and Robert Bach, "Transforming Socialist Emigration: Lessons from Cuba and Vietnam," *In Defense of the Alien* 12 (1990): 89–103.

16. Myron Weiner notes that much of the literature on international migration stresses global economic conditions as the key determinants of population movements. According to migration theorists, individuals emigrate if the expected benefits exceed the costs. Thus, changes in local conditions (such as wages or labor markets) or changes in the global economy (such as shifts in the terms of trade or capital flows) will create a demand for labor in some regions or countries and a surplus in others. Moreover, uneven economic development and demographic growth among states and a severe maldistribution of income within and between states may stimulate the movement of people across borders in search of greater opportunities. See Myron Weiner, *Security, Stability and International Migration* (Cambridge, Mass.: Center for International Studies, 1991).

17. Harto Harkovirta, *The World Refugee Problem* (Tampere, Finland: Hillside Publications, 1991).

18. For a comprehensive account of state actions that cause migratory movements, see Weiner, op. cit.

19. See Michael Teitlebaum, "Immigration, Refugees, and Foreign Policy," *International Organization* 38 (Summer 1984): 429–50; Gil Loescher, *Refugee Movements and International Security,* Adelphi Paper 268 (London: Brassey's, for International Institute for Strategic Studies, 1992); and Alan Dowty, *Closed Borders* (New Haven, Conn.: Yale University Press, 1987).

20. Weiner, op. cit.

21. Richard Dowden. "Addis Ababa Tricked into a Soft Landing," *The Independent* (May 31, 1991).

22. Stephen Engelberg, "Walesa Warns of Albanian Threat If West Fails on Aid," *International Herald Tribune* (March 19, 1991).

23. Gil Loescher, "Refugee Issues," op. cit.

24. Gil Loescher and John Scanlan, *Calculated Kindness: Refugees and America's Half-Open Door, 1945 to Present* (New York: Free Press, 1986); and Norman Zucker and Naomi Zucker, *The Guarded Gate: The Reality of American Refugee Policy* (San Diego: Harcourt Brace Jovanovich, 1987).

25. See Arthur Helton, "Political Asylum Under the 1980 Refugee Act: An Unfulfilled Promise," *University of Michigan Journal of Law Reform* 17 (1984): 243; and Michael Teitlebaum, op. cit.

26. This is the conclusion of the work of many scholars and of the principal human rights organizations. See, for example, Lawyers Committee for Human Rights, *The Implementation of the Refugee Act of 1980: A Decade of Experience* (New York: Lawyers Committee for Human Rights, March 1990): Amnesty International USA, *Reasonable Fear: Human Rights and United States Foreign Policy* (New York: Amnesty International USA, 1990); and Gil Loescher and John Scanlan, op. cit.

27. As reported by Henry Kamm, "Western Nations Raising Barriers to Refugees Trying to Flee Poverty," *New York Times* (March 27, 1989): 1. See also Mark Gibney, "Foreign Policy: Ideological and Political Factors," in Gil Loescher, ed., *Refugees and the Asylum Dilemma in the West* (University Park, Penn.: Penn State University Press, 1992), pp. 36–53.

28. For background, see John Scanlan and Gilburt Loescher, "U.S. Foreign Policy and Refugee Flow from Cuba: 1959–1980," *Annals of American Academy of Political and Social Science* 487 (May 1983): 116–37.

29. Astri Suhrke, "Indochinese Refugees: The Law and Politics of First Asylum," *Annals of American Academy of Political and Social Science* 487 (May 1983): 102–15; Valerie Sutter, *The Indochinese Refugee Dilemma* (Baton Rouge: Louisiana State University Press, 1990); and Janina Wiktoria Dacyl, *Between Compassion and Realpolitik* (Stockholm: University of Stockholm, 1992).

30. Michael Teitlebaum, op. cit.

31. Norman Zucker and Naomi Zucker, "The Uneasy Troika: U.S. Refugee Policy," *Journal of Refugee Studies* 2 (1989): 359–72.

32. *Refugee Reports* 13 (July 31, 1992): 14.

33. Ibid.: 1–6.

34. Although the grounds for giving all members of these groups automatic refugee status is weak, serious threats continue to face individuals in the former USSR and Vietnam. Resurgent nationalism threatening religious and ethnic minorities in Eastern Europe, the Balkans, and the ex–Soviet Union will continue to cause refugee flight in that region; and Vietnamese boat people will continue to be refused local settlement in Southeast Asia.

35. Independent Commission on International Humanitarian Issues, *Refugees: Dynamics of Displacement* (London: Zed Books, 1986), p. 16.

36. See Robert Chambers, "Rural Refugees in Africa: What the Eye Does Not See," *Disasters* 3 (1979): 381–92.

37. See, for example, Art Hansen, "Managing Refugees: Zambia's Response to Angolan Refugees, 1966–1977." *Disasters* 3 (1979): 375–80.

38. Samuel Makinda, op. cit., pp. 53–62.

39. Jeff Crisp and Nick Cater, *The Human Consequences of Conflict in the Horn of Africa: Refugees, Asylum and the Politics of Assistance* (Cairo, Egypt: International Institute for Strategic Studies and Centre for Political Research and Studies, May 1990).

40. On the other hand, Thai authorities informed the author in Bangkok in March 1992 that they considered it to be in their long-term interest to provide temporary asylum to Burmese refugee students, who would eventually provide the next generation of political leadership in Burma. See also Pierre Jambor, *Indochinese Refugees in Southeast Asia: Mass Exodus and the Politics of Aid* (Bangkok: Ford Foundation, 1992).

41. Robert Kaplan, *Surrender or Starve: The Wars Behind the Ethiopian Famine* (Boulder, Colo.: Westview Press, 1988).

42. This was confirmed by the author's visits to the border camps in 1983 and 1992. For a history of the roots of this policy, see William Shawcross, *The Quality of Mercy: Cambodia, the Holocaust and Modern Conscience* (New York: Simon & Schuster, 1984); and Linda Mason and Roger Brown, *Rice, Rivalry and Politics* (South Bend, Ind.: University of Notre Dame Press, 1983).

43. Gil Loescher, "Humanitarianism and Politics in Central America," *Political Science Quarterly* 103 (Summer 1988): 295–320.

44. Bruce Nichols and Gil Loescher, eds., *The Moral Nation: Humanitarian-*

*ism and U.S. Foreign Policy* (South Bend, Ind.: University of Notre Dame Press, 1989).

45. Larry Minear, *Helping People in an Age of Conflict: Toward a New Professionalism in U.S. Voluntary Humanitarian Assistance* (New York: InterAction, 1988); and Jason Clay, *Politics and the Ethiopian Famine, 1984–1985* (Cambridge, Mass.: Cultural Survival, 1986).

46. Larry Minear, *Humanitarianism Under Siege: A Critical Review of Operation Lifeline Sudan* (Trenton, N.J.: Red Sea Press, 1991).

47. Jason Clay, "Ethiopian Famine and the Relief Agencies," in Bruce Nichols and Gil Loescher, eds., *The Moral Nation: Humanitarianism and U.S. Foreign Policy Today* (South Bend, Ind.: University of Notre Dame Press, 1989), pp. 232–77.

48. Bruce Nichols and Gil Loescher, op. cit.; and Larry Minear, *Helping People in an Age of Conflict,* op. cit.

49. For example, the Eritrean Relief Association and the Relief Society of Tigre were creations of the Eritrean People's Liberation Front and the Tigrean People's Liberation Front, respectively, and both openly endorsed the liberation fronts' political objectives. In the past, the EPLF occasionally denied international agencies access to Eritrea for strategic or political reasons.

50. See Bruce Nichols and Gil Loescher, op. cit.

## Chapter 2. The Origins of the International Refugee Regime

1. Claudena Skran points out the historical interrelatedness of the refugee problem in Claudena Skran, "The International Refugee Regime: The Historical and Contemporary Context of International Responses to Asylum Problems," in Gil Loescher, ed., *Refugees and the Asylum Dilemma in the West* (University Park, Penn.: Penn State University Press, 1992), pp. 8–35.

2. Michael Marrus, *The Unwanted: European Refugees in the Twentieth Century* (New York: Oxford University Press, 1985).

3. See, for example, Michael Marrus, ibid.; Malcom Proudfoot, *European Refugees, 1930–1952: A Study in Forced Population Movement* (London: Faber & Faber, 1957); and Joseph Schechtman, *European Population Transfers, 1939–1945* (New York: Oxford University Press, 1946).

4. For a discussion of refugee problems dating back to early modern Europe, involving the expulsion of Jews from Spain in the fifteenth century and of Huguenots from France in the seventeenth century, see Aristide Zolberg, Astri Suhrke, and Sergio Aguayo, *Escape from Violence: Conflict and the Refugee Crisis in the Developing World* (New York: Oxford University Press, 1989). For a treatment of European refugee problems in the nineteenth and twentieth centuries, see Michael Marrus, op. cit.

5. Independent Commission on International Humanitarian Issues, *Modern Wars: The Humanitarian Challenge* (London: Zed Books, 1986).

6. Internal wars and civilian casualties have increased dramatically in the late twentieth century. The latest manifestations of this are the mass outfluxes of Kurds in the aftermath of the 1991 Gulf War, of Somalis fleeing vicious interclan conflict, and of Muslims, Croats, and Serbs caught up in the increasingly brutal ethnic wars in former Yugoslavia.

7. The literature on nationalism is extensive. See Alfred Cobban, *Nationalism and Self-Determination* (London: Oxford University Press, 1969); Anthony

Smith, *The Ethnic Origin of Nations* (Oxford: Basil Blackwell, 1986); Hans Kohn, *Nationalism: Its Meaning and History* (Princeton, N.J.: D. Van Nostrand, 1955); and James Mayall, *Nationalism and International Society* (Cambridge: Cambridge University Press, 1990). For an analysis of the relationship between the process of nation-building and the generation of refugee flows, see Aristide Zolberg, "The Formation of New States as a Refugee Generating Process," *Annals of American Academy of Political and Social Science* 467 (May 1983): 24–38.

8. Claudena Skran, *The International Refugee Regime and the Refugee Problem in the Inter-War Period* (Oxford University Press, forthcoming).

9. Ibid.; also Michael Marrus, op. cit.

10. For general background, see Leo Kuper, *Genocide: Its Political Uses in the Twentieth Century* (New Haven, Conn.: Yale University Press, 1982).

11. For background, see Inis Claude, *National Minorities: An International Problem* (Cambridge, Mass.: Harvard University Press, 1955).

12. John Hope Simpson, *The Refugee Problem* (London: Oxford University Press, 1939); and Michael Marrus, op. cit.

13. For more details, see Michael Marrus, op. cit.; and John Hope Simpson, op. cit.

14. C. A. Macartney, *National States and National Minorities* (New York: Russell & Russell, 1968).

15. John Hope Simpson, op. cit.; and Michael Marrus, op. cit.

16. Simpson, op. cit., p. 192.

17. Claudena Skran, "Profiles of the First Two High Commissioners," *Journal of Refugee Studies* 1 (1988): 277–96.

18. The Nansen passport was later extended to include other refugee groups such as Armenian refugees in 1924, Assyrian and Assyro-Chaldeans in 1928, and Saar refugees in 1935. See Louis Holborn, *Refugees: A Problem of Our Time. The Work of the United Nations High Commissioner for Refugees, 1951–1972,* vol. 1 (Metuchen, N.J.: Scarecrow Press, 1975), pp. 8–10.

19. Unless otherwise indicated, information on Nansen and on the League of Nation's activities on refugees is drawn from the following sources: Claudena Skran, "The International Refugee Regime," op. cit.; Claudena Skran's authoritative work, *The International Refugee Regime,* op. cit.; and Michael Marrus, op. cit.

20. Claudena Skran, *The International Refugee Regime,* op. cit.

21. Ibid.

22. Convention Relating to the International Status of Refugees (October 28, 1933), in League of Nations, *Treaty Series,* vol. 159, no. 3363.

23. League of Nations, *Treaty Series,* vol. 192, no. 4461.

24. League of Nations, *Treaty Series,* vol. 198, no. 4634; and by a resolution of the League Council to the Sudeten Germans on January 19, 1939 (League of Nations, *Treaty Series,* vol. 199, no. 72).

25. It is important to remember, however, that, apart from Europe and the Americas, almost the whole world was under the formal or informal control of the European powers, or ruled by overseas Europeans during the 1930s. Therefore, eight signatories is not necessarily an insignificant number.

26. For further details, see Michael Marrus, op. cit.; and Claudena Skran, *The International Refugee Regime,* op. cit.

27. Alan Dowty, *Closed Borders* (New Haven, Conn.: Yale University Press, 1987, pp. 76–78.

28. Robert Conquest, *The Great Terror: Stalin's Purge of the Thirties* (Hammondsworth, England: Penguin Books, 1971).

29. Hannah Arendt, *The Origins of Totalitarianism* (New York: Harcourt Brace Jovanovich), p. 267.

30. For background, see Richard Plender, *International Migration Law* (Leiden: A. W. Sijthoff, 1989).

31. These policies are discussed, among other places, in Henry Feingold, *The Politics of Rescue: The Roosevelt Administration and the Holocaust, 1938–45* (New Brunswick, N.J.: Rutgers University Press, 1970); David Wyman, *Paper Walls: America and the Refugee Crisis, 1938–1941* (Amherst, Mass.: University of Massachusetts Press, 1968); and David Wyman, *Abandonment of the Jews: America and the Holocaust, 1941–1945* (New York: Pantheon Books, 1984).

32. When Germany subsequently resigned from the League of Nations, the High Commissioner was once again made responsible to the Assembly.

33. Cited in Gervase Coles, "Approaches to the Refugee Problem Today," in Gil Loescher and Laila Monahan, eds., *Refugees and International Relations* (Oxford: Clarendon Press, 1988), pp. 409–10.

34. Ibid., p. 410.

35. Gil Loescher and John Scanlan, *Calculated Kindness: Refugees and America's Half-Open Door, 1945 to Present* (New York: Free Press, 1968), p. xvi.

36. Guy Goodwin-Gill, "Different Types of Forced Migration Movements as an International and National Problem," in Goran Rystad, ed., *The Uprooted: Forced Migration as an International Problem in the Post-War Era* (Lund, Sweden: Lund University Press, 1990) pp. 18–19.

37. The most authoritative recent work is Tommie Sjoberg, *The Powers and the Persecuted: The Refugee Problem and the Intergovernmental Committee on Refugees* (Lund, Sweden: Lund University Press, 1991).

38. Eugene Kulisher, *Europe on the Move: War and Population Changes, 1917–1947* (New York: Columbia University Press, 1948), p. 305; John Stoessinger, *The Refugee and the World Community* (Minneapolis: University of Minnesota Press, 1956), pp. 45–48; and Louise Holborn, op. cit., p. 15.

39. J. P. Clark Carey, "Displaced Populations in Europe in 1944 with Partial Reference to Germany," *Department of State Bulletin* 12(300) (March 25, 1945): 491, cited in Gil Loescher and John Scanlan, op. cit., p. 1.

40. Ibid.

41. According to Leonard Dinnerstein, *America and the Survivors of the Holocaust* (New York: Columbia University Press, 1982), p. 28, some 20,000 of the 60,000 survivors died within one week of liberation.

42. Jacques Vernant, *The Refugee in the Post-War World* (New Haven, Conn.: Yale University Press, 1953), pp. 94–95.

43. For example, the U.S. government urged the creation of an umbrella organization, the American Council for Voluntary Agencies in Foreign Service (ACVA), to promote cooperative planning among voluntary agencies for the postwar relief and rehabilitation effort. See Bruce Nichols, *The Uneasy Alliance* (New York: Oxford University Press, 1988).

44. For a more detailed history, see George Woodbridge, *The History of UNRRA* (New York: Columbia University Press, 1950); and Kim Salomon, *Refugees in the Cold War* (Lund, Sweden: Lund University Press, 1991).

45. See Nicholai Tolstoi, *The Silent Betrayal* (New York: Charles Scribners'

Sons, 1977); and Nicholas Bethell, *The Last Secret: Forcible Repatriation to Russia, 1944–47* (London: Andre Deutch, 1974).

46. See Alfred de Zayas, *Nemesis at Potsdam: The Anglo-Americans and the Expulsion of the Germans* (London: Routledge & Kegan Paul, 1977).

47. See Mark Elliot, *Pawns of Yalta* (Champaign, Ill.: University of Illinois Press, 1982), p. 104; and Malcom Proudfoot, op. cit., p. 229.

48. For background, see Malcom Proudfoot, op. cit.

49. For a critical treatment of Western policy, see Mark Elliot, op. cit.

50. See, for example, the debates over repatriation at the United Nations Third Committee during January and February 1946.

51. E. Penrose, "Negotiating on Refugees and Displaced Persons, 1946," in Raymond Dennett and Joseph Johnson, eds., *Negotiating with the Russians* (Boston: 1951), pp. 144–147.

52. Ibid., pp. 144–147.

53. John Stoessinger, op. cit., pp. 41–42.

54. Dean Acheson, *Present at the Creation* (New York: Norton, 1966), p. 201.

55. Louise Holborn, *The International Refugee Organization: A Specialized Agency of the United Nations, Its History and Work, 1947–1951* (London: Oxford University Press, 1956); and Kim Salomon, op. cit.

56. Annex to the Constitution of the International Refugee Organization, Part 1, Section C, Part 1(a), reprinted as Appendix to Senate Report 950, 80th Congress, 2d Session (1948).

57. IRO Constitution, Article 2; Annex, Article 1(c). See also Annex, Part II.

58. Proudfoot, op. cit., p. 401.

59. See John Loftus, *The Belarus Secret* (New York: Alfred A. Knopf, 1982); and Tom Bower, *The Pledge Betrayed: America, Britain and the De-Nazification of Postwar Germany* (Garden City, N.Y.: Doubleday, 1982), cited in Marrus, op. cit., p. 349.

60. For a detailed history of U.S. refugee policy during this period, see Gil Loescher and John Scanlan, op. cit.; and Leonard Dinnerstein, op. cit.

61. Leonard Dinnerstein, op. cit.; and Robert Divine, *American Immigration Policy, 1924–1952* (New Haven, Conn.: Yale University Press, 1957).

62. For the best treatments of resettlement during the IRO period, see John Stoessinger, op. cit.; and Kim Salomon, op. cit.

63. John Stoessinger, op. cit.

64. In contrast to the prevelant policy of self-interest on the part of governments during this period, Turkey decided to admit all Moslem refugees, irrespective of sex, marital status, health, or profession; and Norway chose to receive a large number of sick and handicapped refugees, apparently without taking the labor market or political effects into consideration.

65. Jacques Vernant, op. cit., p. 45.

66. Raymond Dennett and Robert K. Turner, *Documents on American Foreign Relations 1947* (Princeton, N.J.: Princeton University Press, 1949), p. 7.

67. John Lewis Gaddis, *Russia, the Soviet Union and the United States: An Interpretive History* (New York: John Wiley & Sons, 1978).

68. Almost 10,000 Hungarians fled to Austria and Germany after the communist seizure of power in 1946. Following the 1948 coup in Czechoslovakia, about 50,000 Czechoslovakians succeeded in crossing the frontier to Western Europe. In addition, up to 1 million Poles and roughly 400,000 Finns fled areas

annexed to the Soviet Union; and between 1949 and 1952, over 170,000 ethnic Turks were forced out of Bulgaria.

69. George Warren, *The Development of United States Participation in Inter-governmental Efforts to Resolve Refugee Problems* (mimeo, 1967).

## Chapter 3. The Cold War and the Early Development of the UNHCR

1. For general background to these UN debates, see Louise Holborn, *Refugees: A Problem of Our Time* (Metuchen, N.J.: Scarecrow Press, 1975); Guy Goodwin-Gill. "Different Types of Forced Migration Movements as an International and National Problem," in Goran Rystad, ed., *The Uprooted: Forced Migration as an International Problem in the Post-War Era* (Lund, Sweden: Lund University Press, 1990), pp. 15–46; and Kim Salomon, *Refugees in the Cold War* (Lund, Sweden: Lund University Press, 1991), pp. 218–32.

2. For background, see "Travaux Preparatoires of the Convention Relating to the Status of Refugees of 28 July 1951," vols. 1–2, prepared for the United Nations Institute for Training and Research by Paul Weis. See also Paul Weis, "Legal Aspects of the Convention of 28 July 1951 Relating to the Status of Refugees," *The British Yearbook of International Law* 30 (1953); and Nehemiah Robinson, *Convention Relating to the Status of Refugees: Its History, Contents and Interpretation* (New York: Institute of Jewish Affairs, 1953).

3. *Statute of the United Nations High Commissioner for Refugees,* 5 U.N. GAOR Annex 1 at 46, U.N. Doc. A/1775 (1950); and "The 1951 United Nations Convention Relating to the Status of Refugees" (28 July 1951), *United Nations Treaty,* vol. 189, no. 2545, p. 137.

4. "The 1951 United Nations Convention Relating to the Status of Refugees," op. cit.

5. Despite the fact that the United States might well have ratified the 1951 Convention and still admitted many Eastern Europeans, it did not choose to do so. The reason the United States customarily gave for not ratifying the 1951 convention was that its legal system afforded refugees all the rights promised by the Convention. This was true, however, only with respect to such issues as employment and juridical status. Nothing in U.S. law provided absolute protection from *refoulement* (forcible return). Nothing guaranteed that individuals who were not strongly anticommunist could be granted asylum if they could demonstrate fear of persecution. Administrators who customarily refused to deport Russians, Hungarians, and Poles customarily acted otherwise in the cases of Iranians, South Koreans, and Filippinos; and they were barred from admitting any person, however fearful of persecution, who had ever been an "active" member of the Communist Party. See Gil Loescher and John Scanlan, *Calculated Kindness: Refugees and America's Half-Open Door, 1945 to the Present* (New York: Free Press, 1986). In mid-1992, the U.S. government claimed that it was not bound by Article 33 of the Refugee Convention not to forcibly repatriate Haitians determined to be refugees. According to the United States, the Protocol was not "self-executing," meaning that unless and until Congress implemented the Protocol's provisions in domestic law, the Protocol itself could not be interpreted as a source of rights in U.S. legal practice. Moreover, the government maintained that the provision regarding *non-refoulement* in Article 33 applied to refugees "within the territory of a contracting state." Because the Haitians were intercepted in international waters, the govern-

ment maintained that they could not be said to have been returned from the United States. See Bill Frelick, "Haiti: No Room at the Inn," *Refugees* 90 (July 1992): 34–37.

6. For background, see Richard C. Sheldon and John Dutkowski, "Are Soviet Satellite Refugee Interviews Projectable?" *Public Opinion Quarterly* 16 (Winter 1952–1953): 579–94.

7. *Central Intelligence Act,* July 1949.

8. Psychological Strategy Board, Policy Guidance No. D-18/a, "Psychological Operations Plan for Soviet Orbit Escapees, Phase A" (December 20, 1951): 5, David D. Lloyd Collection, Box 3, File: Immigration Memo No. 4, Harry S. Truman Library.

9. Arthur Helton, "Political Asylum Under the 1980 Refugee Act: An Unfulfilled Promise," *Michigan Journal of Law Reform* 17 (1984): 243, 246.

10. Paul Tabori, *The Anatomy of Exile: A Semantic and Historical Study* (London: George C. Harrap, 1972), pp. 260–61.

11. Michael Marrus, *The Unwanted: European Refugees in the Twentieth Century* (New York: Oxford University Press, 1985), p. 354.

12. This was accomplished primarily through passage of the Refugee Relief Act of 1953, the Refugee Escapee Act of 1957, and the Fair Share Refugee Act passed in 1960.

13. *Refugee Relief Act of 1953,* August 7, 1953.

14. For background, see Edward H. Buehrig, *The United Nations and the Palestinian Refugees: A Study in Non-Territorial Administration* (Bloomington, Ind.: Indiana University Press, 1971); David Forsythe, "UNRWA, the Palestinian Refugees, and World Politics" *International Organization* 25 (Winter 1971): 26–45; David Forsythe, "The Palestine Question: Dealing with a Long-term Refugee Situation," *Annals of American Academy of Political and Social Sciences* 467 (May 1983): 89–101; Howard Adelman, "Palestine Refugees, Economic Integration and Durable Solutions," in Anna Bramwell, ed., *Refugees in the Age of Total War* (London: Unwin-Hyman, 1988); and Benny Morris, *The Birth of the Palestinian Refugee Problem: 1947–1949* (Cambridge: Cambridge University Press, 1987).

15. U.S. Congress, House Committee on Foreign Affairs, 81st Congress, 2d session, *Hearings on Palestine Refugees,* February 16, 1950, p. 9, cited in Ronald Scheinman, *The Office of the United Nations High Commissioner for Refugees and the Contemporary International System* (mimeo, 1974), pp. 163–64.

16. Gene M. Lyons, *Military Policy and Economic Aid: The Korean Case* (Columbus, Ohio: Ohio University Press, 1961).

17. Jacques Vernant, *The Refugee in the Post-War World* (New Haven, Conn.: Yale University Press, 1953), pp. 803–15; and William Henderson, "The Refugees in India and Pakistan," *Journal of International Affairs* 7 (1953): 57–66.

18. For background, see Gil Loescher and John Scanlan, op. cit.; George Warren, *The Development of United States Participation in Intergovernmental Efforts to Resolve Refugee Problems* (mimeo, 1967); and Kim Salomon, op. cit.

19. During this same period, the United States refused to support an initiative of the International Labor Organization (which had communist governments among its membership) to move refugees and other elements of surplus population out of Western Europe to resettlement countries overseas. It preferred instead to create its own international agency, ICEM, composed entirely of nations friendly to the United States, to accomplish the same end. See George Warren, op. cit.

20. For an account of the evolution of these programs, see Gil Loescher and John Scanlan, op. cit.

21. For a more detailed treatment of this period, see Ronald Scheinman, op. cit. Information on the early formation and activities of the UNHCR is largely drawn from this work and from Louise Holborn, *Refugees: A Problem of Our Time. The Work of the United Nations High Commissioner for Refugees, 1951–1972* (Metuchen, N.J.: Scarecrow Press, 1975).

22. Jacques Vernant, op. cit.

23. See, for example, Van Heuven Goedhart's report to the ECOSOC of the United Nations. GAOR, Sixth Session, Doc E/2036, June 27, 1951.

24. United Nations General Assembly Resolution 538B (VI), 1952, paragraph 1.

25. GAOR Sixth Session, Third Committee, 382nd meeting, January 10, 1952.

26. Author's interviews with former UNHCR officials, Bernard Alexander (Great Hasely, England, December 1986) and Gilbert Jaeger, (Oxford, November 1986).

27. Author's interview with Bernard Alexander, former chief assistant to G. J. Van Heuven Goedhart (Great Hasely, England, December 1986).

28. For more detailed accounts of the relationship between the U.S. government and voluntary agencies during this period, see Bruce Nichols, *The Uneasy Alliance* (New York: Oxford University Press, 1988); and Gil Loescher and John Scanlan, op. cit.

29. Louise Holborn, op. cit.

30. United Nations General Assembly Resolution 832 (IX), 1954.

31. U.S. Congress, Subcommittee on Foreign Operations Appropriations of the House Committee on Appropriations, 84th Congress, 1st Session, *Hearing on June 28, 1955,* pp. 428, 433, cited in Ronald Scheinman op. cit., pp. 205–6.

32. Ibid., p. 428, cited in Ronald Scheinman, op. cit., p. 206.

33. The United States finally contributed $5.3 million to the UN Refugee Fund.

34. This is the view of the United Nations official who directed the UNHCR's response in the field to the Hungarian refugees. Author's interview with Bernard Alexander (Great Hasely, England, December 1986).

35. United Nations General Assembly Resolution 1006 (ES11) November 9, 1956; and United Nations General Assembly Resolution 1039 (XI), January 23, 1957.

36. Author's interview with Bernard Alexander (Great Hasely, England, December 1986).

37. Despite the temporal and geographical limitations on the 1951 Refugee Convention, the Hungarians were considered to be persons with a well-founded fear of persecution and, hence, to be refugees. In regard to the temporal limitation of the 1951 Convention and its effect on the question of the Convention's application, the High Commissioner informed the Executive Committee that it was reasonable to relate the departure of the refugees from Hungary not merely to the events that had taken place in Hungary in November 1956, but also to fundamental changes that had taken place in that country as a result of World War II.

38. See Gil Loescher and John Scanlan, op. cit., pp. 49–67.

39. For background on the parole provision, see ibid.; and Deborah Anker and Michael Posner, "The Forty Year Crisis: A Legislative History of the Refugee Act of 1980." *San Diego Law Review,* 19 (Winter 1981): 9–89.

40. Author's interviews with Gilbert Jaeger, the UNHCR member of the UN investigation team to Hong Kong (Oxford, December 1986 and January 1988). For background, see Edvard Hambro, *The Problem of Chinese Refugees in Hong Kong* (Leiden: A. W. Sijthoff, 1955).

41. Author's interview with Gilbert Jaeger (Oxford, December 1986).

42. United Nations General Assembly Resolution 1167 (XII), November 26, 1957.

43. United Nations General Assembly Resolutions 1286 (XIII), 1389 (XIV), and 1500 (XV), 1958.

44. United Nations General Assembly Resolution 1129 (XI), November 21, 1956, paragraph 4.

45. United Nations General Assembly Resolution 1166 (XII), November 26, 1957.

46. United Nations General Assembly Resolution 1388 (XIV), November 20, 1959.

47. To a certain extent, the battleground shifted. The view that refugee policy could play a significant foreign policy role continued to dominate White House and State Department thinking about the Caribbean (Cuba and Haiti) and later about Central America. See Gil Loescher and John Scanlan, *Human Rights, Power Politics and the International Refugee Regime: The Case of U.S. Treatment of Caribbean Basin Refugees* (Princeton, N.J.: Center for International Studies, World Order Studies Occasional Papers Series, No. 14, 1985).

## Chapter 4. The International Refugee Regime and Third World Refugees

1. Some East–West migration continued, although on a more limited basis. After the erection of the Berlin Wall in 1961 and until the mid-1980s, some 70,000 people moved annually from East to West. Most of these emigrants were members of ethnic groups with close ties to receiving countries. For example, between 1961 and November 1989, about 840,000 East Germans moved to West Germany, about a quarter of these in 1989. Apart from Czechoslovakia (in the wake of the 1968 Soviet invasion) and Yugoslavia, the Eastern bloc countries succeeded in reducing emigration to a trickle during the 1960s and 1970s. Virtually all who did succeed in leaving found it relatively easy to settle in the West.

2. The most authoritative account of the causes of refugee movements in the developing world is Aristide Zolberg, Astri Suhrke, and Sergio Aguayo, *Escape from Violence: Conflict and the Refugee Crisis in the Developing World* (New York: Oxford University Press, 1989).

3. Ibid., p. 38.

4. Art Hansen, "Once the Running Stops: Assimilation of Angolan Refugees into Zambian Border Villages," *Disasters* 3 (1970): 369–74.

5. Sadruddin Aga Khan, *Legal Problems Related to Refugees and Displaced Persons* (The Hague: Academy of International Law, 1976), p. 14. Citing other UNHCR sources, Zolberg, Suhrke, and Aguayo, op. cit., list the number of refugees recorded in these two countries in 1972 in the range of 50,000–60,000.

6. William Zartman, "Portuguese Guinean Refugees in Senegal," in Hugh C. Brooks and Yassin El-Ayouty, eds., *Refugees South of the Sahara: An African Dilemma* (Westport, Conn.: Negro Universities Press, 1970); and Sadruddin Aga Khan, op. cit., p. 13.

7. Sadruddin Aga Khan, *Human Rights and Massive Exoduses,* ECOSOC doc. E/CN4/1503 (1981): 20; and Diana Cammack, *Africa's Refugees,* mimeo, 1987.

8. For a detailed treatment of this conflict, see Rene Lemarchand, *Rwanda and Burundi* (London: Pall Mall, 1970); and Zolberg, Suhrke, and Aguayo, op. cit.

9. Zolberg, Suhrke, and Aguayo, op. cit., and Louise Holborn, *Refugees: A Problem of Our Time* (Metuchen, N.J.: Scarecrow Press, 1972).

10. Mohamed Awad, "Refugees from the Sudan," in Hugh C. Brooks and Yassin El-Ayouty, eds., op. cit.

11. Abdel Rahman Ahmed El Bashir. *The Problems of Settlement of Immigrants and Refugees in Sudanese Society.* D. Phil. thesis, Oxford University (1978).

12. Richard Lawless and Laila Monahan, eds., *War and Refugees: The Western Sahara Conflict* (London: Pinter Publishers, 1987).

13. This point was emphasized in a resolution of the Pan-African Conference on Refugees held at Arusha, Tanzania, in May 1979, cited in Robert Chambers, "Rural Refugees in Africa: What the Eye Does Not See," *Disasters* 3 (1979): 382.

14. Although the UNHCR was involved in providing assistance to most African refugee movements during this period, some host governments denied it access to refugees within their borders, preferring instead to handle the problem independently. For example, President Sekou Toure of the Republic of Guinea refused to accept any external assistance for refugees from Guinea-Bisseau, and Hastings Banda of Malawi took a similar attitude toward outside aid for those fleeing the anticolonial war in Mozambique (author's interview with Gilbert Jaeger [Oxford, January 1988]).

15. For the particular problems faced by self-settled refugees, see Robert Chambers, op. cit.: 381–92.

16. Author's interview with Felix Schnyder (Locarno, May 1988). The theory of using the "good offices" of UNHCR is fully developed in Schnyder's lecture at the Hague. See Felix Schnyder, "Les aspects juridiques actuel du probleme des refugies," *Recueil* 114 (Leiden: Academie de Droit International, 1965).

17. United Nations General Assembly Resolution 1673 (XVI), December 18, 1961.

18. As noted in chapter 3, a precedent for this had already been established to deal with the outflow of refugees from the 1956 Hungarian Revolution.

19. United Nations General Assembly Resolution 2039 (XX), 1965.

20. "Protocol Relating to the Status of Refugees" (31 January 1967) *United Nations Treaty* vol. 606, p. 267. A number of countries, most notably Italy and Turkey, maintained geographic limitations, through declarations or understandings attached to their ratification of the Protocol.

21. According to Louise Holborn. op. cit., pp. 199–200, the number of ratifications and accessions to the 1951 Convention and the 1967 Protocol almost quadrupled between 1960 and 1970.

22. Author's interview with Gilbert Jaeger (Oxford, December 1986). See also Louise Holborn, op. cit., p. 185.

23. The Organization of African Unity Convention, *Governing the Specific Aspects of Refugee Problems in Africa.* OAU Doc. CM/267/Rev.1 (10 September 1969).

24. Goran Melander, *The Two Refugee Definitions* (Lund, Sweden: Wallenberg Institute, 1986), pp. 9–21.

25. These agencies included the United Nations Development Program (UNDP), the International Labor Organization (ILO), and the Lutheran World Federation, among others. See T. F. Betts, "Zonal Rural Development in Africa," *Journal of Modern African Studies* 7 (1966): 149–53; T. F. Betts, *Integrated Rural Development: Reports 1–4* (Geneva: International University Exchange Fund, 1969). See also Louise Holborn, op. cit., pp. 1085–86, 1238–41, and 1264–81.

26. For an assessment of these programs, see: T. F. Betts, "Evolution and Promotion of the Integrated Rural Development Approach to Refugee Policy in Africa," *Africa Today* 31 (1984): 7–24; Robert Chambers, op. cit.: 381–92; and Art Hansen, op. cit.: 369–74.

27. Gervase Coles, *Voluntary Repatriation* (Geneva: UNHCR, 1985).

28. In Angola, independence was followed by civil war and renewed outflows of refugees.

29. United Nations, ECOSOC Resolution 1655 (LII), June 1972.

30. Sadruddin Aga Khan, op. cit., p. 305.

31. The High Commissioner was called on to facilitate not only the return home of all refugees "from territories emerging from Colonial rule," but also their resettlement. See United Nations General Assembly Resolution 3271A (XXIX), December 10, 1974.

32. Louise Holborn, op. cit., vol. 2, p. 1399.

33. Shelley Pitterman, "International Responses to Refugee Situations: The United Nations High Commissioner for Refugees," in Elizabeth Ferris, ed., *Refugees and World Politics* (New York: Praeger, 1986), p. 49.

34. For a breakdown of UNHCR expenditures, see Shelley Pitterman, "Determinants of International Refugee Policy: A Comparative Study of UNHCR Material Assistance to Refugees in Africa, 1963–1981," in John Rogge, ed., *Refugees: A Third World Dilemma* (Totowa, N.J.: Rowman & Littlefield, 1987), pp. 15–36.

35. Louise Holborn, op. cit., pp. 1401–2.

36. United Nations General Assembly Resolution 2790 (XXVI), December 1971.

37. United Nations General Assembly Resolution 2958 (XXVII), December 1972.

38. United Nations General Assembly Resolution 3460 (XXXIV), 1979.

39. David Collier, ed., *The New Authoritarianism in Latin America* (Princeton, N.J.: Princeton University Press, 1979).

40. The widespread violation of human rights in these countries during this period is well documented by Amnesty International and the International Commission of Jurists, as well as in numerous reports and documents of the United Nations and the Inter-American Human Rights Commission and in hearings before the U.S. Congress.

41. Jorge Balan, *International Migration in the Southern Cone* (Washington, D.C.: Georgetown University, CIPRA, October 1985), cited in Zolberg, Suhrke, and Aguayo, op. cit. Balan estimates that approximately 200,000 Chileans, 200,000 Uruguayans, and 650,000 Argentines left during this period. Although not all were refugees, a large number were escaping political violence.

42. For background to the human rights situation in Chile at the time of the coup and shortly thereafter, see Amnesty International, *Chile* (London: AI Publications, 1974). See also, generally, the record of a hearing before the Senate Judiciary Committee's Subcommittee to Investigate Problems Connected with

Refugees and Escapees, entitled *Refugee and Humanitarian Problems in Chile,* Part 2, 93d Congress, 2d Session (July 23, 1974); and hearings before the House Committee on Foreign Affairs Subcommittees on Inter-American Affairs and on International Organizations and Movements, entitled *Human Rights in Chile,* 93d Congress, 2d Session (December 7, 1973, and May 7 and 23 and June 11, 12, and 18, 1974). The UN Commission on Human Rights and the Inter-American Commission on Human Rights also visited Chile on fact-finding missions and found evidence of gross violations of human rights.

43. The American response to the Chilean refugee problem is discussed in greater detail in Gil Loescher and John Scanlan, *Calculated Kindness: Refugees and America's Half-Open Door, 1945 to Present* (New York: Free Press, 1986), pp. 95–101.

44. Louis Wiesner, *Victims and Survivors: Displaced Persons and Other War Victims in Vietnam, 1954–1975* (New York: Greenwood Press, 1988).

45. Author's interview with Zia Rizvi, former UNHCR Regional Representative in Southeast Asia (New York, January 1983).

46. Norman Zucker and Naomi Zucker, *The Guarded Gate: The Reality of American Refugee Policy* (San Diego: Harcourt Brace Jovanovich, 1987); Loescher and Scanlan, op. cit.; and Norman Zucker, "Refugee Resettlement in the United States: Policy and Problems," *Annals of American Academy of Social and Political Science* 467 (1983): 172–86.

47. Barry Stein, "The Committment to Refugee Resettlement," *Annals of American Academy of Social and Political Science* 467 (1983): 187–201; and Robert L. Bach, "Third Country Resettlement," in Gil Loescher and Laila Monahan, eds., *Refugees and International Relations* (Oxford, Clarendon Press, 1989), pp. 313–31.

48. Dennis McNamara. "The Origins and Effects of 'Humane Deterrence' Policies in South-east Asia," in Gil Loescher and Laila Monahan, eds., op. cit., pp. 123–33.

49. For the rise in expenditures and growth in office, see Ronald S. Scheinman, "Refugees: Goodbye to the Good Old Days," *Annals of American Academy of Social and Political Science* 467 (1983): 88; and Sheila Avrin McLean, "International Institutional Mechanisms for Refugees," in Mary Kritz, ed., *U.S. Immigration and Refugee Policy: Global and Domestic Issues* (Lexington, Mass.: Lexington Books, 1983), p. 177.

50. For background, see Zolberg, Suhrke, and Aguayo, op. cit.; and Gil Loescher, *Refugee Movements and International Security,* Adelphi Paper 268 (London: Brassey's, for International Institute for Strategic Studies, Summer 1992).

51. These groups are termed "refugee warriors" by Zolberg, Suhrke, and Aguayo, op. cit., pp. 275–78.

52. For background, see Jeff Crisp and Nick Cater, *The Human Consequences of Conflict in the Horn of Africa: Refugees, Asylum and the Politics of Assistance* (Cairo, Egypt: IISS and Centre for Political Research and Studies, May 1990).

## Chapter 5. Asylum Crises in the Industrialized World

1. Amnesty International, Americas Watch, United Nations, and OAS reports all documented the widespread human rights violations in El Salvador during the 1980s.

2. The author visited refugee camps for Guatemalans, Salvadorans, and Nicaraguans in Mexico, Honduras, Costa Rica, and Nicaragua in 1986.

3. For background, see Gil Loescher, "Humanitarianism and Politics in Central America," *Political Science Quarterly* 103 (Summer 1988): 295–320.

4. See, for example, Amnesty International, *Iran: Violations of Human Rights* (London: AI, 1987); and Amnesty International, *Iran: Persistent Violations of Human Rights* (London: AI, 1988).

5. The author visited Pakistan in December 1987 and interviewed government officials, voluntary agency officials, and refugees about the conditions of Iranian refugees in Pakistan. See also the preliminary draft report of the Council of Europe, Parliamentary Assembly, Committee on Migration, Refugees and Demography, *The Situation of Iranian Refugees in Turkey* (Strasbourg: December 5, 1988); and Amnesty International reports on human rights conditions in Turkey and in Pakistan.

6. *The Situation of Iranian Refugees in Turkey,* op. cit., p. 6.

7. During the 1980s, a few other governments had programs for emergency resettlement of Central Americans directly from the region. These included Canada (3,000), Australia (2,000), and Sweden (a few hundred).

8. Bill Frelick, *Clinton Haitian Refugee Policy Repeats Old Mistakes* (Washington, D.C.: U.S. Committee for Refugees, January 1993).

9. United Nations High Commissioner for Refugees, Executive Committee, EC/SCR/40, 1985, cited in James Hathaway, "Burden Sharing or Burden Shifting? Irregular Asylum Seekers: What's All the Fuss?" *Refuge* 8 (December 1988): 1.

10. Ibid.; and Gilbert Jaeger, *Study of Irregular Movements of Asylum Seekers and Refugees* (Geneva: UNHCR, 1985).

11. Doris Meissner, former Acting INS Commissioner, makes this point in regard to Central Americans and Haitians in "Central American Refugees: Political Asylum, Sanctuary and Humanitarian Policy," in Bruce Nichols and Gil Loescher, eds., *The Moral Nation: Humanitarianism and U.S. Foreign Policy Today* (South Bend, Ind.: University of Notre Dame Press, 1989) pp. 123–43.

12. A prominent characteristic of the sovereignty of nations is the right to control the entry of aliens into their territory, and states have retained intact their national prerogatives in this area. It can be argued, however, that mandatory visas, sanctions against airlines, and similar measures undermine the basic principles of refugee protection and run counter in spirit to the obligations toward refugees that states have assumed under treaty and in accordance with customary international law. It can also be argued that, in exercising its functions of international protection, the UNHCR must ensure that all asylum seekers, regardless of whether they qualify as Convention refugees, are given access to asylum procedures and are accorded a fair and independent assessment of their claims. States have an obligation to cooperate with the UNHCR in the fulfillment of its mandate.

13. Gil Loescher and John Scanlan, *Calculated Kindness: Refugees and America's Half-Open Door, 1945 to Present.* (New York: Free Press, 1986); and James Silk, *Despite a Generous Spirit: Denying Asylum in the United States* (Washington, D.C.: U.S. Committee for Refugees, December 1986).

14. See, for example, the 1953 Refugee Relief Act, the Refugee Escape Act of 1957, and the Fair Share Refugee Act passed in 1960.

15. Under the "Seventh Preference" of the Immigration and Nationality Act of 1965, 6 percent of the annual numerical limitation on immigration was reserved for "conditional entrants," who, by definition, were required to be refugees—that

is, persons fleeing the threat of persecution in a communist-dominated country, or "any country within the general area of the Middle East."

16. Bill Frelick, "Call Them What They Are—Refugees," in *World Refugee Survey 1992* (Washington, D.C.: U.S. Committee for Refugees, 1992, p. 14.

17. John A. Scanlan and Gilburt D. Loescher, "U.S. Foreign Policy, 1959–1980: Impact on Refugee Flow from Cuba," *Annals of American Academy of Political and Social Science* 467 (May 1983): 116–138; and Silvia Pedraza-Bailey, "Cuban Americans in the United States: the Functions of Political and Economic Migration," *Cuban Studies/Studies Cubanos* 11 ( July 1981/January 1982): 79–87.

18. Gilburt Loescher and John Scanlan, "Human Rights, U.S. Foreign Policy and Haitian Refugees," *Journal of Inter-American Studies and World Affairs* 26 (August 1984): 313–56; and Naomi Flink Zucker, "The Haitians Versus the United States: The Courts as Last Resort," *Annals of American Academy of Political and Social Sciences* 467 (May 1983): 151–62.

19. Loescher and Scanlan, *Calculated Kindness,* op. cit., pp. 95–101.

20. Doris Meissner, op. cit. p. 126.

21. Newsweek described the Cuban influx as a "voyage to freedom." "Sea Lift from Cuba to Key West," *Newsweek* (May 5, 1980), p. 59.

22. "Commissioners Join Cry for U.S. to Accept Cubans," *Miami Herald* (April 7, 1980), p. 8A.

23. These were the words President Carter used at the beginning of the boatlift to describe the attitude the United States would take toward arriving Cubans. "League of Women Voters," Remarks and a Question-and-Answer Session (May 5, 1980), in *Public Papers of the Presidents: Jimmy Carter, 1980–1981* 1 (1981): 833–34.

24. Former White House Assistant Jack Watson, cited in Mario Rivera, "The Cuban and Haitian Influxes of 1980 and the American Response: Retrospect and Prospect," U.S. House of Representatives Committee on the Judiciary, *Oversight Hearings: Caribbean Migration* (Washington, D.C.: Government Printing Office, 1980), appendix 4, p. 292.

25. Author's interviews, with John Scanlan, conducted with State Department and INS officials (May and August 1980).

26. Doris Meissner, op. cit., p. 127.

27. Norman Zucker and Naomi Zucker, *The Guarded Gate: The Reality of American Refugee Policy.* (San Diego: Harcourt Brace Jovanovich, 1987), p. 142.

28. Henry Kamm, "Western Nations Raising Barriers to Refugees Trying to Flee Poverty," *New York Times* (March 27, 1989), p. 1.

29. Bill Frelick, op. cit., p. 14. Frelick notes that "by adding two Middle Eastern regimes opposed by U.S. foreign policy in the 1980s—Iran and Iraq—the percentage of refugees originating from "enemy" regimes from communist dominated lands or the Middle East rises above 99.8 percent, virtually identical to the pattern prior to the *Refugee Act of 1980.*"

30. From 1980 to 1988, the United States admitted 1,140 Bulgarians, 8,896 Czechs, 4,916 Hungarians, 32,735 Poles, 29,087 Romanians, 48,191 Soviets, and 74 Yugoslavs. During the same period, the United States admitted only 107 Salvadorans, no Guatemalans, no Hondurans, and 188 South Africans. See U.S. Department of Health and Human Services, Office of Refugee Resettlement, *Refugee Resettlement Program (1989)* ( January 31, 1989), p. A-11.

31. Mark Gibney, "A 'Well-Founded Fear' of Persecution." *Human Rights*

*Quarterly* 109 (1988): 109–21; and Mark Gibney and Michael Stohl, "Human Rights and U.S. Refugee Policy," in Mark Gibney, ed., *Open Borders? Closed Societies?* (Westport, Conn.: Greenwood Press, 1986), pp. 151–84.

32. For background, see Naomi Flink Zucker, op. cit., 151–62.

33. Lawyers Committee for International Human Rights, *The UNHCR at 40: Refugee Protection at the Crossroads* (Washington, D.C.: Lawyers Committee for International Human Rights, February 1991).

34. *Jean v. Nelson,* 711 F. 2d 1455 (11th Cir. 1983): 1487.

35. Ibid., 1490.

36. *Louis v. Meissner,* 530 F. Supp. 924 (S.D. Fla. 1981): 926.

37. *Jean v. Nelson,* op. cit., 1463.

38. See INS, *Asylum Adjudications: An Evolving Concept and Responsibility for the INS* (Internal Memorandum, June and December 1982). The INS internal report noted that "different levels of proof are required of different asylum applicants. In other words, certain nationalities appear to benefit from presumptive status while others do not." The report contrasts the consideration of Salvadorans with that of seven Polish sailors who jumped ship, applied for, and were granted asylum in Alaska. In contrast to the treatment afforded the Polish sailors, the report noted: "For an El Salvadoran national to receive a favorable asylum advisory opinion, he or she must have 'a classic textbook case.'" See also Office of the U.S. Coordinator for Refugee Affairs, *Country Reports on the World Refugee Situation* (Washington, D.C.: Department of State, August 1982), p. 105; and Gerard F. Seib, "Aliens Seeking Asylum Swamp U.S. Agencies, Stir Debate on Criteria," *Wall Street Journal* (August 11, 1983): 1.

39. Doris Meissner, op. cit., pp. 130–31.

40. For background, see Dennis Gallagher, Susan Forbes Martin, and Patricia Weiss Fagen, "Temporary Safe Haven: The Need for North American–European Responses," in Gil Loescher and Laila Monahan, eds., *Refugees and International Relations* (Oxford: Clarendon Press, 1989), pp. 333–54.

41. U.S. General Accounting Office, *Asylum: Uniform Application of Standards Uncertain—Few Denied Applicants Deported,* GAO/GGD-87-33BR (Washington, D.C.: GAO, January 1987).

42. Ibid., p. 42.

43. INS Statistics provided to author.

44. Bill Frelick, *The Back of the Hand: Bias and Restriction Towards Central American Asylum Seekers in North America* (Washington, D.C.: U.S. Committee for Refugees, October 1988), p. 8.

45. INS statistics provided to author.

46. An estimated 80 percent of the Salvadorans in the United States were not eligible for legalization, having arrived in the country after the January 1, 1982, eligibility cutoff date.

47. Jeffrey Schmalz, "Miami, Saying It's Overburdened, Tells Nicaraguans to Stay Away," *New York Times* (January 14, 1989): 1, 3.

48. Observers continue to criticize both the asylum and refugee procedures and the agencies mandated to implement these policies. See, for example, Amnesty International USA, *Reasonable Fear: Human Rights and United States Refugee Policy* (New York: AIUSA, 1990); and Lawyers Committee for International Human Rights, *The Implementation of the Refugee Act of 1980: A Decade of Experience* (New York: Lawyers Committee for International Human Rights, 1990).

49. According to an August 1992 Amnesty International report, "Haitians

live in permanent fear, while their oppressors are free to kill, torture and terrorize with impunity." "Haiti Torture Rife, Says Amnesty," *The Independent* (August 21, 1992).

50. Cited in Bill Frelick, "Haiti: No Room at the Inn." *Refugees* 90 (July 1992): 35.

51. Bill Frelick, *Running the Gauntlet: The Central American Journey Through Mexico*. (Washington, D.C.: U.S. Committee for Refugees, 1991).

52. Bill Frelick. "Refugees in Mexico: New Law, Old Practices," in U.S. Committee for Refugees, *World Refugee Survey 1992* (Washington, D.C.: U.S. Committee for Refugees, 1992), p. 92.

53. For further treatment, see Gary Rubin, "Are There Too Many People in the Lifeboat? Immigration and the American Dream," in American Jewish Committee, *Issues in National Affairs* (New York: American Jewish Committee, 1992).

54. Robert Reinhold, "In California, New Discussion on Whether to Bar the Door," *New York Times* (December 3, 1991): 1.

55. For background studies, see James Hathaway, "The Conundrum of Refugee Protection in Canada: From Control, to Compliance, to Collective Deterrence," in Gil Loescher, ed., *Refugees and the Asylum Dilemma in the West* (University Park, Penn.: Penn State University Press, 1992), pp. 71–92; Canadian Collection of Papers for the International Symposium at Oxford, *The Refugee Crisis: British and Canadian Responses* (Toronto: York University, Centre for Refugee Studies, 1989); and the chapters on Canada in Howard Adelman, ed., *Refugee Policy: Canada and the United States* (Toronto: York Lanes Press, 1991).

56. The acceptance rate for applicants from China fell from 74 percent in 1989 to 43 percent in 1990 to 21.6 percent in 1991. See *World Refugee Survey 1992* (Washington D.C.: U.S. Committee for Refugees, 1992), p. 109.

57. As reported in *Refuge* 9 (May 1990): 26.

58. For background accounts of Canadian asylum procedures and policies, see James Hathaway, op. cit.; and Howard Adelman, ed., op. cit. For information about Bill C-86, see U.S. Committee for Refugees, *Refugee Reports* 12 (September 30, 1992): 1–7.

59. James Hathaway, op. cit.; and U.S. Committee for Refugees, ibid.

60. Allan Dowty, *Closed Borders* (New Haven, Conn.: Yale University Press, 1987).

61. In the mid-1970s, for example, in what was proportionately the greatest postcolonial influx of any European state, an estimated 600,000 returnees flooded into Portugal after independence was granted to Mozambique and Angola. Similarly, France opened its doors to hundreds of thousands of Algerians in the early 1960s, as well as to Tunisian Jews expelled from Tunisia during the 1967 Arab–Israeli war; and Britain agreed to accept an estimated 28,000 Ugandan Asians following their expulsion by Idi Amin in 1972. Between 1961 and 1977, some 140,000 Cubans took advantage of air links maintained between Havana and Madrid to find asylum in Spain.

62. The major exceptions involved Italian and Spanish guestworkers, who returned home to economies where wages were rising and opportunities for employment were improving.

63. The huge increases in asylum applications at the beginning of the 1980s were largely the result of political and economic unrest in Poland, the refusal of Germany and other governments to grant work permits to a substantial number of immigrant workers (particularly Turks, who, after long periods of residence in

Western Europe, now claimed asylum to avoid being deported to Turkey, where harsh military rule had been imposed in 1980), and the sharply worsening conditions of physical security in certain parts of the Third World, which led many young people (particularly Iranians) who had completed their studies in Europe to try to extend their stay by seeking refugee status. See Philip Rudge, "Fortress Europe," in U.S. Committee for Refugees, *World Refugee Survey: 1986 in Review* (Washington, D.C.: U.S. Committee for Refugees, 1986): pp. 5–12.

64. The character of migration to Europe also changed during the 1980s. Until the oil crisis of the 1970s, about 70 percent of immigration involved foreign workers. Beginning in the mid-1980s, the number of asylum seekers entering Europe annually exceeded the number of foreign workers. Since then, over 80 percent of legal immigration has involved people admitted on social and humanitarian grounds, mainly cases of family reunion and refugees. See Jonas Widgren, "Europe and International Migration in the Future," in Gil Loescher and Laila Monahan, eds., *Refugees and International Relations* (Oxford: Clarendon Press, 1989), pp. 49–61.

65. Statistics about asylum seekers in Europe are notoriously unreliable. For example, during the 1980s a relatively high percentage of asylum seekers applied for asylum in more than one country and therefore are counted two or more times in official refugee statistics. In 1988 the UNHCR estimated that 30 percent of asylum seekers travel to neighboring countries and often submit multiple claims to asylum status (author's interview with UNHCR staff [Geneva, 1988]).

66. Gil Loescher, "The European Community and Refugees," *International Affairs* 65 (Autumn 1989): 617–36.

67. While there is heated dispute over the size and composition of East–West flows, scant hard data are available. The data that follow in the main text are derived from the OECD's SOPEMI reports; the UNHCR; the U.S. Committee for Refugees; the Inter-Governmental Consultations on Asylum, Refugee and Migration Policies in Europe, North America and Australia (IGC); the Refugee Policy Group; papers delivered at a conference held in Vienna in 1991 on the movement of persons coming from Central and Eastern European Countries; and papers delivered at the Rand Corporation conference held in Santa Monica, California, in November 1991 on prospective migration and emigration from the former Soviet Union.

68. Jean-Claude Chesnais, *The USSR Emigration: Past; Present and Future* (Rome: OECD International Conference on Migration, March 1991); Sidney Heitman, *Soviet Emigration Since Gorbachev* (Cologne: Bericht des Bundesinstituts fur ostwissenschaftliche und internationale Studien, 1989); Sidney Heitman, *Soviet Emigration in 1990* (Cologne: Bericht des Bundesinstituts für ostwissenschaftliche und internationale Studien, 1990); Klaus Segbers, *Wanderungs-und Fluchtlings-bewegungen aus der bisherigen UdSSR* (Ebenhausen: Stiftung Wissenschaft und Politik, January 1991); V. Tiskhov, *The Russians Are Leaving* (mimeo, 1991); M. Tillman, *On Some Causes and Trends of the Forced Emigration from the USSR* (mimeo, 1991); Refugee Policy Group, *Migration in and from Central and Eastern Europe: Addressing the Root Causes* (Washington, D.C.: Refugee Policy Group, 1992); F. W. Carter, R. A. French, and J. Salt, *International Migration Between East and West in Europe* (mimeo, 1992); and Jonas Widgren, *East–West Migration: Economic Buffer or Security Threat?* (mimeo, April 1992).

69. For background, see Jeremy Azrael, Patricia Brukoff, and Vladimir Shkolnikov, "Prospective Migration and Emigration from the Former USSR: A Confer-

ence Report." *Slavic Review* 51 (1992): 323–31; and Paul Goble, "Ethnicity and National Conflict in Soviet Politics," in Neil MacFarlane, ed., *The 'Soviet Threat' Revisited* (Kingston, Ont.: Queens University Press, 1992), pp. 31–39.

70. "Abroad Consensus," *The Guardian* (24 May 1991); and Jean-Claude Chesnais, op. cit.

71. For background, see Azrael, Brukoff, and Shkolnikov. op. cit.; Vladimir Kusin, "Refugees in Central and Eastern Europe: Problem or Threat?" *Report on Eastern Europe* (January 18, 1991): 33–43; Anatoli Vishnevsky and Zhanna Zayonchkovskaya, *Internal and International Migrations in the Former Soviet Space* (mimeo, June 1992).

72. Jochen Blauschke, *East–West Migration in Europe and International Aid as a Means to Reduce the Need for Emigration* Geneva: ILO-UNHCR, May 1992), p. 38.

73. For general background, see E. Honekopp, *Migratory Movements from Countries of East-Central and Eastern Europe: Causes and Characteristics, Present Situation and Possible Future Trends: The Cases of Germany and Austria* (Strasbourg: Council of Europe, November 1990).

74. Jean-Claude Chesnais, *Migration from Eastern to Western Europe, Past (1946–1989) and Future (1990–2000)* (Strasbourg: Council of Europe, November 1990); F. W. Carter, R. A. French, and J. Salt, op. cit.; and L. Tomasi, ed., "The New Europe and International Migration." *International Migration Review* 26 (Summer 1992): 229–720.

75. J.-C. Chesnais, *Migration from Eastern to Western Europe,* op. cit.

76. Ibid.

77. Dan Ionescu, "The Exodus," *Report on Eastern Europe* 43 (October 26, 1990): 25–31.

78. Bimal Ghosh, "The Exodus That Could Explode," *Financial Times* (January 23, 1991), p. 15.

79. According to the *World Refugee Survey 1992* (Washington, D.C.: U.S. Committee for Refugees, 1992), p. 68, "The U.S. State Department's annual human rights report stated that more than 100,000 persons were prevented from entering Austria during 1991 or were forced to leave the country at the point of entry. A substantial number of these, said the report, may have qualified for refugee status."

80. About 30 percent of East Europeans admitted will be spouses and children of previously admitted refugees, primarily from Poland and Romania. The remaining admissions will be Romanian and Albanian refugees. *Refugee Reports* 13 (July 31, 1992): 5.

81. Adrian Bridge, "Germany Acts to Curb Refugees," *The Independent,* (December 7, 1992): 1.

82. OECD, *Sopemi 1989* (Paris: OECD, 1990), p. 1.

83. For background, see Johan Cels, "Responses of European States to De Facto Refugees," in Gil Loescher and Laila Monahan, eds., *Refugees and International Relations* (Oxford: Clarendon Press, 1989), pp. 187–216.

84. In 1988, the recognition rate of asylum seekers in the Federal Republic of Germany was 8.1 percent, in France 34.4 percent, in the Netherlands 17.2 percent, in Norway 2.2 percent, in Sweden 25 percent, in Switzerland 5.5 percent, and in Great Britain 13 percent. This represents a sharp drop from previous years. For example, the recognition rate in France in 1983 had been 60 percent, and in Great Britain in 1982 it had been 41 percent.

85. Johan Cels, op. cit., pp. 204–5.

86. For background on events before mid-1989, see Gil Loescher, "The European Community and Refugees," op. cit.

87. Demetrious Papademetriou, D. A. Clark Cobb, R. C. Kramer, B. L. Lowell, and S. J. Smith, *The President's First Report on Implementation and Impact of Employer Sanctions* (Washington, D.C.: Division of Immigration Policy and Research, U.S. Department of Labor, 1991).

## Chapter 6. The Limitations of the International Refugee Regime

1. See Harto Hakovirta. *An Ethical Analysis of Refugee Aid and the World Refugee Problem* (Amsterdam: Workshop on Duties Beyond Borders, ECPR Joint Sessions, April 1987).

2. United Nations, Economic and Social Council, *Draft Report of the United Nations High Commissioner for Refugees* (E/1992/May 1992), p. 56.

3. Ibid., p. 56.

4. These statistics are derived from UNHCR figures and from those provided in research by Harto Hakovirta, *The World Refugee Problem* (Tampere, Finland: Hillside Publications, 1991); Shelley Pitterman, "International Responses to Refugee Situations: The United Nations High Commissioner for Refugees," in Elizabeth Ferris, ed., *Refugees and World Politics* (New York: Praeger, 1986); and E. Ngolle, *The African Refugee Problem and the Distribution of International Refugee Assistance in Comparative Perspective: An Evaluation of the Policies of the Office of the United Nations High Commissioner for Refugees, 1960–1980* (Ph.D. dissertation, 1985).

5. See Testimony of Hiram Ruiz, U.S. Committee for Refugees, before a Joint Hearing of the House Committee on Foreign Affairs, Subcommittees on International Operations and Africa, 101st Congress, 2d Session, May 10, 1990.

6. Refugee Studies Programme, *Data Paper for U.K.–Japan Group* (March 1992), p. 4.

7. Harto Harkovirta, *The World Refugee Problem,* p. 85.

8. Barbara Harrell-Bond, "Humanitarianism in a Strait-Jacket," *African Affairs* 334 (1985): 3–13.

9. Gary Rubin, *Refugee Protection: An Analysis and Action Proposal* (Washington, D.C.: U.S. Committee for Refugees, 1983), p. 36. Unless otherwise indicated, much of the information on the limitations of the UNHCR and of refugee law is drawn from this work.

10. Ibid., p. 28. For a comprehensive background of international refugee law, see Guy Goodwin-Gill, *The Refugee in International Law* (Oxford: Clarendon Press, 1983); Atle Grahl-Madsen, *The Status of Refugees in International Law* (Leiden: A. W. Sijthoff, 1966); and James Hathaway, *The Law of Refugee Status* (Toronto: Butterworths, 1991).

11. See Chapter 5, note 12.

12. For background, see Atle Grahl-Madsen, *Territorial Asylum* (Dobbs Ferry, N.Y.: Oceana Publications, 1980).

13. Lawyers Committee for Human Rights, *The UNHCR at 40: Refugee Protection at the Crossroads* (New York: Lawyers Committee for Human Rights, February 1991).

14. See Lawyers Committee for Human Rights, *Refugee Refoulement: The Forced Return of Haitians Under the U.S. Haitian Interdiction Agreement* (New York: Lawyers Committee for Human Rights, 1990).

15. *The Organization of African Unity Convention Governing the Specific Aspects of Refugee Problems in Africa*. OAU Document CM/267/Rev.1 (September 10, 1969).

16. *The Cartagena Declaration of 1984* (Geneva: UNHCR, 1985).

17. *INS v. Stevic*, 467 U.S. 407, 104 S. Ct. 2489, 81 L. Ed. 2d 321 (1984), p. 2497. In practice, this policy continues despite the court decision of *INS* v. *Cardoza-Fonseca*, 480 U.S. 421, 107 S. Ct. 12078, 94 L. Ed. 2d 434 (1987).

18. *INS* v. *Elias Zacarias*, 502 U.S. Supreme Ct., No. 90-1342 (January 22, 1992).

19. *INS* v. *Elias Zacarias*, Reply Brief for Petitioner, pp. 11–13, cited in Bill Frelick, "Call Them What They Are—Refugees," *World Refugee Survey 1992*, p. 14.

20. Ibid., p. 20.

21. See Johan Cels, *The European Refugee Regime* (Ph.D. dissertation, 1989).

22. "The 1951 United Nations Convention Relating to the Status of Refugees," *United Nations Treaty*, vol. 189, no. 2545 (July 28, 1951), p. 137.

23. Ambassador Brunson McKinley, Deputy Assistant Secretary for Refugee Programs, testifying to the U.S. House Subcommittee on Western Hemisphere Affairs and International Operations on June 11, 1992, cited in *Refugees* 90 (July 1992): 36. The UNHCR has vigorously disputed this interpretation and has argued that Article 33 proscribes the return of refugees in any manner whatsoever.

24. Guy Goodwin-Gill, "Non-refoulement and the New Asylum Seekers," in David Martin, ed., *The New Asylum Seekers: Refugee Law in the 1980s* (Dordrecht, Netherlands: Martinus Nijhoff, 1988): 103–22.

25. As of mid-1992, Hungary, Poland, Romania, and the Czech and Slovak Republic have become signatories.

26. See, for example, Guy Goodwin-Gill, op. cit.; and Atle Grahl-Madsen, op. cit.

27. *UNHCR Handbook on Procedures* (1979), cited in Rubin, op. cit.

28. Larry Minear, U. Chelliah, Jeff Crisp, John Mackinlay, and Thomas Weiss, *United Nations Coordination of the International Humanitarian Response to the Gulf Crisis 1990–1992*, Occasional Paper 13 (Providence, R.I.: Watson Institute for International Studies, Brown University, 1992).

29. United Nations General Assembly, Resolution 46/182 (December 1991).

30. For inadequacies regarding the provision of food rations, see Refugee Studies Programme, *Responding to the Nutrition Crisis Among Refugees: The Need for New Approaches* (Oxford: Report of the International Symposium, March 17–20 1991).

31. For background, see Mary Ann Larkin, Fred Cuny, and Barry Stein, eds., *Repatriation Under Conflict in Central America* (Washington, D.C., and Dallas: Center for Immigration Policy and Refugee Assistance, Georgetown University, and Intertecht Institute, 1991).

32. See Fred Cuny and Barry Stein, "Prospects for and Promotion of Spontaneous Repatriation," in Gil Loescher and Laila Monahan, eds., *Refugees and International Relations* (Oxford: Clarendon Press, 1989), pp. 293–312.

## Chapter 7. Resolving Refugee Problems: Asylum and Development Assistance Policies

1. For background, see Norman Zucker and Naomi Zucker, *The Guarded Gate: The Reality of American Refugee Policy* (San Diego: Harcourt Brace Jovanovich, 1987); and Gil Loescher and John Scanlan, *Calculated Kindness: Refugees and America's Half-Open Door, 1945 to Present* (New York: Free Press, 1986).

2. See *Refugee Reports* 13 (July 31, 1992): 1.

3. U.S. Congress, *House of Representatives Report No. 608,* 96th Congress, 1st Session (1979), p. 13.

4. Gil Loescher and John Scanlan, op. cit.

5. See, for example, John Scanlan, "Regulating Refugee Flow: Legal Alternatives and Obligations Under the Refugee Act of 1980," *Notre Dame Lawyer* 56 (April 1981): 619–43. Norman Zucker and Naomi Zucker, op. cit., p. 276, also make this recommendation, as have numerous human rights advocacy groups.

6. As part of a legal settlement of *American Baptist Churches* v. *Thornburgh,* the INS agreed to affirm that "foreign policy and border enforcement considerations . . . the fact that an individual is from a country whose government the United States supports . . . [and] whether or not the U.S. Government agrees with the political or ideological beliefs of the individuals [are] not relevant to the determination of whether an applicant for asylum has a well-founded fear of persecution" (*Refugee Reports* 11 [December 21, 1990], p. 1).

7. For greater details, see "Backlogs, Old and New, Threaten to Overload New Asylum System," *Refugee Reports* (January 31, 1992), pp. 10–11. The figures for the end of 1992 were provided by Bill Frelick and Naomi Zucker.

8. Cited in Bill Frelick, "Call Them What They Are—Refugees," *World Refugee Survey 1992* (Washington, D.C.: U.S. Committee for Refugees, 1992), p. 17.

9. For an exposition of this view, see Amnesty International, *Harmonization of Asylum Policies in Europe: Amnesty International's Concerns* (London: AI, 1990). See also Philip Rudge, "Asylum Dilemma—Crisis in the Modern World: A European Perspective," in Gil Loescher, ed., *Refugees and the Asylum Dilemma in the West* (University Park, Penn.: Penn State University Press, 1992), pp. 93–110.

10. See James Hathaway, "The Conundrum of Refugee Protection in Canada: From Control, to Compliance, to Collective Deterrence," in Gil Loescher, ed., op. cit., pp. 71–92.

11. Dennis Gallagher, Susan Forbes Martin, and Patricia Weiss Fagen, "Temporary Safe Haven: The Need for North American–European Responses," in Gil Loescher and Laila Monahan, eds., *Refugees and International Relations* (Oxford: Clarendon Press, 1989), p. 334.

12. Refugee Policy Group, *Migration in and from Central and Eastern Europe: Addressing the Root Causes* (Washington, D.C.: Refugee Policy Group, June 1992), pp. 20–21.

13. ILO figures, cited in International Organization for Migration, *Background Document* (Geneva: 9th IOM Seminar on Migration, December 1990), p. 31.

14. Francois Heisbourg, "Population Movements in post–Cold War Europe," *Survival* 33 (1991): 31–43; and Jonas Widgren, op. cit.

15. See, for example, the Final Report of the Commission for the Study of

International Migration and Cooperative Economic Development, and the compendium of papers presented at the International Conference on Migration held in Rome, March 13–15, 1991, under the auspices of OECD and the Italian government (Paris: OECD, 1991); Sharon Stanton Russell and Michael Teitelbaum, *International Migration and International Trade* (Washington, D.C.: World Bank, Discussion Paper 160, 1992); and Demetrious Papademetriou and Philip Martin, eds., *The Unsettled Relationship: Labor Migration and Economic Development* (New York: Greenwood Press, 1991).

16. Final Report, op. cit.

17. According to Demetrious Papademetriou, development weakens the individual's attachment to his traditional way of life and makes him more likely to migrate internally, usually to the capital city. "Unable to find steady work there, and now both better aware of opportunities to work abroad . . . and better able to finance such a trip through income gained from the informal economy, the internal migrant becomes a prime candidate for entering the international migratory flow " (Demetrious Papademetriou, *Migration and Development: Next Steps* [Paris: L'Arche de la Fraternite Foundation, May 1991], pp. 17–18).

18. Jonas Widgren, "International Migration and Regional Stability," *International Affairs* 66 (1990): 753.

19. For example, both France, with 8 percent of its population composed of foreign-born residents, and Germany, with 7.5 percent, have proportionately larger foreign-born populations today than does the United States, with 6 percent. See Doris Meissner, "Managing Migrations," *Foreign Policy* (Winter 1992): 70.

20. Jacques Cuenod, *E. C. Assistance to Regions with Large Numbers of Refugees* (Washington, D.C.: Refugee Policy Group, 1989).

21. For useful background, see Robert Gorman, *Coping with Africa's Refugee Burden: A Time for Solutions* (Dordrecht, Netherlands: Martinus Nijhoff, 1987); Robert E. Mazur, "Linking Popular Initiative and Aid Agencies: The Case of Refugees," *Development and Change* 18 (1987): 451–52; and John Rogge, ed., *Refugees: A Third World Dilemma* (Totowa, N.J.: Rowman & Littlefield, 1987).

22. Hanne Christensen, *Survival Strategies for and by Camp Refugees: Report on a Six Week Exploratory Sociological Field Study into the Food Situation of Refugees in Camps in Somalia* (Geneva: UNRISD, 1982); Hanne Christensen, *Afghan Refugees in Pakistan: From Emergency Towards Self-Reliance: A Report on the Food Relief Situation and Related Socio-Economic Aspects* (Geneva: UNRISD, 1984); and Barbara Harrell-Bond, *Imposing Aid* (Oxford: Oxford University Press, 1986).

23. Barbara Harrell-Bond, op. cit.

24. Refugee Studies Programme, *Background Paper for U.K.–Japan 2000 Group* (March 1992), p. 6. See also Roger Zetter, "Refugees and Forced Migrants as Development Resources: The Greek Cypriot Refugees from 1974," *Cyprus Review* 4 (Spring 1992): 7–39.

25. On this point, see Leon Gordenker, *Refugees and International Politics* (London: Croom Helm, 1987).

26. *International Conference on Central American Refugees (CIREFCA)*, CIREFCA/89/13, Rev. 1, Draft Declaration and Concerted Plan of Action; Jacques Cuenod, "Refugees: Development or Relief," in Gil Loescher and Laila Monahan, eds., op. cit., pp. 219–54; Robert Gorman, *Coping with Africa's Refugee Burden: A Time for Solutions* (Dordrecht, Netherlands: Martinus Nijhoff, 1987); Robert Gorman, "Taking Stock of the Second International Conference on Assistance to

Africa," *Journal of African Studies* 14 (1987): 4–11; and Barry Stein, "Refugee Aid and Development: Slow Progress Since ICARA II," in Howard Adelman, ed., *Refugee Policy: Canada and the United States* (Toronto: York Lanes Press, 1991).

27. Michael Power, *E. C. Assistance to Refugees and Displaced Persons,* presentation at Symposium on Internally Displaced Persons, Georgetown University, October 1989.

28. Jacques Cuenod, "Refugees: Development or Relief?" op. cit.

29. See UNHCR/UNDP Cooperation with Regard to Development Activities Affecting Refugees and Returnees, November 23, 1987. Memoranda of Understanding have also been reached with World Food Program (August 1985), World Bank (October 1987), and IFAD (1988). See United Nations General Assembly Docs. A/AC.96/677 and A/AC.96/696. The UNHCR worked on a number of joint projects with UN development agencies, particularly the World Bank. One example of this cooperation was the World Bank–UNHCR project in Pakistan to provide temporary employment (mainly to Afghan refugees) in areas such as reforestation, irrigation, and road-building. In Sudan, the UNHCR joined a World Bank project to ensure that the "South Kassala Agricultural Project" was enlarged to include refugees living in the project area.

30. United Nations General Assembly Resolution 40/117 (1985) emphasized "the vital importance of the complementarity of refugee aid and development assistance" and called on UNDP to "increase its effort to mobilize additional resources for refugee-related development projects and, in general, to promote and coordinate with the host countries and the donor community the integration of refugee-related activities into national development planning." United Nations General Assembly Resolution 41/122 and 124 (1986) called on the High Commissioner to continue "to put into practice the concept of development-oriented assistance to refugees and returnees . . . in full cooperation with appropriate international agencies" and reiterated its request that UNDP "increase its efforts to mobilize additional resources for refugee-related development projects."

A development approach to refugee situations has also been endorsed by the UNHCR Executive Committee, *Refugee Aid and Development* (U.N. Doc. A/AC.96/645, Annex I, August 28, 1984). See also M. Zollner, *Development Approaches to Refugee Situations* (Geneva: UNHCR informal report, 1986) and *ICVA/UNHCR Workshop on Development Approaches to Refugee Situations, Recommendations and Suggestions* (Geneva: UNHCR, 1986).

31. UNDP has taken a number of measures to ensure closer collaboration with the UNHCR, including appointing a coordinator/liaison officer for refugee-related matters and displaced persons issues within UNDP and establishing a UNDP Task Force.

32. See Jacques Cuenod, *Report on Refugees, Displaced Persons and Returnees,* UN Economic and Social Council, E/1991/109/Add. 1, June 1991; and Erskine Childers and Brian Urquhart, *Strengthening International Response to Humanitarian Emergencies* (New York: Ford Foundation, 1991).

33. See Julia Taft, "A Call to Action for Restructuring U.S. Refugee Policy," in *World Refugee Survey: 1989 in Review* (Washington, D.C.: U.S. Committee for Refugees, 1989), pp. 7–12; Jeffrey Clark, *The U.S. Government, Humanitarian Assistance, and the New World Order: A Call for a New Approach* (Washington, D.C.: U.S. Committee for Refugees, 1991); U.S. Congress, House Select Committee on Hunger, 102d Congress, 2d Session, *The Decade of Disasters: The United Nations' Response,* July 30, 1991.

34. For fuller development of this idea, see Jacques Cuenod, "Refugees: Development or Relief?" op. cit.

35. UN High Commissioner for Refugees, *Establishment of a UNHCR Fund for Durable Solutions* (Geneva: UNHCR Executive Committee, 30th Session, Doc. No. A/AC.96/569, August 31, 1979).

## Chapter 8. Resolving Refugee Problems: Addressing Political Causes

1. Leo Kuper, *Genocide: Its Political Uses in the Twentieth Century* (New Haven: Conn.: Yale University Press, 1981). Kuper argues that sovereignty constituted the central ideology of the United Nations during the post–World War II era, thus making intervention in the internal affairs of states virtually impossible.

2. John Chipman, "The Future of Strategic Studies: Beyond Even Grand Strategy," *Survival* 34 (Spring 1992): 117.

3. Up until 1992, the Office for Research and the Collection of Information (ORCI) had primary responsibility for early warning. Its functions have since been divided between the Political and the Humanitarian Affairs departments, but no one office has been given responsibility for early warning. For background, see the U.N. Joint Inspection Unit report (A/45/649 and Secretary-General's comments in Add. 1, 1990; and B. G. Ramcharan, *The International Law and Practice of Early Warning and Preventive Diplomacy: The Emerging Global Watch* (Dordrecht, Netherlands: Martinus Nijhoff: 1991).

4. The need for effective early warning has been pointed out by numerous analysts. See, for example, Lance Clark, *Early Warning of Refugee Flows* (Washington, D.C.: Refugee Policy Group, 1989); and Leon Gordenker, "Early Warning of Refugee Incidents," in Gil Loescher and Laila Monahan, eds., *Refugees and International Relations* (Oxford: Clarendon Press, 1989), pp. 355–72.

5. See Roberta Cohen, *Introducing Refugee Issues into the United Nations Human Rights Agenda* (Washington, D.C.: Refugee Policy Group, 1990); and Roberta Cohen, *United Nations Human Rights Bodies: An Agenda for Humanitarian Action* (Washington, D.C.: Refugee Policy Group, 1992).

6. United Nations General Assembly Resolution 46/59, December 1991. During the first half of 1992, UN Fact-Finding Missions have been sent to the Trans-Dniester region of Moldova and to Nagorno-Karabakh.

7. Boutros Boutros-Ghali, in *An Agenda for Peace* (New York: United Nations Secretariat, 1992), argues for the establishment of "peace enforcement units drawn from standing national armies, to be available to the U.N. on 48 hours notice."

8. For a good general background to many of the problems, see Larry Minear, Thomas Weiss, and Kurt Campbell, *Humanitarianism and War: Learning the Lessons from Recent Armed Conflicts,* Occasional Paper 8 (Providence, R.I.: Watson Institute for International Studies, Brown University, 1991).

9. See Krister Eduards, Gunnar Rosen, and Robert Rossborough, *Responding to Emergencies: The Role of the UN in Emergencies and Ad Hoc Operations* (Stockholm: Nordic UN Project, September 1990); and Erskine Childers and Brian Urquhart, *Strengthening International Response to Humanitarian Emergencies* (New York: Ford Foundation, 1991).

10. United Nations General Assembly Resolution A/Res/46-182, December 19, 1991.

11. Larry Minear, "Humanitarian Intervention in a New World Order," *Policy Focus* 1 (1992): 1–3; and Charles Keely, "Filling a Critical Gap in the Refugee Protection Regime: The Internally Displaced," *World Refugee Survey 1991* (Washington, D.C.: U.S. Committee for Refugees, 1991), pp. 22–27.

12. This proposal grew out of an earlier recommendation to create a Special Representative for Humanitarian Questions, made by Sadruddin Aga Khan, *Study on Human Rights and Massive Exoduses,* E/CN.4/1503 (December 31, 1981).

13. In 1991, the United Nations estimated that five out of ten Latin Americans lacked access to housing, health care, and education.

14. At an OAS meeting in Santiago, Chile, in 1991, the organization issued a declaration empowering the OAS Secretary-General to call an emergency meeting of the organization whenever a democratically elected government is overthrown. At the 22d General Assembly of the OAS in Nassau, Bahamas, in 1992, the organization reaffirmed its commitment to condemn any attempt to disrupt the democratic order and decided to consider a modification of the OAS Charter that would allow suspension of membership of any government that destroys representative democracy.

15. For the most part, human rights monitoring operations and observance of elections have been initiatives taken by the Secretary-General or have been part of Security Council–sanctioned peacekeeping and peacemaking missions. The UN Commission on Human Rights so far has not been involved in the design and implementation of these innovative initiatives. See Roberta Cohen, *United Nations Human Rights Bodies,* op. cit.

16. United Nations General Assembly Resolution 45/100 on Humanitarian Assistance to Victims of Natural Disasters and Similar Emergency Situations, December 14, 1990. In 1991, the UN Secretary-General recommended a number of measures, including exploring the use of relief corridors for the distribution of emergency aid. See Report of the Secretary-General, *New International Humanitarian Order: Humanitarian Assistance to Victims of Natural Disasters and Similar Emergency Situations,* General Assembly Document A/45/587 (October 24, 1990).

17. Erskine Childers, *United Nations Mechanisms for Intervention and Prospects for Reform* (Uppsala, Sweden: Life and Peace Institute, May 25–26, 1992).

18. Roberta Cohen, *Human Rights Protection for Internally Displaced Persons* (Washington, D.C.: Refugee Policy Group, 1991).

19. Mary Ann Larkin, Frederick Cuny, and Barry Stein, eds., *Repatriation Under Conflict in Central America* (Washington, D.C., and Dallas: Center for Immigration Policy and Refugee Assistance, Georgetown University, and Intertecht Institute, 1991.

20. For detailed case studies, see Anthony Lake and contributors, *After the Wars: Reconstruction in Afghanistan, Indochina, Central America, Southern Africa and the Horn of Africa* (New Brunswick, N.J.: Transaction Publishers, 1991).

21. Ibid., pp. 23–26.

22. Ibid., pp. 25–26. See also Astri Suhrke, *Towards a Comprehensive Refugee Policy: Conflict and Refugees in the Post–Cold War World* (Geneva: ILO-UNHCR, May 1992).

23. Lawyers Committee for International Human Rights, *General Principles Relating to the Promotion of Refugee Repatriation* (New York: Lawyers Committee for International Human Rights, 1992).

# Recommended Reading
# and Sources

Abella, Irving, and Harold Troper. *None Is Too Many*. Toronto: Lester & Orpen Dennys, 1986.

Acheson, Dean. *Present at the Creation*. New York: W. W. Norton, 1966.

Adelman, Howard, ed. *Refugee Policy: Canada and the United States*. Toronto: York Lanes Press, 1991.

———. "Palestine Refugees, Economic Integration and Durable Solutions." In Anna Bramwell, ed., *Refugees in the Age of Total War* (London: Unwin Hyman, 1988), pp. 295–311.

Aga Khan, Sadruddin. *Legal Problems Related to Refugees and Displaced Persons*. The Hague: Academy of International Law, 1976.

———. *Study on Human Rights and Massive Exoduses*. ECOSOC doc. E/CN 4/1503, 1981.

———. "Towards a Humanitarian World Order." *Third World Affairs* (1985): 105–12.

Aguayo, Sergio. *International Aid in the Case of Central American Refugees and Displaced Persons*. Geneva: ILO/UNHCR, 1992.

Aguayo, Sergio, and Patricia Weiss-Fagen. *Central Americans in Mexico and the United States: Unilateral, Bilateral and Regional Perspectives*. Washington, D.C.: Georgetown University, 1988.

Aleinikoff, Alexander. "Political Asylum in the Federal Republic of Germany and Republic of France: Lessons for the United States." *University of Michigan Journal of Law Reform* 17 (Winter 1984): 183–241.

Aleinikoff, Alexander, and David Martin. *Immigration: Process and Policy*. St. Paul, Minn.: West Publishing, 1985.

Amnesty International. *Harmonization of Asylum Policy in Europe: Amnesty International's Concerns*. London: AI, 1990.

Amnesty International USA. *Reasonable Fear: Human Rights and United States Foreign Policy.* New York: AIUSA, 1990.

Anker, Deborah E., *The Law of Asylum in the United States: A Manual for Practitioners and Adjudicators.* Washington, D.C.: American Immigration Lawyers Association, 1989.

Anker, Deborah E., and Michael Posner. "The Forty Year Crisis: A Legislative History of the Refugee Act of 1980." *San Diego Law Review* 19 (Winter 1981): 9–89.

Anthony, Constance. "Africa's Refugee Crisis: State Building in Historical Perspective." *International Migration Review* 25 (Fall 1991): 574–91.

Appleyard, Reginald. *The Impact of International Migration on Developing Countries.* Paris: Organization for Economic Cooperation and Development, 1989.

———. *International Migration: Challenges for the Nineties.* Geneva: International Organization for Migration, 1991.

Arendt, Hannah. *The Origins of Totalitarianism.* New York: Harcourt Brace Jovanovich, 1958.

Avery, Christopher. "Refugee Status Decision-Making in Ten Countries." *Stanford Journal of International Law* 17 (Winter 1984): 183–241.

Ayoob, Mohammed. "The Third World in the System of States: Acute Schizophrenia or Growing Pains?" *International Studies Quarterly* 11 (1989): 67–79.

Azar, Edward, and Chung-in Moon, eds. *National Security in the Third World: The Management of Internal and External Threats.* Aldershot, England: Edward Elgar, 1988.

Azrael, Jeremy; Patricia Brukoff; and Vladimir Shkolnikov. "Prospective Migration and Emigration from the Former USSR: A Conference Report." *Slavic Review* (1992).

Bach, Robert. "Transforming Socialist Emigration: Lessons from Cuba and Vietnam," *In Defense of the Alien* 12 (1990): 89–103.

Balan, Jorge. *International Migration in the Southern Cone.* Washington, D.C.: Center for Immigration Policy and Refugee Assistance, Georgetown University, 1985.

Bethell, Nicholas. *The Last Secret: Forcible Repatriation to Russia, 1944–47.* London: Andre Deutch, 1974.

Betts, T. F. "Evolution and Promotion of the Integrated Rural Development Approach to Refugee Policy in Africa." *Africa Today* 31 (1984): 7–24.

———. *Integrated Rural Development: Reports 1–4.* Geneva: International University Exchange Fund, 1969.

———. "Zonal Rural Development in Africa." *Journal of Modern African Studies* 7 (1966): 149–53.

Beyer, Gregg. *Improving International Response to Humanitarian Situations.* Washington, D.C.: Refugee Policy Group, 1987.

Blaschke, Jochen. *East–West Migration in Europe and International Aid as a Means to Reduce the Need for Emigration.* Geneva: ILO/UNHCR, 1992.

Böhning, W. R. "Integration and Immigration Pressures in Western Europe." *International Labour Review* 130 (1991): 445–58.

Bower, Tom. *The Pledge Betrayed: America, Britain and the De-Nazification of Postwar Germany.* Garden City, N.Y.: Doubleday, 1982.

Bramwell, Anna, ed. *Refugees in the Age of Total War*. London: Unwin Hyman, 1988.

Breitman, Richard, and Alan Kraut. *American Refugee Policy and European Jewry, 1933–1945*. Bloomington, Ind.: Indiana University Press, 1987.

Brooks, Hugh, and Yassin El-Ayouty, eds. *Refugees South of the Sahara: An African Dilemma*. Westport, Conn.: Negro Universities Press, 1970.

Brown, Francis, ed. *Refugees*. Special issue of *Annals of American Academy of Political and Social Science* 203 (1936).

Buehrig, Edward. *The United Nations and the Palestinian Refugees: A Study in Non-Territorial Administration*. Bloomington, Ind.: Indiana University Press, 1971.

Cels, Johan. *The European Refugee Regime*. Ph.D. dissertation, University of Notre Dame, 1989.

———. *A Liberal and Humane Policy for Refugees and Asylum Seekers: Still a Realistic Option?* London: European Consultation on Refugees and Exiles, 1986.

Center for Migration Studies. *International Migration Review*. Journal of human migration and refugee movements. Staten Island, N.Y.: CMS. Quarterly.

Chambers, Robert. "Hidden Losers? The Impact of Rural Refugees and Refugee Programs on Poorer Hosts." *International Migration Review* 20 (1986): 245–63.

———. "Rural Refugees in Africa: What the Eye Does Not See." *Disasters* 3 (1979): 381–92.

Chesnais, Jean-Claude. *Migration from Eastern to Western Europe, Past (1946–1989) and Future (1990–2000)*. Strasbourg: Council of Europe, 1990.

———. *The USSR Emigration: Past, Present and Future*. Paris: Organization for Economic Cooperation and Development, 1991.

Childers, Erskine. *United Nations Mechanisms for Intervention and Prospects for Reform*. Uppsala, Sweden: Life and Peace Institute, May 1992.

Childers, Erskine, and Brian Urquhart. *Strengthening International Response to Humanitarian Emergencies*. New York: Ford Foundation, 1991.

———. "A World in Need of Leadership: Tomorrow's U.N." *Development Dialogue* 1–2 (1990): 1–111.

Chipman, John. "The Future of Strategic Studies: Beyond Even Grand Strategy." *Survival* 34 (Spring 1992): 109–31.

Chopra, Jarat, and Thomas Weiss. "Sovereignty Is No Longer Sacrosanct." *Ethics and International Affairs* 6 (1992): 95–117.

Clark, Jeffrey. *The U.S. Government, Humanitarian Assistance, and the New World Order: A Call for a New Approach*. Washington, D.C.: U.S. Committee for Refugees, 1991.

Clark, Lance. *Early Warning of Refugee Flows*. Washington, D.C.: Refugee Policy Group, 1989.

Clark, Lance, and Barry Stein. *Older Refugee Settlements in Africa*. Washington, D.C.: Refugee Policy Group (1985).

Claude, Inis. *National Minorities: An International Problem*. Cambridge, Mass.: Harvard University Press, 1955.

Clay, Jason. *Politics and the Ethiopian Famine, 1984–1985*. Cambridge, Mass.: Cultural Survival, 1986.

Cobban, Alfred. *Nationalism and Self-Determination*. London: Oxford University Press, 1969.

Cohen, Roberta. *Human Rights Protection for Internally Displaced Persons*. Washington, D.C.: Refugee Policy Group, 1991.

——. *Introducing Refugee Issues into the United Nations Human Rights Agenda*. Washington, D.C.: Refugee Policy Group, 1990.

——. *United Nations Human Rights Bodies: An Agenda for Humanitarian Action*. Washington, D.C.: Refugee Policy Group, 1992.

Coles, Gervase. *Our Role and Responsibility for the Solution of the Refugee Problem*. Geneva: UNHCR, 1983.

——. *Solutions to the Problem of Refugees and the Protection of Refugees: A Background Study*. Geneva: UNHCR, 1989.

——. *Voluntary Repatriation: A Background Study*. Geneva: UNHCR, 1985.

Commission for the Study of International Migration and Cooperative Economic Development. *Unauthorized Migration: An Economic Development Response*. Washington, D.C.: Commission for the Study of International Migration and Cooperative Economic Development, July 1990.

Conquest, Robert. *The Great Terror: Stalin's Purge of the Thirties*. Hammondsworth, England: Penguin Books, 1971.

Crisp, Jeff, and Nick Cater. *The Human Consequences of Conflict in the Horn of Africa: Refugees, Asylum and the Politics of Assistance*. London: International Institute for Strategic Studies, 1990.

Cuenod, Jacques. *E.C. Assistance to Regions with Large Numbers of Refugees*. Washington, D.C.: Refugee Policy Group, 1989.

——. *Report on Refugees, Displaced Persons and Returnees*. U.N. Economic and Social Council, E/1991/109/Add. 1, June 1991.

Dacyl, Janina. *Between Compassion and Realpolitik*. Ph.D. dissertation, University of Stockholm, 1992.

Darbellay, Alina. "The Journey: Movements of Migrants and Refugees." *Oxford International Review* 3 (Winter 1991).

de Zayas, Alfred. *Nemesis at Potsdam: The Anglo-Americans and Expulsions of the Germans*. London: Routledge & Kegan Paul, 1979.

Dinnerstein, Leonard. *America and the Survivors of the Holocaust, 1941–1945*. New York: Columbia University Press, 1982.

Dirks, Gerald. *Canada's Refugee Policy*. Montreal: McGill–Queens University Press. 1977.

Divine, Robert. *American Immigration Policy, 1924–1952*. New Haven, Conn.: Yale University Press, 1957.

Donnelly, Jack. "International Human Rights: A Regime Analysis." *International Organization* 40 (Summer 1985): 249–70.

Dowty, Alan. *Closed Borders: The Contemporary Assault on Freedom of Movement*. New Haven, Conn.: Yale University Press, 1987.

Drüke, Louise. *Preventive Action for Refugee-Producing Situations*. Frankfurt: Peter Lang, 1990.

D'Souza, Frances, and Jeff Crisp. *The Refugee Dilemma*, Minority Rights Group Report No. 43. London: Minority Rights Group. February 1985.

Eduards, Krister; Gunnar Rosen; and Robert Rossborough. *Responding to Emergencies: The Role of the U.N. in Emergencies and Ad Hoc Operations*. Stockholm: Nordic U.N. Project, September 1990.

El Bashir, Abdel Rahman Ahmed. *The Problem of Settlement of Immigrants and Refugees in Sudanese Society*. D. Phil. Thesis, Oxford University, 1978.

Elliot, Mark. *Pawns of Yalta*. Champaign, Ill.: University of Illinois Press, 1982.

European Consultation on Refugees and Exiles. *A Refugee Policy for Europe*. London: European Consultation on Refugees and Exiles, 1987.

Fagen, Patricia Weiss, and Susan Forbes Martin. *Safe Haven Options in Industrialized Countries*. Washington, D.C.: Refugee Policy Group, 1987.

Federal Republic of Germany Interministerial Working Group. *Refugee Concept*. Bonn: Federal Ministry of the Interior, 25 September 1990.

Feingold, Henry. *The Politics of Rescue: The Roosevelt Administration and the Holocaust, 1938–45*. New Brunswick, N.J.: Rutgers University Press, 1970.

Ferris, Elizabeth. *Central American Refugees and the Politics of Protection*. New York: Praeger, 1987.

———. "The Politics of Asylum: Mexico and the Central American Refugees." *Journal of Inter-American Studies and World Affairs* 26 (August 1984): 357–84.

———, ed. *Refugees and World Politics*. New York: Praeger, 1985.

———, ed., *The Challenge to Intervene: A New Role for the United Nations*. Uppsala: Life & Peace Institute, 1992.

Forbes Martin, Susan. "Emigration, Immigration and Changing East-West Relations." Washington, D.C.: Refugee Policy Group, November 1989.

Ford Foundation. *Refugees and Migrants: Problems and Program Responses*. New York: Ford Foundation, 1983.

Forsythe, David. *Humanitarian Politics: The International Committee of the Red Cross*. Baltimore: Johns Hopkins University Press, 1977.

———. "The Palestine Question: Dealing with a Long-Term Refugee Situation." *Annals of American Academy of Political and Social Science* 467 (May 1983): 89–101.

———. "The United Nations and Human Rights, 1945–1985." *Political Science Quarterly* 100 (Summer 1985): 249–70.

———. "UNRWA, the Palestinian Refugees, and World Politics." *International Organization* 25 (1971): 26–45.

Frelick, Bill. *The Back of the Hand: Bias and Restriction Towards Central American Asylum Seekers in North America*. Washington, D.C.: U.S. Committee for Refugees, 1988.

———. "Call Them What They Are—Refugees." *World Refugee Survey 1992* (1992): 12–17.

———. "Haiti: No Room at the Inn." *Refugees* 90 (July 1992): 34–37.

———. *Running the Gauntlet: The Central American Journey Through Mexico*. Washington, D.C.: U.S. Committee for Refugees, 1991.

Gaddis, John Lewis. *Russia, the Soviet Union and the United States: An Interpretive History*. New York: John Wiley & Sons, 1978.

Gallagher, Dennis, ed. "Refugees: Issues and Directions." *International Migration Review* 20 (Summer 1986): 141–534.

Gallagher, Dennis, and Janelle Diller. *CIREFCA: At the Crossroads Between Uprooted People and Development in Central America*. Washington, D.C.: Commission for the Study of International Migration and Cooperative Economic Development, Working Papers, No. 27, March 1990.

Gallagher, Dennis; Susan Forbes Martin; and Patricia Weiss Fagen. *Of Special Humanitarian Concern: U.S. Refugee Admissions Since Passage of the Refugee Act*. Washington, D.C.: Refugee Policy Group, 1985.

Garvey, Jack. "Toward a Reformulation of International Refugee Law." *Harvard International Law Journal* 26 (1985): 483–500.

Ghoshal, Animesh, and Thomas Crowley. "Refugees and Immigrants: A Human Rights Dilemma." *Human Rights Quarterly* 5 (August 1983): 327–47.

Gibney, Mark, ed. *World Justice? U.S. Courts and International Human Rights.* Boulder, Colo.: Westview Press, 1991.

————, ed. *Open Borders? Closed Societies? The Ethical and Political Questions.* Westport, Conn.: Greenwood Press, 1988.

————. "A Well-Founded Fear of Persecution." *Human Rights Quarterly* 109 (1988): 109–21.

Gilad, Lisa. *The Northern Route.* St. John's, Newf.: Memorial University of Newfoundland, 1990.

Goble, Paul. "Ethnicity and National Conflict in Soviet Politics." In Neil MacFarlane, ed., *The 'Soviet Threat' Revisited* (Kingston, Ont.: Queens University Press, 1992): 31–39.

Golden, Ronny, and Michael McConnell. *Sanctuary: The New Underground Railroad.* Maryknoll, N.Y.: Orbis Books, 1986.

Goodwin-Gill, Guy. *International Law and the Movement of Persons Between States.* Oxford: Clarendon Press, 1978.

————. *The Refugee in International Law.* Oxford: Clarendon Press, 1983.

Gordenker, Leon. *Refugees in International Politics.* London: Croom Helm, 1987.

Gorman, Robert. *Coping with Africa's Refugee Burden: A Time for Solutions.* Dordrecht, Netherlands: Martinus Nijhoff, 1987.

Grahl-Madsen, Atle. *The Status of Refugees in International Law.* 2 vols. Leiden: A. W. Sijthoff, 1966, 1972.

————. *Territorial Asylum.* Dobbs Ferry, N.Y.: Oceana Publications, 1980.

Gurr, Ted Robert. "Ethnic Warfare and the Changing Priorities of Global Security." *Mediterrenean Quarterly* 1 (1990): 82–98.

Hakovirta, Harto. *An Ethical Analysis of Refugee Aid and the World Refugee Problem.* Amsterdam: Workshop on Duties Beyond Borders, April 1987.

————. *Third World Conflicts and Refugeeism: Dimensions, Dynamics and Trends of the World Refugee Problem.* Helsinki: Finnish Society of Sciences and Letters, 1986.

————. *The World Refugee Problem.* Tampere, Finland: Hillside Publications, 1991.

Hambro, Edvard. *The Problem of Chinese Refugees in Hong Kong* (Leiden: A. W. Sijthoff, 1955).

Hammer, Thomas. *European Immigration Policy: A Comparative Study.* Cambridge: Cambridge University Press, 1985.

Hansen, Art. "Managing Refugees: Zambia's Response to Angolan Refugees, 1966–1977." *Disasters* 3 (1979): 375–80.

Hansen Art, and D. Smith, eds. *Involuntary Migration and Resettlement: The Problem and Responses of Dislocated People.* Boulder, Colo.: Westview Press, 1982.

Hanson, Christopher. "Behind the Paper Curtain: Asylum Policy vs. Asylum Practice." *New York University Review of Law and Social Change* 7 (Winter 1978), 107–41.

Harff, Barbara, and Ted Robert Gurr. "Toward Empirical Theory of Genocides and Politicides: Identification and Measurement of Cases Since 1945." *International Studies Quarterly* 32 (1988): 359–71.

Harkavy, Robert, and Stephanie Neuman, eds. *The Lessons of Recent Wars in the Third World.* Lexington, Mass.: Lexington Books, 1985.

Harrell-Bond, Barbara. "Humanitarianism in a Strait-Jacket." *African Affairs* 334 (1985): 3–13.

———. *Imposing Aid*. Oxford: Oxford University Press, 1986.

———. "Repatriation: Under What Conditions Is It the Most Desirable Solution for Refugees? An Agenda for Research." *African Studies Review* 31 (1988): 41–69.

Hathaway, James. *The Law of Refugee Status*. Toronto: Butterworths, 1991.

———. "Reconceiving Refugee Law as Human Rights Protection." *Journal of Refugee Studies* 4 (1991): 113–31.

———. "A Reconsideration of the Underlying Premise of Refugee Law." *Harvard International Law Journal* 31 (1990): 129–83.

———. "Selective Concern: An Overview of Refugee Law in Canada." *McGill Law Journal* 33 (1988): 474–515.

Häusermann, Julia. *Root Causes of Displacement: The Legal Framework for International Concern and Action*. London: Rights and Humanity, 1986.

Heisbourg, Francois. "Population Movements in Post–Cold War Europe." *Survival* 33 (1991): 31–43.

Helton, Arthur. "The Legality of Detaining Refugees in the United States." *Review of Law and Social Change* 14 (1986).

———. "Political Asylum Under the 1980 Refugee Act: An Unfulfilled Promise." *University of Michigan Journal of Law Reform* 17 (1984): 243.

Hitchcox, Linda. *Vietnamese Asylum Seekers*. Oxford: St. Antony's College, 1990.

———. *Vietnamese Refugees in Southeast Asian Camps*. Basingstoke, England: Mac-Millan, 1990.

Hoffman, Stanley, "Delusions of a New World Order," *New York Review of Books* (April 9, 1992): 37–42.

Holborn, Louise. *The International Refugee Organization: A Specialized Agency of the United Nations, Its History and Work, 1946–52*. London: Oxford University Press, 1956.

———. *Refugees, A Problem of Our Time: The Work of the United Nations High Commissioner for Refugees*. 2 vols. Metuchen, N.J.: Scarecrow Press, 1975.

Hull, Elizabeth. *Without Justice for All*. Westport, Conn.: Greenwood Press, 1985.

*Human Rights Quarterly*. Baltimore: Johns Hopkins University Press. Quarterly.

Humphrey, Derek, and Michael Ward. *Passports and Politics*. London: Penguin Books, 1974.

Independent Commission on International Humanitarian Issues. *Modern Wars: The Humanitarian Challenge*. London: Zed Books, 1986.

———. *Refugees: The Dynamics of Displacement*. London: Zed Books, 1986.

Intergovernmental Committee for Migration, and Research Group for European Migration Problems. *International Migration*. Review on the role of migratory movements in the contemporary world, in English/French/Spanish. Geneva: ICM. Quarterly.

*International Bibliography of Refugee Literature*. Geneva: International Refugee Integration Resource Center, 1985.

*International Journal of Refugee Law*. Oxford: Oxford University Press. Quarterly.

*Interpreter Releases*. Information service on asylum, immigration, naturalization, and related matters. Washington, D.C.: Federal Publications. Weekly.

Jaeger, Gilbert. *Status and International Protection of Refugees*. San Remo: International Institute of Human Rights, 1978.

———. *Study of Irregular Movements of Asylum Seekers and Refugees*. Geneva: UNHCR, 1 August 1985.

Jambor, Pierre. *Indochinese Refugees in Southeast Asia: Mass Exodus and the Politics of Aid*. Bangkok: Ford Foundation, 1992.

Joly, Daniele, and Robin Cohen. *Reluctant Hosts: Europe and Its Refugees*. Aldershot, England: Gower, 1987.

Joly, Daniele, with Clive Nettleton. *Refugees in Europe*. London: Minority Rights Group, October 1990.

Kaplan, Robert. *Surrender or Starve: The Wars Behind the Ethiopian Famine*. Boulder, Colo.: Westview Press, 1988.

Keely, Charles. "Filling a Critical Gap in the Refugee Protection Regime: The Internally Displaced." *World Refugee Survey 1991* (1991): 22–27.

———. *Global Refugee Policy: The Case for a Development Oriented Strategy*. New York: Population Council, 1981.

Kennedy, David. "International Refugee Protection." *Human Rights Quarterly* 8 (February 1986): 9–69.

Kerll, H. "New Dimensions of the Global Refugee Problem and the Need for a Comprehensive Human Rights and Development-Oriented Refugee Policy." In Guy Goodwin-Gill, ed. *International Human Rights Law: The New Decade: Refugees Facing Crisis in the 1990s*. Oxford: Oxford University Press, September 1990: 237–51.

Kibreab, Gaim. "Local Settlements in Africa: A Misconceived Option?" *Journal of Refugee Studies* 2 (1989): 468–90.

———. *The State of Art Review of Refugee Studies in Africa*. Uppsala, Sweden: Uppsala Papers in Economic History, 1991.

Knorr, Klaus. "Military Trends and Future World Order." *Jerusalem Journal of International Relations* 11 (1989): 68–95.

Koehn, Peter. *Refugees from Revolution: U.S. Policy and Third World Migration*. Boulder, Colo.: Westview Press, 1991.

Kohn, Hans. *Nationalism: Its Meaning and History*. Princeton, N.J.: D. Van Nostrand, 1955.

Kritz, Mary, ed. *U.S. Immigration and Refugee Policy: Global and Domestic Issues*. Lexington, Mass.: D. C. Heath, 1983.

Kritz, Mary; Charles Keely; and Sylvano Tomasi, eds. *Global Trends in Migration Theory and Research in International Population Movements*. Staten Island, N.Y.: Center for Migration Studies, 1981.

Kritz, Mary; Lin Lean Lim; and Hania Zlotnik, eds. *International Migration Systems: A Global Approach*. Oxford: Clarendon Press, 1992.

Kulischer, Eugene. *Europe on the Move: War and Population Changes 1917–1947*. New York: Columbia University Press, 1948.

Kuper, Leo. *Genocide: Its Political Uses in the Twentieth Century*. New Haven, Conn.: Yale University Press, 1981.

Kusin, Vladimir. "Refugees in Central and Eastern Europe: Problem or Threat?" *Report on Eastern Europe* (18 January 1991): 33–43.

Lake, Anthony, and contributors. *After the Wars: Reconstruction in Afghanistan, Indochina, Central America, Southern Africa and the Horn of Africa*. New Brunswick, N.J.: Transaction Publishers, 1991.

Larkin, Mary Ann; Frederick Cuny; and Barry Stein. *Repatriation Under Conflict in Central America*. Washington, D.C., and Dallas: Georgetown University and Intertecht, 1991.

Lawless, Richard, and Laila Monahan, eds. *War and Refugees: The Western Sahara Conflict*. London: Pinter, 1987.

Lawyers' Committee for International Human Rights. *General Principles Relating to the Promotion of Refugee Repatriation*. New York: Lawyers' Committee for International Human Rights, 1992.

————. *The Implementation of the Refugee Act of 1980: A Decade of Experience*. New York: Lawyers' Committee for International Human Rights, 1990.

————. *Refugee Refoulement: The Forced Return of Haitians Under the U.S.–Haitian Interdiction Agreement*. New York: Lawyers' Committee for International Human Rights, 1990.

————. *Uncertain Haven*. New York: Lawyers' Committee for International Human Rights, 1991.

————. *The UNHCR at 40: Refugee Protection at the Crossroads*. New York: Lawyers' Committee for International Human Rights, 1991.

Levy, Deborah. *Transnational Legal Problems of Refugees: 1982 Michigan Yearbook of International Legal Studies*. New York: Clark Boardman, 1982.

Loescher, Gil. "Humanitarianism and Politics in Central America." *Political Science Quarterly* 103 (Summer 1988): 295–320.

————. "The European Community and Refugees." *International Affairs* 65 (1989): 617–36.

————. "Mass Migration as a Global Security Issue." *World Refugee Survey 1991* (1991): 7–15.

————, ed. *Refugees and the Asylum Dilemma in the West*. University Park, Penn.: Penn State University Press, 1992.

————. *Refugee Movements and International Security*. Adelphi Paper 268. London: Brassey's, for International Institute for Strategic Studies, 1992.

Loescher, Gil, and Laila Monahan, eds. *Refugees and International Relations*. Oxford: Clarendon Press, 1989.

Loescher, Gil, and John Scanlan. *Calculated Kindness: Refugees and America's Half-Open Door*. New York and London: Free Press and Macmillan, 1986.

————, eds. *The Global Refugee Problem: U.S. and World Response*. Special issue of the *Annals of American Academy of Political and Social Science* 467 (1983).

————. *Human Rights, Power Politics, and the International Refugee Regime: The Case of U.S. Treatment of Caribbean Basin Refugees*. Princeton, N.J.: Princeton University Center for International Studies, World Order Studies Occasional Paper Series, No. 14, 1985.

————. "Human Rights, U.S. Foreign Policy and Haitian Refugees." *Journal of Inter-American Studies and World Affairs* 26 (August 1984): 313–56.

Loftus, John. *The Belarus Secret*. New York: Alfred A. Knopf, 1982.

MacAlister-Smith, Peter. *International Humanitarian Assistance: Disaster Relief Organizations in International Law and Organization*. Dordrecht, Netherlands: Martinus Nijhoff, 1985.

Macartney, C. A. *National States and National Minorities*. New York: Russell & Russell, 1968.

Mainz, Beatrice. *Refugees of a Hidden War: The Aftermath of Counterinsurgency in Guatemala*. Albany, N.Y.: State University of New York Press, 1988.

Makinda, Samuel. *Security in the Horn of Africa*. Adelphi Paper 269. London: Brassey's, for International Institute for Strategic Studies, 1992.

Marrus, Michael. *The Unwanted: European Refugees in the Twentieth Century*. New York: Oxford University Press, 1985.

Martin, David. "Large-Scale Migrations of Asylum-Seekers." *American Journal of International Law* 76 (1982): 598–609.

———, ed. *The New Asylum Seekers: Refugee Law in the 1980's.* Dordrecht, Netherlands: Martinus Nijhoff, 1988.

Mason, Linda, and Roger Brown. *Rice, Rivalry and Politics.* South Bend, Ind.: University of Notre Dame Press, 1983.

Matas, David. *Closing the Doors: The Failure of Refugee Protection.* Toronto: Summerhill Press, 1989.

Mayall, James. "Nationalism and International Security after the Cold War." *Survival* 34 (Spring 1992): 19–35.

———. *Nationalism and International Society.* Cambridge: Cambridge University Press, 1990.

Mazur, Robert. "Linking Popular Initiative and Aid Agencies: The Case of Refugees." *Development and Change* 18 (1987): 451–52.

McNeill, William, and Ruth Adams. *Human Migrations: Patterns and Policies.* Bloomington, Ind.: Indiana University Press, 1978.

Meissner, Doris. "Managing Migrations." *Foreign Policy* (Winter 1992): 66–83.

Melander, Goran. *Refugees in Orbit.* Geneva: International Universities Exchange Fund, 1978.

———. *The Two Refugee Definitions.* Lund, Sweden: Raoul Wallenberg Institute, 1987.

Meyer, Anne. *Annotated Bibliography on Sanctuary.* Champaign, Ill.: Urbana Ecumenical Committee on Sanctuary, 1986.

Minear, Larry. "Civil Strife and Humanitarian Aid: A Bruising Decade." *World Refugee Survey—1989 in Review* (1989): 13–19.

———. *Helping People in an Age of Conflict: Toward a New Professionalism in U.S. Voluntary Humanitarian Assistance.* New York: InterAction, 1988.

———. "Humanitarian Intervention in a New World Order." In *Policy Focus* (Washington, D.C.: Overseas Development Council, 1992): 1–3.

———. *Humanitarianism Under Siege: A Critical Review of Operation Lifeline Sudan.* Trenton, N.J.: Red Sea Press, 1991.

Minear, Larry; Thomas Weiss; and Kurt Campbell. *Humanitarianism and War: Learning the Lessons from Recent Armed Conflicts.* Occasional Paper 8. Providence, R.I.: Institute for International Studies, Brown University, 1990.

Minear, Larry; U. Chelliah; Jeff Crisp; John Mackinlay; and Thomas Weiss. *United Nations Coordination of the International Humanitarian Response to the Gulf Crisis, 1990–1992.* Occasional Paper 13. Providence, R.I.: Watson Institute for International Studies, Brown University, 1992.

Morris, Benny. *The Birth of the Palestinian Refugee Problem.* Cambridge: Cambridge University Press, 1987.

Nafziger, J. "International Law Bearing on the Entry of Aliens Regardless of Refugee Status." In *The Refugee Problem on Universal, Regional and National Level* (Thessaloniki, Greece: Institute of Public International Law and International Relations of Thessaloniki, 1987), pp. 513–36.

Nanda, Ved, ed. *Refugee Law and Policy.* Westport, Conn.: Greenwood Press, 1989.

Nash, Alan, ed. *Human Rights and the Protection of Refugees Under International Law.* Halifax, N.S.: Institute for Research on Public Policy, 1988.

Netherlands Institute of Human Rights. *Report of the International Conference "Refugees in the World: The European Community's Response,"* The Hague, 7–8

*December 1989*. Utrecht: Netherlands Institute of Human Rights; Amsterdam: Dutch Refugee Council, 1990.

Newland, Kathleen. *Refugees: The New International Politics of Displacement*. Worldwatch Paper 43. Washington, D.C.: Worldwatch Institute, March 1981.

Newman, Frank, and David Weissbrodt. *International Human Rights*. Cincinnati: Anderson Publishing, 1990.

Ngolle, E. *The African Refugee and the Distribution of International Refugee Assistance in Comparative Perspective: An Evaluation of the Policies of the Office of the U.N. High Commissioner for Refugees 1960–1980*. Mimeo (1985).

Nichols, Bruce. *The Uneasy Alliance: Religion, Refugee Work, and U.S. Foreign Policy*. New York: Oxford University Press, 1988.

Nichols, Bruce, and Gil Loescher, eds. *The Moral Nation: Humanitarianism and U.S. Foreign Policy Today*. South Bend, Ind.: University of Notre Dame Press, 1989.

OAU Secretary-General. *Secretary-General's Report on the Root Causes of the Refugee Problem in Africa*. Addis Ababa: Organization of African Unity, Secretary-General, May 1990.

Organization for Economic Cooperation and Development. *The Future of Migration*. Paris: OECD, 1987.

———. *International Conference on South–North Migration*. Paris: OECD, 1991.

———. *SOPEMI: Continuous Reporting on Migration*. Paris: OECD, Annual.

Paludan, Anne. *The New Refugees in Europe*. Geneva: International Exchange Fund, 1974.

Papademetriou, Demetrious. *Migration and Development: Next Steps*. Paris: L'Arche de la Fraternité Foundation, May 1991.

Papademetrious, Demetrious, and P. Martin, *The Unsettled Relationship: Labor Migration and Economic Development*. New York: Greenwood Press, 1991.

Papademetrious, Demetrious, and Mark Miller, eds. *The Unavoidable Issue: U.S. Immigration Policy in the 1980s*. Philadelphia: Institute for the Study of Human Issues, 1983.

Pedraza-Bailey, Silvia. "Cuban Americans in the United States: The Functions of Political and Economic Migration." *Cuban Studies* 11 (July 1981/January 1982): 79–87.

Penrose, Edith. "Negotiating on Refugees and Displaced Persons, 1946." In Raymond Dennett and Joseph Johnson, eds., *Negotiating with the Russians* (Boston: Little, Brown, 1951), pp. 144–67.

Pitterman, Shelly. "Determinants of International Refugee Policy: A Comparative Study of UNHCR Material Assistance to Refugees in Africa, 1963–1981." In John Rogge, ed. *Refugees: A Third World Dilemma* (Totowa, N.J.: Rowman & Littlefield, 1987), pp. 15–36.

———. "International Responses to Refugee Situations: The United Nations High Commissioner for Refugees." In Elizabeth Ferris, ed. *Refugees and World Politics* (New York: Praeger, 1986), pp. 43–81.

Plender, Richard. *Basic Documents in International Migration Law*. Dordrecht, Netherlands: Martinus Nijhoff, 1988.

———. *International Migration Law*. Leiden: A. W. Sijthoff, 1989.

Porter, B. *The Refugee Question in Mid-Victorian Politics*. Cambridge: Cambridge University Press, 1970.

Proudfoot, Malcolm. *European Refugees, 1930–1952: A Study in Forced Population Movement*. London: Faber & Faber, 1957.

Ramcharan, B. G. *The International Law and Practice of Early Warning and Preventive Diplomacy: The Emerging Global Watch.* Dordrecht, Netherlands: Martinus Nijhoff, 1991.

Refugee Documentation Project. *Refugee.* Forum for discussion of Canadian and international refugee issues. Toronto: York University, Refugee Studies Centre.

Refugee Policy Group. *Migration in and from Central and Eastern Europe: Addressing the Root Causes.* Washington, D.C.: Refugee Policy Group, June 1992.

Refugee Studies Programme. *Background Paper for U.K.–Japan 2000 Group.* Oxford: RSP, 1992.

———. *Journal of Refugee Studies.* Academic exploration of forced migration and national and international responses. Oxford: Oxford University Press. Quarterly.

Reynell, Josephine. *Political Pawns: Refugees on the Thai–Kampuchean Border.* Oxford: Refugee Studies Programme, 1989.

Robinson, Court. *Burmese Refugees in Thailand.* Washington, D.C.: U.S. Committee for Refugees, 1990.

Robinson, Nehemiah. *Convention Relating to the Status of Refugees: Its History, Contents and Interpretation.* New York: Institute of Jewish Affairs, 1953.

Rogge, John, ed. *Refugees: A Third World Dilemma.* Totowa, N.J.: Rowman & Littlefield, 1987.

Rose, Peter. "The Business of Caring: Refugee Workers and Voluntary Agencies." *Refugee Reports* 4 (1981): 1–6.

———. "The Politics and Morality of U.S. Refugee Policy." *Center Magazine* (September–October 1985): 2–14.

Rubin, Gary. *Refugee Protection: An Analysis and Action Proposal.* Washington, D.C.: U.S. Committee for Refugees, 1983.

———. "Are There Too Many People in the Lifeboat? Immigration and the American Dream." *Issues in National Affairs* (New York: American Jewish Committee, 1992).

Rudge, Philip. "Europe in the 1990s: The Berlin Wall of the Mind." *World Refugee Survey—1989 in Review* (1989): 20–24.

———. "Fortress Europe." *World Refugee Survey—1986 in Review.* (1986): 5–12.

Russell, Sharon Stanton, and Michael Teitlebaum, *International Migration and International Trade.* Washington, D.C.: World Bank Discussion Paper 160, 1992.

Rystad, Goran, ed. *The Uprooted: Forced Migration as an International Problem in the Post-War Era.* Lund, Sweden: Lund University Press, 1990.

Salomon, Kim. *Refugees in the Cold War: Toward a New International Refugee Regime in the Early Postwar Era.* Lund, Sweden: Lund University Press, 1991.

Sayigh, Yezid. *Confronting the 1990s: Security in the Developing Countries.* Adelphi Paper 251. London: Brassey's, for International Institute for Strategic Studies, 1990.

Scanlan, John. "Regulating Refugee Flow: Legal Alternative and Obligation under the Refugee Act of 1980." *Notre Dame Lawyer* 56 (April 1981): 618–46.

Scanlan, John, and Gil Loescher. "Mass Asylum and Human Rights in American Foreign Policy." *Political Science Quarterly* 97 (Spring 1982): 39–56.

Scarritt, James, and Ted Robert Gurr. "Minority Rights At Risk: A Global Survey." *Human Rights Quarterly* 11 (1989): 375–405.

Schechtman, Joseph. *European Population Transfers 1939–45*. New York: Oxford University Press, 1946.

———. *Postwar Population Transfers in Europe 1945–55*. Philadelphia: University of Pennsylvania Press, 1962.

———. *The Refugee in the World: Displacement and Integration*. New York: A. S. Barnes, 1963.

Scheinman, Ronald. *The Office of the United Nations High Commissioner for Refugees and the Contemporary International System*. Mimeo, 1974.

Schmid, Alex. *Research on Gross Human Rights Violations: A Programme*. Leiden: Centre for the Study of Social Conflicts, 1989.

Schulz, Richard; Robert Pfaltzgraff; Uri Ra'anan; William Olson; and Igor Lukes. *Guerrilla Warfare and Counter-Insurgency: U.S. Soviet Policy in the Third World*. Lexington: Lexington Books, 1989.

Segal, Aaron, ed. *Population Patterns in the Caribbean*. Lexington, Mass.: D. C. Heath, 1975.

Shawcross, William. *The Quality of Mercy: Cambodia, the Holocaust and Modern Conscience*. New York: Simon & Schuster, 1984.

Silk, James. *Despite a Generous Spirit: Denying Asylum in the United States*. Washington, D.C.: U.S. Committee for Refugees, 1986.

Simpson, John Hope. *The Refugee Problem*. London: Oxford University Press, 1939.

Sjoberg, Tommie. *The Powers and the Persecuted: The Refugee Problem and the Intergovernmental Committee on Refugees (IGCR), 1938–1947*. Lund, Sweden: Lund University Press, 1991.

Skran, Claudena. *The International Refugee Regime and the Refugee Problem in Interwar Europe*. Oxford: Oxford University Press, forthcoming.

———. "Profiles of the First Two High Commissioners." *Journal of Refugee Studies* 1 (1988): 277–96.

Smith, Anthony. *The Ethnic Origin of Nations*. Oxford: Basil Blackwell, 1986.

———. *Nationalism in the Twentieth Century*. Oxford: Martin Robinson, 1979.

———. *Theories of Nationalism*. London: Duckworth, 1983.

Smyser, William. "Refugees: A Never Ending Story." *Foreign Affairs* 64 (Fall 1985): 154–68.

———. *Refugees: Extended Exile*. New York: Praeger, 1987.

Stein, Barry, and Fred Cuny. "Repatriation Under Conflict." *World Refugee Survey 1991* (1991): 15–21.

Stein, Barry, and Sylvano Tomasi, eds. "Refugees Today." *International Migration Review* 15 (Spring–Summer 1981): 331–93.

Stepick, Alex, and Dale Swartz. *Haitian Refugees in the U.S.* London: Minority Group, 1986.

Stewart, Barbara McDonald. *United States Government Policy on Refugees from Nazism, 1933–1940*. New York: Garland Publishing, 1982.

Stoessinger, John. *The Refugee in the World Community*. Minneapolis: University of Minnesota Press, 1956.

*Strategic Survey*. London: Brassey's, for International Institute for Strategic Studies. Annual.

Suhrke, Astri. *Towards a Comprehensive Refugee Policy: Conflict and Refugees in the Post–Cold War World*. Geneva: ILO/UNHCR, 1992.

Suhrke, Astri, and Aristide Zolberg. "Beyond the Refugee Crisis: Disengagement and Durable Solutions for the Developing World." *Migration* 5 (1989): 69–120.

Sutter, Valerie. *The Indochinese Refugee Dilemma*. Baton Rouge: Louisiana State University Press, 1990.

Tabori, Paul. *The Anatomy of Exile*. London: George C. Harrap, 1972.

Taft, Julia. "A Call to Action for Restructuring U.S. Refugee Policy." *World Refugee Survey: 1989 in Review* (1989): 7–12.

Teitelbaum, Michael. "Right vs. Right: Immigration and Refugee Policy in the United States." *Foreign Affairs* (Autumn 1980): 21–59.

———. "Immigration, Refugees and Foreign Policy." *International Organization* 38 (Summer 1984): 429–50.

Thornberry, Cedric. *Ethnic Minorities and International Law*. Oxford: Clarendon Press, 1990.

Tolstoy, Nikolai. *Victims of Yalta*. London: Hodder & Stoughton, 1977.

Tomasi, Lydio. *In Defense of the Alien*. New York: Center for Migration Studies. Annual since 1983.

———, ed. "International Migrations: An Assessment for the 90's." *International Migration Review* 23 (Fall 1989): 393–765.

———, ed. "The New Europe and International Migration." *International Migration Review* 26 (Summer 1992): 229–720.

Tucker, Robert; Charles Keely; and Linda Wrigley, eds. *Immigration and U.S. Foreign Policy*. Boulder, Colo.: Westview Press, 1990.

United Nations, Economic and Social Council. *Draft Report of the United Nations High Commissioner for Refugees*. E/1992/May 1992.

United Nations High Commissioner for Refugees. *The State of the World's Refugees*. New York: Viking Penguin, forthcoming.

———. *Collection of International Instruments Concerning Refugees*. Geneva: UNHCR, 1979.

———. *Handbook on Procedures and Criteria for Determining Refugee Status under the 1951 Convention and the 1967 Protocol Relating to the Status of Refugees*. Geneva: UNHCR, 1979.

———. "Note on International Protection." In *Forty-first Session of the Executive Committee of the High Commissioner's Programme, 1990* (Geneva: United Nations, 27 August 1990).

———. *Refugees*. Magazine on international refugee situations and issues. Geneva: UNHCR. Monthly.

United Nations High Commissioner for Refugees, Refugee Documentation Centre. *Refugee Abstracts*. Abstracts of International literature on refugees. Geneva: UNHCR, RDC. Quarterly.

U.S. Committee for Refugees. *Refugee reports*. News service on national and international refugee issues. Washington, D.C.: USCR/ACNS. Monthly.

———. *World Refugee Survey*. Washington, D.C.: USCR. Annual.

U.S. Department of State, Bureau for Refugee Programs. *World Refugee Report*. Washington, D.C.: U.S. Department of State, Annual.

U.S. General Accounting Office. *Asylum: Uniform Application of Standards Uncertain—Few Denied Applicants Deported*. Washington, D.C.: GAO, 1987.

U.S. House of Representatives. Select Committee on Hunger. 101st Congress, 2d Session. *The Decade of Disasters: The United Nations' Response*. Washington, D.C.: U.S. Government Printing Office, July 30, 1991.

U.S. Select Commission on Immigration and Refugee Policy. *U.S. Immigration*

*Policy and the National Interest.* Washington, D.C.: U.S. Government Printing Office, 1981.

Vernant, Jacques. *The Refugee in the Post-War World.* New Haven, Conn.: Yale University Press, 1953.

Warren, George. *The Development of United States Participation in Intergovernmental Efforts to Resolve Refugee Problems.* Mimeo, 1967.

Wasserstein, Bernard. *Britain and the Jews of Britain, 1939–1945.* Oxford: Clarendon Press, 1979.

Weiner, Myron. "On International Migration and International Relations." *Population and Development Review* 11 (1985): 441–55.

———. "People and States in a New Ethnic Order." *Third World Quarterly* 13 (Fall 1992): 317–32.

———. *Security, Stability and International Migration.* Cambridge, Mass.: Center for International Studies, 1991.

Weiss, Paul. "Human Rights and Refugees." *Israel Yearbook on Human Rights* 1 (1971): 35–50.

———. "Legal Aspects of the Convention of 28 July 1951 Relating to the Status of Refugees." *British Yearbook of International Law* 30 (1953): 478–520.

———. "The 1967 Protocol Relating to the Status of Refugees and Some Questions of the Law of Treaties." *British Yearbook of International Law* (1976): 39–70.

———. *Travaux Preparatoires of the Convention Relating to the Status of Refugees of 28 July 1951.* Geneva: U.N. Institute for Training and Research, 1991.

Weiss, Thomas, ed., *Humanitarian Emergencies and Military Help in Africa.* New York: St. Martin's Press, 1990.

Widgren, Jonas. "International Migration and Regional Stability." *International Affairs* 66 (October 1990): 749–66.

Wiesner, Louis. *Victims and Survivors: Displaced Persons and Other War Victims in Vietnam, 1954–1975.* Westport, Conn.: Greenwood Press, 1988.

Woodbridge, George. *The History of UNRRA.* New York: Columbia University Press, 1950.

World Council of Churches. *Refugees.* Newsletter. Geneva: WCC, Monthly.

Wyman, David. *The Abandonment of the Jews: America and the Holocaust, 1941–45.* New York: Pantheon, 1985.

———. *Paper Walls: America and the Refugee Crisis, 1938–41.* Amherst, Mass.: University of Massachusetts Press, 1968.

Zetter, Roger. "Refugees and Forced Migrants as Development Resources: The Greek-Cypriot Refugees From 1974." *Cyprus Review* 4 (Spring 1992): 7–39.

Zolberg, Aristide. "The Next Waves: Migration Theory for a Changing World." *International Migration Review* 23 (1989): 403–30.

———. "International Factors in the Formation of Refugee Movements." *International Migration Review* 20 (Summer 1986): 151–69.

Zolberg, Aristide; Astri Suhrke; and Sergio Aguayo. *Escape from Violence: Conflict and the Refugee Crisis in the Developing World.* New York: Oxford University Press, 1989.

Zucker, Norman, and Naomi Flink Zucker. *The Guarded Gate: The Reality of American Refugee Policy.* San Diego: Harcourt Brace Jovanovich, 1987.

———. "The Uneasy Troika in U.S. Refugee Policy: Foreign Policy, Pressure Groups, and Resettlement Costs." *Journal of Refugee Studies* 2 (1989): 359–72.

# Index